The Blue Guides

Please write to us with your suggestions and corrections for the next edition of the guide. Writers of the best letters will be awarded a free Blue Guide of their choice.

If you would like to be included on our mailing list for information about Blue Guides, please write to us at Freepost, A & C Black (Publishers) Ltd, Cambridgeshire, PE19 3EZ

Blue Guide

ISTANBUL

John Freely

A & C Black · London

W W Norton · New York

Fourth edition, June 1997

Published by A & C Black (Publishers) Limited
35 Bedford Row, London WC1R 4JH

A CIP catalogue record of this book is available from the British Library.

ISBN 0–7136–4514–8

Published in the United States of America by
WW Norton and Company Inc.
500 Fifth Avenue, New York, NY 10110

Published simultaneously in Canada by
Penguin Books Canada Limited
10 Alcorn Avenue, Toronto
Ontario M4V 3BE

ISBN 0–393–31746–3 USA

Cover photograph: view from the Süleymaniye Mosque over Yeni Mosque to the Bosphorus by Peter Wilson. **Title page illustration**: the türbe of Süleyman.

John Freely was born in Brooklyn, New York, in 1926. He joined the US Navy at the age of 17 and was on active duty during the last two years of World War II, serving in the Pacific, India, Burma and China. After the war he went back to school and received a PhD in Physics from New York University in 1960, later doing post-doctoral studies in the History of Science at Oxford. He first went to Istanbul in 1960 to teach physics at the old Robert College, now the University of the Bosphorus, to which he returned in 1993 after intervals of living and working in New York, Boston, London, Athens and Venice. His first book was *Strolling Through Istanbul*, co-authored by Hilary Sumner-Boyd, published in 1972. Since then he has written more than 20 books on travel archaeology and architecture, including Blue Guide Boston and Cambridge. His most recent book is *Istanbul, The Imperial City*, published in 1996.

Printed Butler and Tanner Ltd, Frome and London

Introduction

Istanbul, with a population estimated at twelve million and increasing rapidly, is by far the largest city in Turkey. Few cities in the world can compare with it in the beauty of its setting or in the number and grandeur of its historic monuments. This Blue Guide is designed to be the most comprehensive guide to Istanbul in any language, giving not only a complete and accurate description of its monuments, but also providing all of the background and practical information that travellers will need to enjoy all aspects of their stay in this incomparable city.

Istanbul is the only city in the world that stands upon two continents. The main part of the city, which is located at the southeastern tip of Europe, is separated from its suburbs in Asia by the Bosphorus, the beautiful and historic strait that cuts through from the Black Sea to the Sea of Marmara, the ancient Pontus and Propontis. The European part of the city is divided by the Golden Horn, an inlet of the sea that is fed by two streams known as the Sweet Waters of Europe. The oldest section of the city, Stamboul, is on the right bank of the Golden Horn; on the lower left bank is the port quarter of Galata, with the more modern neighbourhoods stretching out along the hills above the Bosphorus. (The words Istanbul and Stamboul are corruptions of the Greek stin poli, meaning 'in the city', or 'to the city', phrases that are still used by Greeks when referring to the imperial capital once known as Constantinople, and before that as Byzantium.)

Stamboul itself forms a roughly triangular promontory, bounded on the north by the Golden Horn, on the south by the Sea of Marmara, and on its landward side by its ancient defence-walls. At Saray Burnu, the point that forms the apex of this promontory, the Bosphorus and the Golden Horn meet and flow together into the Marmara, together forming what the Byzantine historian Procopius referred to as the city's 'garland of waters'.

The Practical Information section includes a brief introduction to the Turkish language—travellers to Istanbul are urged to learn a few words and phrases of basic Turkish, for this will enable them to meet the people of this fascinating city and learn something of their way of life. The Background Information provides an introduction to the history, architecture and art of Istanbul, so that you can fully appreciate the Byzantine and Ottoman monuments of the city.

There is no other city in the world like Istanbul, and those who come to know it invariably fall under its spell, for it is truly enchanting. Iyi Yolculuklar!, which means have a pleasant journey.

Contents

Maps and Plans

Using this Guide

Asterisks (*) indicate places of special interest or excellence. Double asterisks (**) denote monuments of extraordinary interest, those that should not be missed on a visit to Istanbul.

Abbreviations. In addition to generally accepted and self-explanatory abbreviations, the following occur in the *Guide*:

Blv.	*Bulvar* (Boulevard)
Cad.	*Caddesi* (Avenue)
C	Century
c	*circa* (about, concerning a date)
km	kilometres
m	metres
Mey	*Meydan* (Square)
Pl.	Reference to page and square number in Atlas at the end of the book
Rte	Route
Sok.	*Sokak* (Street)
SS.	Saints
TL	Turkish *Lira*
TTOK	Turkish Touring and Automobile Club

Practical Information

This part of the Blue Guide is meant to assist travellers in planning their journey to Istanbul and to enjoy their stay in the city. The practical information contained in this section is based on the author's long residence in the city and has been completely revised and updated for this new edition.

■ Sources of Information

General information on Istanbul can be obtained from the overseas offices of the Ministry of Tourism. In Great Britain enquiries should be addressed to the Turkish Tourism and Information Office at 170/173 Piccadilly, London W1V 9DD, ☎ 0171-355-4207, fax 0171-491-0773. There are also offices in the USA at 821 United Nations Plaza, New York, NY 10017, ☎ (212) 687-2194, fax (212) 599-7568, and at 1717 Massachusetts Avenue, NW Suite 306, Washington DC 20036, ☎ (202) 429-9844, fax (202) 429-5649).

The books listed in the Bibliography (see above) provide useful information on Istanbul and on Turkey in general, including the history of the city and its art and architecture, as well as works on its many historical monuments.

There are two detailed atlases and city directories: the Euro-City Istanbul Atlas published by Dünya Süper Dağıtım Ticaret ve Sanayı A. S.; and the Istanbul A–Z, published by Ayda Limited; both are available at all large bookshops, where less detailed maps can also be purchased.

■ When to Visit

Istanbul has a temperate climate and you can enjoy a visit here throughout the year, although it can be rainy in winter, when the smog from low-grade fuel pollutes the air. Spring is the most beautiful time in Istanbul, when judas trees bloom along the hills of the Bosphorus and wisteria embowers the old wooden mansions on the Princes' Isles. The heat of summer is usually tempered by the meltem, the fresh breeze that blows down the Bosphorus from the Black Sea, though when the dreaded lodos blows in from the south across the Marmara the heat and humidity can be unpleasant for two or three days at a time. Early autumn is also a wonderful time, marked by the annual migration of myriads of storks, who rise up from the Princes' Isles and other nesting places in great thermal spirals before flying south along the meridians to Egypt.

■ Plan of Visit

The 21 itineraries in this Guide are designed so that each takes a day or less. The four principal monuments of the city are treated as separate routes, while the other itineraries take one through all parts of the old city and its most historic suburbs. To follow all of them in some detail would require several weeks. For those with only a short time at their disposal the following places should not be missed:

1. The Golden Horn, Yeni Cami, the Spice Bazaar, and the Cağaloğlu Baths (Ch. 1).
2. Haghia Sophia (Ch. 2).
3. Topkapı Sarayı (Ch. 3).
4. Haghia Eirene, the Archaeological Museum, the Çinili Köşk, the Museum of the Ancient Orient (Ch. 4).
5. The Hippodrome, the Palace of Ibrahim Paşa, the Mosque of Sultan Ahmet I, and the Church of SS. Sergius and Bacchus (Ch. 5).
6. The Basilica Cistern, the Column of Constantine and the Mosque of Sultan Beyazit II (Ch. 6).
7. The Covered Bazaar (Ch. 7).
8. The Mosque of Rüstem Paşa (Ch. 8).
9. The Süleymaniye (Ch. 9).
10. The Church of St. Saviour in Chora (Kariye Camii; Ch. 13).
11. The Theodosian Walls (Ch. 16).
12. The Shrine and Cemetery of Eyüp (Ch. 17).
13. The Galata Tower (Ch. 18).
14. The Bosphorus, Dolmabahçe Palace, Rumeli Hisarı, Sadberk Hanım Museum, and Beylerbey Palace (Ch. 19).

For those with more limited time in Istanbul, the sights that should not be missed are Haghia Sophia, Topkapı Sarayı, the Basilica Cistern, the Süleymaniye, Kariye Camii, and the Bosphorus.

■ Formalities

Passports and visas
You must have a valid passport to enter Turkey. Citizens of the UK, the Republic of Ireland, and the USA require a visa to enter Turkey. Visas can be purchased at the arrival point; at the time of writing the charge is £10 for citizens of the UK and Ireland or $20 for those of the USA. Those who wish to remain in Turkey for more than three months must apply for a residence permit, which may be granted to those who can prove that they are employed in Turkey or have adequate financial means to support their stay. Otherwise, foreigners can leave the country before the end of the three month limit, and then after an interval of at least one day, usually in Greece, they can return for another three months, a practice than can be continued more or less indefinitely.

Health regulations
Vaccination and inoculation are not required for travellers entering Turkey from Europe and North America. As far as health precautions are concerned, it is best to drink only bottled water, which is widely available. If you do have stomach trouble, drink plenty of water and stick to plain food. It is wise to take out health insurance before you go.

Currency regulations
Not more than $5000 worth of Turkish currency may be brought into or taken out of the country. There is no limit on the amount of foreign currency that may be brought into Turkey. When entering Turkey, foreign currency and travellers'

cheques may be exchanged for Turkish currency at exchange bureaux (Kambio). When exchanging money, retain your receipt, for this will allow you to exchange your unused Turkish currency when you leave the country.

Customs regulations

Apart from the occasional spot-check, visitors to Turkey are seldom asked to open their baggage for inspection. On entering Turkey you are allowed to bring in your personal belongings, sporting, camping, and photographic equipment, 1.5 kg of coffee, a litre of alcohol, 200 cigarettes, 50 cigars and five litres of wine or spirits. If you are carrying a portable radio, tape-recorder or electric type-writer they may be recorded in your passport, in which case you must have these in your possession when you leave the country. The same applies to antiques or any other valuable items. Antiquities may not be taken out of Turkey under any circumstances, so if you buy anything old (and here the definition of what is an antique is quite vague) be sure to have it validated by the merchant from whom you purchase it. It is also necessary to do this when purchasing Turkish rugs and carpets.

Motoring

Private cars may be brought into Turkey for up to three months without a carnet de passage or triptych, although trailers and caravans require a customs document. Drivers must have an international driving licence, car registration papers, and international green card insurance. The licence and engine number of your car will be recorded in your passport, and you will not be able to leave the country without it unless you have it officially sealed in a customs ware-house. For stays longer than three months it is necessary to apply to the Turkish Touring and Automobile Club (TTOK) (see address below) for a triptych.

Private yachts

Yacht owners in possession of a Transit Log may keep their boats in Turkish waters for up to two years for wintering or maintenance. Certain marinas are licenced for the storage of foreign yachts for a period of up to five years. On arrival in Turkish waters owners should proceed to the nearest port of entry.

■ Getting to Istanbul

Travel agents

There are many accredited travel agencies and tour operators in the UK and the USA who sell travel tickets to Istanbul and book accommodation there. A booklet listing these is available from Turkish Tourism and Information Offices (see above under Sources of Information).

By air

Regular air services between London and Istanbul are provided by both British Airways (BA) and Turk Hava Yolları (THY), the Turkish national airline. THY also has direct flights to Istanbul from the USA, while Delta Airlines has flights from the USA to Istanbul via Frankfurt

By sea

Turkish Maritime Lines (Denizcilek Bankası) operates a passenger liner and car-ferry from Venice to Turkish ports. Information can be obtained from Sunquest Holidays, 9 Grand Parade, Green Lanes, London N4 1JX, ☎ 0181-800 8030.

By rail

The Istanbul Express has a daily service from Munich, Vienna and Athens. This train is usually very crowded with Turkish workers and their families returning from Germany, and there are often long delays.

By bus

There is a direct bus service to Istanbul from Paris (with a connection to London). Information can be obtained from Eurolines, ☎ 01582-404-511 or from the National Express Office, Buckingham Palace Road, Victoria, London SW1, ☎ 0171-730 0202.

By road

Motorists heading from London now generally avoid the route through the Balkans because of the unsettled conditions there. Most motorists now head down to Italy and take a car ferry across the Adriatic to Igoumenitsa, from where it is an easy two-day drive across northern Greece and Turkish Thrace to Istanbul. (Those in a hurry can make this drive in one day.)

■ Transport in Istanbul

Buses and trams

The city has an extensive network of buses and trams, many of which go out to the suburbs along the Marmara and both the European and Asian shores of the Bosphorus. Buses bear signs showing their route and destination. Before boarding a bus or tram you must buy a single ticket (*bilet*); these are available at special kiosks along the route or from itinerant sellers at central bus stops, who charge a small amount extra. There is a special double-decker bus service that runs along the European shore of the Bosphorus from Emirgan to the Galata Bridge, and from there to the Spice Bazaar to Sultanahmet; the fare is twice that of normal buses, but it is well worth it.

An old-fashioned tramway line has now been laid out along the whole length of Istiklal Cad., which has become a pedestrian mall between Taksim and Tünel.

A modern tramline, the Metro, goes from the Galata Bridge to Sultanahmet and then along Divan Yolu through the centre of the old city to the bus terminal outside the Theodosian walls.

Taxis

Taxis all have meters and are required to use them, so that it should not be necessary to bargain about fares. If the meter is not on just say 'saat' (which means 'clock') to the driver. Most drivers are honest and courteous.

Cars

Travellers motoring in Turkey can obtain free assistance and advice from the Turkish Touring and Automobile Society (Türkiye Turing ve Otomobil Kurumu, or TTOK). Their main office in Istanbul is at Birinci Oto Sanayı Sitesi Yanı, Dördüncu Levent, ☎ 282-8140.

Car rental
The largest car-rental agency is Avis, which has offices at the following places: Airport, ☎ 663-0646; Cihangir, ☎ 249-7941; Hilton Hotel, ☎ 233-7752, fax 231-6244.

Train service
The Orient Express has its terminus at Sirkeci Station, ☎ 527-0051. A commuter train runs out along the Marmara coast from Sirkeci to the beach resort at Florya; service is frequent and inexpensive. Trains on the Asian side have their terminus at Haydarpaşa Station in Kadıköy, ☎ (216) 336-0475.

Tünel
This is the venerable funicular railway that ascends from Karaköy (near the Galata end of the Galata Bridge) to the lower end of Istiklal Cad.

Ferries
Ferries leave from on and around the Galata Bridge to all parts of the city and its suburbs. Locations of the various lines are posted on the bridge and on the quays on both banks of the Golden Horn; schedules and itineraries are posted at all ferry stations. (See below for help in reading ferry-schedules.)

Ferries on the upstream side of the Galata Bridge go up the Golden Horn (Haliç), calling at various stations on both shores before reaching the last stop at Eyüp. Ferries for the Princes' Isles (Adalar) and the Asiatic suburbs on the Marmara shore leave from the landing on the downstream side of the bridge, while Bosphorus (Boğaziçi) ferries depart from the quay on the right bank of the Golden Horn, downstream from the Galata Bridge. The large maritime station in Galata, at the confluence of the Bosphorus and the Golden Horn, is the terminus for longer-range ferries. Information on ferry schedules can be obtained by ·calling 244-4233.

The fares are very low and the ferries are quite comfortable and usually not too crowded. And there is no more exciting way to see the city, particularly when steaming up the Bosphorus on a fine day. Special tour tickets are available that allow you to use any ferry during the course of a day, so that you can make unlimited stops anywhere along the Bosphorus.

A new high-speed sea-bus service has been established, with its main terminals at the Karaköy and Kabataş iskeles. The service links the Asian suburb of Bostancı with Istanbul and Ataköy, a European suburb on the Marmara shore near the Yeşilköy airport. Information on sea-bus schedules can be obtained by calling ☎ 560-7291.

Reading a ferry-schedule and buying a ticket. Timetables are posted on all ferries and ticket booths. There are two sets of timetables, one for Sundays and holidays (Pazar Günü ve Tatil Günü) and one for weekdays (Pazardan Başka). The timetables give the stations and arrival and departure times for the three lines that terminate on or around the Galata Bridge (Köprü), with separate listings for each direction. The lines are:

1. Up and down the Golden Horn (Haliç)
2. To and from Üsküdar, Kadıköy, the Princes' Isles (Adalar) and Yalova
3. Up and down the Bosphorus (Boğaz or Boğaziçi)

The names and times for the ferry-stations on the European shore of the Marmara are printed in black, while those on the Asian shore are printed in red. In purchasing a ticket, simply tell the clerk the name of your destination, the class of ticket, and whether you want a one-way or round-trip ticket. The following vocabulary will enable you to read the timetables and to purchase a ticket.

Köprüdan Boğaza	from the Galata Bridge to (up) the Bosphorus
Boğazdan Köprüye	from (down) the Bosphorus to the Galata Bridge
Köprüdan Halıça	from the Galata Bridge to (up) the Golden Horn
Halıçdan Köprüye	from (down) the Golden Horn to the GalataBridge
Köprüdan Adalara	from the Galata Bridge to the Princes' Isles
Adalardan Köprüye	from the Princes' Isles to the Galata Bridge

Kalkış (K.)	Departure time
Varış	Arrival time
Hat, Hatti	Itinerary
Günleri yapılı	Days operating
Günleri yapılmaz	Days not operating
Hergün	Daily
Expres	Express
Gidiş	One-way ticket
Gidiş-Geliş	Round-trip ticket
İyi yolculuklar	Have a pleasant journey

■ Useful Addresses

Information bureaux (Danışma). Ministry of Tourism Regional Directorate, Meşrutiyet Cad. 57, Galatasaray, ☎ 243-3472. There are information offices in the Hilton Arcade, ☎ 233-0592; the Maritime Passenger Terminal (Yolcu Salonu) in Karaköy, ☎ 249-5776; in Sultanahmet Square, ☎ 518-1802; at Sirkeci Station, ☎ 511-5888; and at Yeşilköy Airport, ☎ 663-0793.

Tourist police. Headquarters in Bahçekapı (near Sirkeci Station), ☎ 527-4503; also offices at Alemdar Karakol, near the Blue Mosque; the Maritime Passenger Terminal in Galata; Sirkeci Station; and at Yeşilköy Airport.

Airlines and travel agents. Almost all airlines and travel agents have their offices on Cumhuriyet Cad. between the Hilton and Taksim Square. BA is at No. 10, ☎ 234-1300; THY is at No. 131, ☎ 225-0556; Delta, ☎ 231-2339, and Türk Express, ☎ 230-1515 (the local affiliate of American Express) are in the Hilton Arcade.

Shipping line. Turkish Maritime Lines has its main office at the Maritime Passenger Terminal in Karaköy, ☎ 249-9292.

Post offices (PTT). Central Post Office, Yeni Postahane Sok. 25 (near Sirkeci Station) (open 08.00–21.00 daily, including Sunday); branch post offices on Istiklal Cad. just off Galatasaray Square (open 09.00–17.00, Mon–Fri, 09.00–13.00, Sat), and just off Taksim Square (open 09.00–19.00, Mon–Fri, 09.00–13.00, Sat).

Hospitals (Hastahane). American Hospital (Amiral Bristol Hastahane), Güzelbahçe, Nisantaşı, ☎ 231-4050; German Hospital, Sıraselviler Cad., Taksim, ☎ 293-2150; International Hospital, Yeşilköy, ☎ 663-3000; Taksim First-Aid Hospital, Sıraselviler Cad., Taksim, ☎ 252-4300.

Consulates. UK, Meşrutiyet Cad. 34, Tepebaşı (just off Galatasaray Square), ☎ 252-6436; USA, 106 Meşrutiyet Cad. (next to the Pera Palas Hotel), ☎ 251-3602.

Banks. Any bank with a 'Kambiyo' sign will change money or cash travellers' cheques. The following are some of the largest Turkish and foreign banks in Istanbul:
Akbank, Sabancı Centre, 4 Levent, Istanbul; ☎ 270-0044, fax 269-7383.
Chase Manhattan Bank, Yıldız Posta Cad. Dedeman Ticaret Merkezi, Kat (Floor) 11, Esentepe; ☎ 275-1280, fax 275-9932.
Citibank, Büyükdere Cad. 100, Esentepe; ☎ 268-7700, fax 288-7760.
Koç American Bank, Barbaros Bulvarı, Koca Iş Merkezi, Beşiktaş; ☎ 274-7777, fax 267-2927.
Osmanlı Bankası, Voyvoda Cad. 35–37, Karaköy; ☎ 252-3000, fax 244-6471.
Türk Boston Bank, Maya Akar Centre, Büyükdere Cad. 101, B. Bl. Kat 17 D79, Esentepe; ☎ 274-5222.
Yapi ve Kredi Bankası, Yapı Kredi Plaza, Büyükdere Cad., Levent, Istanbul; ☎ 280-1111; fax 280-1670.
Midland Bank, Cumhuriyet Cad. 8, Elmadağ Han, Kat 2-3, Elmadağ; ☎ 231-5560, fax 230-5300.

Note: Because of the extremely high inflation rate and frequent currency devaluations, it has been impossible to quote prices or exchange rates in this Guide. For information on prices and exchange rates consult your travel agent or bank before leaving for Turkey.

Personal security and behaviour
Crime in Istanbul is low by US or European standards, and most areas of the city are perfectly safe at night. Women would be best advised not to walk unaccompanied at night. You should be alert for purse-snatchers and pickpockets, even in the daytime. Codes of dress are much the same as in cities in Europe or the US, although women would be advised to dress somewhat conservatively, and in a mosque women must wear a scarf and long sleeves.

Disabled travellers
Many of the pavements in Istanbul now have ramps for the disabled. But apart from this there are very few facilities for the disabled.

■ Hotels and Pensions

Hotels in Istanbul range from luxurious establishments with international standards to simple inns used by Anatolian peasants. The hotels listed below are some of those that cater largely to foreign travellers. Omission of a hotel from this list does not imply any adverse judgement, nor does inclusion imply any guarantee of satisfaction. Hotels that are licensed and controlled by the Ministry of Tourism are officially categorised, according to their accommodation, as ***** (De luxe), **** (First Class), *** (Second Class), ** (Third Class), and * (Fourth Class). There are also several hotels operated by the Turkish Touring and Automobile Club (TTOK), all of them in splendidly restored Ottoman edifices. These and a number of other hotels, many of them in restored Ottoman buildings, operate under a special licence, designated as S.

The following is a selection of centrally located hotels in the various categories other than the lowest. They are grouped according to their location, first those in the Old City, and then those in the so-called Modern City, including the suburbs along the Bosphorus. (Note: Unless otherwise noted, all telephone numbers are on the European side of the city, for which the code number is 212, whereas the code for the Asian side and the Princes' Isles is 216. To call a number on the other side of the Bosphorus, first dial 00 and then the appropriate number.)

The Old City

Arcadia (****), Dr. Imren Öktem Sok. 1; ☎ 516-9696, fax 516-6118. A large modern hotel centrally located behind Ibrahim Paşa Sarayı; restaurant with roof terrace looking out over the monuments of the First Hill.

Armada (S), Ahırkapı Sok., Ahırkapı; ☎ 638-1370, fax 518-5060. A modern hotel in the old quarter on the Marmara slope of the First Hill below the Hippodrome and the Blue Mosque; restaurant serving traditional Turkish dishes.

Ayasofya Pansiyonlar (S), Soğuk Çeşme Sok., Sultanahmet; ☎ 513-3660, fax 513-3669. A street of charming old Ottoman mansions along the outer walls of Topkapı Sarayı, all elegantly restored and furnished in period decor by the TTOK. Several restaurants, including one in a converted Roman cistern (Sarnıç Lokantası), an outdoor café, bars, a Turkish bath, and a library with a unique collection of books about Istanbul as well as old prints and maps of the city.

Empress Zoe (S), Akbıyık Cad., Adliye Sok. 10, Sultanahmet; ☎ 518-2504, fax 518-5699. An imaginatively restored old Ottoman house in the old quarter below the Blue Mosque; roof terrace looking out over the Marmara and garden café adjoining picturesque 15C Turkish bath.

Four Seasons (*****), Tevfikhane Sok. 1, Sultanahmet; ☎ 638-8529, fax 638-8530. Brand new hotel created in a late Ottoman building formerly used as a prison, restored without altering its external appearance, with restaurant serving traditional Ottoman cuisine.

Kalyon (****), Sahilyolu, Sultanahmet; ☎ 234-3200, fax 638-1111. On the shore road below the Blue Mosque. overlooking the Marmara; restaurant with garden looking out across the strait to the Asian side of the city and the Princes' Isles.

Kariye (S), Kariye Camii Sok. 18, Edirnekapı; ☎ 534-8414, fax 521-6631. Old Ottoman building restored by the TTOK on the street next to Kariye Camii;

restaurant (Asithane) serving traditional Turkish cuisine, dining al fresco in garden during summer.

Konuk Evi (S), Soğukçeşme Sok., Sultanahmet; ☎ 514-0120, fax. 514-0213. Another old Ottoman mansion beautifully restored by the TTOK, set in a spacious courtyard with its restaurant in a former greenhouse.

Pierre Loti (***), Piyerloti Cad. 5, Çemberlitaş; ☎ 518-5700, fax 516-1886. Small centrally located hotel on street leading off Divan Yolu from Constantine's Column.

President (****), Tiyatro Cad. 25, Beyazit; ☎ 516-6980, fax 516-6999. Large, modern and very centrally located hotel near the Covered Bazaar, with restaurant, two American bars and a pub.

Yeşil Ev (S), Kabasakal Sok. 5, Sultanahmet; ☎ 517-6785, fax 517-6780. An old Ottoman mansion next to the Blue Mosque and behind the Baths of Roxelana, beautifully restored by the TTOK; restaurant with tree-shaded garden around a cascade fountain.

The Modern City and suburbs

Büyük Londra (**), Meşrutiyet Cad. 117, Tepebaşı; ☎ 245-0670, fax 245-0671. The oldest hotel in the city, built in the late 1870s on what was then a fashionable avenue overlooking the Golden Horn; now well restored and modernised.

Ceylan Inter-Continental Istanbul (*****), Taksim; ☎ 231-2121, fax 231-2180. Completely refurbished de luxe hotel on Taksim Square; three restaurants and a cafeteria, rooftop terrace with panoramic view, two outdoor swimming pools (one for children).

Çırağan Palace Kempinski (*****), Çırağan, Beşiktaş; ☎ 258-3377, fax 259-6686. Outstanding de luxe hotel housed in a splendidly restored mid 19C Ottoman palace on the Bosphorus. Turkish and Italian restaurants; outdoor swimming pool on the edge of the Bosphorus.

Conrad Istanbul (*****), Beşiktaş, ☎ 227-3000, fax 259-6667. Outstanding new de luxe hotel overlooking the Bosphorus and the gardens of Yıldız Palace. Turkish and Italian restaurants; indoor and outdoor swimming pools.

Divan (*****), Cumhuriyet Cad. 2, Elmadağ, Taksim; ☎ 231-4100, fax. 248-8527. One of the oldest of the modern de luxe hotels, now refurbished; restaurant and an American bar that was once a favourite of Turkish and foreign writers.

Hyatt Regency (*****), Taşkışla Cad., Taksim; ☎ 225-7000, fax 225-7007. New de luxe hotel near Taksim Square; Turkish and Italian restaurants; outdoor swimming pool and tennis courts.

Hilton (*****), Cumhuriyet Cad., Harbiye; ☎ 231-4650, fax 240-4165. The oldest of the modern de luxe hotels, built at a time when there was plenty of open space in the area, so that it is surrounded by extensive and well-kept grounds, with an outdoor swimming pool. Excellent Chinese restaurant (Dragon) as well as three other dining rooms with Turkish and international cuisine.

Kervansaray (****), Taksim; ☎ 235-5000, fax 253-4378. Modern hotel on Taksim Square; Turkish and European restaurants; roof terrace.

Marmara (*****), Taksim; ☎ 251-4696, fax 244-0509. De luxe hotel on Taksim Square; restaurant with Turkish, Italian and French specialities as well as brassiere for lunch and supper; rooftop lounge with panoramic view.

Pera Palas (****), Meşrutiyet Cad. 98, Beyoğlu; ☎ 251-4560, fax 251-4089. The first of Istanbul's grand hotels, opened in 1895 for travellers arriving on the Orient Express. It has been the setting for a number of murder mysteries, most notably those of Agatha Christie and Eric Ambler. The decor of the public rooms is evocative of the cosmopolitan Pera of late Ottoman and early Republic times; these include a restaurant with Turkish and Western dishes, a charming patisserie, and the famous bar-room that was the setting for so many real and fictional Levantine intrigues, with a terrace café outside where in summer you can watch the sun setting over the Golden Horn.

Riva (****), Aydede Cad. 8, Taksim; ☎ 256-4420, fax 256-2033. Excellent hotel centrally located near Taksim Square; restaurant with Turkish and international food.

Swissotel The Bosphorus (*****), Maçka; ☎ 259-0101, fax 259-0105. Outstanding de luxe hotel on a wooded hilltop overlooking the Bosphorus. Restaurant with Turkish and international cuisine; indoor and outdoor swimming pools, health and fitness facilities

Taksim Eresin (****), Topçu Cad. 34, Taksim; ☎ 256-0803, fax 253-2247. A modern hotel near Taksim Square; restaurant with Turkish and international dishes.

Yenişehir Palas (***), Meşrutiyet Cad, Oteller Sok. 1/3, Tepebaşı; ☎ 252-7160, fax 249-7507. A moderately priced hotel near the Pera Palas, in the heart of old Pera.

■ Restaurants

Istanbul, with its cosmopolitan atmosphere and its rich mixture of ethnic backgrounds, is particularly well-endowed with excellent restaurants (**lokanta**), which cater to every taste and social class. The gastronomic spectrum includes: the de luxe Western-style restaurants in the modern sections of the city, the excellent kebab lokantas in the old city, the famous fish-restaurants along the Bosphorus, and the simple little working-men's cookshops found all over the city. It would be impractical to list all of the good restaurants in the city, for there are so very many in every category, so what follows is just a selection.

The list does not include the restaurants in the de luxe and first class hotels. These are often excellent, but travellers wishing to experience something of the flavour of Turkey are advised to eat in those restaurants which the Turks themselves frequent. The most popular are the old-fashioned **meyhanes,** taverns that serve traditional Turkish meze, or hors d'oeuvres, along with beer and raki.

The inflation rate in Turkey is so high that it is meaningless to quote prices, other than the following general guide: $ Modest, $$ Medium, $$$ Expensive.

Asır (also called Hasır) ($), Kalyoncukulluk Cad. 94/1, Beyoğlu (just off Tarlabaşı Cad. next to the police station); ☎ 250-0557. One of the very few Greek meyhanes left in the city; wonderful atmosphere reminiscent of the Beyoğlu of times past.

Bekriye ($), Birinci Cad. 90, 2nd floor, Arnavutköy; ☎ 257-0469. Informal meyhane in a charming old Turkish house on the Bosphorus; set menu with simple but interesting Bosnian and Macedonian meze.

Boncuk ($), Nevizade Sok., Beyoğlu; ☎ 243-1219. Outstanding meyhane with Armenian meze. The best food of the score or so meyhanes on this colourful and wonderfully lively street off the Galatasaray fish-market.

Çatı ($$), Istiklal Cad, Orhan Apaydın Sok 20/7 (top floor); ☎ 251-0000. A favourite for those dining after the theatre and cinema; live music; closed Sun.

The China ($$), Lamartin Cad. 17, Taksim; ☎ 250-6263. The oldest Chinese restaurant in Istanbul and still one of the best; closed Sun.

Çiçek Pasajı ($), Istiklal; Cad. Galatasaray. An alleyway lined with lively meyhanes, of which the best is probably **Seviç**, Bayram'in Yeri (No. 8), ☎ 244-2867. Simple menus consisting mostly of traditional meze, served with beer or raki.

Club 29 Çubuklu ($$$), Paşabahçe Yolu 24, Çubuklu; ☎ (216) 322-2829. Restaurant with outstanding European and Turkish food on a terrace overlooking the Bosphorus on the Asian shore, along with bar, disco and swimming pool. Free boat service from Istinye on the European shore

Darüzziyafe ($$), Şifahane Cad. 6; ☎ (212) 511-8414. Outstanding restaurant housed in the former imaret of the Süleymaniye complex; specialises in Ottoman cuisine.

Deniz Park (Aleko'nun Yeri) ($$), Daire Sok. 9, Yeniköy; ☎ 262-0515. One of the very few Greek fish restaurants remaining on the Bosphorus; superb view of the strait, particularly under a full moon.

Develi ($$), Balıkpazarı, Gümüş Yüzük Sok. 7, Samatya; ☎ 585-1189. Turkish meat restaurant, founded in 1912, on the Marmara shore in Samatya, one of the oldest quarters of the city, with specialities from southeastern Anatolia; terrace open in summer.

Façyo ($$$), Kireçburnu Cad. 13, Tarabya; ☎ 262-0024. The oldest fish restaurant in Tarabya, the beautiful cove on the European shore of the Bosphorus.

Four Seasons ($$), Istiklal Cad. 509, Tünel; ☎ 293-3941. An elegant restaurant with Turkish and international cuisine.

Galata Meyhane ($$), Istiklal Cad., Orhan Apaydın Sok. 11, Beyoğlu; ☎ 293-1139. A modern version of an old-fashioned Beyoğlu meyhane, with live music six nights a week; closed Sun.

Hacı Baba ($$), Istiklal Cad. 49, Beyoğlu; ☎ 244-1886.

Hamdi Et Lokantası ($), Tahmis Cad., Kalçın Sok. 17; ☎ 528-0390. Local lokanta frequented by those who work in the market quarter down by the Golden Horn; specialises in kebabs from southeastern Anatolia.

Imroz ($), Nevizade Sok., Beyoğlu; ☎ 249-9073. Old-fashioned meyhane owned by a Greek from the Aegean isle of Imroz; specialises in traditional Greek and Turkish meze.

Karaca ($$), Yahya Kemal Cad. 10–12; ☎ 265-9720. Excellent fish restaurant opposite the old iskele, or pier, in the village of Rumeli Hisarı. The upper deck commands a view of the middle Bosphorus between the fortress of Rumeli Hisarı and the Fatih Mehmet Bridge.

Konyalı ($$), Topkapı Sarayı, Sultanahmet; ☎ 513-9696. Excellent restaurant and cafeteria in the Fourth Court of Topkapı Palace, with a superb view of the confluence of the Bosphorus and the Golden Horn and across the strait to the Asian shore.

Kör Agop ($$), Kumkapı Meydanı; ☎ 517-2334. An old Armenian lokanta, the best of the many fish restaurants in Kumkapı, the ancient quarter on the Marmara shore.

Körfez ($$$), Körfez Cad. 78, Kanlıca; ☎ (216) 4160-4314. A de luxe fish restaurant in a cove on the Asian shore of the middle Bosphorus; customers are ferried across by a boat from Rumeli Hisarı.

Pandeli ($$), Mısır Çarşısı I, Eminönü; ☎ 527-3909. An old Greek restaurant above the entrance to the Spice Bazaar; traditional Turkish cuisine as well as international dishes.

Rejans ($$), Emir Nevruz Sok. 17, Galatasaray, Beyoğlu; ☎ 244-1610. An old-fashioned White Russian restaurant that has been operating since the early 1930s; the most popular specialities are borscht, piroshky, beef stroganoff, chicken kievsky, and game birds in season, served with lemon vodka.

Seoul ($$$), Nispetiye Cad. 42, Etiler; ☎ 263-6087. Excellent Korean restaurant, with a large garden open in the summer.

Sultanahmet Köftecisi ($), Divanyolu Cad 12 A, Sultanahmet; ☎ 513-1438. An extremely popular lokanta specialising in köfte; it is said to serve more customers a day than any other restaurant in Turkey.

Yakup 2 ($), Asmalımescit Sok. 35–37, Tünel; ☎ 249-2925. An old-fashioned meyhane with excellent Turkish food; much loved by Turkish journalists and other writers as well as all else who know and love this raffish quarter of old Beyoğlu.

■ Turkish Food and Drink

The Turkish cuisine is one of the best and most varied in the world, and in Istanbul you can dine like a Sultan, if you know how and what to order. This is no problem in a lokanta, the simple restaurants where the working-class people eat, for there you simply walk up to the counter and choose what you want from the pots on the steam table. But in higher-class restaurants the procedure is more complex. Traditionally, you begin with cold hors d'oeuvres (soğuk meze), selected from a huge tray. Then, if you wish to, you can order a few hot hors d'oeuvres (sıcak meze). After that comes the main course, which may be followed by a sweet (tatlı) and a cup of Turkish coffee (kahve).

The menu below includes most of the popular dishes that are served in Istanbul restaurants:

Soğuk Meze, Cold Hors d'Oeuvres

beyaz peynir white goat cheese
beğin brain
biber dolması stuffed green peppers
cacık chopped cucumbers with yogurt and garlic
domates dolması stuffed tomatoes
imam bayıldı (literally, The Imam Fainted) aubergines with parsley
kaser peynir hard cheese resembling cheddar

lahana dolması stuffed cabbage
lakerda salted bonito
midye pilakısı mussels cooked with olive oil and served cold
tarama carp roe
yaprak dolması stuffed green peppers
zeytin olives

Salata, Salads

çoban salata (Shepherd's salad) chopped peppers, tomatoes, lettuce, cucumbers, and celery
domates salatası tomato salad
fasulye ezmesi dried kidney bean salad
ispanakoku salatası spinach root salad
marul Romaine lettuce

pancar salatası beet salad
patates ezmesi mashed potato salad
patlıcan salatası aubergine salad
piyaz dried white kidney bean salad
salatalık salatası cucumber salad
yeşil salata green salad
yoğurtlu kabak salatası zucchini sala with yogurt

Sıcak Meze, Hot Hors d'Oeuvres

Among the most popular hot meze dishes are the various types of börek, thin layers of pastry with various fillings, such as the following:

etli börek börek with minced meat filling
ispanaklı börek börek with spinach
mantarlı börek börek with mushroom

pastırmılı börek börek with a filling of dried spiced beef
peynerli börek börek with cheese filling
tavuklu börek börek with chicken filling

Other popular hot meze dishes are the following:

arnavut ciğer chopped liver and onions
beğin tavası fried brain
et sauté thin slices of meat sautéed in tomato and pepper sauce
izgara köfte grilled meat balls
kabak kızartması fried zucchini

koç yumurtası fried sheep's testicles
menemen eggs scrambled with green and red peppers and white cheese
midye tavası fried mussels
midye dolması fried mussels served in the shell and stuffed with pilav
patates köfte potato croquettes

Etler, Meat Dishes

Meat (and fish) may be prepared in several ways: grilled (izgara), fried (tava), roasted (kızartma), in casserole (güveç), grilled on a skewer (şiş). The general types of meat are the following:

ciğer liver
dana veal
kiyma minced meat
kuzu budu rostosu roast leg of lamb

kuzu lamb
pirzola lamb chops
sığır beef
yaban domuz wild boar

Among the most popular meat dishes are the various types of kebabs:

bahçevan kebabı meat cooked with all of the vegetables one would find in a typical kitchen garden
Bursa kebab döner kebab served with yogurt and tomato sauce, sometimes called Iskender kebab
çöp kebab same ingredients as in tas kebab, but cooked in a wax-paper envelope
döner kebab pressed lamb cooked on a rotating spit over a charcoal fire and carved off in thin slices

islim kebabı meat and aubergines cooked in a covered casserole
kâğıt kebab meat, vegetables, and herbs in a wine sauce, and cooked in a wax-paper envelope
şiş kebab lamb skewered on a spit with tomatoes and onions and grilled over a charcoal fire
tas kebab lamb stew with rice and vegetables

Other popular meat dishes are:

güveç meat or poultry baked together with vegetables in a casserole

hünkâr beğendi ('The Sultan's Favourite') puréed aubergine served with chicken or meat

kadın budu ('The Lady's Thigh') ground meat and rice first formed into oval patties and then dipped into beaten eggs and fried

karnıyarık ('Belly Split-Open') ground meat cooked together with aubergines

kış türlüsü a winter (kış) dish cooked with meat, carrots, celery, potatoes, and leeks

Balık, Fish

alabalık trout
barbunya red mullet
çinakok a species of small bluefish
dil sole
kalkan turbot
kılıç swordfish
kılıç şişte swordfish skewered on a spit and cooked over a charcoal fire

lüfer bluefish
levrek bass
mercan bream
palamut bonito
tekir small red mullet
üskümrü mackerel

Tavuk, Poultry

tavuk chicken (it also means poultry in general)
çerkez tavuk (Circassian chicken) chicken with walnut sauce
pılıç young chicken
pılıç dolması stuffed roast chicken
pılıç kâğıta chicken cooked in a wax-paper envelope
tavukklu beğendi chicken in egg purée

tavuklu güveç chicken casserole
bıldırçın quail
çulluk woodcock
hindi dolması stuffed turkey
kaz goose
keklik partridge
ördek duck
sülün pheasant

Sebze, Vegetables

bezelye peas
bamyas okra
biber green pepper
çalı fasulye green string beans
domates tomatoes
enginar artichoke
fasulye green beans
fasulye pılakısı white beans
havuç carrots
hıyar cucumber
ispanak spinach
kabak zucchini

karnıbahar cauliflower
kereviz root celery
kuskonmaz asparagus
lahana cabbage
maydonoz parsley
pancar beets
patates potatoes
patlıcan aubergine
pirasa leeks
pirinç rice (*pilav* when cooked)
salatalık cucumbers
soğan onion

Çorba, Soup

domateslı çorbası tomato soup
domateslı pirinç çorbası tomato and rice soup

düğün çorbası (Wedding Soup) soup with meat, vegetables, eggs, and paprika

işkembe çorbası tripe soup
kırmızı mercimek çorbası red lentil
   soup

mercimek çorbası lentil soup
tavuk çorbası chicken soup
yayla çorbası beef soup with yogurt

Meyva, Fruit
çilek strawberry
elma apple
erik plum
grepfrut grapefruit
incir fig
karpuz watermelon
kavun melon

kiraz cherry
muz banana
portakal orange
şeftali peach
üzüm grapes
vişne sour cherry

Tatlı, Sweets and Puddings
aşure ('Noah's Pudding') sweet
   pudding with walnuts, raisins, and
   peas
ayva kompostu stewed quince
ayva marmaladı quince marmalade
baklava many-layered pastry filled
   with walnuts, baked and soaked in
   syrup
bal kabağı tatlısı pumpkin dessert
bülbül yuvası ('The Nightingale's
   Nest') shredded wheat with pista-
   chios and syrup
dondurma ice cream
ekmek kadayıfı crumpet in syrup
gül receli rose jam
helva dessert made with farina and
   flour mixed with nuts and served
   with cinnamon

kadın gobeği ('The Lady's Navel')
   doughnut soaked in syrup
lokma flour dessert fried in oil and
   soaked in syrup
muhallebi pudding made from milk,
   rice, and rose-water
portakal peltesi orange pudding
revani dessert made with farina, flour,
   and eggs soaked in syrup
sarığı burma rich, flaky dessert with
   nut filling
sütlaç rice pudding
tulumba tatlısı rich flour dessert with
   almond flavouring
yogurt tatlısı pudding made with
   yogurt and eggs

Drinks

When dining, Turks like to drink **rakı**, a strong (87% proof) anise-flavoured drink. They rarely drink it straight, mixing it half-and-half with water, when it turns milky white. Rakı is definitely an acquired taste, but when you get used to it it goes very well with Turkish food. In recent years Turks have begun to drink more wine (**şarap**) with their meals. Most restaurants have a wide selection of red (*kırmızı şarap*), white (*beyaz şarap*), and rosé (*pembe şarap*) wines. The most drinkable brand of wine is Kavaklıdere, whose white wine is labelled Çankaya and the red Yakut. There are two brands of bottled beer, Tuborg and Efes which can occasionally be found on tap. Tekel, the government monopoly, also puts out vodka (*votka*), cognac (*kanyak*) and gin (*cin*), which are not particularly recommended, as well as a variety of liqueurs, all of which are very sweet.

   Soft drinks include Fruko, a lemon drink, as well as Coca-Cola and Pepsi Cola. Turks wash down their food with copious quantities of bottled water (*su*) and mineral water (*maden suyu*), which is excellent and cheap. They also drink *ayran*, a kind of liquid yogurt, which goes very well with Turkish foods. Here and there in the old city you can find a **bozahane**, a café that sells boza, a delicious drink made from millet and slightly fermented. And an excellent breakfast drink, particularly in winter, is *salep*, a thick beverage made from powdered orchid root and served piping hot. The salep goes very well with a *simit*, a kind of ring-shaped pretzel, which are carried in huge stacks by itinerant vendors. They are quite delicious, and make an excellent snack when strolling around town.

All Turkish meals end with coffee (*kahve*), served in a small cup with varying amounts of sugar (*şeker*). If you want no sugar in your coffee say *sade*, a little sugar: *az şekerli*, medium-sweet: *orta şekerli*, sweet: *şekerli*. You can also order tea (*çay*), which is served in a small bell-waisted glass with several cubes of sugar on the side. The tea is usually bitter and of very inferior quality, but you will probably end up drinking it anyway, because it is such a basic element in the Turkish way of life.

■ Museums and Monuments

The table below gives the hours of admission to the various museums and monuments in Istanbul. The mosques of Istanbul are not included on this list; they are open during the five occasions of daily prayer, and often at other times as well. The larger mosques are open throughout the day. The smaller ones may be closed between the hours of prayer, but if you stand patiently by the front door someone will usually fetch the caretaker, who will open up the mosque for you. Shoes must be taken off at the door and placed on a shelf, usually inside the mosque. Shorts should not be worn when visiting mosques, and women should wear a head-scarf and cover their arms.

The opening hours listed below may vary by half-an-hour or an hour depending on the season. All museums and monuments are closed on the following national holidays: 23 April, 1 May, 19 May, 27 May, 30 August, 29 October. They are also closed during the religious holidays of Şeker Bayram and Kurban Bayram, whose dates are regulated by the Islamic lunar calendar.

Hours of admission to the museums and monuments of Istanbul
Ahrida Synagogue, Kürkçü Çeşme Sok. 15, Balat, ☎ 521-5710; permission to visit can be obtained from the Chief Rabbinate (Hahambaşılığı), Yemenici Sok. 23, Tünel, ☎ 244-8794.
Archaeological Museums (Arkeologi Müzeleri), Sultanahmet, ☎ 520-7740): Archaeological Museum: 09.30–16.30; Museum of the Ancient Orient (Eski Şark Eserli Müzesi): 09.30–12.00, Çinili Köşk: 13.00–16.30; all closed Mon.
Aşıyan Museum (Aşıyan Müzesi), Aşıyan Yokuşu, Bebek, ☎ 263-6986): 09.00–17.00; closed Mon, Thu.
Atatürk Museum (Atatürk Müzesi), Halaskargazi Cad. 250, Şişli, ☎ 240-6319: 09.30–16.30; closed Thu, Sun.
Aynalıkavak Palace, Kasımpaşa-Hasköy Yolu, Hasköy, ☎ 256-9750: open 09.00–17.00; closed Mon, Thu.
Basilica Cistern (Yerebatan Saray), Yerebatan Cad. Sultanahmet Square, ☎ 522-1259: 09.00–17.00; open every day.
Beylerbey Palace, Beylerbey, ☎ 321-9320: 09.30–16.00; closed Mon, Thu.
Calligraphy Museum (Hat Sanatler Müzesi), Beyazit Square, ☎ 527-5851: 09.00–16.00; closed Sun, Mon.

Caricature Museum, Karacılar Cad., Barbaros Bulvarı, ☎ 521-1264; 09.00-17.00 daily.

Carpet and Kilim Museum (Halı ve Kilim Müzesi), Sultanahmet, ☎ 518-1330: 09.30–12.00, 13.00–16.00; closed Sun, Mon.

Dolmabahçe Palace, Beşiktaş, ☎ 258-5544: 09.00-16.00; closed Mon, Thu.

Fethiye Camii (Church of the Pammakaristos), Fener, ☎ 522-1750: permission to visit must be obtained from the Haghia Sophia Museum.

Fire Brigade Museum (Itfaiye Müzesi), Itfaiye Cad. 9, Fatih, ☎ 524-1126: 09.30–14.30; closed Mon.

Galata Mevlevi Dervish Monastery and Museum of Divan Literature (Divan Edebiyatı Müzesi), Galip Dede Cad. 15, Tünel, ☎ 245-4141: 09.30–16.30; closed Mon.

Galata Tower (Galata Kulesi), Büyükhendek Sok., Şişhane, ☎ 245-1160: 08.00–21.00 daily.

Haghia Eirene (Aya Ireni): open only during recitals.

Haghia Sophia (Aya Sofya), Sultanahmet, ☎ 522-1750: 09.30–16.30; closed Mon.

Ibrahim Paşa Palace and the Museum of Turkish and Islamic Art (Türk ve Islam Eserleri Müzesi), At Meydanı 46, Sultanahmet, ☎ 518-1385: 10.00–17.00; closed Mon.

Ihlamur Palace, Ihlamur Cad., Beşiktaş, ☎ 261-2991: 09.00–17.00; closed Mon, Thu.

Kariye Camii (Church of St. Saviour in Chora), Kariye Camii Sok., Edirnekapı, ☎ 631-9241: 09.30–16.30; closed Tue.

Istanbul (Çelik Gülersoy) Library (Istanbul Kitaplığı), Soğukçeşme Sokağı, Sultanahmet; ☎ 512-5730: 10.00–12.00, 13.30–16.30, Mon, Wed, Fri.

Rahmi M. Koç Industrial Museum, Hasköy Cad. 27, Sütluce, ☎ 265-7153: 10.00–17.00; closed Mon.

Küçüksu Palace, Küçüksu: 09.00–16.00; closed Mon, Thu.

Lighting & Heating Systems Museum (Aydınlatma ve Isıtma Araçları Müzesi), Turistic Yol Altı 12, Büyük Çamlıca, tel (216) 328-5680: open daily 09.00–17.00.

Maslak Palace, Büyükdere Cad., Maslak, ☎ 276-1022: 09.00–17.00; closed Mon, Thu.

Military Museum (Askeri Müze), Harbiye, ☎ 233-7115: 09.00–17.00; closed Mon, Tue.

Mosaic Museum (Mozayik Müzesi), Arasta Sokağı, Sultanahmet, ☎ 518-1205: 09.00–17.00; closed Tue.

Municipal Museum (Şehir Müzesi), Yıldız Sarayı, Barbaros Blv., ☎ 258-5344; 09.30–16.30; closed Thu.

Naval Museum (Deniz Müzesi), Beşiktaş, ☎ 261-0040: 09.30–17.00; closed Mon, Tue.

Painting and Sculpture Museum (Resim ve Heykel Müzesi), Beşiktaş. ☎ 261-4298: 12.00–16.00; closed Mon, Thu.

Reform Movement Museum (Tanzimat Müzesi), Gülhane Parkı, ☎ 512-6384: 09.00–17.00; open daily.

Rumeli Hisarı Fortress, Rumeli Hisarı, ☎ 263-5305: 09.30–17.00; closed Mon.

Sadberk Hanım Museum, Büyükdere Cad. 27–29, Sarıyer, ☎ 242-3813: 10.30–17.00; closed Wed.

Sait Faik Abasıyanık Museum, Çayır Sok. 15, Burgaz, ☎ 228-1647: open Tue– Fri, 09.00–13.00, 14.00–17.00, Sat, 09.00–13.00; closed Sun, Mon.

Theodosius Cistern, Eminönü Belediye Basbakanlığı, Klod Farer Cad.: open 09.00–17.00; closed Sun.

Topkapı Sarayı, Sultanahmet, ☎ 512-0480: 09.30–17.00, Harem 10.00–16.00; closed Tue.

Women's Library and Cultural Centre (Kadın Eserleri Kütüphanesi ve Bilgi Merkezi), Fener Mahallesi, Haliç 34220, Istanbul, ☎ 534-9550, fax 523-7408: open Sat, Sun, Mon, 13.00–19.00, Tue, Thu, Fri, 10.00–19.00; closed Wed.

Yedikule (Castle of the Seven Towers), Yedikule, ☎ 585-8933: 09.30–17.00; closed Mon.

Yıldız Palace Museum (Yıldız Sarayı Müzesi), Barbaros Blv., Beşiktaş, ☎ 258-3080/ext 380; Şale Köskü and Marangozhane: 10.00–16.00; closed Mon, Tue.

▌ Entertainment

The Istanbul Festival. From mid-June through mid-July each year there is an international cultural festival in Istanbul, in which outstanding artists from all over the world give performances in the city. Many of these performances are held in settings of great beauty and historic interest, as was the case when Mozart's *Abduction from the Seraglio* was put on in Topkapı Sarayı. For information and tickets consult the office of the Istanbul Festival at the Atatürk Kültür Merkezi in Taksim Square, ☎ 293-3133.

Atatürk Cultural Centre (Atatürk Kültür Merkezi), Taksim Square, ☎ 251-5600; puts on a full season of opera, ballet and symphonic music, featuring both Turkish and foreign artists.

Aksanat Cultural Centre (Aksanat Kültür Merkezi), Akbank Building, Istiklal Cad., Beyoğlu, ☎ 252-3500; exhibition, arts and music centre and arts workshop.

Cemal Reşit Rey Concert Hall, Harbiye, ☎ 240-5012; used for chamber orchestra recitals and other musical performances.

Folk-dancing
The Turkish National Folk-Dance Group is one of the best ethnic dance-groups in the world. The number and variety of Turkish folk-dances reflects the great depth and diversity of the cultures that have flourished in Anatolia and that have been assimilated by the people of Turkey. The Group performs in the colourful native costumes of the various regions of Anatolia where the dances originate and they are accompanied by the lively music from those areas. Performances are given at both the **Açık Hava Tiyatrosu** (Open-Air Theatre) near the Hilton, and also in **Rumeli Hisarı**, the ancient Ottoman fortress on the European shore of the Bosphorus.

Cinemas
Akmerkez, Akmerkez Shopping Mall, Etiler, ☎ 282-0505
Alhazar, Istiklal Cad. 179, Beyoğlu, ☎ 245-7538
Atlas, Istiklal, Cad. 209, ☎ 243-7576

Beyoğlu, Istiklal Cad. Halep Pasajı 140, ☎ 251-3240
Dünya, Istiklal Cad., Fitaş Pasajı 24–26, ☎ 252-0162
Emek, Istiklal Cad, Yeşilçam Sok. 5, ☎ 293-8439
Feriye, Sabancı Cultural Centre, Ortaköy, ☎ 236-2864
Fitaş, Istiklal Cad., Fitaş Pasajı 24–26, ☎ 249-0166
Kent, Halaskargazi Cad. 281, Şişli, ☎ 241-6203
Site, Halaskargazi Cad. 291, Şişli, ☎ 247-6947

Night clubs and discos

All of the de luxe hotels have night clubs with dancing and shows. A selection of other night clubs and discos are the following:
Alem, Köybaşı Cad. 10, Yeniköy, ☎ 223-0012
Eylül, Birinci Cad. 23, Arnavutköy, ☎ 256-4980
Galata Tower Night Club, Galata Tower, ☎ 245-1160
Hayal Kahvesi, Istiklal Cad., Büyükparmakkapı Sok. 19, Beyoğlu, ☎ 244-2558
Kervansaray, Elmadağ, ☎ 247-1630
Orient House, Beyazit, ☎ 517-6163
Pasha, Muallim Naci Cad. 142, Ortaköy, ☎ 259-7061
Parisienne, Elmadağ, ☎ 247-6362
Roxy, Arslan Yatağı Sok. Sıraselviler, Taksim, ☎ 249-4839

◼ General Information

Emergencies

hospital *hastahane*
doctor *doktor*
pharmacy *eczane*
first aid *ilk sihhi imdad*
sick *hasta*
I'm sick *Hastayim*
I want a doctor *Doktor istiyorum*
There's a fire! *Yangın var!*

Emergency telephone numbers

Ambulance: 112
Police: 155
Fire: 110
Telephone enquiries: 118

National holidays

The Turkish National Holidays, when all offices, shops, schools, banks and museums are closed, are as follows: 23 April (National Sovereignty Day and Children's Day), 1 May (Spring Day), 19 May (Sport Day), 27 May (Constitution Day), 30 August (Victory Day), and 29 October (Republic Day). There are also two religious holidays when all of the above places are closed; these are Şeker Bayram (3 days) and Kurban Bayram (4 days). The dates of these holidays are regulated according to the Muslim lunar calendar and thus occur 12 days earlier each year.

Opening hours

Offices: weekdays 09.00–12.00, 13.30–17.00; Sat, 09.00-13.00; closed Sun, holidays.
Shops (varies): weekdays 09.00–13.00, 14.00–19.00; Sat, 09.00–12.00, 13.00–19.00; closed Sun, holidays.

Banks: 09.00–13.00, 14.00–17.00 (09.00–14.00 in summer); Sat, 09:00–12.00.
Covered Bazaar: 08.00–18.30 every day except Sun.

Shopping malls
Two giant new shopping malls have recently been opened in Istanbul; these are:
Akmerkez, Etiler, ☎ 282-0170
Galleria: Ataköy (outside the city on the Marmara shore near the airport), ☎
559-9560

Telephones and postal information
Stamps (*Posta pulu*) are sold only at post offices (for location see Useful
Addresses, above). Special delivery is called *expres* (*patınıtuker*) and registered
mail is *taahhütlü*. Telegrams may also be sent at post offices. There are numerous
telephones (*telefon*) all over the city, particularly at kiosks, and also in post
offices. They are operated by metal discs called *jetons*, which may be purchased
at Post Offices. Most cities in the USA and Europe can now be dialled direct from
Istanbul; this can be done most conveniently at the larger hotels, where there
are English-speaking telephone operators.

Newspapers (gazete) and books (kitap)
Most British newspapers and the *International Herald Tribune* are on sale in the
highest-class hotels, in foreign-language bookshops, and at a few centrally located
kiosks. There is a good English-language newspapers, the *Daily News*. There are
several bookshops (*kitabevi*) that have a fairly large supply of books in English; the
best is *Robinson Crusoe*, Istiklal Cad. 389, Tünel, Beyoğlu, ☎ 293-6868.

Religious services
Protestant: Christ Church (Anglican), Serdarı Ekrem Sok. 82, Tünel, ☎ 251-
5616; St. Helena's, British Consulate, Galatasaray, ☎ 244-4228; Dutch Chapel
(non-denominational), Postacılar Sok. 4, Beyoğlu, ☎ 244-5212. **Roman
Catholic**: St. Espirit, Cumhuriyet Cad. 250B (across from the Hilton), ☎ 248-
0910; St. Antoine, Istiklal Cad. 325, Beyoğlu, ☎ 244-0935; St. Louis des
Français, Postacilar Sok. 11, ☎ 244-1075. **Jewish**: Neve Shalom Synagogue,
Büyük Hendek Sok. 67, Beyoğlu, ☎ 244-7566. **Greek Orthodox**: Haghia
Trianda, Meselik Sok. 11/1, Taksim, ☎ 244-1358.

Barbershops (berber) and hairdressers (küafor)
There are barbershops and hairdressing salons in all of the top hotels.

Toilets (tuvalet)
Signs read WC or OO. Men is Baylara or Erkeklere; Women is Bayanlara or
Kadınlara. There are also large public toilets in the Karaköy and Eminönü pedestrian underpasses, in the Hippodrome, next to the Galatasaray Lisesi, and behind
the water-distribution building in Taksim Mey. There are public toilets in most
mosque courtyards.

■ The Turkish Language

Turkish primer. Although Turkish may look and sound a bit strange at first, it is not really a difficult language. With a little work and practice, a visitor can soon learn enough basic Turkish to communicate with the people of Istanbul. (An excellent primer is *Teach Yourself Turkish* by Geoffrey Lewis, Hodder & Stoughton, London.)

The sounds of Turkish. All letters have one and only one sound; no letters are silent, although the ğ is almost silent. Vowels have their short continental value; i.e. **a** as in father (the rarely used â sounds rather like ay), **e** as in get, **i** as in sit, **o** as in doll, **u** as in bull; ı (undotted) is between i and u, somewhat as the final a in Anna; **ö** is as in German or the u in further; **ü** is as in German or the French u in tu. Consonants are as in English except for the following: **c** as j in jam, **ç** as ch in church; **g** always hard as in give, never soft as in gem; **ğ** is almost silent, tending to lengthen the preceding vowel; **s** is always unvoiced as in sit, never like z; **ş** is as s in sugar. Turkish is very lightly accented, most often on the last syllable, but all syllables should be clearly and almost evenly articulated.

Numbers

1	*bir*	14	*on dört*	80	*seksen*
2	*iki*	15	*on beş*	90	*doksan*
3	*üç*	16	*on altı*	100	*yüz*
4	*dört*	17	*on yedi*	101	*yüz bir*
5	*beş*	18	*on sekiz*	200	*iki yüz*
6	*altı*	19	*on dokuz*	300	*üç yüz*
7	*yedi*	20	*yirmi*	1000	*bin*
8	*sekiz*	21	*yirmi bir*	1001	*bin bir*
9	*dokuz*	30	*otuz*	1,000,000	*bir milyon*
10	*on*	40	*kırk*	one-half	*yarım*
11	*on bir*	50	*elli*	one and one-half	*bir büçük*
12	*on iki*	60	*altmış*		
13	*on üç*	70	*yetmış*	zero	*sıfır*

Clock and calendar

day *gün*
Sunday *Pazar*
Monday *Pazartesi*
Tuesday *Salı*
Wednesday *Çarşamba*
Thursday *Perşembe*
Friday *Cuma*
Saturday *Cumartesi*
month *Ay*
January *Ocak*
February *Şubat*
March *Mart*
April *Nisan*

May *Mayıs*
June *Haziran*
July *Temmuz*
August *Auğustos*
September *Elul*
October *Ekim*
November *Kasım*
December *Aralık*
week *hafta*
hour, time *saat*
What time is it? *Saat kaç?*
one o'clock *saat bir*
ten past two *ikiyi on geçiyor*
twenty to five *beşe yirmi var*

at six o'clock   *saat altıda*
morning   *sabah*
noon   *oğle*
afternoon   *oğleden sonra*
evening   *akşam*

night   *gece*
today   *bugün*
yesterday   *dün*
tomorrow   *yarın*
year   *yil, sene*

Everyday words and expressions

Hello   *merhaba*
I   *ben*
we   *biz*
you   *sen* (singular), *siz* (plural)
he, she, it   *o*
they   *onlar*
this   *bu*
that   *şu* (near), *o* (remote)
Where?   *Nerede?*
here   *burada*
there   *şurada* (near), *orada* (remote)
When?   *Ne zaman?*
Why?   *Niçin?*
What?   *Ne?*
Yes   *Evet*
No   *Hayır*
very, much   *çok*
little   *az*
large   *büyük*
small   *küçük*
and   *ve*
good   *iyi*
very good   *çok iyi*
bad   *fena*
very bad   *çok fena*
now   *şimdi*
later   *sonra*
before   *evvel*
fast   *çabuk*
slow   *yavaş*
open   *açık*
closed   *kapalı*
forbidden   *yasak*
please   *lütfen*

Thank you   *Tesekkürederim (or simply 'merci')*
What do you want?   *Ne istiyorsunuz?*
I want tea   *Çay istiyorum*
I don't want tea   *Çay istemiorum*
Is there any tea?   *Çay var mi?*
There isn't any tea   *Çay yok*
Do you understand?   *Anliyormusun?*
I understand   *Anliyorum*
I don't understand   *Anlamiyorum*
How are you?   *Nasilsiniz?*
I'm fine   *Iyiyim.*
Not so good   *Şöyle böyle*
nice, pretty   *güzel*
very nice   *cok güzel*
Good morning   *Gün aydın*
Good evening   *Iyi akşamlar*
Good night   *Iyi geceler*
Sir   *Efendim*
Mr   *Bay*
Mrs   *Bayan*
man   *adam*
men   *adamlar*
woman   *kadın*
What is your name?   *Isminiz ne?*
Where are you from?   *Nerelisiniz?*
I'm English/American   *Ben Ingliz/Amerikalı*
Welcome   *Hoş geldiniz* (in response one says *Hoş bulduk*)
Goodbye   Allahısmarladık (said by the person leaving), *Güle güle* (said by the person who remains)

Getting around town

Street   *Sokak*
Road   *Yol*
Avenue   *Caddesi*
Boulevard   *Bulvar*
Square   *Meydan*
bus   *otobüs*

taxi   *taxi*
train   *tren*
What time does the train leave/arrive?   *Tren ne zaman kalkıp/variyor?*
car   *oto*
petrol   *benzin*

Taxi *Taxi*
Train *Tren*
What time does the train leave/arrive?
Tren ne zaman kalkıp/variyor?
car *oto*
petrol *benzin*
station *istasyon*
ticket *bilet*

right *sağ*
left *sol*
straight ahead *doğru*
mosque *cami*
church *kilise*
museum *müze*
cinema *sinema*
theatre *tiyatro*

At the hotel

Hotel *Otel*
room *oda*
Do you have a room? *Oda var mı?*
Yes, there is a room *Oda var*
There is no room *Oda yok*
For how many people? *Kaç kişi?*
One person *Bir kişi*
Two people *İki kişi*
For how many days/nights? *Kaç
    gün/gece?*
How many rooms/beds? *Kaç
    oda/yatak?*
single room *tek oda*

double room *çift oda*
toilet *tuvalet*
bath *banyo*
with bath *banyolu*
without bath *banyosuz*
shower *duş*
hot water *sıcak su*
soap *sabun*
towel *havlu*
toilet paper *tuvalet kâğıt*
key *anahtar*
The bill, please *Hesap, lütfen*

At the restaurant

restaurant *lokanta*
meal *yemek* (it also means 'to eat')
menu *yemek listesi*
waiter *garson*
What is there to eat? *Yemek ne var?*
knife *bıçak*
fork *çatal*
spoon *kaşık*
plate *tabak*
napkin *pecete*
glass *bardak*

cup *fincan*
bottle *şişe*
water *su*
milk *süt*
bread *ekmek*
salt *tuz*
pepper *biber*
without oil *yağsız*
(A more detailed vocabulary is given
    in the section on Turkish food.)

In the market

market *pazar*, or *çarşı*
shop *dukkan*
How much is this? *Bu, ne kadar?*
Too much *Çok pahalı*
Cheap *Ucuz*
How many? *Kaç tane?*
one item *bir tane*

one more *bir tane daha*
bigger *daha büyük.*
smaller *daha küçük.*
half a kilo *yarım kilo.*
250 grams *iki yüz elli gram*
money *para*
Do you have change? *Bozuk para var
    mı?*

Stamboul—the Old City

The name Stamboul generally refers to that part of the city which was once called Constantinople; that is, the area bounded on the south by the Sea of Marmara, on the north by the Golden Horn, and on the landward side by the Theodosian walls. Modern Istanbul extends far beyond those limits, including within its boundaries the European and Asian suburbs along the Marmara coast, as well as both shores of the Bosphorus out almost as far as the Black Sea. There are now four bridges across the Golden Horn. The first of these is the Galata Bridge, about 1km above the confluence of the Golden Horn and the Bosphorus. The second is the Atatürk Bridge, another kilometre up the Golden Horn. A third bridge spans the Horn a short distance inside the Theodosian walls, and a fourth just outside the walls is used by the ring road.

1 · The Galata Bridge to the First Hill

The **Galata Bridge** (Pl. 11,1) is the focal point of Istanbul's colourful and turbulent daily life. Throughout the day and early evening a steady stream of pedestrians and traffic pours across the bridge between Karaköy and Eminönü, the busy squares at its Galata and Stamboul ends.

The upper level of the Galata Bridge is an excellent vantage-point from which to orient yourself before setting out to explore the city. Looking towards the eastern tip of Stamboul you see **Saray Burnu** (Pl. 11,2), the point where the Golden Horn and the Bosphorus meet and flow together into the Marmara. Above Saray Burnu, on what was once the acropolis of ancient Byzantium, there are the pavilions and gardens of **Topkapı Sarayı** (Pl. 11,4), the imperial residence of the Sultan and his court in Ottoman times. To the right of the Saray, on the summit of the First Hill, is the majestic edifice of **Haghia Sophia** (Pl. 11,3), the former cathedral of Byzantine Constantinople.

The most prominent monument on the Second Hill is **Nuruosmaniye Camii** (Pl. 10,4), a baroque mosque framed by a pair of minarets. The Third Hill is crowned by the **Süleymaniye** (Pl. 10,2), the great mosque complex of Süleyman the Magnificent, which dominates the skyline of the old city as seen from the bridge. On the foreshore between these two hills stands **Yeni Cami** (Pl. 10,2), the large mosque that looms over the Stamboul end of the Galata Bridge, while farther off to the right, in the midst of the market quarter, is the smaller **Mosque of Rüstem Paşa** (Pl. 10,2).

The Fourth Hill is surmounted by **Fatih Camii** (Pl. 5,8), the Mosque of the Conqueror, whose dome and four minarets can be seen in the middle distance, some way in from the Golden Horn. Atop the Fifth Hill, on the edge of the ridge above the Golden Horn, stands the **Mosque of Selim I** (Pl. 5,6), flanked by a pair of minarets. Just visible in the distance are the dome and two minarets of **Mihrimah Camii** (Pl. 4,6); this marks the summit of the Sixth Hill, some 2km in from the Golden Horn and just inside the Theodosian walls. Across the Golden Horn the skyline is dominated by the huge, conical-capped **Galata Tower** (Pl. 7,7), the last remnant of the medieval Genoese town of Galata.

Skyline of the old city from the Sea of Marmara

The south bank of the Golden Horn around the present Galata Bridge was in Byzantine times the principal port and commercial quarter of the city. During the latter period of the Byzantine Empire this part of the city was given over to various Italian city-states, some of which had obtained trading and commercial concessions as early as the 11C. The area above the Galata Bridge was the territory of the Venetians, which included piers, warehouses, and the residences of the merchants and their families. The area below the bridge belonged to the Amalfians; beyond that was the concession of the Pisans, followed by that of the Genoese, who also controlled the town of Galata.

The area at the Stamboul end of the Galata Bridge, where Yeni Cami now stands, was in earlier centuries a Jewish quarter, wedged in between the concessions of the Venetians and the Amalfians. The Jews who resided here were members of the schismatic Karaite sect, who broke off from the main body of Orthodox Jewry in the 8C. The Karaites continued to live in this quarter until the end of the 16C, when they were evicted to make way for the construction of the first mosque on this site; they were then resettled across the Golden Horn in Hasköy, where some of their descendants continue to live today.

*Yeni Cami

Yeni Cami (Pl. 11,1), the New Mosque, is one of the most familiar landmarks in the city, standing as it does at the Stamboul end of the Galata Bridge. It was the last large mosque to be built in the city during the classical period of Ottoman architecture. Although it cannot stand comparison with the great imperial mosques built earlier in that era, it does possess a certain grandeur, an effect that is enhanced by its dramatic setting beside the Golden Horn.

The name of the building is an abbreviation of Yeni Valide Camii, the New Mosque of the Valide Sultan. The first stage in the construction of the mosque began in 1597, under the sponsorship of the Valide Sultan Safiye, mother of Mehmet III. The original architect was Davut Ağa, a former apprentice of the great Sinan. Davut Ağa died in 1599, however, and was replaced by Dalgiç Ahmet Çavuş. Dalgiç Ahmet Çavuş remained chief architect until 1603, when the death of Mehmet III halted construction of the mosque, for his mother then lost her power in the Saray. The unfinished mosque was then destroyed by fire in 1660. Later in that year the fire-black-

Yeni Cami

ened ruins of the mosque attracted the attention of the Valide Sultan Turhan Hadice, mother of Mehmet IV, who decided to rebuild it as an act of piety. The architect Mustafa Ağa was placed in charge of the project, which was completed in 1663 according to the original design.

Exterior. Like all of the imperial mosques in Istanbul, Yeni Cami is preceded by a monumental courtyard on its west side. The ceremonial entrance to the courtyard, now unused, is at the centre of the west end of the avlu, where a grand flight of steps leads up to an ornate portal. A calligraphic inscription over the gateway reads: 'Health be with you; should you be worthy, enter in for eternity.'

Today you enter the avlu through smaller gateways at its northeast and southeast corners. The courtyard is square in plan, measuring 39m on a side along its outer walls. Around its interior there is a portico carried by a peristyle of 20 columns, with a pretty octagonal şadırvan in the centre. The şadırvan serves merely a decorative function, and the ritual ablutions are performed at water-taps along the south wall of the mosque. The façade of the mosque under the porch is decorated with tiles and faience inscriptions forming a frieze. The two centre columns of the portico that frame the entrance to the mosque are of a most unusual and beautiful marble not seen elsewhere in the city.

The external form of the mosque reflects its internal plan. The central area of the interior is defined by four great piers that ultimately support the central dome. This central dome is flanked by semidomes along both axes of the mosque, with smaller domes at each corner of the building and still smaller domes beside these, two each at the northeast and southeast corners, and three each above the northwest and southwest corners. The north and south sides of the mosque have two storeys of porticoed galleries that produce a charming effect. Notice how the four great piers are continued above the building as tall octagonal turrets. Smaller turrets rise in steps on either side of the semidomes, producing with them and the central dome a symmetrical cascading impression. The two minarets, which are entered from within the mosque, rise from the northwest and southwest corners of the building. Both of them have three şerefes with superbly sculptured stalactite parapets.

At the northeast corner of Yeni Cami there is a very interesting and unusual building, through the centre of which a great arched portal allows you to pass around behind the mosque. This is a **kasır**, or **royal pavilion**, entered by the

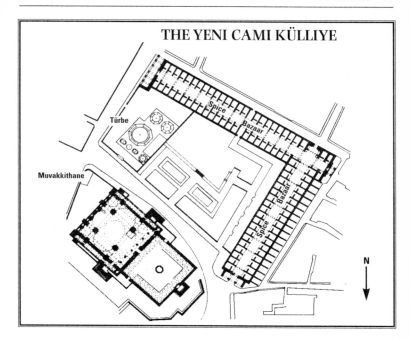

THE YENI CAMI KÜLLIYE

ramp beside the mosque. This ramp leads to a suite of rooms (not open to the public) built over the archway, and from there a door leads to the royal loge within the mosque. The suite included a salon, a bedchamber and a toilet, with kitchens on the lower level, and served as a pied-à-terre for the royal family when they attended services.

Interior. The floor plan of the mosque is a square 41m on a side. On the sides and rear there is a colonnade of slender marble columns connected by alternating large and small arches, which vary in shape from ogee to pointed to round. This colonnade supports the upper gallery, which has a fine marble parapet.

The central area of the interior is defined by the four huge piers that are the main support of the dome. From these piers rise four great arches, and between them four squinches make the transition from square to circle. Upon the circle so formed rests the dome, which is 17.5m in diameter and has its crown 36m above the floor. The interior space is extended by the semidomes along the east–west axis of the mosque, with smaller domes above each corner of the nave and still smaller domes above the corners of the galleries.

The royal loge is at the northeast corner of the gallery; this is screened off by a gilded grille to shield the Sultan and his family from the public gaze when they attended services. This loge is connected by a long passageway to the royal pavilion at the northeast corner of the mosque.

The blue, green and white tiles on the walls are of inferior quality, since the great age of Turkish ceramics ended half a century before the mosque was completed. Nevertheless, the interior furnishings of the mosque are quite elegant in detail, particularly the mihrab, which is decorated with gilded stalactites, and the mimber, which is surmounted by a conical canopy carried on marble columns.

Precincts. The original külliye of Turhan Hadice included the mosque, a hospital, a primary school, a mausoleum, two fountains, a public bath, and a market, with the proceeds of the latter two institutions contributing to the support of the rest of the foundation. The hospital, the public bath, and the primary school have been destroyed, but the other institutions remain, although only the market is now open to the public.

The market of the Yeni Cami complex is the handsome L-shaped building to the south and west of the mosque. It is called the *****Mısır Çarşısı**, the **Egyptian Market**, because it was originally endowed with the Cairo imposts. In English it is more commonly known as the **Spice Bazaar**, because it was famous for selling spices and medicinal herbs. Spices and herbs are still sold there, but the bazaar now deals in a wide variety of other commodities making it, perhaps, the most popular market in the city. There are 88 vaulted rooms in all, as well as chambers above each of the entryways at the ends of the two halls. The main entrance is through the monumental gatehouse near the southwest corner of Yeni Cami, an impressive building that gives an imperial Ottoman touch to the busy market square outside.

The domed building at the east end of the mosque garden is the **türbe** of the Yeni Cami külliye. Turhan Hadice, foundress of the mosque, is buried there. Buried beside her is her son, Mehmet IV, and five later sultans: Mustafa II, Ahmet III, Mahmut I, Osman III and Murat V.

The small building to the west of the türbe is the **library**; this was built by Turhan Hadice's grandson, Ahmet III. Across the street from the türbe, at the corner of the wall enclosing the garden of the mosque, is a tiny polygonal building with a quaintly shaped dome. This was the **muvakithane**, the house and workshop of the müneccim, the mosque astronomer. The müneccim regulated the times for the five occasions of daily prayer and fixed the exact times of sunrise and sunset during Ramazan, beginning and ending the daily fast which is required during that period. It was also his duty to determine the day on which each month of the Muslim lunar calendar commenced, beginning with the appearance of the first sickle moon in the western sky just after sunset.

We now head eastward from Yeni Cami Meydanı on Bankacılar Cad., which at the first intersection becomes Hamidiye Cad. At the near corner on the right we see the **sebil** of the Yeni Cami külliye, now used for commercial purposes. In Ottoman times attendants in the sebil would have handed out cups of water free to passersby.

Here we make a short excursion up the street to the right, Şeyhülislam Hayri Efendi Cad., stopping just beyond the alleyway on the left, Zahire Borsası Sok. There on the left we come to a building on whose façade there are a series of reliefs between the windows, the uppermost ones in the form of five-pointed stars. This is the Yıldız Dede Tekkesi, a former dervish lodge that also included a hamam. The tekke was founded shortly after the Turkish Conquest by Yıldız Dede, a Turkish holy man who was Fatih's court astrologer. This is evident in his name for in Turkish yıldız means 'star', whereas Dede, or 'Grandfather', is one of the words used in Turkish to designate a saint, another being Baba, or 'Father'. According to Evliya Çelebi, the 17C Turkish chronicler, Yıldız Dede built his hamam on the site of an ancient synagogue, perhaps one belonging to the Karaite Jews, since it stood in their quarter.

We now retrace our steps as far as Zahire Borsası Sok, an L-shaped alley that takes us out to Hamidiye Cad. At the bend in the alley we pass on our right the **Ticaret Borsası**, the Istanbul Stock Exchange. This is housed in part of the medrese of Sultan Abdül Hamit I (see below), which takes up the rest of that side of the alleyway and the block beyond it.

At the end of the alley we turn right on Hamidiye Cad., and so passing the famous confectionary of Şekerci Hacı Bekir, founded here in 1777. The founder, Hacı Bekir, was chief Şekerci, or Confectioner, in the reign of Abdül Hamit I; he is renowned for his creation of lokum, or Turkish Delight, which was first sold in this shop.

The huge building that takes up the whole block on the opposite side of Hamidiye Cad. is the fourth Vakıf Hanı, built by the architect Kemalettin Bey in the years 1911–26. This was built on the site of the imaret of Abdül Hamit's külliye, standing opposite the Sultan's medrese and türbe.

At the near corner on the right we see the **türbe of Abdül Hamit I** (1774–89), adjoining the corner of his medrese. Buried alongside Abdül Hamit I is his son, the mad Mustafa IV. The külliye also included a sebil, which was displaced when Hamidiye Cad. was widened some years ago.

A short distance farther along the avenue intersects Ankara Cad., which leads uphill from the Golden Horn to the ridge that joins the First and Second Hills. **Ankara Cad**. follows approximately the course of the defence-walls that Septimius Severus built around the town of Byzantium c AD 200.

To the left of the intersection is **Sirkeci Station**, the last stop for trains from Europe to Istanbul. The station was built by the German architect Jachmund in 1887–89 as the terminus for the Orient Express, which then made its first through run from Vienna to Istanbul.

We now turn right to follow Ankara Cad. as it curves uphill along the valley between the First and Second Hills. After crossing the next intersection we see on our left the buildings of the **Vilayet**, the headquarters of the Governor of the Istanbul Province. This was originally the headquarters of the Grand Vezir, for whom the main building of the Vilayet was erected in 1844. As we pass the Vilayet we see beyond it the great edifice of Haghia Sophia, with Haghia Eirene off to the left.

At the next corner we see on our right the **Iranian Consulate**, built in 1866 by the Italian architect Domenico Stampa. We turn left here to enter Prof. K. Ismail Gürkhan Cad. About 100m along on the left is the entrance to the men's section of the *Cağaloğlu Hamamı (Pl. 11,3), the most famous and beautiful Turkish bath in Istanbul. The entrance to the women's section is around the corner to the left. The hamam was built in 1741 by Mahmut I, who used the revenues from the baths to pay for the upkeep of the library that he endowed in the nave of Haghia Sophia.

Interior. The layout of the men's bath is conventional, in that the bathers pass from the camekan through the rather small soğukluk into the hararet, with all three chambers laid out in a straight line. But in the women's baths the camekan is not in

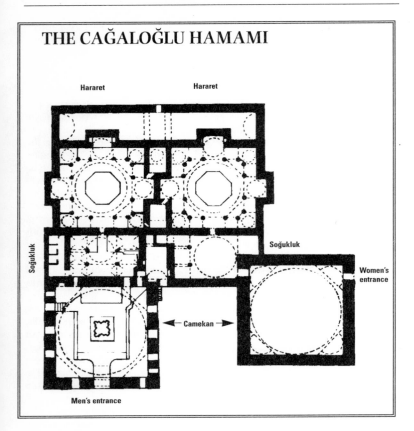

THE CAĞALOĞLU HAMAMI

line with the other two chambers but set off to the side, with one of its corners joining a corner of the soğukluk. As in most Turkish baths, the most elaborate chamber is the hararet, which has the same form in both the men's and women's sections. This is an open cruciform chamber, with its central dome supported by a circlet of columns and with domed side chambers in the arms of the cross.

We continue to the next main intersection, where we turn left on Alay Köşkü Cad., which runs downhill as far as Alemdar Cad. At the last turning on the left before reaching the avenue we come to **Beşir Ağa Camii** (Pl. 11,3), a small mosque complex raised on a platform.

The complex was built in 1745 by Beşir Ağa, Chief Black Eunuch in the reign of Mahmut I. In addition to the mosque, the külliye consisted of some shops, which occupied the vaults in the platform beneath the building, a medrese, and a dervish tekke. The tekke is no longer occupied by dervishes, since their various orders were disbanded in the early years of the Turkish Republic. The pretty baroque sebil on the corner was also part of Beşir Ağa's foundation.

We go on to Alemdar Cad., where to our left we see a large ornamental gateway with a projecting canopy in the Turkish rococo style. This is the famous **Sublime Porte**, which in former times led to the palace and offices of the Grand Vezir, the Ottoman equivalent of the Prime Minister. The first palace on this site was built by Sokollu Mehmet Paşa when he became Grand Vezir in 1564, during the last years of Süleyman's reign. From that time onwards most of the business of the Ottoman Empire was conducted here, behind the Sublime Porte. Hence the gateway came to stand for the government itself, and ambassadors were accredited to the Sublime Porte rather than to the Ottoman Empire, just as to this day ambassadors to Great Britain are accredited to the Court of St. James. The present gateway was built early in the reign of Abdül Mecit I, dating to about 1840. It now leads to various offices of the Vilayet, the main entrance to which is on Ankara Cad.

Across the avenue from the Sublime Porte there is a large polygonal gazebo built into a defence tower of the Saray wall. This is the **Alay Köşkü**, the Review Pavilion, originally constructed in about 1565 and rebuilt in 1819. The interior consists of several rooms reached by a ramp rising from just inside the gate of Gülhane Park. From the latticed windows of this kiosk the Sultan could observe the comings and goings at the palace of his Grand Vezir across the way. The kiosk also served as a pavilion from which the Sultan could review military parades or the fabulous Processions of the Guilds that were held from time to time in the earlier centuries of Ottoman rule in Istanbul. The Alay Köşkü is now used as an exhibition hall.

We now turn right on Alemdar Cad., which leads uphill past the entrance to Gülhane Park (see p 83). As we do so we pass a neo-classical building that now houses a government office. This was built in 1875 as a Military College, housing the faculty of Forensic Medicine.

After the next turning we come on our right to **Zeynep Sultan Camii**, a small baroque mosque, (Pl. 11,3). This was built in 1769 by the architect Mehmet Tahir Ağa for Princess Zeynep, a daughter of Ahmet III. In form the mosque is merely a square room covered by a dome, with a square projecting apse to the east and a porch with five bays to the west. The walls are built with alternating courses of brick and stone, and the cornice of the dome undulates to follow the extradoes of the round-arched windows, all of which makes the building look more like a Byzantine church than an Ottoman mosque. The külliye also included a primary school, which stands at the corner of the street just below the mosque, and the picturesque little cemetery where the foundress and members of her family and household are buried. The elaborate rococo sebil outside the cemetery gate is not an original part of the foundation. It was built in 1778 as part of the külliye of Abdül Hamit I and was moved to its present location when Hamidiye Cad. was widened some years ago.

We now continue up Alemdar Cad. After crossing the side street just beyond Zeynep Sultan Camii we stop and look to our right, where a short stretch of crenellated wall is just visible over the building in front of it. This is the apse of the Byzantine church of the **Theotokos** (Mother of God) **in Chalcoprateia**, of which only this and a short stretch of the north wall remain. Chalcoprateia means 'the Copper Market', which is where the church was built c 450 by the Empress Pulcheria, sister of Theodosius II and wife of the Emperor Marcian.

The handsome though sombre building that occupies most of the left side of the street is the recently restored **Soğuk Kuyu Medresesi** (Pl. 11,3), a work of the great Ottoman architect Sinan. The medrese was commissioned by Cafer Ağa, Chief White Eunuch in Topkapı Sarayı in the reign of Süleyman the Magnificent. After Cafer's death in 1557 the work was continued by his brother Gazanfer Ağa, who succeeded him as Chief White Eunuch, and the medrese was completed by Sinan in 1559–60. The hillside slopes quite sharply here, so Sinan first erected a vaulted brick substructure to support the medrese and its court-yard. The entrance to the medrese is approached from the street running parallel to the west end of Haghia Sophia, where a little alleyway leads down to the inner courtyard of the building. The principal rooms of the medrese are arrayed around the courtyard, with the dershane, or lecture-hall, in the large domed chamber to the left as you enter, and the hücre, or students' cells, laid out around the other three sides of the cloister. The medrese now serves as a very attractive little bazaar of old Turkish arts and crafts.

Alemdar Cad. now brings us to the summit of the First Hill, which in the early centuries of the Byzantine Empire was the imperial quarter and the centre of the political and religious life of the city. The long park to the right, the **Atmeydanı**, occupies the site of the Hippodrome, the huge arena that played such an important and dramatic role in the public life of Byzantine Constantinople.

The area immediately to the east of the Atmeydanı is dominated by the huge Sultan Ahmet Camii (Pl. 11,5), better known to foreigners as the **Blue Mosque** (see p 85). The area between the Blue Mosque and Haghia Sophia was the site of the Augustaeum, the principal square of ancient Constantinople. The long park beyond the far end of the modern square here was the site of the Byzantine Senate, which formed the east side of the Augustaeum. At the southeast corner of the Augustaeum stood the Chalke, or Brazen House, the monumental vestibule of the Great Palace. Nearby were the Baths of Zeuxippus, the largest public bathing establishment in the ancient city. The Baths stood on about the same site as the Hamam of Roxelana, the handsome Ottoman building that forms the east side of the park between the Blue Mosque and Haghia Sophia. On its north side the Augustaeum gave access to the church of Haghia Sophia and the Patriarchal Palace, the centre of the religious life of the Byzantine Empire. Just to the west of the Augustaeum there was another large square, the Basilica, a porticoed stoa surrounded by some of the most important public institutions in the city, including the University of Constantinople, the central law-courts of the Byzantine Empire, the principal public library, and a large outdoor book-market.

2 · **Haghia Sophia

Haghia Sophia (in Turkish, Ayasofya; Pl. 11,3) is one of the most extraordinary buildings in the history of architecture. It was the cathedral of Byzantine Constantinople for more than a thousand years, and then for nearly five centuries after the Turkish Conquest it was one of the most important mosques of Istanbul before being converted into a museum.

■ **Admission**. The museum and its precincts are open 09.30–16.30 every day except Mon.

Haghia Sophia

History and architecture of the church

The present edifice of Haghia Sophia is the third church of that name to stand upon this site. The first church was completed c 360, in the reign of Constantius, son and successor of Constantine the Great, and was dedicated to Haghia Sophia, the Divine Wisdom, an attribute of Christ. This church was burnt down on 9 June 404 during a riot by the supporters of St. John Chrysostom, the Patriarch, who had been removed from his see by the Empress Eudoxia, wife of the Emperor Arcadius. A new church was later built on the same site by Theodosius II, son and successor of Arcadius, and dedicated on 10 October 415. This structure, which is known to archaeologists as the Theodosian church, was destroyed by fire on 15 January 532, the first day of the Nika Revolt. Justinian began work on the present church just a month after the end of the rebellion, on 23 February. The Emperor appointed as head architects Anthemius of Tralles and Isidorus of Miletus, the two greatest mathematical physicists of the age. Anthemius died during the first year of construction, but Isidorus carried the project through to completion late in 537 and it was dedicated on 26 December of that year.

During the construction a number of structural crises had occurred, due partly to the rapidity with which the building had been erected, and also because of the enormous stresses caused by the vast and shallow dome. Then the structure was weakened by a series of earthquakes that shook the city between 553 and 557, and on 7 May 558 the eastern part of the dome collapsed, along with the arch and semidome on that side of the church. The original architects were no longer alive, so Justinian entrusted the task of rebuilding the church to a nephew of Isidorus, Isidorus the Younger. Isidorus decided to change the design of the dome, making it less shallow so as to reduce the lateral stresses. The reconstruction project was completed late in 563 and the church was rededicated on Christmas Eve of that year.

A series of earthquakes in the 9C–10C damaged the building and caused cracks to appear in the dome, until finally in 989 part of the dome and the eastern arch collapsed. Basil II entrusted the reconstruction to Trdat, an Armenian architect, and on 13 May 996 the church was once again reopened. The church interior suffered grievously in the Latin sack of Constantinople in 1204, when it was stripped of all of its sacred relics and other precious objects. During the Latin Occupation Haghia Sophia served as the Roman Catholic cathedral of the city, and a campanile was erected near the northwest corner of the building.

Following the recapture of Constantinople by the Byzantines in 1261 Haghia Sophia was reconsecrated as a Greek Orthodox sanctuary, after which the campanile was taken down and the church refurbished and redecorated. The dome suffered another partial collapse on 19 May 1346, and the church was closed until the reconstruction was completed in 1355. But during the last century of Byzantine rule Haghia Sophia was allowed to fall into serious disrepair, sharing in the general decay of the dying city, and travellers to Constantinople in that period report that the church was partially in ruins.

The last Christian liturgy in Haghia Sophia began shortly after sunset on Monday, 28 May 1453. Constantine XI Dragases arrived an hour or so before midnight and prayed there silently for a time before returning to his post on the Theodosian walls, where he died the following morning when the city fell to the Turks. Within hours the Turkish soldiers broke into Haghia Sophia and carried off those they found there into bondage, ending the final Christian liturgy in the church.

Conversion to a mosque. Mehmet II, now known as Fatih, or the Conqueror, made his triumphal entry to the city on the afternoon of 29 May and rode directly to Haghia Sophia. After inspecting the building he ordered that it should be converted into a mosque immediately, and the following Friday he attended the first Muslim service to be held in Aya Sofya Camii, the Mosque of Haghia Sophia.

This conversion required some structural additions and changes, including the erection of a minaret at the southeast corner of the building and the construction of a mihrab and mimber, along with other furnishings used in Muslim services. Fatih and his successors continued to keep Haghia Sophia in good repair throughout the Ottoman period, for it was one of the principal imperial mosques of the city and was always held in great veneration. The last and most thorough of these restorations was commissioned by Abdül Mecit I and was carried out in 1847–49 by the Swiss architects Gaspare and Giuseppe Fossati. During the course of this restoration, the surviving figurative mosaics were cleared of the whitewash and plaster with which they had been covered earlier in the Ottoman period. When the project was complete the mosaics were covered over once again, in order to protect them from further damage.

In April 1932 Thomas Whittemore and other members of the Byzantine Institute began the task of uncovering and restoring the mosaics, and at that time Haghia Sophia was closed to prepare the building for its reopening as a museum in 1934. Restoration of the mosaics was not completed until 1964, when the galleries of Haghia Sophia were for the first time opened to the public.

The church of Haghia Sophia

Exterior. Haghia Sophia was laid out so that its apse faced in the direction of sunrise at the time of the winter solstice; thus it is oriented some 33 degrees south of east. In order to simplify the description of its plan, it will be assumed that its apse faces due east.

The main ground plan of the building is a rectangle, approximately 70m in width and 75m in length. At the centre of the east wall there is a projecting apse, semicircular within and three-sided on the exterior, while to the west the church is preceded by a narthex and exonarthex. Above the central part of the rectangular area there is an enormous dome, with smaller semidomes to east and west and conches over the apse and the four corners. These cover the central area of the nave, which is flanked by side aisles with galleries above that extend around the south side of the church above the narthex.

This was the basic form of the church as it was originally planned, but structural crises during the construction and subsequent damage due to earthquakes necessitated the erection of **buttresses** on all sides of the building. The oldest of these are the two pairs of very tall buttresses built against the north and south walls of the church. These were built during Justinian's reign, either in the latter part of the original construction or in the rebuilding of the dome in 558–63. The pillar-like outer parts of these buttresses were added in 1317 by Andronicus II to provide additional support for the building. The four massive flying-buttresses against the west gallery were added in the second half of the 9C. The arch buttresses and retaining walls at the east side of the church were erected by Fatih soon after the Conquest.

Fatih also built the brick **minaret** at the southeast corner of the building; this replaced a temporary wooden minaret which had been erected over the southeast buttress when Haghia Sophia was converted into a mosque. Selim II built the stone minaret at the northeast corner in 1574, and the two stone minarets at the northwest and southwest corners were added a year or so later by his son and successor, Murat III. All three of these stone minarets are works of Sinan, who also restored all of the buttresses and the fabric of the building.

In addition to these repairs and additions, a number of subsidiary structures were erected in the precincts of Haghia Sophia during both the Byzantine and Ottoman periods; these minor monuments will be examined after visiting the church itself.

Atrium and narthexes. Justinian's church was preceded on its west side by an **atrium**, a porticoed arcade that enclosed an area 47.7m wide and 32.3m deep. The portico has now completely disappeared and what remains of the site of the atrium, roughly its eastern half, is occupied by the garden to the west of Haghia Sophia, where the present entrance to the museum is located. The columns and other ancient architectural fragments arrayed in the garden to the left were unearthed in Istanbul in the past half-century. In the courtyard to the right we see the şadırvan of Aya Sofya Camii, a rococo structure built c 1740 by Mahmut I.

We now head towards the entrance of the building itself, which is on the middle of its west side. As we approach the entrance we see on our left an excavation pit, where we look down upon the remains of the **Theodosian church**, excavated in 1935. Some blocks of the reliefs remain in the pit, while other huge architectural fragments have been arrayed farther to the north in the atrium.

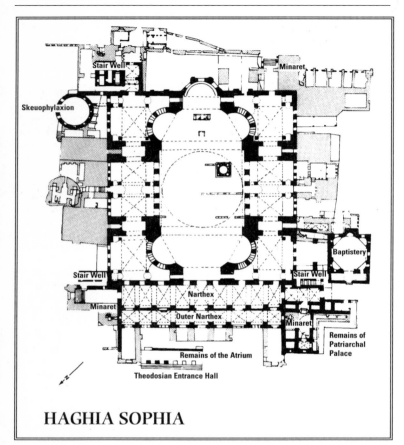

HAGHIA SOPHIA

What remains in situ is chiefly the foundations of a monumental entrance-porch, which is shown in an architectural drawing to the left of the entrance to the exonarthex. These remains show that the Theodosian church was a basilica comparable in size to the present structure. It well deserved the name by which it was generally known and which it passed on to its successor: Megale Ekklesia, the Great Church.

We now enter the church and find ourselves in the exonarthex. This was originally entered through the three doors at the centre and one each at the north and south ends of the portico, with great arched windows piercing the other four bays. This outer vestibule comprises nine cross-vaulted bays separated by arches, as does the narthex. Within the bays of the narthex to the right of the entryway we see a number of huge rectangular panels of mosaic pavement stacked edgeways along the walls. These are from the Great Palace of Byzantium and were discovered during excavations in the 1930s on the slope of the First Hill just below the Blue Mosque, where the most interesting mosaics are preserved in situ in the Mosaic Museum (see p 99). In the last bay of the exonarthex we see a huge Byzantine sarcophagus in verd antique. This contained the remains of the Empress Eirene, wife of John II Comnenus (1118–43), and it was originally in the church of the Pantocrator which they erected on the Fourth Hill.

Five doors in alternate bays lead from the exonarthex into the narthex, which is about twice as high and wide as the outer vestibule. The piers and walls of the narthex are revetted with superb marble panels. According to Paul the Silentiary, who wrote a long poem celebrating the rededication of Haghia Sophia by Justinian in 563, these and other marbles in the church came from all over the Empire. In order to obtain the elaborate symmetrical patterns of each panel, thin blocks of marble were cut in two, sometimes in four, and opened out like a book so that the natural veining of the stone was duplicated and quadruplicated, giving the unique natural designs that add so much to the beauty of the interior.

Beneath the Turkish painted decoration on the vaults of the narthex we can see here and there portions of the original **mosaic decoration**. According to the Silentiary, this mosaic decoration originally covered the great dome, the semidome, the north and south tympanum walls, and the vaults of the narthex, aisles, vestibules and galleries, a total area of more than 1.5 hectares. This decoration, much of which has survived, consists of large areas of plain gold ground adorned around the edges of architectural forms with bands of geometrical or floral designs in various colours. Simple crosses in outline on the crowns of vaults and the soffits of arches are constantly repeated, and, according to the Silentiary, there was a cross of this kind on the crown of the great dome. It is clear from the Silentiary's description that in Justinian's time there were no figurative mosaics in the church. The figurative mosaics that have survived are all from after the Iconoclastic period, which ended in 843.

Doors open off from each bay of the narthex into the nave, with the largest one at the centre, flanked by a pair of somewhat smaller portals, and with two pairs of still smaller doors to either side. The monumental central door from the narthex into the nave was known as the **Imperial Gate**; this was reserved for the use of the Emperor and the Patriarch and those who accompanied them in processions. Above the centre of the brass cornice of this door there is an embossed decoration in very low relief showing a dove flying straight down above an open book, which rests upon a throne framed by two pillars and an arch. The book is inscribed with these words from the tenth chapter of the Gospel according to St. John, in which Jesus addresses the Pharisees: 'Our Lord spoke: "I am the door of the sheep; by me, if any man enter he shall be saved, and shall go in and out, and shall find pasture"'.

In the lunette above the Imperial Gate there is a figurative mosaic, the second of those uncovered in 1932. The mosaic shows Christ seated upon a jewelled throne, his feet resting upon a stool. He raises his right hand in a gesture of blessing, and in his left hand he holds a book with this inscription: 'Peace with you, I am the Light of the World'. At the left a crowned figure prostrates himself before the throne, his hands outstretched in supplication. Above, on either side of the throne, there are two roundels, the one on the left containing a bust of the Blessed Virgin and the other an angel carrying a staff or wand. It is thought that the imperial figure depicts the Emperor Leo VI, the Wise, and the mosaic is dated to the period of his reign, 886–912.

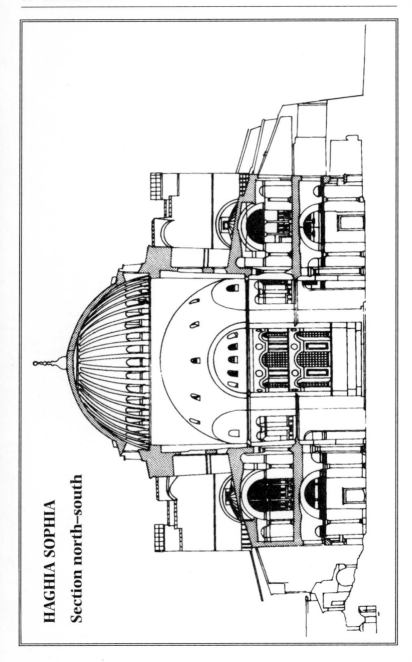

HAGHIA SOPHIA
Section north–south

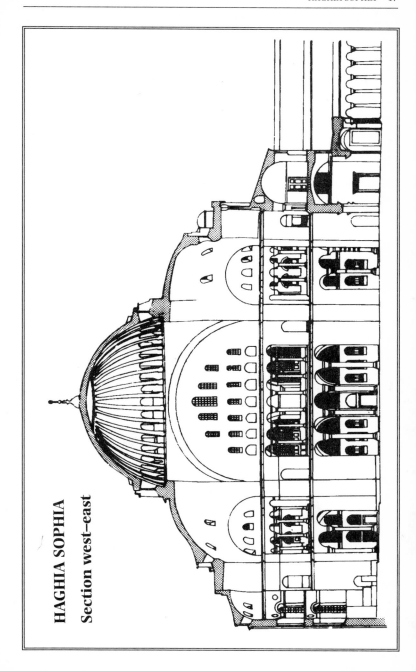

HAGHIA SOPHIA
Section west–east

The nave. Here we enter the nave, inevitably pausing to look upon the vast interior of the church, particularly the fabled dome. The main support for the **dome** is provided by four enormous and irregularly shaped **piers** standing in a square approximately 31m on a side. From these piers rise four great arches, between which four pendentives make the transition from the square to the circular base of the dome. Upon the cornice of this circular base rests the slightly elliptical dome, of which the east–west diameter is about 31m and the north–south approximately 33m, with the crown soaring 56m above the floor, about the height of a fifteen-storey building.

The dome has 40 ribs which intersect at the crown, separated at the base by 40 windows. To the east and west smaller pairs of subsidiary piers support the two great semidomes, each pierced by five windows, which give the nave its vast length. The central arches to north and south are filled with tympanum walls pierced by 12 windows, seven in the lower range, five in the upper.

Between the great piers on the north and south four monolithic columns of verd antique support the galleries, while above six columns of the same marble carry the tympanum walls. At the four corners of the nave there are semicircular exedrae covered by conches, in each of which there are two massive columns of porphyry below and six of verd antique above. At the east, beyond the subsidiary piers, a semicircular apse projects beyond the east wall of the church, covered by a conch.

To the north and south of the main piers there are lateral piers, which are joined structurally with the four main buttresses on those sides, consolidating the fabric of the church. These divide the side aisles and the galleries above into six large compartments on each floor, three on either side, joined to one another by great arches springing between the piers. The north and south compartments on either side consist of a single bay and those at the centre have two bays each, all of them domical cross-vaults surrounded by half-barrel vaults. These vaults are supported internally by a double colonnade within each aisle, with pairs of rectangular pillars at the ends of each aisle and verd antique columns in between.

Columns, capitals and other marbles. The **capitals** of the columns are unique and famous. There are several different types, but they are all alike in having the surface decoration of acanthus leaves and palm foliage so deeply undercut that they produce an effect of white lace on a dark ground. Most of the capitals are of the bowl type, including all of those in the nave and gallery arcades. There, Ionic volutes support a decorated abacus beneath which the bowl-shaped body of the capital is adorned with acanthus leaves. In the centre of these capitals, at both front and back, there are the imperial monograms of Justinian and Theodora.

The capitals of the 16 verd antique columns of the aisles are of similar type but smaller in scale. Those of the eight pillars at the ends of the aisles are much the same, only there the bowl, instead of becoming circular towards its base, remains rectangular throughout.

One of these pillars, that which is sheathed in brass at the northwest corner of the north aisle, is the subject of a medieval legend that still has believers today. Antony of Novgorod, who visited Haghia Sophia in 1200, reports it thus: 'One sees at the side of the church the column of St. Gregory the Miracle-Worker. St. Gregory appeared near this column, and the people kiss it and rub their breasts and shoulders against it to be cured of their pains'. Credulous pilgrims have worn a hole in the brass plate and into the pillar itself, for the moisture contained in the cavity has always been considered a cure for eye diseases and a nostrum for fertility.

There are also many legends concerning the provenance of the various columns in the church, but there is every

Gallery colannade in Haghia Sophia

reason to believe that most or all of them were specially quarried for Haghia Sophia. From the Silentiary's description there can be little doubt that the verd antique columns in the nave and galleries were expressly hewn for Haghia Sophia from the famous quarries near Molossis in Thessaly. But there is a possibility that the eight porphyry columns in the exedrae, which differ from one another in height and diameter, may have been taken from an ancient building, but if so there is no evidence as to its identity.

The only other kind of marble used for columns in the church comes from the ancient quarries on the isle of Proconnesus in the Marmara. This is a soft white stone streaked with grey or black, and is used for the 24 aisle columns of the gallery and the eight rectangular pillars at the ends of the aisles on the ground floor. The pavement of the church, the frames of the doors and windows, and parts of the wall surfaces are also made of this marble.

Other types of decoration in rare marbles are also found in the church. The great square of opus Alexandrinum in the pavement towards the southeast of the nave is the most noteworthy of these. This is made up mostly of circles of granite, red and green porphyry, and verd antique. According to Antony of Novgorod, the Emperor's throne stood upon this square at the time of his coronation, surrounded by a bronze enclosure.

There are also some interesting marble panels above the inner side of the Imperial Gate, in which slabs of verd antique alternate with inlaid panels of various marbles. At the top is an elaborate ciborium with drawn panels revealing a cross on an altar; lower down are other panels with ovals of porphyry, those at the bottom surrounded by pairs of stylised dolphins with foliate tails gobbling up tiny squid with waving tentacles. In the spandrels above the nave there is a superb frieze of sectile work with scrolls of trees and flowers, with the figures of birds perched on the twigs.

The mosque of Haghia Sophia

When Haghia Sophia was converted into a mosque, the mihrab and mimber were oriented towards Mecca, which is some 10 degrees south of the main axis of the church. These undistinguished structures date from the Fossati restorations of 1847–49, as does the Sultan's loge against the northeast pier. The Fossatis were also responsible for the six huge green levhas, or painted wooden plaques, that hang from the piers at gallery level. These were done by the calligrapher Mustafa Izzet Efendi and bear in golden letters the Sacred Islamic Names, those of Allah, the Prophet Mohammed, and the first four Caliphs: Abu Bekr, Umar, Othman, and Ali.

The inscription in the dome is also by Mustafa Izzet Efendi. This is a quotation from the Kuran, reading: 'In the name of God the Merciful and Pitiful; God is the light of Heaven and Earth. His light is Himself, not that which shines through glass or gleams in the morning star or glows in the firebrand'.

The oldest objects now remaining in Haghia Sophia from the Ottoman period are the two beautiful **lustration urns** of Proconnesian marble in the west exedrae. These are late classical or early Byzantine urns to which have been added Turkish lids. According to Evliya Çelebi, these were gifts of Murat III, who also built the large müezzin mahfili beside the southeast pier and the smaller enclosures for chanters against the other three piers. The marble **Kuran kursu** in the north arcade was presented to the mosque by Murat IV, and the very elegant library in the south aisle was built by Mahmut I in 1739. The **library**, which was endowed with the revenues of the Çağaloğlu Baths (see p 37), consists of several domed rooms enclosed with metal grilles. These rooms, housing some 5000 Ottoman books and manuscripts, are revetted with superb Iznik tiles of the 16C, which the Sultan found stored in the Saray.

The mosaics in the nave. The largest and most beautiful of the surviving mosaics in the nave appears in the ****conch of the apse**. This mosaic depicts the Virgin Mary with the Christ Child on her knees; she is dressed in flowing robes of blue with a small cross on the fold of the mantle over her head and one on each shoulder; her right hand rests upon her son's shoulder and her left upon his knee. Jesus is dressed in gold and wears sandals on his feet; his right hand is raised in blessing while his left hand holds a scroll. The Virgin sits on a simple bench-like throne adorned with jewels. Beneath her are two cushions, the lower one green, the upper one embroidered with clubs like those on playing-cards, while her feet rest upon a plinth-like stool, also bejewelled.

At the bottom of the arch that frames the apse there is a colossal figure of the Archangel Gabriel; he wears a divitision, an undergarment, over which is thrown a chlamys, a cloak of white silk; his great wings, reaching nearly to his feet, are of brightly coloured feathers, mostly green, blue and white. In his right hand he holds a staff, in his left a translucent globe through which can be seen his thumb. Although the upper part of his left side and the top of his wings are lost, he is a fine and striking figure.

Opposite, on the north side of the arch, there are only a few feathers remaining from the wings of the Archangel Michael. On the face of the apse conch there remain the first three and the last nine letters of an inscription in Greek, of which the whole of the middle part is now missing. The inscription was an iambic distich that once read in full: 'These icons the deceivers once cast down the pious emperors have again restored'.

The apse mosaic was unveiled by the Patriarch Photius on Easter Sunday 867; this was a most momentous occasion, for it signified the final triumph of the Orthodox party over the Iconoclasts and celebrated the permanent restoration of sacred images to the churches of Byzantium. The two pious sovereigns referred to here are Michael III, the Sot, and his protégé, Basil I, whom Michael had made co-emperor the previous May and who would the following September murder his benefactor and usurp the throne for himself.

Three other mosaic portraits are located in **niches** at the base of the north tympanum wall and are visible from the nave. In the first niche from the west there is St. Ignatius the Younger, who was twice Patriarch of Constantinople (847–58, 867–77); in the central niche is St. John Chrysostom, once Patriarch of Constantinople (398–404); and in the fifth niche from the west is St. Ignatius Theophorus of Antioch. All three of these mosaics are dated to the last quarter of the 9C.

Recent restorations have revealed mosaics on the **soffit** of the great eastern arch that frames the apse. These have not yet been restored and are only faintly visible, although one of them can be identified as the Virgin. These were done immediately after the restoration of 1346–55.

The only other mosaics that are visible from the nave are the six-winged angels in the **east pendentives**. (Those in the west pendentives are imitations in paint done by the Fossatis at the time of their restoration in 1847–49.) These are the only figurative mosaics that were not plastered over during the Ottoman period, although during their restoration the Fossatis did cover the faces with gold-starred medallions, which are still in place. The east pendentives were probably destroyed when that side of the dome collapsed in 1346; the mosaics would therefore post-date the restoration of 1346–55.

The galleries. The public entryway to the galleries is at the north end of the narthex, where a door leads into the north vestibule. From there an inclined ramp leads up to the northwest corner of the galleries. The Silentiary and other ancient sources write that the galleries in Haghia Sophia served as the gynaceum, the women's quarters. However, there is reason to believe that the two eastern bays of the south gallery were reserved for the use of the royal family and, on occasion, for synods of the Greek Orthodox Church. The north and south galleries have the same plan as the side aisles below them, with a series of four cross-vaulted bays in succession with smaller barrel-vaulted bays, while the west gallery, which is above the narthex, is a broad barrel-vaulted hall with nine windows on the west framed by pillars. The throne of the Empress of Byzantium was located just behind the balustrade at the centre of the west gallery; the spot is marked by a disc of green Thessalian marble set into the pavement, framed by a pair of coupled columns of green marble.

Three of the four surviving mosaics in the galleries are located at the far end of the south side, beyond the first bay. That part of the south gallery is partially screened off by two pairs of false doors of marble with elaborately ornamented panels, the so-called **Gates of Heaven and Hell**. Between them is the actual doorway, surmounted by a slab of translucent Phrygian marble, above which a wooden beam carved with floral designs in low relief forms a cornice to the whole gateway. This gateway is certainly not an original part of the church but a later addition, and it was probably erected to close off the far end of the south gallery when it was used for synods of the Greek Orthodox Church.

The latest in date of the **mosaics** in the gallery is located to the right of the entrance to the bay beyond the marble screen, on the east wall of the lateral pier. This is the ****Deesis**, an iconographic type in which Christ is flanked by the Blessed Virgin and St. John the Baptist, who are shown interceding with him on behalf of mankind. Here John is shown to the right, an expression of agonised grief on his ascetic face, and on the left the young and wistful Virgin casts her gaze shyly downward, while between them Christ holds up his right hand in a gesture of blessing. Although two-thirds of the mosaic is now lost, the features of the three figures in the portrait are still completely unmarred. This superb mosaic is dated to the second half of the 13C, and is one of the finest extant works of art from the Palaeologian renaissance.

Set into the pavement just opposite the Deesis there is a **sarcophagus** lid inscribed in Latin capital letters with the name Henricus Dandolo. Dandolo, Doge of Venice, was one of the generals of the Fourth Crusade, and though nearly 90 years old and almost blind he led the charge that broke through the Byzantine defences on 13 April 1204. Dandolo died in Constantinople on 16 June 1205, after which he was buried here in the gallery of Haghia Sophia.

The other **two mosaics in the south gallery** are located on the east wall of the church, at the far end of the last bay. The oldest of these is on the left, next to the apse, where Christ is shown between the figures of an emperor and empress of Byzantium. Christ is shown enthroned, his right hand raised in a gesture of benediction, his left holding the book of Gospels. At the left of the scene the Emperor is shown offering a money-bag, and on the right the Empress is holding an inscribed scroll. Above the Emperor's head an inscription reads: 'Constantine, in Christ, the Lord Autocrat, faithful Emperor of the Romans, Monomachus'. Above the head of the Empress there is this inscription: 'Zoe, the most pious Augusta'. The scroll in her right hand has the same legend as that over the Emperor's head, save that the words Autocrat and Monomachus are omitted for want of space.

It is evident that all three heads and the two inscriptions concerning Constantine have been altered. This has led to the identification of the imperial figures as the Empress Zoe, daughter of Constantine VIII and one of the few women to rule Byzantium in her own right (1042), and her third husband, Constantine IX Monomachus (1042–55). It has been suggested that Constantine is the third imperial figure to be shown with Zoe in the mosaic, replacing her second husband, Michael IV (1034–41), who in turn replaced her first husband, Romanus III Argyrus (1028–34), with the Emperor's head and the identifying inscription being changed on each accession. The mosaic in its present state is thus dated to 1042 or shortly afterwards.

The third of the mosaics in the south gallery is located on the wall to the right of the Zoe mosaic, separated from it by a window. In the centre of this mosaic the Blessed Virgin is depicted holding the Christ Child; to the left an emperor is shown offering a bag of gold, while on the right a red-haired empress holds forth a scroll. The imperial figures are identified by inscriptions as: 'John, in Christ the Lord, faithful Comnenus', and 'Eirene, the most pious Augusta'. The mosaic extends onto the narrow panel of side wall at right-angles to the main composition; here is the figure of a young prince, identified by an inscription as 'Alexius, in Christ, faithful Emperor of the Romans, Porphyrogenitus'. These are portraits of the Emperor John II Comnenus; his wife Eirene, daughter of King Ladislaus of Hungary; and their eldest son Alexius. The main panel has been dated to 1118, the year of John's accession to the throne, and the portrait of Alexius to 1122, when at the age of 17 he became co-emperor with his father. Alexius did not live to succeed John, dying shortly after his coronation. The Emperor was known in his time as Kalo John, or John the Good. The Byzantine historian Nicetas Choniates wrote of John that 'he was the best of all the emperors, from the family of the Comneni, who ever sat upon the Roman throne'. Eirene was noted for her piety and her kindness to the poor, for which she is revered as a saint in the Greek Orthodox Church.

The **fourth of the surviving mosaics** in the galleries is located high on the east face of the northwest pier. This panel represents the Emperor Alexander, who ascended to the throne in May 912, succeeding his elder brother, Leo VI. 'Here comes the man of thirteen months', said Leo with his dying breath, as he saw his despised brother coming to pay his last respects. This cynical prophecy was fulfilled in June of the following year, when Alexander died of apoplexy during a drunken game of polo. The mosaic portrait of Alexander is dated to the brief period of his reign. The portrait shows him standing full-length, wearing the gorgeous ceremonial costume of a Byzantine emperor: crowned with a camelaucum, a conical, helmet-shaped coronet of gold with pendant pearls; draped in a loros, a long gold-embroidered scarf set with jewels; and shod in gem-studded crimson boots. Four medallions flanking the imperial figure bear the legend: 'Lord help the servant, the orthodox and faithful Emperor Alexander'.

The Vestibule of the Warriors. We now return to the narthex and continue straight ahead to the door at its southern end, passing into the chamber beyond it. This was called the Vestibule of the Warriors, since the troops of the Emperor's bodyguard waited here for him while he was in the church. The vestibule is a long and narrow chamber of somewhat irregular plan, being some 0.6m wider at the south than at the north. It is roofed by three cross-vaults of unequal size that bear no relationship to the room below, a fact that has led some authorities to suggest that the vestibule was added after the original construction of the church. If so, the addition must have been made soon afterwards, perhaps during the reconstruction of 558–63, because the gold mosaics on the vault are from Justinian's reign.

The panel in the lunette above the doorway at the inner end of the vestibule was the first figurative mosaic to be uncovered in the restoration project that began in 1932. The mosaic depicts the Blessed Virgin enthroned in an hieratic pose, holding the Christ Child in her lap, as she receives two crowned and haloed figures. The figure on the right, identified by an inscription as 'Constantine, the great Emperor among the Saints', offers the Virgin a model of a walled town representing Constantinople. The figure on the left, identified as 'Justinian, the Illustrious Emperor', offers her a model of a church symbolising Haghia Sophia. The mosaic is dated to the last quarter of the 10C.

The precincts of Haghia Sophia

There are a number of minor monuments of some interest in the precincts of Haghia Sophia, some of them dating from Byzantine times and others from the Ottoman era. These precincts are open during the same hours as the museum, except for the buildings and grounds in the restricted area just to the north of the church.

The Imperial Ottoman tombs. As we leave the church we pass on our left a window that looks into the former **baptistery** of Haghia Sophia. (This is not open to the public.) In 1623 it was converted into a mausoleum to house the remains of the mad Sultan Mustafa I, who died shortly after he was deposed by the Janissaries on 10 September of that year. A quarter of a century later the mad Sultan Ibrahim was interred here too, on 10 September 1648, after he had been deposed and executed on the orders of his mother, the Valide Sultan Kösem.

The domed buildings in the garden to the south of Haghia Sophia are all imperial Ottoman **tombs**. The earliest in date is the **türbe of Selim II** (1566–74), which was completed in 1577. This türbe is important because it is a work of Sinan, and also because both the exterior entrance façade and the whole of the interior are revetted with superb Iznik tiles. The building is square, with an outer dome resting directly on the exterior walls, while within, a circlet of columns supports the inner dome.

The **türbe of Murat III** (1574–95) stands just beside that of Selim II, his father; this fine building was completed in 1599 by Davut Ağa, the successor to Sinan as Chief of the Imperial Architects. It is hexagonal in plan, also with a double dome, and is revetted with Iznik tiles comparable in quality to those in Selim's türbe. Built up against Murat's türbe is the little building called the **Türbe of the Princes**, which contains only the tiny catafalques of five infant sons of Murat IV (1623–40), who died during one of the many plagues that ravaged the Harem.

The latest in date of the türbes in the garden beside Haghia Sophia is that of **Mehmet III** (1596–1603), son and successor of Murat III. The türbe, which stands at the eastern end of the garden, was completed by the architect Dalgıç Ahmet Çavuş in 1603, the year of the Sultan's death. It is octagonal in plan, with a double dome, and is also revetted with superb Iznik tiles.

Minor Ottoman structures. The other Ottoman structures in the courtyard of Haghia Sophia are of very minor importance. The building just to the right of the exit is a primary school built by Mahmut I in 1740. It is very typical of the little Ottoman one-room schoolhouses of that period, consisting of just a porch and a square chamber covered by a dome. This **schoolhouse** was used for the education of the children of the clergy and staff of the Haghia Sophia Mosque. To the left of the exit there is a little domed structure built by the Fossatis in 1847–49. This was the **muvakithane**, the house and workshop of the mosque astronomer, whose sundial can still be seen on the façade of Haghia Sophia.

The ***Hamam of Roxelana** is located on the east side of the park between Haghia Sophia and the Blue Mosque. This splendid public bath was commissioned by Süleyman the Magnificent in the name of his wife Haseki Hürrem, better known in the West as Roxelana. The hamam was designed by Sinan and was completed by him in 1556. It is a double hamam, one end being for men and the other for women. Each end of the building consists of a great entrance hall covered with a vast dome; from there you pass through a corridor with three small domes to the hararet, the steam-room, which is also domed and surrounded by a series of little chambers for bathing. Note the charming symmetry of the building and its gracious lines; it is one of the most attractive and elaborate of the Turkish baths in the city. The hamam has been splendidly restored and is now open to the public as an exhibition gallery for Turkish carpets.

The street that runs past the east end of Haghia Sophia was known in Byzantium as the **Embolos of the Holy Well**. This was a porticoed way by which the Emperor could walk from the Chalke, the monumental vestibule of the Great Palace of Byzantium, to the Holy Well, a sacred spring that issued forth near the southeast corner of Haghia Sophia. From there the Emperor could enter Haghia Sophia directly, passing through the large portal that can still be seen in the east bay of the south aisle.

Farther along this street, at the northeast corner of the church, there is a large Turkish gateway in the rococo style. This is the rear entrance to the garden north of Haghia Sophia (closed to the public). The gateway leads to a building known in Byzantium as the **skeuophylakion**, the treasury of Haghia Sophia, where all the precious objects and sacred vessels of the church were kept. This two-storey building, which stands just to the east of the northeast buttress, is circular in plan and covered with a dome.

Archaeological studies have indicated that the skeuophylakion is older than Justinian's church, and some authorities believe that it served as the treasury of the original church of Haghia Sophia which was completed by Constantius. There is another domed building south of the skeuophylakion, built in between the two north buttresses. This dates to the 16C and was an **imaret**, or free kitchen, which served the clergy and staff of the Mosque of Haghia Sophia.

Restored Ottoman houses

Just opposite the rear gate of Haghia Sophia is the monumental ***street-foun-tain of Ahmet III**, which stands just to the right of the outer entrance to Topkapı Sarayı. This is one of the most beautiful and elaborate of the monumental Ottoman fountains in Istanbul, and is a particularly fine example of Turkish rococo architecture.

***Soğuk Çeşme Sokağı**, the Street of the Cold Fountain, leads off to the left at this point, passing between the precincts of Haghia Sophia and the outer defence-walls of Topkapı Sarayı, leading downhill to the gateway of Gülhane Park. The old Ottoman houses that line the right side of the street, backing against the defence-walls of the Saray, have in recent years been completely restored and sumptuously decorated by the Turkish Touring and Automobile Club (TTOK), directed by Çelik Gülersoy. The houses now form the Ayasofya Pansionlar, a luxuriously appointed hotel complex operated by the TTOK. The largest of the buildings, an Ottoman konak dating from the early 19C, now serves as the **Istanbul Library of the Çelik Gülersoy Foundation**, which houses a rich collection of books on Istanbul and old prints depicting the city in Ottoman times. During the course of the reconstruction of Soğuk Çeşme Sokağı an ancient cistern of the late Roman period was discovered along the lower section of the street, just behind the Soğuk Kuyu Medresesi. The cistern is now the Sarnıç Lokantası, a de luxe restaurant operated by the TTOK, where you can dine in Roman splendour in a most extraordinary setting.

3 · **Topkapı Sarayı

Topkapı Sarayı (Pl. 11,4) was for more than four centuries the imperial residence of the Ottoman sultans. In addition to its historical and architectural interest, it houses extraordinary collections of porcelain, armour, fabrics, jewellery, miniatures, calligraphy, and many precious objects and works of art that once belonged to the sultans and their court.

■ **Admission**. Topkapı Sarayı is open 09.30–17.00 except for the Harem, whose hours are 10.00–16.00; closed Tue. Tickets are purchased in the gateway to the Second Court. A separate ticket must be purchased to gain admission to the Harem.

When Fatih captured Constantinople in 1453, he found the palaces of the Byzantine emperors in such ruins as to be uninhabitable. He then chose a large overgrown area on the broad peak of the Third Hill as the site of his first imperial residence. Here he constructed an extensive complex of buildings and gardens which later came to be known as Eski Saray, the Old Palace. A few years later he decided to build a new palace on the north side of the First Hill, on what had been the acropolis of ancient Byzantium. He began by ringing the acropolis with a massive wall, which extended from the Byzantine sea-walls along the Marmara to those along the Golden Horn. (The new palace eventually took its name from the main sea-gate in this wall; this was Topkapı, the Cannon Gate, so-called because it was flanked by two enormous cannon that threatened all shipping approaching Saray Burnu. This twin-towered gateway was destroyed in the 19C.)

Fatih constructed the palace buildings on the high ground of the acropolis, while on the slopes of the hill and along the shore he laid out extensive parks and gardens. This was done during the period 1459–65, after which the Sultan and his court took up residence in Topkapı Sarayı, leaving the Old Palace as a residence for the women of his departed father's harem. The Harem in Topkapı Sarayı in its present state dates largely from the reign of Murat III (1574–95), with extensive reconstruction and additions chiefly under Mehmet IV (1648–87) and Osman III (1754–57), while the isolated pavilions of the Fourth Court date from various periods.

In 1574, 1665 and 1856 serious fires devastated large sections of the palace, so that many of the older buildings have disappeared, particularly those in the First Court. Nevertheless the three inner courtyards and the buildings around them remain much the same as they were in the 15–16C.

Topkapı Sarayı was much more than just the private residence of the Sultan and his court. It was the seat of the supreme executive and judicial council of the Empire, the Divan, and it housed the largest and most select of the training schools for the imperial civil service, the Palace School. The Saray was laid out to accommodate these various institutions, each in its own buildings around the four main courtyards. The residential section of the palace extended along the west side of the three inner courts, with the Harem, the women's quarters to the south and the Selamlık, the residence of the Sultan and the royal princes, to the north. During the great days of the Ottoman Empire the population of the palace is estimated to have been between 3000 and 4000.

Topkapı Sarayı continued as the principal imperial residence for nearly four centuries, until in 1853 Sultan Abdül Mecit I moved into the new palace of Dolmabahçe on the Bosphorus. The old palace on the First Hill was thereafter little used until 1924, when Topkapı Sarayı was converted into a museum. In the years since then the Saray has undergone a continuous process of renovation and restoration; the high-point came in the 1960s with the opening of part of the Harem to the public.

The First Court

The main entrance to the palace grounds, now as in Ottoman times, is through **Bab-ı Hümayün**, the Imperial Gate, opposite the northeast corner of Haghia Sophia. This monumental gateway was erected by Fatih in 1478. Originally there was a second storey, demolished in 1867 when Sultan Abdül Aziz surrounded the gate with the present marble frame and lined the niches on either side with marble. In Ottoman times these niches often displayed the severed heads of rebels or those convicted of serious crimes. The rooms in the gateway housed the Kapıcıs, or guards, of whom 50 were on watch at all times of the day and night. The older part of the arch contains four beautiful calligraphic inscriptions, one recording the erection of the gate by Fatih and the other three quotations from the Kuran. The tuğra, or imperial monogram, is that of Fatih, and other calligraphic inscriptions record the reconstruction of the gateway by Abdül Aziz in 1867.

The Imperial Gate leads to the **First Court** of Topkapı Sarayı. This was sometimes called the Courtyard of the Janissaries, as they assembled here when on duty in the palace, up until their destruction in 1826 by Mahmut II.

The First Court formed the outer grounds of Topkapı Sarayı, and was not considered to be part of the palace proper. To the right of the entryway there once stood the palace infirmary. Farther off to the right a road leads down to what was once part of the outer gardens of the Saray (not open to the public), and before that the grounds of the Great Palace of Byzantium. The rest of the right side of the First Court consists of a blank wall behind which were the palace bakeries, famous for the superfine white bread baked for the Sultan and the chosen few upon whom he bestowed it. These buildings, several times burned down and reconstructed, now serve as workrooms for the Topkapı Sarayı museum.

To the left of the entryway stands the Byzantine church of Haghia Eirene, which most travellers visit after completing a tour of Topkapı Sarayı (see p 72). Until 1826 the church served as an arsenal for the Janissaries, and later in the 19C it was used as a storehouse for antiquities, principally old Ottoman armaments.

During Ottoman times the area between Haghia Eirene and the Saray defence-walls was the site of a quadrangle that housed the Straw Weavers and the Carriers of Silver Pitchers, with a central courtyard where the palace firewood was stored. Still standing behind a high wall north of Haghia Eirene are the buildings of the **Darphane**, which housed the Imperial Mint and the Outer Treasury. These buildings have recently been restored, and in the summer of 1996 they served as an exhibition area for the Habitat Conference. Just to the north of the Darphane a road leads down to Gülhane Park and the museums that stand on its upper terrace (see p 72); during Ottoman times this area also formed part of the lower gardens of the palace.

Near the far right-hand corner of the First Court there is a fountain known as **Cellad Çeşmesi**, the Executioner's Fountain, so named because the Chief Executioner of the palace cleaned his hands and sword there after performing his duties. The fountain is flanked by two truncated pillars called by the Turks 'Example Stones'. The examples were the severed heads of executed criminals and rebels.

At the far end of the First Court is **Bab-üs Selam**, the Gate of Salutations, better known as **Orta Kapı**, or the Middle Gate. This was the entryway to the Inner Palace, through which only authorised persons could pass, and only on foot. This is a much more impressive entryway than the Imperial Gate and it preserves its original appearance to a greater extent. The gateway is typical of the military architecture of Fatih's time, with its twin octagonal towers capped with conical roofs. The gatehouse itself is surmounted by a crenellated parapet with sloping merlons, concealing a patrol-walk broad enough to hold several cannon. The double-arched doorway is closed by two pairs of splendid doors, the outer one of which bears the date 1524/25.

Above the outer gate is the tuğra of Süleyman the Magnificent and a calligraphic inscription giving the Islamic creed: 'There is no God but God, and Mohammed is his Prophet'. Between the two doorways there is a large central chamber, which now serves as the entrance to the Topkapı Sarayı museum. To the right of this chamber there are several rooms that once housed the head gatekeepers; one of these chambers was used as a waiting-room for foreign

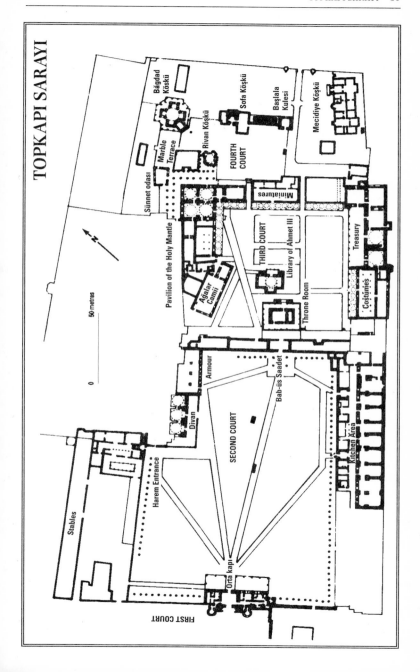

TOPKAPI SARAYI

FIRST COURT

Stables

Harem Entrance

Orta Kapı

SECOND COURT

Divan

Armour

Bab-üs Saadet

Kitchen Area

Ağalar Camii

Pavilion of the Holy Mantle

THIRD COURT

Library of Ahmet III

Throne Room

Costumes

Treasury

Miniatures

Sünnet odası

Marble Terrace

Bağdad Köşkü

Rivan Köşkü

FOURTH COURT

Sofa Köşkü

Başlala Kulesi

Mecidiye Köşkü

N

0   50 metres

ambassadors or other foreign visitors who had an audience with the Grand Vezir or the Sultan (a very rare occurrence). To the left are smaller rooms for the lower-ranking gatekeepers, along with a cubicle for the Chief Executioner and a tiny cell for prisoners awaiting execution.

The Second Court

The enormous **Second Court**, some 130m long and 110m in width at its south end, appears much as it did when it was first laid out in the time of Fatih. The main path through the court is flanked by ancient cypresses and plane trees, with rose bushes growing alongside the other pathways, giving it a tranquil park-like atmosphere. In Ottoman times this was known as the **Court of the Divan**, the Imperial Council, which met in the domed chambers at the far left corner of the courtyard. The Divan and the Inner Treasury beyond it are the only buildings in the courtyard, with the remainder of its periphery consisting simply of blank walls faced by colonnaded porticoes with antique marble columns and Turkish capitals. Beyond the colonnade the whole of the right side of the courtyard is occupied by the kitchens of the palace, while beyond the wall to the left are the Royal Stables, a mosque, and some dormitories, none of which are open to the public at present. (Some of the carriages from the stables are occasionally on view in a gallery to the right of the gate near the southwest corner of the First Court.)

> The Court of the Divan seems to have been designed essentially for the pageantry connected with the transaction of the public business of the Empire. Here, four times a week, the Divan met to deliberate on administrative matters or to discharge its judicial functions. On such occasions the whole courtyard was filled with a vast throng of magnificently dressed officials and the corps of palace guards and Janissaries at least 5000 people on ordinary days, but more than twice that number when some special ceremony was being held. Even at such times an almost total silence prevailed throughout the courtyard, a fact commented upon with astonishment by the travellers who witnessed it.

The Divan. From the Middle Gate five paths radiate to various parts of the courtyard, with the second from the left leading to the Divan. This building, together with the Inner Treasury, projects from the northwest corner of the courtyard and is dominated by the square tower with a conical roof that is such a conspicuous landmark of the Saray. This complex dates in essentials from the time of the Conqueror, though much altered in subsequent periods. The tower was originally lower and had a pyramidal roof; the present structure with its Corinthian columns was built for Mahmut II in 1820.

The Divan complex consists of the Council Chamber (the first room on the left), the Public Records Office, and the Office of the Grand Vezir. The first two rooms, both of which are square and covered by a dome, open widely into one another under a great arch. Both chambers were badly damaged by fire in 1574, and were immediately afterwards restored by Murat III, probably under the supervision of Sinan. During the reign of Ahmet III they were redecorated in a rather charming rococo style, but in 1945 the Council Chamber was restored to appear as it was after the repairs by Murat III. The lower walls are revetted in

Iznik tiles of the best period, while the upper parts of the walls, as well as the vaults and the domes, retain faded traces of their original arabesque painting.

Around three sides of the room there is a low couch covered with Turkish carpets, the divan from which the Council took its name. Here sat the members of the Council: the Grand Vezir in the centre opposite the door, the other vezirs on either side of him in strict order of rank. Over the Grand Vezir's seat there is a grilled window looking into a small room in the tower; this was called the Eye of the Sultan because from his hiding-place he could witness the proceedings of the Council without being observed. The Records Office, which has retained its 18C decor, served as an archive for Divan records and for documents that might be needed at Council meetings. From here a door led to the Grand Vezir's office, though the present entrance is from under the elaborate portico with its richly painted rococo ceiling.

The Inner Treasury. Adjacent to the three rooms of the Divan complex is the Inner Treasury, a long chamber with eight domes in four pairs supported internally by three massive piers. This building dates from the late 15C or the early 16C. Here, and in the vaults below, were stored the tax receipts and tribute money as they arrived from all over the Empire. These funds were kept here until the quarterly pay-days for the use of the Council in meeting the expenses of government, and at the end of each quarter what remained unspent was transferred to the Imperial Treasury in the Third Court.

The Inner Treasury is now used to display the Saray's *Collection of Arms and Armour*. As you would expect, this is especially rich in Turkish arms and armour of all periods, including many objects that belonged to the sultans themselves.

Around the corner from the Divan, directly under the south side of the Divan Tower, is the **Carriage Gate**, one of the two main entrances to the Harem. Guided tours of the Harem start here; check at the Information Desk for scheduled departure times of tours led by English-speaking guides. Most visitors on a first visit to Topkapı Sarayı prefer to postpone their tour of the Harem until they have seen the rest of the palace, returning to the Carriage Gate from the Fourth Court.

Just to the left of the Carriage Gate a doorway leads to the dormitory of the Halberdiers-with-Tresses, which is at present not open to the public. The Halberdiers-with-Tresses were so called because they wore headdresses in which two tufts of horse-hair hung down before their eyes, designed to prevent them from getting a good look at the women when they delivered firewood to the Harem.

The remainder of the west side of the Second Court is occupied by a long portico where various inscriptions in old Turkish script are displayed; they have been assembled from demolished Ottoman buildings all over Istanbul.

Returning to the Middle Gate, we now take the right-hand path towards the Saray kitchens. On the way notice the enormous Byzantine capital lying near the portico; this was excavated outside the Imperial Gate some years ago, along with another capital of the same type that is now in the corridor of the kitchen area, near the southernmost gateway. Both capitals are dated 5C–6C AD.

The *Palace Kitchens. Beyond the three gateways in the east portico a long, narrow courtyard runs the entire length of the area. The palace kitchens open off from this on the east, while the rooms on the west served as storerooms, except for two that were used as mosques by the kitchen staff. The kitchens consist of a long series of ten spacious chambers with lofty domes on the Marmara side—a conspicuous feature of the Istanbul skyline—and equally lofty dome-like chimneys on the side of the courtyard. The two southernmost domes go back to Fatih's time, the other eight to that of Beyazit II, while the cone-like chimneys in front of them are additions by Sinan, who reconstructed much of this area after the devastating fire of 1574.

Today the kitchens are used to display the **Porcelain Collection**, the Saray's incomparable collection of Chinese porcelain and other china and glassware. The Chinese collection, which is housed in the three southernmost rooms, is considered to be the third richest and most varied in the world, surpassed only by those at Peking and Dresden. The collection, of which 4584 pieces are exhibited out of a total of 10,512, was begun by Beyazit II, and augmented by Selim I and above all by Süleyman the Magnificent. The last two kitchens at the north end have been restored to their original appearance and are used for a fascinating display of antique Turkish cooking utensils, including platters, bowls, ladles and kazans, bronze cauldrons of prodigious size, all of which were once used in the Saray kitchens.

The small building with three domes at the north end of the courtyard is variously identified as the confectioner's mosque or as an olive-oil refinery and soap-factory; doubtless it served different purposes at different times. It now houses an interesting collection of Turkish glass from the Beykoz and other Istanbul factories of the 18C–19C, some of it very lovely.

Leaving the kitchen precincts, we now approach **Bab-üs Saadet**, the Gate of Felicity. This is the entryway to the Third Court and to the strictly private and residential areas of the palace, which in Ottoman times was called the House of Felicity. The gateway itself was originally built in Fatih's time, though it was reconstructed in the late 16C and thoroughly redecorated in the rococo style in the 18C. At the time of his accession and on holidays, the Sultan sat before the gate on his gold and emerald Bayram Throne to receive the homage of his subjects and officials.

The Third Court

Just beyond the inner threshold of the Bab-üs Saadet stands the Arz Odası, the *Throne Room. Although this structure is in the Third Court, it belongs by function and use rather to the Second, for here was played out the last act of the ceremonies connected with the meetings of the Divan. Here, at the end of each session of the Council, the Grand Vezirs and the other high officials of the realm waited on the Sultan and reported to him upon the business transacted and the decisions taken, which could not be considered final until they had received the royal assent. Here also the ambassadors of foreign powers were presented to the Sultan upon their arrival and departure.

The Throne Room occupies a small building with a heavy and widely overhanging roof supported on a colonnade of antique marble columns. The foundations date from Fatih's time, but most of the superstructure dates to the reign of Selim I (1512–20); inscriptions record restorations by Ahmet III (1703–30) and Mahmut II (1808–39). The room was restored yet again in more recent times, after having been badly damaged in the fire of 1856.

The Palace School. Apart from the Throne Room, the Treasury, and the Pavilion of the Holy Mantle, all the buildings in and around the Third Court were devoted to the various branches of the Palace School. The School was organised in six divisions, or Halls; the two introductory schools, Küçük Oda (Small Hall) and Büyük Oda (Large Hall), occupied the entire south side, to left and right respectively, of the Bab-üs Saadet. Here also were the quarters of the White Eunuchs, and their Ağa, who were in charge of the administration and discipline of the School. If a boy was talented in any field, he would pass from this introductory school to one of the four vocational Halls.

The Seferli Koğusu, or Campaign Hall, stands on the raised part of the east side of the Court. The north side of the Court, opposite the Bab-üs Saadet, was occupied by the Hasine Koğusu, the Hall of the Treasury, on the right, next to the Treasury itself, and the Kiler Koğusu, the Hall of the Commissariat. Finally, the last and highest of the vocational schools, the Has Oda Koğusu, the Hall of the Privy Chamber, occupies a large building on the west side of the Court between the Pavilion of the Holy Mantle and Ağalar Camii, the principal mosque of the School.

> This elaborately organised school for the training of the Imperial Civil Service appears to be unique in the Islamic world. It was founded and its principles laid down by Fatih, though later sultans added to and modified it. The pages who attended the school came from the Christian subjects of the Empire and likely youths captured in war. They entered at various ages from 12 to 18 and received a vigorous training, intellectual and physical, which in contrast to the usual Islamic education was largely secular and designed specifically to prepare the students for the administration of the Empire. There can be no doubt that the brilliant success of the Ottoman state in the earlier centuries of its existence was to a large extent due to the training its administrators received in the Palace School.

*The Imperial Costume Collection. Turning to the right from the Bab-üs Saadet, we pass the building which was once the Büyük Oda. This building burned down in 1856 but has since been reconstructed and is now used for museum offices. We then come to the Seferli Koğusu, which is preceded by a domed colonnade supported by a row of handsome Byzantine columns in verd antique. The Hall is a long room divided into three aisles by two rows of pillars supporting barrel-vaults. It houses the Imperial Wardrobe, a fascinating collection of costumes of the Ottoman sultans from Fatih's time onwards. There are over 1300 of them in the Saray's collection, of which a few of the most splendid and interesting are on display.

**The Treasury. The rest of the east side of the court is taken up with the rooms, on a slightly lower level, of the pavilion of Mehmet II, which served him and several later sultans as a selamlık, or suite of reception rooms. The vaults below were used as the Privy Treasury and gradually the rooms themselves were turned over to the Treasury as storerooms. It is curious that these rooms, some of the finest in the palace and with an unrivalled view, should from the 17C onward have been used as mere storerooms, even the superb open loggia at the corner having at one time been walled in. The loggia has been opened again and the rooms are used for the display of the palace treasures; it is altogether an astonishing collection, admirably mounted and displayed.

Entering the **first room** on the right, the most notable object on view is an *ebony throne** inlaid with ivory and mother-of-pearl, made for Murat IV. Also of interest are several narghilahs, or water-pipes, with cut-crystal bases and mouthpieces set with diamonds; little coffee-cup holders, including one set with small rose-coloured diamonds, and an enamelled gold pen-box encrusted with gems. The star attractions in the **second room** include the *Eve Throne**, so called because it was used by the sultans, beginning with Ahmet I, in ceremonies that took place on the eve of festivals; the famous *Topkapı Dagger**, made for Mahmut I, with three great emeralds on the sides and one on the top that opens to reveal a watch; a suit of armour that belonged to Murat IV; robes, turbans and aigrettes belonging to various sultans, including one made for his own use by Süleyman, who was an accomplished goldsmith.

The most notable exhibits in the **third room** include a *throne presented by Nadir Shah of Iran to Mahmut I, an elaborate oval seat plated with gold and set with emeralds, rubies and pearls in an enamel base; a Kuran case encrusted with gems, belonging to Mehmet III, with floral design in diamonds on the cover; a gold-plated belt, armlet and goblet belonging to Shah Ismail, part of the loot taken by Selim I in his victorious Persian campaign of 1514; and a golden reliquary for the supposed hand of St John the Baptist. The **fourth room** features the golden *Bayram Throne** first used by Murat III in 1579; the Kaşık Elması, an 86-carat diamond, the fifth-largest in the world, worn by Mehmet IV in the aigrette of his turban on his accession to the throne in 1648; an 80-carat diamond that belonged to Ahmet I; along with jewel-studded pendants, aigrettes and other precious objects belonging to various sultans.

In the centre of the Court, standing by itself, is the **Library of Ahmet III**, erected in 1719 near the site of an older pavilion with a pool. It is an elegant little building of Proconnesian marble consisting of three domed areas flanked by three loggias with sofas and cupboards for books; although 18C, the decoration is still almost wholly classical.

The two main buildings on the north side of the Court were both damaged in the fire of 1856; the nearest one was entirely reconstructed and now serves as offices for the Director of the Museum. The farther one, beyond a passage leading to the Fourth Court, houses the **Exhibition of Turkish and Islamic Art**. The ground floor has changing exhibitions of Islamic miniatures, while the upper gallery displays portraits of all of the Ottoman sultans. From an artistic point of view the **miniature collection** is perhaps the supreme treasure of the Saray. The collection is said to number more than 13,000, of which only a few are exhibited at any one time.

The oldest miniatures in the collection are in the so-called Fatih Album, whose works, tentatively ascribed to Mohammed Siyah Kalem, are from Iran and dated variously from earlier than the 13C to the second half of the 15C. The oldest Ottoman works are by Matrakci Nasuh, court-painter of Süleyman, including 137 miniatures illustrating the stages of the Sultan's campaign into Iraq in 1537. One of these miniatures shows Süleyman's fleet sailing down the Golden Horn, with both Istanbul and Galata represented in accurate detail. Other

Double colonnade of the Privy Chamber

miniatures are in three albums commissioned by Murat III, one of the books illustrating a procession of the guilds held in 1583 to celebrate the circumcision feast of the future Mehmet III, which lasted for 57 days. The latest in date of the imperial albums was composed in 1720 to commemorate the circumcision feast of four sons of Ahmet III; here the miniatures are by Levni, one of the two greatest Ottoman painters, the other being Nigâri, whose finest work is a portrait of Süleyman in his last years.

In the last building on the north side of the courtyard, beyond another passage leading to the Fourth Court, there is a chamber known as the **Treasury of the Sword Bearer**. This is now used to exhibit some of the Saray's fascinating **Clock Collection**, which includes priceless timepieces from all periods in the history of the palace, only a portion of which are on display.

The west side of the Court is occupied by the following buildings, going from north to south: the Pavilion of the Holy Mantle, the Hall of the Privy Chamber, and the Mosque of the Ağas. The first will be visited presently; meanwhile, a few words will suffice for the other two. Has Oda, the Hall of the **Privy Chamber**, was the highest of the vocational divisions of the Palace School. It was limited to 40 pages in immediate attendance upon the Sultan, and included the highest of the officials in the Inner Palace. These chambers are now used for temporary exhibitions. Beyond the Has Oda, the building that juts out at an angle is **Ağalar Camii**, the Mosque of the Ağas, the principal place of worship of the Palace School. Though dating from the time of the Conqueror, it has been much remodelled and now houses the Library of the Saray.

*The Pavilion of the Holy Mantle. A portal at the northwest corner of the courtyard gives entrance to **Hirka-i Saadet Dairesi**, the chambers where the relics of the Prophet Mohammed and other sacred objects are preserved. These relics, of which the Prophet's mantle is the most sacred, were brought from Egypt by Selim I after his conquest of that country in 1517, when he assumed the title of Caliph. For centuries these relics were guarded here and displayed on state occasions only to the Sultan, his family, and his immediate entourage; in 1962 the present exhibit was arranged and opened to the public. The Pavilion itself consists of four domed rooms forming a square, with a fifth domed room opening off to the left of the southwest chamber. The foundation and plan of the Pavilion date to the reign of the Conqueror; at that time and until the mid 19C it formed part of the Has Oda, or Selamlık. Murat III partly reconstructed the rooms and revetted them with tiles, and Mahmut II added some rather unfortunate embellishments.

The kiosks in the Portico of Columns. A door in the right wall of the northeast room of the Pavilion leads into the open L-shaped Portico of Columns. This portico adjoins two sides of the Pavilion of the Mantle, with kiosks opening off from the east and west ends. The one to the east is the **Rivan Köşkü**, built in 1636 by Murat IV to commemorate his capture of Rivan (modern Erivan), in the Caucasus. It is a cruciform room entirely revetted in Iznik tiles dating from just after the greatest period, but still beautiful, while the outside has a polychrome revetment of marble. The kiosk at the west end of the portico is the **Sünnet Odası**, the Circumcision Room; this was built for Sultan Ibrahim in 1641, and for the next two centuries the circumcision rites of young Ottoman princes were carried out here. Both the interior and exterior of the kiosk are covered with ceramic tiles; none of these is from Ibrahim's own time but they range in date from the earliest Iznik style in cuerda seca technique through the great period in the second half of the 16C and the early 17C.

The Fourth Court

The Sünnet Odası stands at the south end of a broad marble terrace overlooking the Golden Horn. This terrace forms the west end of the Fourth Court, which is not really a courtyard but a garden on several levels, adorned with a number of pavilions. At the southeast corner of the terrace there is a large marble pool with a cascade fountain at its centre, once the scene of aquatic revels staged for Crazy Ibrahim by the women of his harem. On the left side of the terrace there is a curving balustrade of white marble carved in openwork design. At the centre of this balustrade, hanging high out over the lower gardens of the Saray, there is a charming little balcony covered by a domed canopy in gilded bronze carried on four slim bronze pillars. An inscription on the canopy records that the balcony is called **Iftariye** and was made in 1640 for Sultan Ibrahim. The balcony takes its name from the Iftar, the festive meal taken after sunset in the holy month of Ramazan, which ends the daily fast.

At the north end of the terrace stands the ****Baghdad Köşkü**, built in 1638 by Murat IV to commemorate his capture of Baghdad the previous year. The kiosk is cruciform in plan and its wide overhanging eaves are carried by an arcade of slender marble columns. The columns are crowned with lotus capitals and the voussoirs of the arches are in alternating white and coloured marble with

The Marble Terrace in the Fourt Court

serrated edges. The walls inside and out are sheathed in ceramic tiles, chiefly blue and white. The interior is furnished with carved wooden cabinets and coffee-tables inlaid with mother-of-pearl, and the window-recesses on four sides are lined with embroidered divans. One of the eight walls is taken up with a splendid bronze chimney-piece, while the other seven are graced by stained glass windows in two courses. The dome of the kiosk is adorned with elaborate arabesques on a crimson ground, painted on leather.

A staircase beside the pool leads down into what was once the garden of Ahmet III, one of the sites of his fabulous Tulip Festivals. At the centre of the garden there is a charming pavilion known as the **Sofa Köşkü**. The pavilion is believed to have been built for Ahmet III, probably as a pied-à-terre for his use during the Tulip Festival; in 1752 the building was redecorated in the rococo style by Mahmut I. Farther on there is a low tower called **Hekimbaşı Kulesi**, the Tower of the Chief Physician.

Across the road is a pavilion standing on a marble terrace; this is the **Mecidiye Köşkü**, the last building to be erected in the Saray before it was abandoned as an imperial residence. This kiosk was erected in about 1840 for Abdül Mecit I, and is entirely Western in style. In recent years its lower floor and terrace have been converted into a branch of the Konyalı restaurant, from which there is a panoramic view out across the Marmara to the Asian suburbs of the city.

**The Harem

We now return to the Court of the Divan (the Second Court) to visit the Harem. At present about a score of rooms, passageways and courtyards are open to the public on guided tours, including most of the more important and impressive chambers.

The Harem was not an original part of the palace as laid out by Mehmet II. Fatih seems to have designed Topkapı Sarayı primarily as the administrative centre of his Empire, reserving the Old Palace on the Third Hill for his court and his harem. This arrangement was maintained by his three immediate successors: Beyazit II (1481–1512), Selim I (1512–20), and Süleyman the Magnificent (1520–66), at least during the early years of his reign. According to tradition, Süleyman allowed Roxelana to install herself in Topkapı Sarayı, but probably only in wooden pavilions, and his son Selim II (1566–74) seems to have followed this. The first permanent structures in the Harem appear to have been built during the reign of Selim's son Murat III (1574–95).

The **Carriage Gate** took its name from the fact that the Harem ladies entered their carriages here when they were allowed to go for an outing. Above the gateway is an inscription giving the date 1588. The gateway opens into a small, dark vestibule called **Dolaplı Kubbe**, the Dome with Cupboards (**1**); this is followed by a larger chamber revetted with fine tiles, which served as a **guard-room** (**2**). On the left a door opens to a long passage leading down to the gardens of the Saray, and another gives access to the mosque of the Black Eunuchs; while on the right a door opens into the Divan tower. Straight ahead is the long, narrow **Courtyard of the Black Eunuchs** (**3**). The left side of the courtyard is bordered by an arcade of ten marble columns with lotus capitals, above which hang wrought-iron lamps that once lighted the way to the Carriage Gate. The building to the rear of the porch, which is revetted in ceramic tiles, was the **barracks** of the Black Eunuchs (**4**); an inscription in the courtyard bears the date 1668–69, indicating that this part of the Harem was rebuilt by Mehmet IV after the great fire of 1665.

At the far end of the courtyard a staircase on the left leads up to the Schoolroom of the Princes, where the young sons of the Sultan received their primary education; these are pretty rooms with good tiles, but they are not open to the public. Just beyond the Schoolroom a door leads to the apartments of the Kızlar Ağası, the Chief Black Eunuch; these too are closed to the public.

At the far end of the Courtyard of the Black Eunuchs is the **Cümle Kapısı**, the Main Gate (**5**), which opens into the Harem proper. This leads to a second guard-room (**6**), from the left side of which a long, narrow corridor stretches to the open **Courtyard of the Cariyeler** (**7**), or women servants. On the right side of this courtyard there are three suites of rooms for the chief women officials of the Harem: the Head Stewardess, the Treasurer, and the Chief Laundress. Their domed and tiled rooms are very attractive, particularly as they overlook the lower gardens of the Saray. The long staircase just beyond the three suites leads down to a large courtyard on a much lower level, once the site of the Harem hospital.

Just beyond the Cümle Kapısı a gateway opens onto a wide corridor which extends the entire east side of the Harem; this is the **Altın Yol**, the Golden Way, a name which often appears in the history of the palace. At the very beginning of the corridor an opening on the left leads to the large open **Courtyard of the Valide Sultan** (**8**). The Valide Sultan reigned over the Harem and frequently dominated her son, the Sultan, and through him the Empire. Her *apartments, which occupy most of the west side of the courtyard on two levels, were well

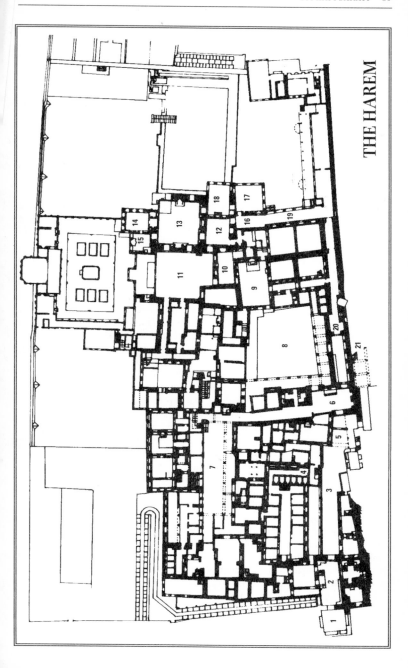

THE HAREM

placed for her to exercise her often nefarious influence, for they are in the centre of the Harem. The rooms of the Valide's apartment are small but quite attractive, with tiled walls and painted ceilings; unfortunately they are not yet open to the public.

At the northwest corner of the courtyard a doorway leads into the *Ocaklı Oda, the Room with a Hearth (9), a beautifully tiled chamber dominated by a large and splendid bronze chimney-piece. On the right a door leads to the suites of the First and Second Kadınlar, the two highest ranking women in the Sultan's harem. On the left a door opens into a smaller chamber called *Çeşmeli Oda, the Fountain-Room (10). The pretty çeşme, or wall-fountain, after which the room is named, bears the date 1665–66, and so it appears that both this room and the Ocaklı Oda are part of Mehmet IV's reconstruction after the fire of 1665. The two rooms served as antechambers between the Harem and the Sultan's own apartments.

A doorway leads from the Çeşmeli Oda into the **Hünkâr Sofası, the Hall of the Emperor (11), the largest and grandest room in the palace. Divided by a great arch into two unequal sections, the larger section is domed and the smaller, slightly raised, had a balcony above. The upper part of the room—dome, pendentives and arches—has been restored to its original appearance. However, the lower part retains the unfortunate baroque decorations added by Osman III (1754–57). This Hall was a reception room where the Sultan gave entertainments for the women of the Harem: the balcony was used by the musicians. This splendid chamber is believed to have been constructed for Murat III (1574–95), in which case the architect would surely have been Sinan.

A door at the northeast corner of the Hünkâr Sofası leads into a small but lavishly tiled **antechamber** (12). This once-elegant little room was badly disfigured during a reconstruction in the late 16C or the early 17C, when it was cut in half right through the dome to make space for an adjacent apartment (see below). This antechamber leads into the **Salon of Murat III (13), the most splendid room in the palace. The Salon is dated by an inscription to 1578; unlike the Hünkâr Sofası, it has retained the whole of its original decoration. The walls are sheathed in Iznik tiles from the greatest period of their manufacture; the panel of plum blossoms surrounding the elegant bronze chimney-piece is especially noteworthy, as is the calligraphic frieze which runs around the room. Opposite the fireplace there is an elegant three-tiered cascade fountain of carved polychrome marble set in a marble embrasure. The beauty of the decoration and the perfect and harmonious form of the room identify it as a work of Sinan.

Opening off the west side of the Salon there is a small chamber known as the *Library of Ahmet I (14), built in 1608–09. This is one of the most delightful rooms in the palace. The library is adorned with finely carved wooden bookshelves and cabinets inlaid with sea-tortoise shell and mother-of-pearl, and its walls are revetted with blue and green tiles almost as beautiful as those in the salon. The room is lighted by windows on two sides, affording sweeping views across the Marmara and up the Bosphorus and the Golden Horn.

A marble doorway in the south wall of the library leads to an even lovelier chamber, the **Dining-Room of Ahmet III (15), constructed in 1705–06. Its walls are panels of lacquered wood decorated with paintings of brightly coloured flowers in garlands and vases, of heaped bowls of fruit, and, in one corner, a group of yellow-feathered ducklings following their mother. These decorations are characteristic of the Tulip Period, when European rococo art and architecture made its first appearance in Istanbul.

To the east of the Salon of Murat III there are a pair of very handsome rooms known as the **Double Kiosk** (**17** and **18**). It is not known exactly when or for what purpose the apartments in the Double Kiosk were built, but they must date from the end of the 16C, or the first years of the 17C, as their tiles are of the very greatest period and perhaps the most beautiful in the palace. The first room has a dome magnificently painted on canvas, while the ceiling of the inner room is flat but also adorned with superb painted designs. The second room also has a wonderful brass-gilt fireplace, on each side of which, above, are two of the most gorgeous tile panels in existence. Beyond the fireplace the paving stones have been removed to reveal, at a depth of about 30cm, another pavement and a surbase of tiles, also of the greatest period, but of a totally different design and colour from those that now revet the two rooms. This was the level of the Salon of Murat III, which was cut in half to provide space for the first of the two rooms in the Double Kiosk.

The colonnaded corridor that runs past the Double Kiosk is called, for some unknown reason, the **Consultation-Place of the Jinns** (**19**). This leads out to an open courtyard known as Gözdelere Taşlığı, the Terrace of the Favourites, which overlooks the lower gardens of the palace. On the right side of the terrace is a long wooden building in two storeys which once housed the Sultan's favourite women. These rooms are undergoing restoration but are not open to the public.

At the far end of the colonnaded corridor the **Golden Way** (**20**) leads off to the right and brings us to **Kuşhane Kapısı**, the Birdcage Gate (**21**), where in 1651 the Valide Sultan Kösem was killed by the Chief Black Eunuch, Tall Süleyman. Guided tours of the Harem end at this point, after which those who have seen the rest of Topkapı Sarayı can make their way back to the Middle Gate, leaving the House of Felicity.

4 · The Lower Gardens of the Saray

The lower gardens of Topkapı Sarayı extended from the outer walls of the palace down to the shores of the Marmara and the Golden Horn. The gardens on the Marmara side of the palace have long since vanished, but those on the slope of the First Hill leading down to the Golden Horn and Saray Burnu have been preserved in Gülhane Park. The main entrance to the park is on Alemdar Cad., beside the Alay Köşkü, but it is also possible to enter the grounds through a gate in the west wall of the First Court of Topkapı Sarayı, just beyond the church of Haghia Eirene. The latter entrance is the most convenient for those who have just completed a tour of the Saray, for it enables you to visit Haghia Eirene and then go on to tour the museums that are located on the upper terrace of Gülhane Park: the Archaeological Museum, the Museum of the Ancient Orient, and the Çinili Köşk.

**Haghia Eirene

Haghia Eirene (Pl. 11,3) is the second largest Byzantine church in the city, surpassed in size only by Haghia Sophia.

■ **Admission**. The church is only open to the public when it is being used for exhibitions or concerts.

According to tradition, the original church of Haghia Eirene was the cathedral of Byzantium before Constantine the Great established his capital here. This church was dedicated to Haghia Eirene, the Divine Peace, an attribute of Christ, complementary to his personification of the Divine Wisdom. The church was rebuilt by the Emperor Constantius (337–61). At the time of the Nika Revolt, in 532, Haghia Eirene and Haghia Sophia were totally destroyed by fire. After the revolt was put down Justinian began a project to rebuild both churches; the new church of Haghia Eirene was probably completed at about the same time as Haghia Sophia, in 537. The new churches of the Divine Wisdom and the Divine Peace were thenceforth closely linked and formed two parts of what was essentially one religious establishment, both of them administered by the Patriarchate and served by the same clergy. Haghia Eirene was almost destroyed in 564, when a fire ruined the atrium and part of the narthex, but it was immediately restored by Justinian, then in the last year of his life. In October 740 the church was severely damaged by an earthquake, after which it was restored, either by Leo III or his son, Constantine V.

It appears that since that date no other major catastrophes have befallen the church, therefore the building you see today dates from Justinian's time, with the exception of 8C repairs and minor Turkish additions. After the Conquest Haghia Eirene was enclosed within the outer walls of Topkapı Sarayı, serving as an arsenal for the Janissaries until they were annihilated in 1826. In the late 19C the building became a storehouse for antiquities, principally old Ottoman armaments. The building was restored in the 1980s and is now used for exhibitions and concerts.

Exterior. The church is rectangular in plan, 42.2m long and 36.7m wide, with a five-sided apse projecting from the east wall, and to the west a narthex preceded by an atrium. The central area of the nave is covered by a dome carried on a high drum, with peaked roofs to its north, east and south, and a lower domical vault to the west. The ancient architectural fragments arrayed around the building are from excavations on the First Hill. The ground around the church has risen some 5m above its original level and the present entry is through a Turkish porch and outbuildings outside the west end of the north aisle. From there a ramp leads down to the level of the interior.

Interior. The church is a basilica of a very unusual type, as can be seen from an examination of its plan. The central nave is flanked by a pair of side aisles, above which there is a gallery that also surmounts the narthex. The central area of the nave is covered by the great **dome**, some 15.5m in diameter. The dome is supported primarily by four huge piers standing on the corners of a square. Between these piers there are four great circular arches; pendentives then make

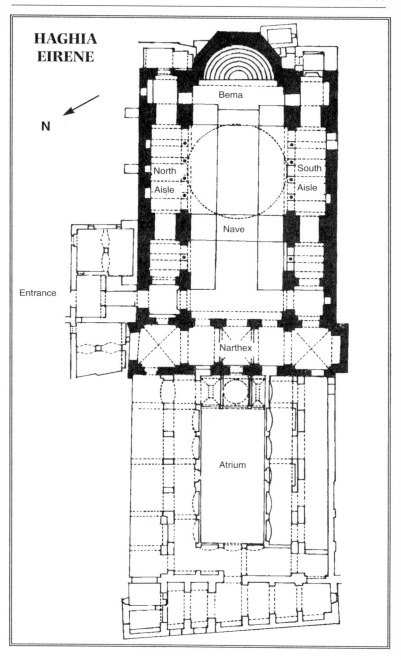

HAGHIA EIRENE

N

Bema

North Aisle

South Aisle

Nave

Entrance

Narthex

Atrium

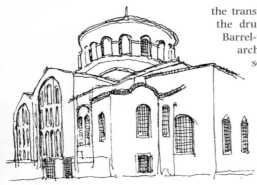

Haghia Eirene

the transition to the circular base of the drum that carries the dome. Barrel-vaults open off from these arches to the north, east and south, with a conch covering the apse. Another pair of piers at the west end of the nave support an elliptical domical vault, from which barrel-vaults open off to the north and south.

The wide **nave** is separated from the side aisles by the usual colonnade: there are four monoliths on either side between the main piers, and another one on either side between the west piers, and a pair of subsidiary piers which help to support the west ends of the north and south galleries. Around the periphery of the semicircular apse there is a **synthronon**, the only one in the city to have survived from the Byzantine period. This has six tiers of seats for the clergy, with doors at either side leading to an ambulatory which runs beneath the fourth tier.

In the conch of the apse a **mosaic cross** in black outline stands on a pedestal of three steps, against a gold ground with a geometric border. The inscription here is from Psalm lxv, 4 and 5; that on the bema arch is from Amos ix, 6, with alterations. In both cases parts of the mosaic have fallen away and letters have been painted in by someone who was indifferent to both grammar and sense. There is some difference of opinion concerning the dating of these mosaics; one theory is that they date from the reconstruction after the earthquake of 740, the other, that they are from Justinian's reign. The decorative mosaics in the narthex, which are similar to those in Haghia Sophia, are almost certainly from Justinian's period.

At the west end of the nave a rather attractive Turkish wooden staircase leads to the galleries. At the west end of the nave five doors lead from the church into the **narthex**, a vestibule of five bays. The central bay of the narthex and those at either end are groin-vaulted; the two in between are barrel-vaulted. From the narthex five doors originally led into the atrium, but three of these have been blocked up. The **atrium** has been rather drastically altered; the whole of the inner peristyle is Turkish, as well as a good many bays of the outer. However, most of the outer walls date from the Byzantine period: they are curiously irregular, the north portico is considerably longer than the south, thus the west wall of the atrium is not parallel to the narthex.

The two porphyry sarcophagi in the courtyard are from the imperial mausoleum in the church of the Holy Apostles, destroyed at the time of the Turkish Conquest. The sarcophagi, which date from 4C–6C AD, were brought here when Haghia Eirene became a storehouse for antiquities. Four others of the same type and period are now arrayed outside the Archaeological Museum (see below).

The ruins to the south of Haghia Eirene, between the church and the outer walls of the Saray, are off-limits to the public, but you can walk in discreetly for a cursory examination. These are the remains of the **Hospice of Samson**, partially excavated in 1946. Procopius, Justinian's court chronicler, writes that between Haghia Sophia and Haghia Eirene 'there was a certain hospice, devoted to those that were at once destitute and suffering from serious illness, namely those who had lost their property and their health. This was erected in early times by a certain pious man, Samson by name.' Procopius goes on to report that the Hospice of Samson was destroyed by fire during the Nika Revolt of 532—along with Haghia Sophia and Haghia Eirene—and that it was rebuilt and considerably enlarged by Justinian.

We now leave the First Court of the Saray, by the road to the left beyond the Darphane, which leads down to the lower gardens of the Saray. The road is flanked on both sides by ancient columns, capitals, sarcophagi and architectural fragments, an overflow from the museums on the terrace below. We then come to the gateway of the courtyard shared by the Archaeological Museum (Arkeologi Müzesi), the Museum of the Ancient Orient (Eski Şark Eserleri Müzesi), and the Tiled Pavilion (Çinili Köşk).

**The Archaeological Museum*

■ **Admission**. The Archaeological Museum is open 09.30–16.30, Museum of the Ancient Orient 09.30–12.00, Çinili Köşk, 13.00–16.30; all three museums are closed Mon.

Courtyard. Around these buildings, as well as in the gardens to the left of the courtyard, antiquities of all sorts are arrayed. The most noteworthy of these are the four huge porphyry sarcophagi in front of the Archaeological Museum; they too were originally in the imperial mausoleum of the church of the Holy Apostles.

The most interesting objects in the café garden are two colossal gorgon heads identical to those in the Basilica Cistern (see p 100); these are from the Forum of Constantine (see p 104) on the Second Hill.

The **Archaeological Museum** (Pl. 11,3) has one of the world's richest collections of antiquities, principally from Anatolia and the surrounding regions in the Near East and the eastern Mediterranean.

The first systematic attempt in the Ottoman Empire to collect and preserve the nation's antiquities began in 1846, during the regime of Abdül Mecit I. The project was initiated by Fethi Ahmet Paşa, son-in-law of Mahmut II, who contacted governors all over the Ottoman Empire and directed them to collect all of the movable works of art from within their provinces and ship them to Istanbul. These antiquities were at first stored in Haghia Eirene, and when that was full the Çinili Köşk was used as a storehouse, beginning in 1874. The modern history of the Museum dates from 1881, when the archaeologist Osman Hamdi Bey was made director. The Archaeological Museum was first opened to the public on 13 June 1891, and new wings were added in 1902 and 1908. A new museum was added behind the old museum and was dedicated in 1991, with its newest gallery, devoted to Istanbul Through the Ages, opened in 1994.

Facing the door in the entrance lobby is a colossal statue of the god Bes, the Cypriot Hercules, who is shown holding up the headless form of a lioness; the gaping holes in his loins was probably the site of a gigantic phallus (1C–3C AD, Amanthus, Cyprus).

We now turn left from the entrance, passing on our left the museum shop and on our right the entrance to the new museum, to which we will return after seeing all of the galleries on the ground floor.

The next gallery is devoted to **Osman Hamdi Bey** (1842–1910), the founder of the Archaeological Museum, with photos showing his life and highlights of his career. The stairway leads to the upper floors of the new museum.

The next two rooms contain a number of extraordinary **sarcophagi** found in an excavation directed by Osman Hamdi Bey in 1887 in the royal necropolis at Sidon in Syria. These sarcophagi belonged to a succession of kings who ruled in Phoenicia between the mid 5C BC and the latter half of the 4C BC. Just inside the doorway of the first room we come to the (#800) *Tabnit Sarcophagus (6C BC), the earliest of the sarcophagi found at Sidon. This is a so-called anthropoid sarcophagus, in the form of a diorite mummy-case. The Egyptian hieroglyphic inscription on the lid records that the sarcophagus originally belonged to an Egyptian commander named Peneptah. Below this another inscription, in the Phoenician alphabet, states that the second owner of the sarcophagus was Tabnit, King of Sidon, whose mummy is now exposed in the glass case just beyond.

Also on exhibition here are (#369), the *Lycian Sarcophagus (end 5C BC), and (#367), the *Satrap Sarcophagus (2nd half 5C BC). The first of these is decorated with scenes from the life of the deceased, who from his appearance has been identified as a satrap, or oriental potentate. The second, which is from Lycia, on the southwest coast of Asia Minor, is decorated on its sides with a lion-hunt and a boar-hunt, and on its ends with the figures of centaurs and sphinxes.

Entering the next room, we pass three undecorated temple-like sarcophagi and then come to the most famous work of art in the museum, the so-called (#370) **Alexander Sarcophagus** (late 4C BC), the latest in date of the funerary monuments in the royal necropolis of Sidon to be excavated. The sarcophagus was originally believed to have been that of Alexander the Great himself, for it is adorned with sculptures in deep, almost round relief, showing the Emperor in scenes of hunting and battle. But Alexander is known to have been buried in Alexandria. The sarcophagus has now been identified as belonging to Abdalonymos, who became King of Sidon in 333 BC after Alexander defeated the Persians at the battle of Issus, which apparently inspired the battle scenes in the reliefs.

We now return to the entrance lobby and continue on into the southern wing of the museum, which is devoted to classical sculpture.

The first gallery here has **sculptures of the archaic period** (700–480 BC). The free-standing statues here are idealised representations of a young man, known in Greek as a kouros, or a young woman, a kore. These were placed as dedicatory offerings in temples of Apollo and Artemis. The most notable are the head of a (#1645) kouros from Samos (6C BC) and a legless kouros (#5536) from Cyzicus (c 550–540 BC), the face in both cases wreathed in the haunting smile characteristic of archaic Greek sculpture. (#1945) is a headless statue of a seated male figure (mid 6C BC) from the Branchidae, the famous family of oracles at the temple of Apollo in Didyma, found in Miletus. Other sculptures are in the form of reliefs on stelae used as funerary monuments. The most notable of these is (#2813), a relief (6C BC) showing a long-haired youth driving a chariot drawn by two horses, from Cyzicus.

The next hall contains sculptures from the period of Persian rule in Anatolia. The two most notable examples are (#5761/5764 and 5763), funerary stelae (5C BC) from Daskylion, both with reliefs showing funeral processions in which mourners are following a cart carrying a sarcophagus.

The next hall is devoted to **Attic grave stelae** with reliefs as well as other sculptures of the classical period. The most notable stelae are: (#1142), with a relief of a young athlete from Nisyros (c 480–460 BC); (#85), a young warrior, from Pella (c 430–420 BC); and (#80), a man bidding farewell to his two young sons, from Amisus (Samsun) (end of 5C BC). The two most notable **sculptures** in the round are the head of a horse (#398), provenance

To Topkapı Sarayı

Entrance

Archaeological Museum (ground floor)

Museum of the Ancient Orient

Tea Gardens

Çinili Köşk

THE MUSEUMS

unknown (second half of 5C BC); and a statue of Athena (#435) from Leptis Magna in Libya, a Roman copy of an original from the end of the 5C BC.

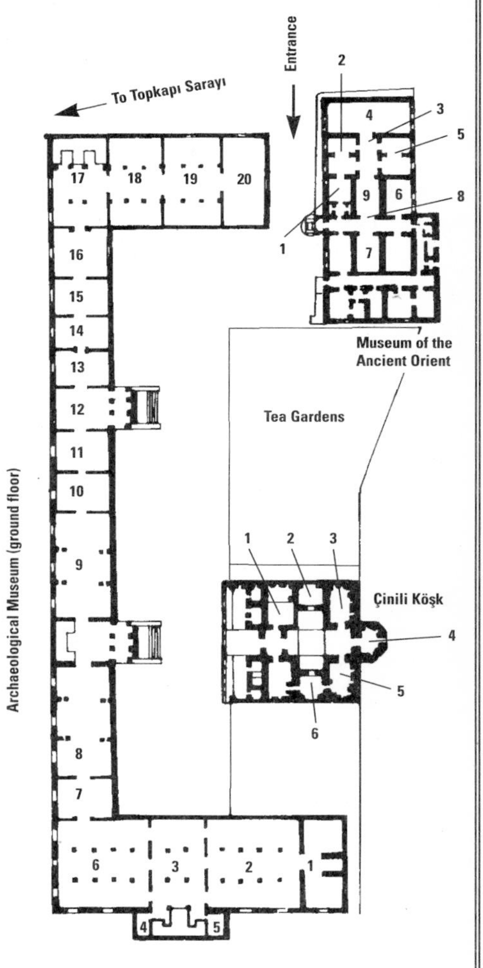

The following gallery exhibits **sculptures of the Hellenistic period**, the two most famous works being representations of Alexander the Great. (#1138) is a superb **head of Alexander from Pergamum, a work from the first half of the second century BC after an original of the 4C BC by Lysippos. (#709) is an outstanding life-size *statue of Alexander from Magnesia ad Sipylum (Manisa), an original work dating from the mid 3C BC. Other interesting works are

(#764), a relief of a Dionysiac dancer from Pergamum (end of 3C BC); a statue (#363) of Hermaphroditus, the bisexual offspring of Hermes and Aphrodite, from Pergamum (3C BC); and a statue (#400) of Marsyas, from Tarsus, a Roman copy of an original from the 3C BC.

The next gallery has **sculpture from Tralles and Magnesia** on the Maeander. The most famous work here is the ****Ephebos of Tralles** (#1191). This statue represents a youth resting after exercise; he is shown standing in a relaxed attitude with a cape draped over his shoulders, a wistful smile on his face (late 1C BC-early 1C AD). (#1189) is a Caryatid from Tralles (1C AD); this is similar to those in the Erechtheion on the Athenian Acropolis, where a kore serves as a column with her headdress as the capital. (#605) is a statue of a matron named Baebia, from Magnesia on the Maeander (mid 1C BC).

We now enter the first hall of the south wing, which is devoted to **Hellenistic and Roman sculpture**. Beside the door on the left is a Herm (#1433), a statue of the god Hermes in which only his head and genitals are represented on a stele. An inscription on the stele (2C AD), found in Pergamum, states that it is a copy of the famous Herm by Alkamenes, which stood just outside the Propylaia on the Athenian Acropolis. In the centre of the room we see a colossal head (#358) of the poetess Sappho, from Smyrna (Izmir), a Roman copy of a Hellenistic original.

The left side of the hall is devoted to Roman portrait busts of the 1C–4C AD. These include portraits of the emperors Augustus (#39), Tiberius (#2163), Claudius (#87), Marcus Aurelius (#5129), Lucius Verus (#2646), Antoninus Pius (#1604), Severus Alexander (#4811), Commodus (#4492), Diocletian (#4864), and Constantine the Great (#5296); as well as the empresses Agrippina the Elder (#2164), and Faustina the Younger (#5130). Among the works in the right side of the room is a relief (#1242) honouring Euripides, from Smyrna (1C BC–1C AD); the dramatist is being presented with a tragic mask by Skene, the personification of the theatre, while Dionysus looks on with approval. (#1028) is a relief of a Muse playing the lyre (2C BC).

The next hall has **sculptures from Ephesus, Miletus and Aphrodisias**. The principal work from Ephesus is a large reclining statue of Oceanus (#4281), from the 2C AD. The sculptures from Miletus include statues of Apollo Kitharados (#2000) and five Muses (#1993, 1994, 1999, 2002, 2007), all dating from the 2C AD. The works from Aphrodisias, exhibited in an area dedicated to the Turkish archaeologist Kenan Erim (1929–91), include statues of Valentinian II (#2264, late 4C AD), a Roman judge (#2265, c AD 425–450), a young matron (#2269, 2C AD); a relief of a Gigantomachia (#1613), or battle between the Olympian gods and the Giants (2C AD), and a pillar (#2272, 2C AD) decorated with reliefs of animals and Erotes among foliage.

The last hall in this wing is devoted to **sculpture of the Roman imperial period**. To the left of the entryway is a colossal statue of Tyche (#4410), the Goddess of Fortune, who is shown holding the child Plutos, the God of Wealth, while above them there is a profusion of fruits and flowers in a cornucopia, the horn of plenty; this is from Prusias ad Hypium and is tentatively dated to the 2C AD. In the centre of the wall opposite the door is a colossal statue of Zeus (#172), from Gaza (2C AD). Other works here include a group of statuettes of Erotes in a cock-fight (#57–58), from Tarsus (2C AD); statue of the lady Cornelia Antonina (#2645), from Antioch in Pisidia (2C AD); statue of

Dionysus (#1236), from Synnada (1C–2C AD); statuette of Pan (#26), from Tirnovo in Bulgaria (early 3C AD); statue of Artemis (#61), from Cyrene in Libya (copy of original from 2C BC).

We now return to the entrance lobby and continue on into the next room, where we turn right to enter the new museum. Here we see the **Children's Museum**, which opened in the summer of 1996, the most prominent exhibit being a large model of the Trojan horse. Beyond the stairway we see the reconstructed front of the archaic temple of Athena in Assos (6C BC). This will be the major exhibit of the **Hall of the Classical Sculpture of Anatolia**, which is still under preparation.

Istanbul Through the Ages. This gallery, which opened in the summer of 1995, is on the first floor of the new museum.

The first exhibits show the very earliest sites of human habitation in the environs of Istanbul. The most notable site is the Yarımburgaz Cave on the European shore of the Marmara, where archaeologists have unearthed evidence of human settlement dating back some 350,000 years. A glass case contains the complete skeleton of a man from Pendik, on the Asian shore of the Marmara, dated to the sixth millennium BC. The oldest object found in Istanbul itself is a baked clay jar (#104) unearthed in the Hippodrome and dated to the sixth millennium BC.

The next exhibition area is devoted to objects from the ancient Greek city-state of Byzantium, the oldest of them dating to the 7C BC. These include pottery and other artefacts, as well as a large number of tombstones from the early cemeteries of the city, with reliefs showing the deceased and their family and belongings.

The area at the end of the first corridor is concerned with the Haliç, or Golden Horn. The most striking exhibit here displays sculptures from a nymphaeum, or monumental fountain, of the 2C AD excavated at Silahtarağa above the Golden Horn. The sculptures represent a Gigantomachia. The Olympians, who include Selene, Artemis and Apollo, are done in white marble, while the Giants, of whom only fragments survive, are in grey limestone. Above are three marble busts, a man flanked by two women.

The other exhibition areas are all devoted to Byzantine Constantinople. The displays are arranged topographically, with each area devoted to one or more of the Byzantine monuments or areas or aspects of the city in the period 330–1453. The first of these is ancient Chalcedon (see ch. 20), now the suburb of Kadıköy on the Asian shore of the Marmara. The displays that follow include Constantinople's harbours; hydraulic works, including cisterns; the Theodosian Walls (ch. 16); the sea walls along the Golden Horn (ch. 14) and the Marmara (ch. 5); the Augustaeum (ch. 1); the churches of Haghia Sophia (ch. 2), Haghia Eirene (ch. 4) and SS. Sergius and Bacchus (ch. 5); the Great Palace of Byzantium (ch. 5); the Hippodrome (ch. 5); the Palaces of Antiochus and Lausus (ch. 5); the area within the walls of Topkapı Sarayı (ch. 4); the Forum of Theodosius (ch. 7); the Forum and Column of Constantine (ch. 6); Kalenderhane Camii (church of the Kyriotissa, incorrectly identified here as St. Saviour Akataleptos) (ch. 8); Bodrum Camii (church of the Myrelaion) (ch. 8); the Hebdomon (Bakırköy) and Rhegium (Küçükçekmece); the Forum and Column of Arcadius (ch. 15); the church of St. John of Studius (ch. 15); the church of St. Polyeuktos (ch. 11); the Column of Marcian (ch. 11); the Palace of Blachernae (ch. 14); the Church of the Holy Apostles (ch. 11); the Church of Constantine Lips (ch. 11); Kariye Camii (the church of St. Saviour in Chora) (ch. 13); the church of the Pantocrator (ch. 10); the Church of the Pammakaristos (Fethiye Camii) (ch. 12); Galata (ch. 18); the Princes' Isles (ch. 21); and the Bosphorus (ch. 19). In the last gallery we see a length of the huge chain that was used by the Byzantines to close the Golden Horn in times of siege. Beyond that is an exhibition of coins from ancient Byzantium and Byzantine Constantinople.

We now continue in turn to the galleries on the two upper floors.

Anatolia and Troy Through the Ages (new museum, second floor). This hall is arranged chronologically, beginning at the north end; the display cases on the right side of the hall have objects from the different levels of Troy, while those on the left display antiquities of the various prehistoric periods from sites elsewhere in Anatolia.

The exhibit at the north end of the hall explains the topography of the site and the history of the excavations by Heinrich Schliemann, Wilhelm Dörpfeld, Carl W. Blegen, and Manfred Korfmann. The exhibition areas that follow on the right have objects from Troy I (3000–2500 BC), Troy II (2500–2300 BC), Troy III (2300–2100 BC), Troy IV (2100–1900 BC), Troy V (1900–1700 BC), Troy VI (1700–1275 BC), Troy VIIa (1275–1240 BC), Troy VIII (700–350 BC), Troy IX (350 BC–AD 400). The exhibition areas on the left side of the wall have objects from other sites in Anatolia, ranging in time through the Upper Palaeolithic (350,000–12,000 BC), Mesolithic (12,000–8000 BC), Neolithic (8000–4500 BC), and Chalcolithic (4500–3000 BC) periods, the Bronze Age (3000–1200 BC, the Dark Ages of Anatolia (1200–700 BC), and the archaic (700–480 BC) period.

At the south end of the hall there is a gallery devoted to Phrygia in the archaic period, with photographs of the extraordinary rock-carved Phyrigian sanctuaries and sculptures of the fertility goddess Cybele-Kubaba. A display case has antiquities from Phrygian sites in western Anatolia, most notably the huge bronze cauldrons that are the most distinctive works of this culture.

Cultures of Anatolia's Neighbours (new museum, third floor). This floor is dedicated to antiquities from cultures bordering on Anatolia, including those from Cyprus, Syria and Palestine. The most striking exhibit on this floor is at the north end of the hall, where we see a hypogeum, or subterranean tomb, from Palmyra (Syria). This is modelled on an original hypogeum in the Valley of the Tombs built by the Yarhai family in AD 108; the sculptural portraits are original and came from different hypogea in Palmyra.

In leaving the new museum we pass through a room on the second floor of the old museum. The glass cases here contain clay **votive figurines** of the classical and Hellenistic figurines. In the centre of the room is a colossal bronze statue of the Emperor Hadrian from Nicomedia, mid 2C AD. From the window here you have an excellent view of the Çinili Köşk, the next stop on our itinerary.

**The Çinili Köşk

The Çinili Köşk (Pl. 11,3), or Tiled Pavilion, was built by Fatih in 1472 as an outer pavilion of Topkapı Sarayı, serving as a pied-à-terre for the Sultan on occasions when he wanted to escape the crowded confines of the Inner Palace. At the time when the Çinili Köşk was built, a large level area was cleared in front of it so that the young princes and palace pages could play cirit, a form of polo, and enabling the Sultan to look on from the elevated front porch of the pavilion. The pavilion continued in use until 1856, when the imperial residence was shifted to Dolmabahçe Palace. It was abandoned until 1874, when it was converted into a storehouse for antiquities. During the 1950s the Çinili Köşk was thoroughly restored to its original condition and converted into a museum.

Exterior. The kiosk is laid out in two almost identical storeys (the lower one completely visible only at the rear), cruciform in plan with chambers in the corners of the cross. It has a deeply recessed entrance alcove on the main floor entirely revetted in tiles of various kinds, most of them tile mosaic in turquoise and dark blue. On the back wall these form simple geometrical designs, but in the deep soffit of the arch there is an inscription in a geometricised form of Cufic calligraphy. On the three faces of the vault at the height of the lintel of the door there is a long double Persian inscription in the beautiful cuerda seca technique. The main inscription is in white letters on a dark blue ground. Above and entwined with this is a subordinate inscription in yellow, with the tendrils of a vine meandering in and out between the letters, the whole encased in a frame of deep mauve with flowers of dark blue, turquoise and white.

Interior. The interior consists of a central salon in the shape of an inverted Latin cross with a dome over the crossing. The cross is extended by a vestibule at the entrance end, an apse-like room at the far end, and two eyvans or open alcoves (now glassed in) at the ends of the shorter arms, with additional chambers at the corners of the cross. All of these rooms were once tiled and many of them still are, with triangular and hexagonal panels of turquoise and deepest blue, sometimes with superimposed gold designs. (The lower floor is not open to the public.)

In the first room, to the left of the entrance vestibule, there is a small selection of Selçuk tiles—mostly wall tiles of enamel and majolica ware—of the 12C–14C. The principal exhibit in the central salon is the superb mihrab from the mosque of Ibrahim Bey at Karaman, in central Anatolia, one of the most splendid works from the height of the great Iznik period. The second room, to the left, has tiles of the transitional period from Selçuk to Ottoman, i.e.14C–15C. The third and fourth rooms contain some of the best Iznik ware of the 16C and early 17C. The last two rooms contain ceramics from the 18C–19C, some of it pretty but Europeanised and lacking the brilliance and superb craftsmanship of the earlier work. The best of these are exhibited in the last room; these are charming plates made in the 19C in Çanakkale, on the Dardanelles.

**Museum of the Ancient Orient*

The Museum of the Ancient Orient (Pl. 11.3) was erected in 1883 and originally housed the Institute of Fine Arts. It was converted into a museum in 1917, and after restoration it reopened in 1974. The entrance to the museum is flanked by two basalt lions of the neo-Hittite period, dated c 800 BC; these were talismans to frighten enemies away from the gateway of the city.

A stairway leads from the entrance lobby to the floor above, where we turn left to enter **room 1**. This contains an exhibition of objects from Arabia and Nabatea in the pre-Islamic period. Flanking the entryway there are torsoes of two red sandstone statues of kilted male figures (#7805, 7806), one of which has retained its head (3C–1C BC). Other exhibits of interest include #7611: a superb relief with the heads of five bulls above a floral design, flanked by two giraffe heads (2C AD); (#7608): an Arabic inscription of the 6C mentioning the name of Christ. One of the cases contains tombstones, funerary offerings, tomb furniture, and other objects, as well as statuettes of seated deities (1C BC–1C AD). Elsewhere in the room there are two reliefs, one of a robed warrior and the other of a mythological creature with the head of a bearded man and body of a lion, both dated 4C–1C BC.

Room 2 is devoted to ancient Egyptian objects, ranging in date from the rise of the First Dynasty (c 3200 BC) to the beginning of the Ptolomaic Dynasty (310 BC). These include sphinxes, stelae, tombstones, mummy cases, funerary pottery, tomb furnishings, votive offerings, statuary and architectural fragments. Three mummy cases (#10891, 10892, 10866) bear inscriptions identifying the deceased as priests and priestesses of Amon. The small containers are canopic jars, with lids in the form of animal heads; these preserved the various internal organs of the deceased, the various heads symbolising the gods who protected these parts until they were reunited with the body in the next world.

Room 3 is the far end of the corridor to the right of the stairway, with room 9 constituting the other end. Room 3 has on its walls colourful *tile panels with the figures in relief of lions and mythological beasts. These panels are from Babylon, dating from the reign of Nebuchadnezzar II (605–562 BC); they formed part of the monumental processional way that led from the Ishtar Gate to the sanctuary where the New Year's festival was held. A case contains antiquities from three different periods in Mesopotamian history: the Halaf Culture (fifth millennium BC), the Fifth Cultural Period in Nineveh (third millennium BC); and the Old Sumerian Period (fourth to third millennium BC). To the right of the doorwas leading into room 4 there is a representation of Lamassu, a demon who guarded Assyrian doorways (9C BC).

Room 4 contains antiquities from Mesopotamia and the Urartian culture, which flourished in eastern Anatolia at the beginning of the first millennium BC. The most important exhibits here are several **tiles with stamped inscriptions** dating from the period 2222–2198 BC, the oldest-known examples of printed writing. There is also a *bronze bar marked with various lengths and a *basalt duck representing a standard weight; these are dated c 2000 BC and are the oldest standard measures in existence. An alcove contains objects from the New Sumerian period (2144–200 BC), including a statue of King Gudea, the most powerful ruler of that era. Nearby there is a diorite statue of Puzur Ishtar, Governor of Mari (c 2000 BC), copied from the original in the Berlin Museum. Elsewhere in the room there are cases with objects from the

Kassite or Middle Babylonian period (c 1600–900 BC), as well as from the Old Assyrian (c 1350–1200 BC), Mittanian (c 1500–1300 BC), Middle Assyrian (c 1200–1100 BC), and New Assyrian periods (9C BC), the latter including a large basalt statue of King Shalmaneser III (858–824 BC).

Room 5 is devoted mostly to antiquities from the New Assyrian period, along with some of the oldest inscriptions in existence. The most historic of the inscriptions here is the famous *****Code of Hammurabi** (#Ni 2358), dated 1750 BC, the world's oldest recorded set of laws. Also of great interest is a Babylonian ***tablet** (#U93103), dated c 320 BC, recording astronomical observations, one of the earliest extant scientific records.

Room 6 has mostly Urartian and Assyrian works. Opposite the entrance there are a basalt altar (#7761) and a fragmentary floor mosaic (#7760), both of them Urartian works of the 7C BC found at Toprakkale near Lake Van in eastern Turkey. On the walls there are Assyrian reliefs from the palaces of Tiglath-Pileser III (745–727 BC), Sennacherib (705–688 BC) and Ashurbanipal (669–629 BC).

Room 7 is devoted mostly to objects of the Hatti and Hittite cultures of Anatolia. The earliest work of the Hatti, who preceded the Hittites in Anatolia, is a fragment of a vase with a relief of a monstrous fertility god, dated c 3000 BC. Another Hatti work is a bronze standard in the form of a solar disk surmounted by two stags outlined in a braided halo, dating from early in the third millennium BC. The most historic work here is the famous ****Treaty of Kadesh** (#115), dated 1269 BC, recording the end of a war between the forces of Ramses II of Egypt and Hattusilas, the Hittite emperor. Other exhibits include works of the Chalcolithic era (c 5500–3000 BC), as well as the Old Hittite Kingdom (c 1700–1450 BC), Hittite Empire (1450–1200 BC), Late Hittite (1200–700 BC), and neo-Hittite (10C–9C BC).

Room 8 has mostly works of the Assyrian, neo-Hittite and Aramean cultures. The most striking exhibit here is the Ivriz Kaya relief (#7869), a plaster copy of the original; this shows a diminutive king offering gifts of grain and fruit to a gigantic god, a neo-Hittite work of the 8C BC. Another interesting relief (#7723), from the palace of the Aramean king Barrakab, shows four musicians in a procession, the two in front playing lyres and the other tambourines, dated to the third quarter of the 8C BC.

Room 9 forms the opposite end of the corridor that began as room 3, and its walls exhibit more the panels of the processional way that led to the Ishtar Gate in Bablyon. To the right there is a basalt stele (#7786) with a relief showing a Hittite warrior, a fine work of the Aramean dynasty dated to the 9C–8C BC.

Gülhane Park. The road from the First Court of Topkapı Sarayı continues downhill to the south end of Gülhane Park, where the Soğuk Çeşme Gate leads out to Alemdar Cad.

The park occupies part of the site of the ancient city of Byzantium, whose outer defence circuit followed much the same course as the outer walls of Topkapı Sarayı. During the summer months Gülhane Park is a very popular gathering place for the ordinary people of Istanbul, with the main street of the park flanked by shops, eating places, cafés, sideshows, playgrounds, children's rides, the Istanbul Zoo, and an outdoor theatre for concerts of folk music and other musical and theatrical productions.

Halfway along on the right is the Tanzimat Müzesi (Reform Movement Museum; open every day 10.30–17.00). This commemorates the Hatti Şerif, or imperial decree, signed here in the Gülhane pavilion by Sultan Abdül Mecit on 3 November 1839, initiating the first reforms in the Ottoman government. The exhibits in the museum include paintings, photos and memorabilia of the leaders of the Reform Movement.

Some distance beyond the museum a sign points to the right for the **Akvaryum**, or Aquarium. This is housed in a late Roman cistern dated c AD 300–20, its brick roof supported by two columns in three rows of four each.

Near the far end of the park we see on our right a number of marble columns and other ancient architectural fragments. This has been identified as the **Orphanage of St. Paul**, founded by Justin II (564–78). It was rebuilt by Alexius I Comnenus (1081–1118); then in the reign of Michael VIII Palaeologus (1259–82) it was used to house the University of Constantinople.

From here a path on the leads to a hill overlooking Saray Burnu. On top of the hill stands one of the very oldest but least known monuments in the city; this is the so-called **Goth's Column*, a granite monolith 15m high surmounted by a Corinthian capital. The name of the column comes from the laconic inscription in Latin on its base: 'To Fortune, who returns by reason of the victory over the Goths'. Some scholars have ascribed this column to Claudius II Gothicus (268–70) and others to Constantine the Great, both of whom won notable victories over the Goths, but there is no firm evidence either way. According to the Byzantine historian Nicephorus Gregoras, the column was once surmounted by a statue of Byzas the Megarian, the eponymous founder of Byzantium.

After leaving Gülhane Park we cross the shore highway to **Saray Burnu**, the promontory at the confluence of the Bosphorus and the Golden Horn. From here there is a splendid view up the Bosphorus and across to the suburbs on the Asian shore. At the centre of the park there is a large bronze **statue** of Kemal Atatürk (1881–1938), the Father of modern Turkey and the first President of the Turkish Republic. This monument, made in 1926 by the Austrian sculptor Kripple, was the first statue of a Turk ever to be erected in this country.

We now begin walking back along the highway towards the Galata Bridge. A few hundred metres along we come to a handsome Ottoman structure built directly at the water's edge. This is **Sepetçiler Köşkü**, the Kiosk of the Basket-Weavers. Built by the guild of the basket-weavers in 1647 for Sultan Ibrahim, it served as a sea-pavilion and boat-house for Topkapı Sarayı. Here the Sultan and his entourage would board one of his barges to be rowed up the Bosphorus or the Golden Horn for a day's outing. The kiosk was reconstructed in the 1980s and now serves as the **International Press Centre**. The substructures on which the kiosk is built are part of the Byzantine sea-walls of Constantinople, as evidenced by inscriptions recording repairs by several emperors.

From the Sepetçiler Köşkü you can walk along the shore road back to the Galata Bridge. The first part of this walk is rather difficult, passing lines of buses and lorries, but then the rest of the way lies along the quays past the ferry terminal, one of the liveliest places in the city, with a magnificent view up the Golden Horn.

5 · Around the Hippodrome

**Sultan Ahmet Camii*

Sultan Ahmet Camii (Pl. 11,5), the **Blue Mosque**, is one of the most prominent landmarks in Istanbul, with its graceful cascade of domes and semidomes, and its six slender minarets accentuating the corners of the building and the court-yard.

The Blue Mosque was founded by Ahmet I, who in 1609 directed the architect Mehmet Ağa to begin construction. The mosque and all of its associated pious foundations were completed in 1616, just a year before the Sultan's death at the age of 27. For the next 250 years most reigning sultans chose to perform their Friday noon prayers at the Blue Mosque, because of its proximity to Topkapı Sarayı, and the imperial processions to and from the mosque were the high point of Istanbul life during that period. Even after Topkapı Sarayı was abandoned as the imperial residence, Sultan Ahmet Camii continued to hold pride of place as one of the two supreme imperial mosques of the city, sharing that honour with the Süleymaniye, an eminence that both mosques retain today.

Exterior. Sultan Ahmet Camii is preceded by a **courtyard** as large in area as the mosque itself, with monumental entryways at each of the three sides. The gate at the centre of the west side is the grandest of these; its outer façade is decorated with a calligraphic inscription by Dervish Mehmet, the father of Evliya Çelebi. The courtyard is in the classic style, bordered by a peristyle of 26 columns forming a portico covered by 30 small domes. At the centre of the courtyard there is a handsome octagonal **şadırvan** which, like the one at Yeni Cami, now serves only a decorative purpose. The ritual ablutions are actually performed at water taps in the outer courtyard, beneath the graceful arcade which forms part of the north and south walls of the avlu.

The four **minarets** at the corners of the mosque each have three şerefes, while the pair at the far corners of the courtyard have two each. The minarets are fluted and the şerefes have sculptured stalactite parapets.

The central **dome** of the mosque is flanked by semidomes on all four sides, with those to north and south surrounded by three smaller semidomes and those to east and west by two each, and with small full domes above the four corners of the building. The four piers supporting the main dome continue above the building as tall octagonal turrets capped with domes, while smaller round turrets flank each of the corner domes, all of which creates a harmonious cascade from the main dome down through the clustering semidomes, turrets and smaller domes. The north and south façades of the building have two storeys of porticoed galleries.

The **main entrance** to the mosque itself is at the east end of the courtyard, with smaller entrances from the outer courtyard beside the central minarets on the north and south sides. (Tourists are asked to enter the mosque through the north door and are restricted to the rear half of the mosque, so as not to disturb the faithful at their prayers.)

THE MOSQUE OF SULTAN AHMET I

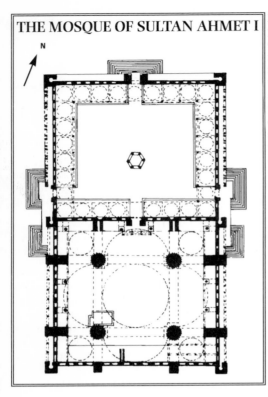

Interior. The interior plan, like that of Yeni Cami and the other imperial mosques of the city, recalls in a general way that of Haghia Sophia; although in this case there are also great differences. It is very nearly a square (51m long by 53m wide) covered by a dome (23.5m in diameter and 43m high) resting on four pointed arches and four smooth pendentives. To east and west there are semidomes which are themselves flanked by smaller semidomes. Thus far, the plan is not unlike that of Haghia Sophia. But in the Blue Mosque, instead of tympanic arches to north and south, there are two more semidomes, each surrounded by three smaller semidomes, making a quatrefoil design. The main support for the great dome comes from four colossal free-standing columns, 5m in diameter, which are divided in the middle by a band and ribbed above and below with convex flutes.

The mosque is flooded with light from its 260 **windows**. These were once filled with Turkish stained glass of the early 17C which would have softened the incoming sunlight. The original windows have been lost because of lack of maintenance during the latter years of the Ottoman Empire; now they are slowly being replaced by inferior modern imitations. The painted **arabesques** in the domes and the upper parts of the building are feeble in design and crude in colouring. This is almost always the case in these modern imitations of a type of decoration that was in the 16C–17C richly elaborate in design and sombrely magnificent in colour. Here the predominant colour is an overly bright blue, from which the building derives its popular name of the Blue Mosque.

What is original and very beautiful in the decoration of the interior is the revetment of **tiles** on the lower part of the walls, especially in the galleries. These are Iznik tiles of the best period and they merit close observation. The magnificent floral designs display the traditional lily, carnation, tulip and rose motifs, as well as cypresses and other trees; these are all in exquisite colours, subtle blues and greens predominating. The **mihrab** and **mimber**, of white

Sultan Ahmet Camii

Proconnesian marble, are also original; they are fine examples of the carved stonework of the early 17C. Of equal excellence is the bronzework of the great courtyard **doors**, and also the woodwork of the doors and window-shutters of the mosque itself, encrusted with ivory, mother-of-pearl and sea-tortoise shell.

Under the sultan's loge, which is in the upper gallery to the left of the mihrab, the wooden ceiling is painted with floral and geometrical arabesques in that exquisite early style in rich and gorgeous colours, of which so few examples remain.

Precincts. The mosque and its courtyard were surrounded by an outer precinct wall, of which only part of the north section remains. This wall separated the mosque from its dependent buildings in the külliye. The **külliye** of Sultan Ahmet Camii was extensive, including a medrese, türbe, hospital, caravansarai, primary school, public kitchen and a market; the rents from these helped defray the expenses of the other pious foundations in the mosque complex. The hospital, caravansarai and market were destroyed in the 19C, and the public kitchen is now incorporated into the structure of the School of Industrial Arts, which stands at the south end of the Hippodrome. The primary school, which has recently been restored, is elevated above the north wall of the outer precinct of the mosque.

The large medrese, dwarfed somewhat by the scale of the mosque itself, is just outside the precinct wall toward the northwest, near the very large square **türbe**. Ahmet I is buried here, along with his wife Kösem and three of his sons: Osman II, Murat IV, and Prince Beyazit. All of these institutions were closed to the public, but quite recently the türbe has been opened.

A ramp at the northeast corner of the mosque leads up to the **hünkâr kasrı**, the imperial pavilion, a suite of rooms used by the Sultan whenever he came here for services, with an internal passageway leading to the royal loge within the mosque. The hünkâr kasrı is now used to house the *****Kilim Museum**, a remarkable collection of carpets from all over Turkey and covering all periods of Ottoman history, including a number that were made for use in the Sultan's tent when he was on campaign. (The Kilim Museum is open 09.30–12.00, 13.00–16.00; closed Sun, Mon.)

Beneath the kible end of the prayer room of the mosque there are huge vaulted structures that once served as storerooms and stables; these handsome chambers have recently been restored to serve as a **Rug Museum*, exhibiting works ranging from the 15C to the 19C, including rare and beautiful examples. This museum has a separate entryway from the courtyard below the mosque on that side, just above the recently restored Ottoman market street on Kaba Sakal Sok. (The Rug Museum is open 09.30–12.00, 13.00–16.00; closed Sat, Sun.)

***Hippodrome*

The square in front of the Blue Mosque covers the site of the ancient Hippodrome (Pl. 11,5), one of the most famous monuments in Byzantine Constantinople.

The original Hippodrome was constructed c AD 200 by the Emperor Septimius Severus, when he rebuilt the town of Byzantium. Constantine the Great reconstructed and enlarged the Hippodrome, adorning it with works of art from all over the Roman Empire. It has often been remarked that just as Haghia Sophia was the centre of the religious life of Constantinople, so was the Hippodrome the focal point of its civil activities. Many of the great events in the history of the Byzantine Empire took place here, beginning with the solemn inaugural rites of the new capital on 11 May 330. The triumphs of victorious generals and emperors were celebrated here, and on several occasions the remains of deposed rulers were exposed for public abuse in the arena. But the Hippodrome functioned primarily as a sports centre, where the regular programme of chariot races and circuses served as a diversion for the people of the city.

The turbulent mobs of the Hippodrome were originally divided into four factions: the Greens, Blues, Whites and Reds. In the early centuries of Constantinople the Blue and Green factions began to achieve dominance, and eventually the Whites and Reds were absorbed by the other two groups. Traditionally, the Blues were recruited from the upper and middle classes and were orthodox in religion and conservative in politics, while the Greens were lower class and radical both in their religious beliefs and in their politics. The social, religious and political polarisation between the two factions was the source of constant dissension during the early history of the Byzantine Empire. The worst of these disturbances was the Nika Revolt in 532, which ended when Justinian's general Belisarius trapped 30,000 partisans in the Hippodrome and slaughtered them there. This broke the political power of the popular factions in the Hippodrome, and they were never again a serious problem for the reigning emperor.

The Hippodrome was 480m long and 117.5m wide: according to one estimate it could seat about 100,000 spectators. Down the long central axis of the arena there was a raised terrace called the spina, or spine; this was adorned with a line of statues, obelisks, and columns, three of which are still standing in situ. The royal enclosure, the Kathisma, was probably at the middle of the east side of the Hippodrome, where the Emperor and his party could enter directly from the Great Palace. The straight north end of the arena, where chariots, performers and spectators entered through vaulted passageways, was at the north end of the present park. The semicircular south end, the sphendone, is today concealed by buildings at that end of the square. At the top of the outer wall an arcade of columns, with an epistyle in the classical manner, ran around the structure. Many of these columns were still standing a century after the Turkish Conquest, but in 1550 they were pulled down and used for building material. The final destruction of the Hippodrome occurred in 1609, when what remained of the structure was demolished to make way for the mosque of Sultan Ahmet I. The site of the arena became a public square, as it is still today, and was given the appropriate name of **At Meydanı**, the Square of Horses.

Near the north end of the At Meydanı there is a domed structure known as the **Fountain of Kaiser Wilhelm II**. The Kaiser donated the funds to build this fountain in 1895, on the occasion of his visit to Abdül Hamit II, and it was completed three years later.

The Egyptian Obelisk and the Hippodrome, a drawing by William Bartlett c 1838

The first of the ancient monuments on the spina, beginning at the north end of the Hippodrome, is the **Egyptian Obelisk**. This was originally commissioned by the Pharaoh Thutmose III (1549–1503 BC), who erected it at Deir el Bahri opposite Thebes in Upper Egypt to commemorate one of his campaigns in Syria and his crossing of the Euphrates River. The obelisk was originally about 60m tall and weighed some 800 tonnes, but it broke apart during shipment to Constantinople in the 4C AD, and only the upper third survived. This fragment lay on the seashore where it was unloaded for some years, until it was finally erected on its present site by Theodosius I in 390.

The obelisk is mounted on four brazen blocks resting on a marble base with sculptured reliefs. The scenes on the four sides of the base represent Theodosius I and his family in the Kathisma, as they look down at various events taking place in the arena below. On the north side of the base the Emperor is shown supervising the erection of the obelisk, with the operations shown on the lower block. On the west he is depicted with his family as he receives homage from a group of kneeling captives; standing beside Theodosius is his nephew Valentinian II, ruler of the western part of the Roman Empire, and flanking them are the Emperor's two eldest sons, Honorius and Arcadius, who would themselves later become Emperors of West and East, respectively. On the south side the royal family is shown watching a chariot race, and on the east Theodosius is represented standing between Honorius and Arcadius, holding a laurel wreath in his hand as he prepares to crown the winner of the race. Below the Kathisma, in this last scene, you can see the faces of the crowd in the Hippodrome; their faces, like those of the royal family, have been badly eroded by the elements. At the bottom of the panel there are dancing maidens, in a line, accompanied by three musicians.

Inscriptions in Greek and Latin on the base praise Theodosius and his Prefect Proclus for erecting the obelisk; the Latin inscription says that thirty days were required to do the job, while the one in Greek says that it took thirty-two days. The total height of the monument including the base is about 26m and its base represents the original level of the race-course, about 4.5m below the present surface of the ground.

At the centre of the spina stands the so-called **Serpentine Column**. The three intertwined bronze serpents that form the column were the base of a trophy which once stood in the Temple of Apollo at Delphi, dedicated to the god by the 31 Greek cities who defeated the Persians at Plataea in 479 BC. The base of the column was uncovered in 1920, revealing the names of the cities inscribed on the lower coils of the serpents. The column was brought from Delphi by Constantine the Great; it seems to have stood at first in the courtyard of Haghia Sophia and was erected in the Hippodrome only at a later date. There are several stories about what became of the missing serpent heads, but the most likely one is that they were chopped off by a drunken member of the Polish Embassy, one night in April 1700. The upper part of one of the serpent heads was found in 1847 and is now in the Archaeological Museum.

The third of the ancient monuments on the spina is a roughly built *pillar* of stone 32m high that stands near the south end of the At Meydanı. The 16C French traveller Petrus Gyllius called it the Colossus, but most modern writers refer to it, incorrectly, as the Column of Constantine Porphyrogenitus. Both names stem from the Greek inscription on its base, where the pillar is compared to the Colossus of Rhodes, and where it is recorded that the pillar was restored and sheathed in bronze by the Emperor Constantine VII Porphyrogenitus (913–59). But the inscription also states that the pillar was decayed by time; thus it must date from an earlier period, perhaps to that of Theodosius I or Constantine the Great.

**Palace of Ibrahim Paşa*

Opposite the Blue Mosque on the west side of the At Meydanı we see the Palace of Ibrahim Paşa which now houses the **Museum of Turkish and Islamic Art**.

■ **Admission**. The palace and the museum are open 10.00–17.00; closed Mon.

The original palace here on the western side of the Hippodrome was acquired in 1524 by Ibrahim Paşa, a Greek convert to Islam who became an intimate companion of Süleyman the Magnificent during the early years of the Sultan's reign. In 1523 Ibrahim was appointed Grand Vezir and the following year he married Süleyman's sister Hadice. Some idea of the enormous wealth and influence that Ibrahim had at this time can be gained from even a casual glance at the palace, the grandest private residence ever built in the Ottoman Empire, far greater in size than any of the buildings of Topkapı Sarayı itself. But his great wealth wealth and power lead to Ibrahim's downfall and in 1536 Süleyman had him executed. Immediately afterwards all of Ibrahim's wealth and possessions, including the palace on the At Meydanı, were confiscated by the State.

The great hall, that part of the palace which fronts on the At Meydanı, was in Ibrahim's time the Audience Room for the Grand Vezir, and afterwards it was probably the site of the High Court of Justice. Later it seems to have been used as a barracks for unmarried Janissaries and also as a prison. By the beginning of the present century much of the palace was in ruins, but in recent years it has been restored and now houses the Museum of Turkish and Islamic Art.

Exterior. After passing through the entrance-lobby you enter the northeast corner of the great central courtyard; this has been very attractively restored, with marble paving around a garden, and with a balcony overlooking the At Meydanı. Part of the north wing on the lower floor has been fitted out as an old-fashioned Istanbul coffee-house, a charming place to have a drink before or after seeing the exhibits in the museum.

Before going through the exhibits, stand in the courtyard to survey the structure of the palace. Visible here is the main part of the original palace of Ibrahim Paşa. There was another section of almost equal size adjoining the present structure to the northeast, apparently an enormous han-like edifice, which has vanished except for the wing nearest the At Meydanı. The most important part of the present structure is the great hall, which takes up most of the upper level of the south wing on the side overlooking the At Meydanı; this would have been Ibrahim Paşa's Hall of the Divan, and the two large chambers to its west would have been the antechambers to this.

The long western or inner chamber of the palace on its upper floor has at its

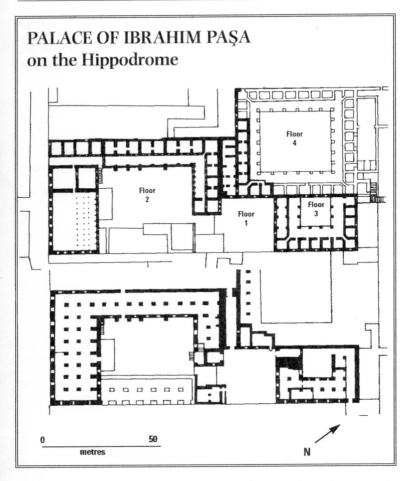

PALACE OF IBRAHIM PAŞA
on the Hippodrome

Floor 4

Floor 2

Floor 1

Floor 3

0   50
metres

N

rear a row of 13 cell-like cubicles opening onto a long corridor with a stone sofa overlooking the garden. This corridor turns the corner to pass along the north wing, which is only half as long as the south wing, with five cells along the inner side and a sixth overlooking the courtyard. The southern end of the corridor here is connected by a stairway with the courtyard, the entrance below being through a foyer with a great round-arched entryway.

The lower level of the palace around the courtyard consists of a series of splendid vaults, supported by a single row of piers in the north and west wings, creating two aisles, while in the south wing there is a triple row of piers, one engaged in the walls on the courtyard side, thus creating three aisles there. Some of these vaults are used to house the ethnological collection of the Museum of Turkish and Islamic Art, while other collections are on the upper level of the palace.

Interior. The usual route through the museum is via the round-arched foyer next to the entryway at the northeast corner of the courtyard, going up the stairway to the upper level. The principal collections of the museum are housed in the cells of the north and west wings, as well as in the great hall and its two antechambers in the south wing, from where a stairway leads back to the courtyard, and from there one can enter the great vaults to see the ethnological collection.

The main collections on the upper floor include rare and beautiful works from all periods of the Turkish and Islamic world, including objects from the Ummayid, Abbasid, Mamluk, Selçuk, Beylik, and Ottoman periods, ranging in date from the 7C–19C. The collections include carpets, manuscripts and calligraphy, miniatures, woodwork, stonework, ceramics and glassware, metalwork, carpets and folk-arts; altogether an extraordinary exhibit, superbly displayed. The ethnological collection includes tents and other objects belonging to the Yürük, the nomadic Turkish people of Anatolia.

At the southwest corner of the At Meydanı a narrow street named Şehit Mehmet Paşa Yokuşu leads off to the south, winding down towards the Marmara. At the second turning on the left, the street passes on the right, the remains of Helvacı Camii, a mosque founded in 1546 by one Iskender Ağa. Unfortunately, this has fallen into ruins and is no longer of any interest.

Farther down the street on the left there is a very interesting dervish monastery, whose entrance is half-way down the side street and on the right. This was built in 1692 by Ismail Bey and is known as the **Özbekler Tekkesi**. It is rather crudely designed, but its form is unique because of the steep descent of the hill on which it is built. The little domed gatehouse leads to an anteroom, opposite which there is the large and handsome mescit-zaviye, the room where the dervish ceremonies took place. On the right is a small porticoed courtyard with the cells of the dervishes; on the left is another courtyard of cells on two storeys, the lower level being reached by a staircase behind the zaviye. The building has been restored and is now being used as a hostel for university students.

**Sokollu Mehmet Paşa Camii*

Şehit Mehmet Paşa Yokuşu continues downhill past the walled garden of a mosque, after which it turns left to continue past the lower wall of the enclosure. Here is the entrance to Sokollu Mehmet Paşa Camii (Pl. 10,6), one of the most beautiful of the smaller mosques in Istanbul, a minor masterpiece by Sinan.

The mosque was built by Sinan in 1571–72 for Sokollu Mehmet Paşa, one of the most outstanding Grand Vezirs in the history of the Ottoman Empire. Sokollu Mehmet, the son of a Bosnian priest, was taken into the Janissary Corps as a youth and was educated in the Palace School at Topkapı Sarayı. His outstanding genius brought him early preferment and he rose rapidly in the Ottoman hierarchy, becoming Grand Vezir under Süleyman the Magnificent in 1565. He continued to hold that post under Süleyman's son and successor, Selim II, and married the Sultan's daughter, the Princess Esmahan, in whose honour he built this mosque. (The mosque is officially named after Esmahan, but it is more commonly associated with her more famous husband.) After Selim's death in 1574, Sokollu Mehmet Paşa served as Grand Vezir under Murat III until 1579, when he was murdered by a mad soldier in the Divan.

Exterior. The **courtyard** of the mosque is enchanting in design. It served, as in the case of many mosques, as a medrese, with the scholars living in the little domed cells under the portico. Each cell had a single window, a fireplace, and a recess for storing bedding, books and personal belongings. Instruction was given in the dershane, the large domed room over the staircase in the west wall, and also in the mosque itself. Notice the charming ogive arches of the portico and the fine **şadırvan** in the centre. The porch of the mosque forms the fourth side of the court; in the lunettes of the windows there are some striking and elegant inscriptions in blue and white faience.

SOKOLLU MEHMET PAŞA CAMII

Interior. Entering the building, you are delighted by the harmony of its lines, the lovely soft colour of the stone, the marble decoration, and, above all, by the tiles. In plan the mosque is a hexagon inscribed in an almost square rectangle, and the whole is covered by a dome, counter-balanced at the corners by four small semidomes. There are no side aisles, but around three sides there is a low gallery supported on slender marble columns with typical Ottoman lozenge capitals. The polychrome of the arches, whose voussoirs are of alternate green and white marble, is characteristic of the period.

The **tile decoration** of the mosque has been used with singularly charming effect. Only selected areas of the walls have been sheathed in tiles: the pendentives below the dome, a frieze of floral design, and the exquisite central section of the east wall. The latter panel frames the mihrab with tiles decorated in vine and floral motifs in turquoise on a background of pale green, interspersed with panels of fine calligraphy with white letters on a deep blue field. The fine marble mimber is surmounted by a tall conical cap, sheathed in the same turquoise tiles that frame the mihrab. Above the mihrab the framed arch in the east wall is pierced by elegant stained glass windows, whose bright spectrum of colours complements the cool tones of the faience flowers below.

Above the entrance portal a small specimen of the wonderful painted decoration of the classical period can be seen. It consists of very elaborate arabesque designs in rich and varied colours. Also above the door, surmounted by a design in gold, there is a fragment of black stone from the Kaaba in Mecca; other fragments can be seen in the mihrab and mimber.

After leaving the mosque courtyard by the main gateway, turn left and then right at the next corner on to **Kadirga Liman Cad**. This picturesque old street soon leads to a large open square, much of which is now given over to a park and playground. This is the pleasant area known as **Kadirga Limanı**, which means literally the Galley Port. As its name suggests, this was originally a seaport, long since silted up and built over. The port was originally dug and put in shape by the Emperor Julian the Apostate in 362. In about 570 Justin II redredged and enlarged the port and named it after his wife Sophia. It had to be continually redredged but remained in use until after the Turkish Conquest. By about 1550, when the French traveller Petrus Gyllius saw it, only a small part of the harbour remained, and now even this is gone.

In the centre of the square, Kadirga Liman Meydanı, there is a very striking and unique monument. This is the **namazgah of Esma Sultan**, daughter of Ahmet III, which was built in 1779. It is a great rectangular block of masonry. On two faces there are fountains with calligraphic inscriptions; the corners have ornamental niches, while the third side has a staircase leading to the platform on top. This is the only surviving example in Stamboul of a namazgah, or outdoor place of prayer, in which the direction of Mecca is indicated by a niche, but otherwise entirely without furniture or decoration.

We now retrace our steps on Kadirga Liman Cad, and continue on to its intersection with Küçük Ayasofya Cad. Just beyond the corner we see on our right the huge dome of an abandoned Ottoman hamam. This is the **Çardaklı Hamam**, built in 1503 by Hüseyin Ağa, Chief Black Eunuch under Beyazit II.

**Saints Sergius and Bacchus

We now turn right on Küçük Ayasofya Cad. After a few steps this brings us to Küçük Aya Sofya Camii, the former church of SS. Sergius and Bacchus (Pl. 11,5).

> The church was begun by Justinian in 527, the first year of his reign, and it was completed before 536. He dedicated the church to SS. Sergius and Bacchus, two Roman soldiers martyred for their faith and later the patron saints of Christians in the Roman army. SS. Sergius and Bacchus belongs to that extraordinary period of prolific and fruitful experiment in architectural forms which produced, in Constantinople, buildings so ambitious and so different as the present church, Haghia Sophia itself, and Haghia Eirene—to name only the surviving monuments—and in Ravenna, San Vitale, the Baptistery, and Sant' Apollinare in Classe. It is as if the architects were searching for new modes of expression suitable to a new age. The domes of this period are especially worthy of note: the great dome of Haghia Sophia is of course unique, but the dome of SS. Sergius and Bacchus is no mere small-scale version of it, being quite different in design and very extraordinary on its own account.
>
> The church was finally converted into a mosque in the first decade of the 16C by the Chief Black Eunuch Hüseyin Ağa, whose tomb can be seen in the garden to the north of the mosque. SS. Sergius and Bacchus is known in Turkish as Küçük Aya Sofya Camii, the Mosque of Little Haghia Sophia, because of its supposed resemblance to the Great Church.

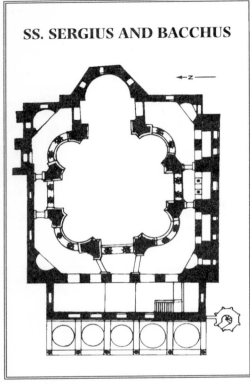

SS. SERGIUS AND BACCHUS

Interior. In plan the church is an irregular octagon crookedly inscribed in a very irregular rectangle. It is difficult to account for these irregularities, but they may be partly due to the fact that SS. Sergius and Bacchus was one of a pair of contiguous churches and had perhaps to be slightly deformed to accommodate its neighbour. The neighbouring church is thought to have been that of SS. Peter and Paul, which was probably located just to the south of the present building.

The method of transition from the octagon to the dome is astonishing: the **dome** is divided into sixteen compartments, eight flat sections alternating with eight concave ones above the angles of the octagon. This gives the dome the oddly undulatory or corrugated effect that is so distinctive when the building is observed from the heights of the First Hill. The octagon has eight polygonal piers with pairs of columns in between, alternately of verd antique and red Synnada marble, both above and below, arranged straight on the axes but curved out into the exedrae at each corner. The space between this brightly coloured, moving curtain of columns and the exterior walls of the rectangle becomes an ambulatory below and a spacious gallery above, reached by a staircase at the south end of the narthex.

The capitals and the classic entablature are exquisite specimens of the elaborately carved and deeply undercut style of the 6C, similar to those in Haghia Sophia. On the ground floor the capitals are of the 'melon' type, in the gallery 'pseudo-Ionic'; a few of them still bear the monogram of Justinian and Theodora, though most of these have been effaced. In the gallery the epistyle is arcaded in a way that became traditional in later Byzantine architecture. On the ground floor, the entablature is still basically classical, trabeated instead of arched, with the traditional architrave, frieze and cornice, but it is very different in effect from anything classical, the impression is of lace. The frieze consists of a long and beautifully carved inscription in twelve Greek hexameters honouring Justinian and Theodora, the two founders, and also St. Sergius, although for some reason St. Bacchus is not mentioned.

Nothing remains of the original interior decoration of the church. The walls, like those of Haghia Sophia, were revetted with veined and variegated marbles, while the vaults and domes glittered with mosaics. As described by Procopius, Justinian's court chronicler: 'By the sheen of its marbles it was more resplendent than the sun, and everywhere it was filled profusely with gold'.

Küçük Aya Sofya Camii, the former church of Saints Sergius and Bacchus

**The Byzantine sea-walls*

A winding lane leads from the outside courtyard of SS. Sergius and Bacchus and passes under the railway line, after which we pass through the yard of a municipal building to make our way out to the Marmara highway. We turn left here to follow a well-preserved stretch of the ancient Byzantine sea-walls along the Marmara.

The Byzantine sea-walls along this part of the Marmara shore were originally constructed by Constantine the Great, ending where his land-walls met the sea at Samatya. When the Theodosian walls were built in the following century, the sea-walls along the Marmara and the Golden Horn were extended to meet them. During the 9C the Marmara walls were almost completely rebuilt by the Emperor Theophilus, who sought to strengthen the city's maritime defences against the Arabs. The Marmara defences consisted of a single line of walls 12–15m high with 188 towers at regular intervals. These walls stretched from Saray Burnu to the terminus of the Theodosian walls on the Marmara, a total distance of 8km, and were pierced by 13 sea-gates. Although much of the fortifications along the Marmara have been destroyed in modern times, particularly during the building of the railway in the 1870s, that which remains is still grand and impressive, particularly the walls and towers below the First Hill.

Almost immediately in front of SS. Sergius and Bacchus there is a small postern gate, undoubtedly designed for the use of the monastery that was once attached to the church. Closer inspection shows that the posts of the gateway are carved with a long inscription in Greek, containing a conflation or cento from Habakkuk and Psalms. It is believed that these gateposts once formed the base of the celebrated equestrian statue of Justinian that stood in the Augustaeum.

Just before the first exit from the highway we see an array of ancient column fragments that have been re-erected beside the walkway. These are all from the Great Palace of Byzantium, whose fragmentary ruins continually come to light in construction projects along the Marmara slope of the First Hill.

A short way after crossing the highway exit we come to the ruins of a handsome postern known in Turkish as **Çatladi Kapı**, or the Cracked Gate. The marble sides and archway of the gate are finely carved with acanthus-leaf decorations as well as a large monogram of Justinian. This postern is probably the one that was called the Imperial Marine Gate, since it appears to have been one of the entrances to the Great Palace from Porta Leonis, the Emperor's private harbour. This port took its name from the statues of the two lions that flanked the Imperial Marine Gate. These are the lions now in the Archaeological Museum.

The gateway gave entrance to the ***Palace of Bucoleon**, one of the seaside pavilions of the Great Palace. The remains can be seen just beyond the next tower in the sea-walls; here you see the east loggia of the palace, with its three huge marble-framed windows and a vaulted room behind them. Below the windows some projecting corbels indicate that a balcony ran along the façade, suspended over a marble quay below. Notice the curious-looking row of large square marble slabs built into the lower part of the wall; these are the bottoms of Doric capitals of the 5C BC, doubtless from some ancient temple that stood nearby.

These ruins are virtually all that remains of the Great Palace of Byzantium whose pavilions and gardens covered the Marmara slopes of the First Hill. The Palace was first built by Constantine the Great when he founded his new capital. Much of the Palace was destroyed during the Nika Revolt in 532, but it was rebuilt and considerably enlarged by Justinian soon after. Several later emperors restored and extended the Palace, adorning it with works of art, most notably Basil I (867–86). The Great Palace was divided into several different establishments: the Sacred Palace and the Palaces of Daphne and Chalke, which were located near the present site of the Blue Mosque; the Palaces of Magnaura and Mangana, which stood to the southeast of Haghia Sophia, on the slope of the First Hill leading down to the Marmara; and the seaside Palace of Bucoleon.

The Great Palace served as the imperial residence until the sack of Constantinople by the Crusaders in 1204. After the recapture of the city in 1261 it was found to be in a state of advanced decay and was never afterwards restored. Instead, the later emperors abandoned the palaces by the Marmara and took up their residence in the Palace of Blachernae, in the northwest corner of the city. At the time of the Turkish Conquest the Great Palace was completely in ruins. Shortly after he entered the city, Sultan Mehmet the Conqueror walked through the ruined halls of the palace and was so saddened that he recited a melancholy distich by the Persian poet Saadi: 'The spider is the curtain-holder in the Palace of the Caesars. The owl hoots its night call on the Towers of Aphrasiab.'

The tower that forms the angle in the defence-walls just to the east of Bucoleon was once the Pharos, the lighthouse of Constantinople. In modern times the lighthouse has been relocated farther to the east along the sea-walls. About 400m east of the lighthouse we come to an ancient entryway in the sea-walls. The Byzantine name of this gateway is unknown, but in Ottoman times it was called Ahır Kapı, the **Stable Gate**, because it led to the imperial mews in the lower gardens of the Saray. The gateway is still used by those going out to the Marmara, and we will return to it after making an excursion farther eastward along the sea walls.

Incili Köşk and St. Saviour Philanthropus

There are two minor monuments of some historic interest along the walls past Ahır Kapı. The first of these is about 500m along, just beyond the modern lighthouse. This is a marble structure called **Incili Köşk**, the Kiosk of the Pearl, the only Ottoman sea-pavilion still standing along the Marmara shore. An inscription on the wall-fountain built into this kiosk gives the name of its founder as Sinan Paşa and the date 1578.

A short distance beyond the Incili Köşk we see the façade of an ancient church built into the sea-walls, with blocked-up doors, window niches, and a huge arch rising to the top of the wall. This is all that remains of the **church of St. Saviour Philanthropus**, built in the first half of the 12C by Alexius I Comnenus.

Those agile enough to climb up to the top of the sea-wall above the church can see the remains of another ancient structure on the other side of the railway tracks. The ruins there have been identified as those of the **church of St. George of the Mangana**. This was built by Constantine IX Monomachus (1042–55), who was buried there.

We now return to Ahır Kapı, where we re-enter the city through the double Byzantine gate, the only surviving portal in the ancient sea-walls. We turn right inside and follow a street that soon passes under the railway line, where we turn right again. This brings us to **Ishakpaşa Cad.**, a street lined with picturesque old houses built up against the outer defence walls of Topkapı Sarayı.

At the point where the road veers to the right, following a bend in the walls, we see a mosque and hamam flanking the side street on the left, which is known as Akbıyık Cad., the Avenue of the White Moustache.

The mosque, on the left at the beginning of Akbıyık Cad. is **Ishak Paşa Camii**, and the abandoned haman across from it to the right is part of the same complex. The complex was built in 1483 by Ishak Paşa, who served as Grand Vezir under both Fatih and Beyazit II. The mosque has been restored recently, but the hamam, one of the oldest in the city, is beginning to fall into ruins.

We follow Ishakpaşa Cad. to the next corner, where we turn left on Kutlugün Sok. There we pass on our right the new **Four Seasons Hotel**, which is housed in the reconstructed Sultanahmet Prison. The prison was built in the last years of the Ottoman Empire and was completed in 1917, probably by the architect Vedat Tek. The prison was closed in the 1970s and was abandoned until its restoration as a hotel.

At the end of Kutlugün Sok. we turn right, after which we turn left at the next corner, crossing Mimar Mehmet Ağa Cad. This brings us to Torun Sok., the Street of the Grandchild, which parallels the bazaar street below the Blue Mosque. Halfway along Torun Sok. we come on our right to the rear entrance of the ***Mosaic Museum** (Pl 11,5).

■ **Admission**. The Mosaic Museum is open 09.00–17.00; closed Tue.

The exhibits in the museum were discovered during excavations made in 1935 to search for the remains of the Great Palace of Byzantium. These excavations revealed extensive mosaic pavements as well as columns, capitals and other architectural fragments, all of which are now arrayed in the garden of the museum. The ruins were identified as being the northeast portico of the Mosaic Peristyle, a colonnaded walkway which may have led from the imperial apartments of the palace to the Kathisma, the royal enclosure on the Hippodrome.

The mosaics depict lively scenes such as a tiger hunt, a bear eating a young stag, a donkey throwing his rider, a bear chasing a young man, a fight between an elephant and a lion, and a wolf devouring its prey, as well as an interesting scene depicting a mock chariot race between two spectators in the Hippodrome. Another fascinating panel depicts a bearded young man with a Christ-like appearance, though the figure has not yet been identified. There has been considerable discussion about the date of these mosaics, but current opinion is that they were made c AD 500.

The upper entrance of the museum leads us on **Kaba Sakal Cad.**, the Avenue of the Bushy Beard, where we turn right. This is an early 17C Ottoman market street that has been completely restored, its flanking arcade of ancient shops now serving the tourist trade.

At the end of the arcade we turn left on Mimar Mehmet Ağa Cad. and then right on to the extension of Kaba Sakal Cad., which passes on its left the Haseki Hürrem Hamamı (see p 205). Opposite the hamam we see two restored Ottoman buildings, a medrese and a konak, or town house. The first of these is the **Kaba Sakal Medresesi**, founded in the 18C by the Şeyhülislam Mehmet Efendi. The medrese has been beautifully restored and now houses the **Istanbul Crafts Market**. Each of the chambers around the courtyard of the medrese is occupied by an artisan practising old Ottoman crafts, including engraving, bookbinding, embroidery, carving on bone, and doll-making. These restorations were carried out by the TTOK, directed by Çelik Gülersoy, which now operates the splendidly restored 19C konak as a luxurious hotel, the **Yeşil Ev**, or Green House.

There is an extremely pleasant café-restaurant in the rear courtyard of Yeşil Ev, centred on an elegant Ottoman selsebil, or cascade fountain. This is a perfect place to stop for lunch after the long walk around the Hippodrome.

6 · The Hippodrome to Beyazit Square

**Yerebatan Saray*

This route begins outside the entrance to Haghia Sophia. From there we cross the tramline and go a short way up the left side of the street opposite, Yerebatansaray Cad. This brings us to a small building that serves as the entrance to an enormous underground cistern called Yerebatan Saray, the Underground Palace (Pl.11,3), known in English as the **Basilica Cistern**.

■ **Admission**. Yerebatan Saray is open every day from 09.00–17.00.

The structure is called the Basilica Cistern because it lay beneath the Stoa Basilica, the great public square on the First Hill. This reservoir was rebuilt by Justinian after the Nika Revolt in 532, possibly as an enlargement of an earlier cistern constructed by Constantine the Great. Throughout the Byzantine period the Basilica Cistern was used to store water for the Great Palace and the other buildings on the First Hill. After the Conquest it served Topkapı Sarayı and the palace gardens. Nevertheless, general knowledge of the cistern's existence seems to have been lost until it was rediscovered c 1547 by Petrus Gyllius.

Interior. Yerebatan Saray is by far the largest of the many underground cisterns in the city remaining from Roman times. It is 138m long (the longitudinal axis is in the direction of the street above) by 64.6m wide. (Compare this to the plan of Haghia Sophia, which is 75m long and 70m wide.) The 336 columns of the cistern are arranged in 12 rows of 28 each, separated by 4m and with a height of 8m. (Ninety of these columns in the southeast corner of the cistern were walled off at the end of the 19C and are not visible today.) Most of the

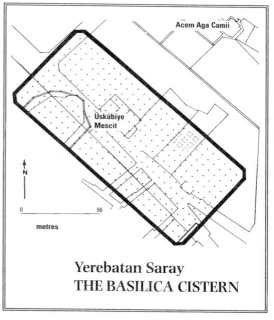

columns are topped by Byzantine Corinthian capitals; these have imposts above them that support little domes of brick constructed in a herring-bone pattern.

In the far-left corner of the cistern two of the columns are mounted on ancient classical bases supported by the heads of Gorgons one of them upside down and the other on its side. (The Gorgons in Greek mythology were three sisters, one of whom, Medusa, was slain by Perseus.) These Gorgon heads and the two we have seen outside the Archaeological Museum were, as we have noted, originally in the Forum of Constantine (see below). The two heads here were probably put in place when Justinian rebuilt the Basilica Cistern after the Nika Revolt in 532.

Along Divanyolu Caddesi

The exit from the cistern leaves us on Alemdar Cad., where we turn right and make our way back to the beginning of **Divanyolu Cad.**, which we will more or less follow for the rest of this itinerary. This avenue follows the route of the ancient Mese, or Middle Way, the main thoroughfare of Byzantine Constantinople. This continued to be the principal artery of the city in Ottoman times because it led from the vicinity of Topkapı Sarayı to the centre of Stamboul. Consequently, the modern avenue here is lined with monuments of the imperial Ottoman centuries, along with some ruined remnants of the Byzantine Empire. Its Turkish name, the Road of the Divan, comes from the fact that it was the principal approach to Topkapı Sarayı for the thousands who attended the tri-weekly meetings of the Divan.

At the beginning of Divanyolu on the right there is an Ottoman **suterazi**, or water-control tower. The marble shaft at the foot of the suterazi was discovered during excavations in 1965. This was part of the Miliarium Aureum, the Golden Milestone, also known as the Milion. The Milion was a triumphal archway that stood at the beginning of the Mese; it served as the reference point for the milestones on the Via Egnatia, the great Roman road that extended from Byzantium to Durres (Durazzo) on the Albanian coast of the Adriatic. During Byzantine times it was surmounted by statues of Constantine the Great and his mother Helena, who stood holding the True Cross between them.

About 100m along Divanyolu we come on our left to **Firuz Ağa Camii**. This was constructed in 1491 for Firuz Ağa, Chief Treasurer in the reign of Beyazit II. Firuz Ağa Camii is of interest mainly because it is one of the few examples in Istanbul of a mosque of the `pre-classical' period, that is, of those built before 1500. This is the architectural style that flourished principally in the city of Bursa when it was the capital of the Ottoman Empire, in the century before the Conquest. Firuz Ağa Camii is quite simple in form, consisting merely of a square room covered by a windowless dome resting on the walls, the so-called single-unit type of mosque. The building is preceded by a little porch of three bays, while the minaret, unusually, is on the left side. The tomb of the founder, in the form of a marble sarcophagus, is on the terrace beside the mosque. Firuz Ağa Camii is an elegant little building, perhaps the most handsome of the early mosques of its type in the city.

Just beyond Firuz Ağa Camii a little park borders an open area excavated in the 1950s. The ruins exposed in these excavations are so fragmentary that it is difficult to determine their identity. It is thought that they are the ruins of two adjacent palaces, those of Antiochus and Lausus, noblemen of the early 5C AD. The grander of these is the **palace of Antiochus**, an hexagonal building with five deep semicircular apses, between each pair of which there are circular rooms. Early in the 7C the palace of Antiochus was converted into a martyrium for the body of St. Euphemia of Chalcedon, a Christian maiden who was martyred for her faith c 300. The martyrium is elaborately decorated with 13C frescoes representing scenes from the life and martyrdom of St. Euphemia, along with a striking picture of the Forty Martyrs of Sebaste; these are preserved in rather poor condition under a shed at the rear of the site. (This is not open to the public.) The silver-plated casket of St. Euphemia is preserved in the church of St. George in the Greek Orthodox Patriarchate in the Fener (see p 192).

Once past these ruins we continue along Divanyolu for a short distance and then take the second street on the left, Işık Sok., which leads uphill to a square known as Binbirdirek Meydanı. On the south side of the square there is a little building which serves as the entrance to another ancient underground cistern; this is known in Turkish as ****Binbirdirek**, the Cistern of a Thousand-and-One Columns (pl.11,5).

■ **Admission.** The cistern is not officially open to the public. However, there is a bekçi, or watchman, who for a modest tip will unlock the door and lead you down into the cistern. The steps are broken and slippery and the railing has rusted away in many places, so you must proceed with caution.

Interior. Unlike Yerebatan Saray, the cistern is dry, and so you can walk about and appreciate the grandeur of this extraordinary structure. The cistern was originally about 19m high from the floor to the top of the little brick domes in herring-bone design, but over the centuries mud has accumulated to a depth of some 4.5m. The columns are in two tiers bound together by curious stone ties. There were originally 224 double columns in 16 rows of 14 each, but 12 of these were walled in not long after the cistern was completed. The impost capitals are plain except that some of them are inscribed with the monograms of the stonemasons.

The dimensions of Binbirdirek are 64m by 56.4m, giving it a floor area of some 3610 sq m; this makes it the second largest underground cistern in the city, but still only about a third of the area of Yerebatan Saray. It is thought that the cistern was originally built by Philoxenus, a Roman senator who came to the city with Constantine the Great, although there is evidence that some of the structure dates to the 5C–6C. During the 19C the cistern was used as a spinning-mill and more recently as a storehouse.

On emerging from the cistern we walk to the far end of the square and then turn left on Klod Farer Cad., named after the French novelist Claud Farrere. At the first corner we turn right into Dostluk Yurdu Sok., which at the next corner on the right brings us to Piyer Loti Cad., named for the French novelist Pierre Loti. Directly across the street at the corner we come to the Eminönü Belediye Basbakanlığı building, where a door to the right of the main entrance has a sign indicating the entrance to the **Theodosius Cistern**.

■ **Admission.** The cistern is open 09.00–17.00; closed Sun. The policeman on duty will put on the lights, which only faintly illuminate the cistern. The stairway down to the cistern is in poor repair, so you are restricted to a platform inside the entrance.

Interior. The cistern measures 42.5m by 25m, its brick roof supported by 32 columns of white marble, with some capitals of the Corinthian order and others Doric. The cistern is believed to have been built during the reign of Theodosius II (408–50) by his sister, the Empress Pulcheria, who would later marry her brother's successor Marcian (450–57). The cistern has been restored in recent years and was opened to the public in 1994.

After leaving the cistern we turn left on Piyer Loti Cad., which brings us up to Divanyolu Cad. On the other side of the avenue we see the **türbe of Mahmut II** (1808–39), enclosed by a long garden wall. The türbe was completed in 1840; it was designed in the Empire style then popular in Europe, and is thus a little pompous and formal. Mahmut's son and grandson, Sultans Abdül Aziz and Abdül Hamit II, together with a large number of princes and imperial consorts, are also buried here. The tomb and its extensive garden are now open to the public.

Directly opposite the türbe of Mahmut II, on the left side of Divanyolu Cad., is an elegant Ottoman library. This is one of the buildings of the **Köprülü külliyesi**, whose other institutions are scattered about in the immediate neighbourhood. These buildings were erected in 1659–60 by two members of the illustrious Köprülü family, Mehmet Paşa and his son Fazıl Ahmet Paşa. The Köprülüs are generally considered to have been the most distinguished family in the history of the Ottoman Empire. During the second half of the 17C and the early years of the 18C five members of the family served as Grand Vezir, some of them among the most able of those that ever held that post. The library of the Köprülü külliyesi is a handsome little building with a columned porch and a domed reading-room, constructed in a mixture of brick and stone. The library contains an important collection of books and manuscripts, many of which are state papers and other documents belonging to the two founders.

One block beyond the library and on the same side of the main avenue, which here changes its name to Yeniçeriler Cad. are two other institutions belonging to the Köprülü külliyesi; these are the **mosque and the türbe of Mehmet Paşa**. The türbe is roofed, unusually, with a metal grille. The mosque is a few steps beyond the türbe, projecting out onto the sidewalk of the avenue. The mosque, which is octagonal, was once the lecture hall of the Köprülü medresesi, most of which has now disappeared.

Directly across the avenue from the Köprülü mosque stands the *Çemberlitaş Hamamı, one of the finest extant examples of a classical Turkish bath. This hamam was founded some time before her death in 1583 by the Valide Sultan Nur Banu, wife of Selim II and mother of Murat III. The bath was originally double, but the women's section was destroyed when the avenue was widened some years ago. The entrance to the bath, which has sections for both man and women, is around the corner on the side street.

Just beyond the hamam, at the corner of Yeniçeriler Cad. and Vezirhanı Cad., we come to the ****Column of Constantine**. This is known locally as Çemberlitaş (Pl. 10,4), the Hooped Column, a name that it has given to the adjacent bath and the surrounding neighbourhood.

> The column was erected by Constantine the Great to commemorate the dedication of the city as capital of the Roman Empire on 11 May AD 330. It stood at the centre of the Forum of Constantine, a colonnaded oval portico which is thought to have been similar to that which Bernini later built in front of St. Peter's in Rome. Around the Forum, which was adorned with statues of pagan deities, Roman emperors, and Christian saints, there stood several large public buildings, temples, and churches. All that remains of this grandeur now lies buried beneath 3m of earth, with only the battered column itself surviving.

The column, whose present height is 34.8m, originally had a square pedestal standing on five steps; above this there was a porphyry plinth and column base supporting a shaft of seven porphyry drums. In 416 the column was damaged during an earthquake. As it seemed in imminent danger of collapse, iron hoops were bound around the junctions of the drums to stabilise the shaft. At the summit of the shaft there was a large capital, presumably Corinthian, upon which stood a colossal statue of the Emperor Constantine in the guise of Apollo, with a sceptre in his right hand, the globe of the world in his left, and a crown of brazen sun-rays glittering in his helmet.

The statue fell down and was destroyed during a hurricane in 1106, and some 50 years later Manuel I Comnenus replaced the capital with the present masonry courses and marble block, with a large cross above, which was removed after the Conquest. In 1779 the column was damaged during a great fire that destroyed most of the surrounding neighbourhood, leaving the black scars that you see today. The column was soon afterwards repaired by Abdül Hamit I, who enclosed the base of the column in its present masonry casing, which conceals the lowest porphyry drum. The column was restored during the 1970s, when the ancient iron hoops were replaced.

A short way down the right side of Vezirhanı Cad. is the entrance to another institution of the Köprülü külliyesi, the **Vezir Hanı**. Along with the other buildings in the külliye, the Vezir Hanı was erected in 1659–60 by Mehmet Paşa and his son Fazıl Ahmet Paşa. It served as a hostel for travelling merchants and was also equipped with stables for their animals as well as shops and storerooms for their goods. The Vezir Hanı was also the principal slave-market in Istanbul, until the abolition of slavery in the Ottoman Empire in 1855.

Just beyond the Column of Constantine, on the same side of Yeniçeriler Cad., there is an interesting old mosque, **Atik Ali Paşa Camii**. This is one of the oldest mosques in the city, built in 1496 by Hadım (Eunuch) Atik Ali Paşa, Grand Vezir of Beyazit II. Surrounded by a quiet garden off the busy street, it is an attractive little mosque, particularly from the outside. Its plan is somewhat unusual; it consists of a rectangular room divided into two unequal parts by an arch. The larger west section is covered by a dome, the east by a semidome under which is the mihrab, as if in a sort of great apse. The west section is also flanked to north and south by two rooms with smaller domes. The semidome and the four small domes have stalactite pendentives, a common feature in Ottoman mosques of early date.

Atik Ali Paşa Camii originally had several dependencies: a tekke, an imaret, and a medrese. Of these only a part of the medrese remains; this is across Yeniçeriler Cad. from the mosque, the remainder having been destroyed some years ago when the road was widened. This building, though mutilated, is interesting as being one of the very few medreses of the pre-classical period that survive in the city.

A short distance beyond Atik Ali Paşa Cad., on the same side of the avenue, there is the külliye of **Koca Sinan Paşa**, enclosed by a picturesque marble wall with iron grilles. The külliye consists of a medrese, a sebil, and the türbe of Koca Sinan Paşa, who died in 1595. Koca Sinan Paşa was Grand Vezir under both Murat III and Mehmet III, and was the conqueror of the Yemen. Perhaps the most outstanding element in this very attractive complex of buildings is the türbe, a fine structure with 16 sides. It is built of polychrome stonework, white and rose-coloured, and with a rich cornice of stalactites and handsome window mouldings.

The medrese, which is entered through a gate in the alley alongside, has a charming courtyard with a portico in ogive arches. The sebil, too, is an elegant structure with bronze grilles separated by little columns and surmounted by a hanging roof. The külliye was built in 1593 by Davut Ağa, the successor to

Sinan as Chief Architect of the Ottoman Empire; it has recently been restored.

On the other side of the alley across from the sebil a marble wall with grilles encloses another complex of buildings, the **külliye of Ali Paşa of Çorlu**. This Ali Paşa was a son-in-law of Mustafa II and served as Grand Vezir under Ahmet III, on whose orders he was beheaded in 1711 on the Aegean island of Mytilene. Ali Paşa's head was later brought back to Istanbul and buried in the cemetery of his külliye, which had been completed three years earlier. This külliye, consisting of a small mosque and a medrese, belongs to the transitional period between the classical and baroque styles. Though attractive, there is nothing outstanding about these buildings, although you might notice how essentially classical they still are. The only very baroque features are the capitals of the columns on the porch. The külliye has recently been restored, and the medrese now serves as a hostel for university students.

Directly across the avenue stands the octagonal **mosque of Kara Mustafa Paşa of Merzifon**. This unfortunate Grand Vezir also lost his head, executed by Mehmet IV after the second unsuccessful siege of Vienna in 1683. The buildings were begun in 1669 and finished by the Paşa's son in 1690. This mosque is of the transitional type between classical and baroque; it is of interest as being one of the few mosques with an octagonal plan. This külliye has also been restored in recent years; the medrese has been converted into a research institute commemorating the Turkish poet Yahya Kemal, who died in 1958.

The street beyond this little külliye is called **Gedik Paşa Cad.**; this leads to a **hamam** of the same name on the second turning on the left. This is one of the very oldest baths in the city (c 1475), and it is still in operation. Its founder was Gedik Ahmet Paşa, one of Mehmet the Conqueror's Grand Vezirs (1470–77), commander of the Ottoman fleet at Azov and conqueror of Otranto. This hamam has an unusually spacious and monumental soğukluk consisting of a large domed area flanked by alcoves and cubicles; the one on the right has a very elaborate stalactited vault. The hararet is cruciform except that the lower arm of the cross has been cut off and made part of the soğukluk; the corners of the cross form domed cubicles. The bath has recently been restored and now glistens with bright new marble; it is much patronised by the inhabitants of this picturesque quarter.

**Beyazidiye

At the first cross street beyond Gedik Pasa Cad. the avenue reaches Beyazit Meydanı, one of the busiest intersections in the old city. An underground pedestrian walkway makes it possible to cross safely to the other side of the avenue, from where you walk through the crowded market area to the Beyazidiye, the mosque complex of Beyazit II (Pl. 10,4).

The Beyazidiye was the second great mosque complex to be erected in Istanbul after the Conquest, the first being that of Mehmet II himself (see p 149, Fatih Camii). The külliye was built between 1501 and 1506, and consists of the great mosque itself, along with a medrese, primary school, public kitchen, public bath, and several türbes. Heretofore the architect's name has variously been given as Hayrettin or Kemalettin, but a recent study has shown that the külliye is due to a certain Yakub-şah bin Sultan-şah, who also built a caravansarai at Bursa. His background is unknown and his origin uncertain, but he may have been a Turk. Whatever his origin, he created a work of the very greatest importance, both in its excellence as a building and in its historic significance in the development of Ottoman architecture.

The Beyazit mosque marks the beginning of the great classical period that continued for more than two centuries. Before this time Ottoman architects had been experimenting with various styles of mosques and had often produced buildings of great beauty, as in Yeşil Cami at Bursa or Üç Şerefeli Cami at Edirne; but no definite style had been evolved that could produce the vast mosques demanded by the capital of a world empire. The original mosque of the Conqueror was indeed a monumental building, but as that was destroyed by an earthquake in the 18C, Beyazit Camii remains the earliest extant example of the great imperial mosques of Istanbul.

THE MOSQUE OF SULTAN BEYAZIT II

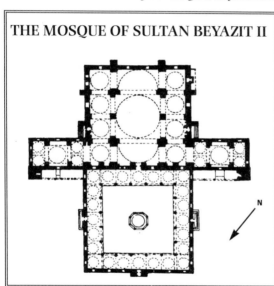

Exterior. Beyazit Camii is entered through what is perhaps the most charming of all the mosque courtyards in Istanbul. A peristyle of 20 ancient columns—porphyry, verd antique, and Syenitic granite—upholds an arcade with red-and-white or black-and-white marble voussoirs. The colonnade is roofed with 24 small domes and three magnificent entrance portals give access to it. The pavement is of polychrome marble and in the centre stands a beautifully decorated şadırvan. (The encircling colonnade of stumpy verd antique columns supporting a dome appears to be a clumsy restoration.) Capitals, cornices, and niches are elaborately decorated with stalactite mouldings. The harmony of proportions, the rich but restrained decoration, the brilliance of the variegated marbles, give this courtyard a quite unique charm.

Interior. An exceptionally fine portal leads into the mosque, which in plan is a greatly simplified and much smaller version of Haghia Sophia. As there, the great central dome and the semidomes to east and west form a kind of nave, beyond which to north and south are side aisles. The arches supporting the dome spring from four huge rectangular piers; the dome has smooth pendentives but rests on a cornice of stalactite mouldings. There are no galleries over

The Beyazidiye mosque

the aisles which open wide into the nave, separated only by the piers and by a single antique granite column between them. This is an essential break with the plan of Haghia Sophia: in one way or another the mosque architects all tried to centralise their plan as much as possible, so that the entire area is visible from any point. At the west side a broad corridor, divided into domed or vaulted bays and extending considerably beyond the main body of the mosque, creates the effect of a narthex. This is a transitional feature, retained from an older style of mosque; it appears only rarely later on.

At each end of this corridor rise the two fine **minarets**, their shafts picked out with geometric designs in terracotta; they stand far beyond the main part of the building in a position which is unique and gives a very grand effect. At the end of the south arm of the corridor a small library was added in the 18C by the Şeh-ül Islam Veliyüttin Efendi. An unusual feature of the interior of the mosque is that the Sultan's loge is to the right of the mimber instead of to the left. The loge is supported on columns of very rich and rare marbles. The central area of the building is approximately 40m on a side, and the diameter of the dome is about 17m.

The mosque precincts. Behind the mosque is the **türbe garden**; Beyazit II is buried here in a simple, well-proportioned türbe of limestone picked out in verd antique. The even simpler türbe of his daughter Selçuk Hatun is nearby. Behind these a third türbe, in a highly ornate Empire style, is that of the Grand Vezir Koca Reşit Paşa, the distinguished leader of the Tanzimat Movement, who died in 1857. Below the east side of the türbe garden facing the street is an arcade of shops originally erected by Sinan in 1580; it had almost disappeared long ago but it was restored during the 1960s.

Just beside these shops is the large double **sibyan mektebi** with two domes and a porch; this is the oldest surviving primary school in the city, since that belonging to the külliye of the Conqueror has disappeared. The school has recently been restored and now houses the hakkı tarık us Research Library. (hakkı tarık us was a journalist who, like the poet e.e. cummings, had an aversion to capital letters.)

Almost opposite the north minaret stands the extremely impressive **imaret** of the külliye. The imaret, in addition to serving as a public kitchen, seems also to have been used as a caravansarai. The various rooms of the imaret line three sides of the courtyard (now roofed in), with the fourth side pierced by the monumental entrance portal. The first room on the right housed an olive press, the second was a grain storeroom, and the third, in the right-hand corner, was the bakery, equipped with two huge ovens. The large domed chamber at the far corner of the courtyard was the kitchen and dining-room. The even larger domed chamber beside it, forming the left third of the complex, served as a stable for the horses and camels of the travellers who were guests at the imaret, while the chamber between the stable and the courtyard was used as a dormitory. The imaret was converted into a library by Abdül Hamit II in 1882; it now houses the **State Library**. This library is an important one, with 120,000 volumes and more than 7000 manuscripts, and the imaret makes a fine home for it.

The **medrese** of the Beyazidiye is at the far west end of the square. It is of the standard form; the cells where the students lived and studied are ranged around four sides of a porticoed courtyard, while the lecture-hall is opposite the entrance portal. This building now serves as the Municipality Library; unfortunately, the restoration and conversion were rather badly done, a lot of cement having been used instead of stone, and with the portico very crudely glassed in. Nevertheless, the proportions of the building are so good and the garden in the courtyard so attractive that the general effect is still quite charming.

The medrese is now also used to house the **Hat Sanatlar Müzesi (Museum of Calligraphic Art)**. The museum is open 09.00–16.00; closed Sun, Mon. The collections of the museum are organised into sections specialising in different types of calligraphic script, including Cufic, Tal'iq, Naksi, Thuluh, and Muhakkak. These are used in Kurans, panels, wooden cut-outs, collages, mirror-writing, representations of the Holy Relics, tuğras (imperial signatures), Hilyes (descriptions of the features and qualities of the Prophet), as well as in embroidered inscriptions, works of women calligraphers, and calligraphic models. There are also examples of calligraphic inscriptions on wood, stone and glass, as well as in title deeds and family trees, and even a talismanic shirt that must have done wonders for its wearer. One of the chambers in the medrese has been set up with life-sized wax models showing a calligrapher instructing his students in this quintessentially Islamic art form.

Beyond the medrese, facing on the main avenue (which here takes the name Ordu Cad.), are the splendid remains of **Beyazit's hamam**. This must have been the most magnificent Turkish bath in the city, and deserves restoration, for the fabric of the building still seems to be essentially in good condition. It was a double hamam; the two sections were almost identical, except that the women's bath was slightly smaller than the men's. Notice the ancient reliefs built into the lower part of the façade near the street corner, including a line of marching soldiers placed upside down in the wall. These are fragments of the triumphal arch that stood in the centre of the Forum of Theodosius. Some remnants of the archway and the forum can be seen on the oppo-site side of Ordu Cad. (see p 121).

On the north side of Beyazit Meydanı you see the ornate entryway to the **University of Istanbul**. The main buildings of the university are the former

The Beyazit tower

Seraskerat or Ministry of War, constructed by the French architect Bourgeois in 1866.

In the courtyard of the University stands the **Beyazit Tower**, built in 1828 by Mahmut II as a fire-watch station. It is some 50m high and is made largely of Proconnesian marble. The tower is no longer open to the public.

7 · The Market Quarter

The lively and colourful area between Beyazit Meydanı and the Golden Horn is the principal market quarter of Istanbul. It is also the industrial centre of the old city, with innumerable small and primitive factories, forges, workshops, ateliers and stores, along with warehouses and depots. Many of these establishments are housed in picturesque old Turkish hans, among which are the most splendid extant examples of Ottoman civil architecture.

A large outdoor market occupies the area in and around the outer courtyard of the Beyazidiye just outside the walls of Istanbul University. The market spills over into **Bakırcılar Cad.**, the Avenue of the Copper-Workers, where most of the coppersmiths in the city make and sell their wares. Many of the streets in this quarter are named after the artisans, tradesmen and merchants who carry on their activities there, just as they have for centuries past.

Just north of the Beyazit mosque there is an open courtyard entered through a stone portal known as Kaşıkçı Kapısı, the Gate of the Spoonmakers. This is *Sahaflar Çarşısı, the Market of the Secondhand Booksellers, which has been located here since the early 18C. The Sahaflar Çarşısı is one of the most interesting and picturesque spots in the city, with bookshops and stalls around the vine-shaded courtyard. In the centre of the courtyard there is a bronze bust of Ibrahim Müteferriker (1674–1745), a Hungarian who was captured by the Turks and became a Muslim, entering the Sultan's service and setting up the first printing press in the Ottoman Empire.

**Kapalı Çarşı

At the far end of the courtyard a stairway leads down to an ancient stone portal known as **Hakkaklar Kapısı**, the Gate of the Engravers, a name that goes back to the time when that guild carried on its activities here. After passing through the gateway, turn right on the narrow street outside, and then a short way along turn left into an entryway of the famous **Kapalı Çarşı**, the **Covered Bazaar** (Pl. 10,4).

> The Kapalı Çarşı was established on its present site by Fatih soon after the Conquest, when it occupied about the same area that it does today. Although it has been destroyed several times by fire, most recently in 1954, the Bazaar is essentially the same in structure and appearance as when it was first built, although much of the fabled Oriental atmosphere of the market has vanished in the past half-century.

Interior. The Kapalı Çarşı is a small city in itself: according to a survey made in 1976, there are more than 3000 shops of various kinds, along with store-houses, workshops, stalls and hans, as well as several lunch-counters, a

The Covered Bazaar, a drawing by William Bartlett c 1838

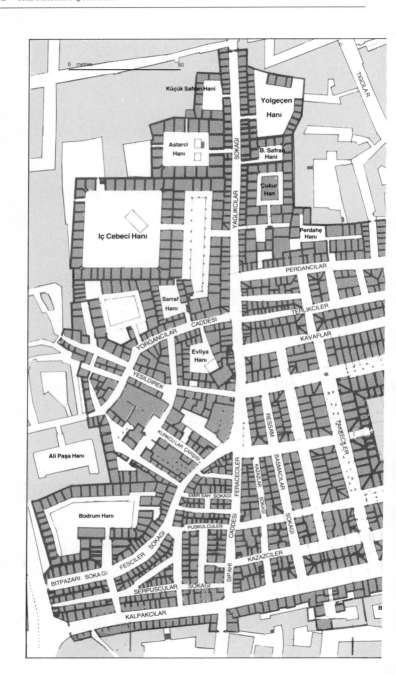

0   metres   50

Küçük Safran Hani

Yolgeçen Hanı

Astarci Hanı

B. Safran Hani

Çukur Han

Iç Cebeci Hanı

Perdahę Hanı

PERDANCILAR

Sarraf Hanı

TERLIKCILER

CADDESI

KAVAFLAR

YORGANCILAR

Evliya Hanı

YESILDIREK

RESSAM

TAKKECILER

KURKCULAR CARSISI

Ali Paşa Hanı

FERACECILER

KAZAZLAR SOKAGI

BASMACILAR

EMIR SAH SOKAGI

CADDESI

SOKAGI

PUSKULCULER

Bodrum Hanı

SIPAHI

KAZAZCILER

FESCILER SOKAGI

BITPAZARI SOKAGI

SERPUSCULAR   SOKAGI

KALPAKCILAR

SOKAGI

YAGLIKCILAR

TIGCILAR

B

THE COVERED BAZAAR

Pastimaci Hanı

SOKAGI

Halicilar Hanı

Tarakçilar Hanı

Imemeli Hanı

Kizlar Ağasi Hanı

Kalci Hanı

Zincirli Hanı

Kasikci Hanı

SOKAGI

SOKAGI

MAHMUT PAŞA CADDESI

SOKAGI

AYNACILAR

Çuhagilar Hanı

SAHAFLAR

KARAKOL SOKAGI

CUHACI HANI

Yarakçi Hanı

KUYUMCULAR

AGA SOKAGI

SOKAGI

MUHAFAZACILAR SOKAGI

KILICILAR CD

Old Bedesten

Nuruosmaniye Cami

KESECILER

Sandal Bedesteni

NUR-I OSMANIYE KAPISI

KOLANCILAR

KALPAKCILAR

Balyaci Han

Kebabçi Han

Rabia Hanı

Yağci Hanı

SOKAGI

teahouse and a restaurant, altogether employing more than 20,000 people.

At first the Kapalı Çarşi seems a veritable labyrinth, but the plan reveals that most of the streets form a fairly regular grid, particularly in the central area of the market, and it is not too difficult to find your way about. Shops selling the same kind of merchandise tend to be congregated in their own streets: thus there is a handsome colonnaded street of oriental rug-merchants, whose wares range all the way from magnificent museum pieces to cheap modern imitations. There is also a glittering street of jewellers and dealers in silver and gold ornaments, whose merchandise spans the spectrum from tawdry costume jewellery to priceless heirlooms.

In the centre of the Bazaar is the great domed hall known as the **Old Bedesten**. This is one of the original structures surviving from Fatih's time. Then, as now, it was used to house the most precious wares, for it can be securely locked and guarded at night. The East portal of the Bedesten is known as **Kuyumcu Kapışı**, the Gate of the Goldsmiths. Above the outer part of the gateway there is the figure in relief of a single-headed Byzantine eagle, the date and origin of which are unknown. The single-headed eagle was the imperial emblem of the Comneni dynasty, who ruled over Byzantium in the 11C–12C. The Gate of the Goldsmiths opens into Inciciler Sok., the Street of the Pearl-Merchants. The third turning on the right from this street leads to the **Sandal Bedesten**, whose main entrance is a few steps down the second turning on the left.

The Sandal Bedesten is a great hall that is thought to have been built early in the 16C, probably during the reign of Beyazit II, when the great increase in Ottoman trade and commerce required an additional market and storehouse for valuables in the Kapalı Çarşi. The internal support for the lofty roof is provided by twelve massive piers, in four rows of three each, supporting 20 brick domes.

The gateway at the far end of the Sandal Bedesten leads out of the Kapalı Çarşi. Turn right here and then take the first turning on the left just opposite Çarşi Kapı, one of the main entrances to the Kapalı Çarşi.

This brings you into the outer courtyard of **Nuruosmaniye Camii** (Pl. 10,4). This is one of the most picturesque mosque courtyards in the city, shaded by plane trees and horse chestnuts, with the mosque on the left and the various buildings of the külliye—the medrese, library, türbe, and sebil—scattered here and there irregularly. The courtyard is always very busy, for it is one of the principal approaches to the Kapalı Çarşi; thus it attracts a colourful collection of beggars, itinerant pedlars, and an occasional Aşık, or wandering Anatolian minstrel.

Nuruosmaniye Camii was begun in 1748 by Mahmut I and completed in 1755 by his brother and successor, Osman III, from whom it takes its name, the Mosque of the Sacred Light (Nur) of Osman. The architect seems to have been a Greek by the name of Simeon, who had probably studied in Europe prior to designing the mosque. For Nuruosmaniye Camii is the first large and ambitious Ottoman building to exemplify the new baroque architectural style then prevalent in western Europe.

Exterior. The whole structure is erected on a low terrace to which irregularly placed flights of steps give access. On the west the mosque is preceded by a porch with five bays, and this is enclosed by a very unusual courtyard with nine domed bays arranged in a semicircle. The two minarets rise from outside the ends of the porch. At the northeast corner of the mosque an oddly shaped ramp supported on wide arches leads to the Sultan's loge. (Note that the arches here, and most of those elsewhere in the building, are semicircular, whereas they are generally pointed in earlier mosques.)

Interior. The mosque consists essentially of a square room covered by a large dome resting on four circular arches in the walls; the form of these arches is strongly emphasised, particularly on the exterior, where the great wheel-shaped arches constitute the most characteristic feature of the building. There is a semi-circular apse for the mihrab at the centre of the east wall and side chambers at the northeast and southeast corners. The Sultan's loge, which is screened off by a gilded metal grille, is in the gallery above the northeast corner.

Nuruosmaniye Camii is an extremely unusual building. It has a certain perverse genius but its proportions are awkward and ungainly and its oddly shaped members seem to have no organic unity. Also, the stone from which it is built is harsh and steel-like in texture and dull in colour. All things considered, the mosque must be pronounced a failure, although a charming one.

*Mahmut Paşa Camii

A gateway at the far end of the outer courtyard of Nuruosmaniye Camii leads out to Vezirhanı Cad. Turn left here and then at the first cross-street, Kılıççılar Sok., turn right into a picturesque little square, from which a gateway leads into the courtyard of a large and venerable mosque. This is Mahmut Paşa Camii (Pl. 10,4), one of the very oldest mosques in the city.

Mahmut Paşa Camii was built in 1462, the first large mosque to be erected in Istanbul. The founder was a Greek of an aristocratic Byzantine family who converted to Islam and joined the Ottoman army, rising to become Grand Vezir under Fatih. Mahmut Paşa proved to be an extremely capable administrator and general, but when his army suffered a severe defeat in Anatolia in 1474 he was beheaded by Fatih.

Exterior. Mahmut Paşa Camii is a very fine example of the so-called 'Bursa style' of mosque architecture, of which very few examples survive in Istanbul. To the west the mosque is preceded by a porch of five bays. Unfortunately, this has been ruined by a clumsy modern restoration, in which the original columns have been replaced by, or encased in, ungainly octagonal piers. Over and beside the entrance portal there are several calligraphic inscriptions in Arabic and Osmanlı (Old Turkish) verse giving the date of foundation and of two restorations, one in 1755 and the second in 1828. The ugly piers undoubtedly belong to the latter restoration, since they are characteristically baroque. The entrance portal itself is also clearly restoration work of the 19C. The single minaret of the mosque rises from the southwest corner of the building, just behind that end of the porch.

Interior. The entryway leads into a narthex; this is a most unusual feature, which in Istanbul mosques is found only here and in the Beyazidiye. The vaults

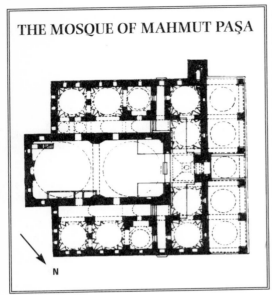

THE MOSQUE OF MAHMUT PAŞA

N

of the narthex are interesting and different from one another. The central bay has a square vault heavily adorned with stalactites. In the first two bays on either side smooth pendentives support domes with 24 ribs; while in the two end bays the domes are not supported by pendentives at all, but by a very curious arrangement of juxtaposed triangles so that the dome rests on a regular sixteen-sided polygon. Other examples of this odd and not unattractive expedient are found in Istanbul only in the west dome of Murat Paşa Camii (see p 201) and in one or two other mosques that belong to the same early period.

The mosque itself consists of a long rectangular room divided in the middle by an arch, thus forming two square chambers each covered by a dome of equal size. On each side of the main hall there is a narrow barrel-vaulted passage that communicates both with the hall and with three small rooms on either side. The two large domes of the great hall of the mosque have smooth pendentives, rather than the stalactited ones usually found in these early mosques. The mihrab and mimber are inferior works of the 18C or later, as are most of the other decorations and mosque furniture. This is a pity, since it spoils the appearance of the mosque interior, making it difficult to recapture its original charm. In the small side chambers some of the domes have smooth pendentives while others are stalactited. The side chambers were called tabhanes, and were used as hostels by travelling dervishes, a feature found only in early Ottoman mosques.

The külliye of Mahmut Paşa also included a hamam, a han, and the founder's türbe. The hamam and han are some distance away (see below), but the türbe is just behind the mosque, in a little graveyard at the end of Kılıççılar Sok. This magnificent and unique **tomb** is dated by an inscription to 1474, the year Mahmut Paşa was executed. It is a tall octagonal building with a blind dome and two tiers of windows. The upper part of the fabric on the outside is entirely encased in a mosaic of tile-work, with blue and turquoise predominating. The tiles make a series of wheel-like patterns of great charm; they are presumably of the first Iznik period (1453–1555), and there is nothing else exactly like them in Istanbul.

Along Kılıççılar Sokak

We now retrace our steps to walk westward along **Kılıççılar Sok.**, the Street of the Sword-Makers. This is one of the most picturesque byways in the city, one of the very few surviving examples of an old Ottoman bazaar street. The left side of the street is lined with an arcade of 18C shops that were once part of the külliye of Nuruosmaniye Camii. On the right side of the street the shops and ateliers are part of the **Çuhacılar Hanı**, the Han of the Cloth-Dealers, which takes up the whole block on that side. This han was built in the early 18C by Nevşehirli Ibrahim Paşa, Grand Vezir in the reign of Ahmet III. The main entrance to the han is through an arched gateway halfway down the street; this brings you into the cluttered inner courtyard, which is lined with an arcade of shops and ateliers.

A portal in the far left-hand corner of the courtyard takes you out to the street running past the east side of the Kapalı Çarşı. A short way down this street and to the right there is an arched gateway that opens on to Mahmut Paşa Yokuşu, one of the principal market streets in the old city.

About 250m down the street you come to the **Mahmut Paşa Hamamı*, an imposing domed building standing off a little to the left. This is part of the Mahmut Paşa külliyesi, dated by an inscription over the entrance portal to 1476, two years after the Grand Vezir's death. Like most of the great Ottoman hamams, it was originally double, but the women's section was torn down to make room for the adjacent han. The men's bath has recently been partially restored for use as a shopping mall. At present shops have been set up only in the camekan; the soğukluk and hararet have not yet been restored, but you can walk in to look at them. The camekan is a huge hall of square plan, 17m on a side, covered by a high dome on stalactited pendentives. The soğukluk is far larger than in most baths, a truly monumental room covered by a dome with spiral ribs and a huge semidome in the form of a scallop shell; on each side are two square cubicles with elaborate vaulting. The hararet is octagonal with five shallow oblong niches, and in the cross axis there are two domed eyvans, each of which leads to two more private bathing cubicles in the corners.

*Medrese of Rüstem Paşa

On leaving the hamam a complicated detour leads to an interesting monument. We take Sultan Mektebi Sok., the street that leads off to the right from Mahmut Paşa Yokuşu directly opposite the hamam, and follow it for about 200m to its end; we then turn left on to Hoca Hanı Sok. and continue for another 50m. This brings us to the *medrese of Rüstem Paşa (Pl. 10,4), Süleyman's son-in-law and Grand Vezir.

This fine building was designed by Sinan, and an inscription records that it was completed in 1550. It has a unique plan for a medrese. The courtyard is octagonal, with a şadırvan in the centre and a colonnaded portico of 24 domes. Behind the portico the cells are also arranged in an octagonal plan, but the building is made into a square on the exterior by filling in the corners with auxiliary rooms, which served as baths and lavatories. One side of the octagon is occupied by the lecture-hall, a large domed room that projects from the square on the outside like a great apse. The medrese has been well restored in recent years, and it is now used as a community services centre.

After returning to the hamam, continue in the same direction down Mahmut Paşa Yokuşu. Many of the buildings on this and the adjacent streets are old Ottoman hans, perhaps several score of them in all. Evliya Çelebi mentions by name more than 25 that already existed by the middle of the 17C, and many others were built during the following century; some go back to the time of the Conquest and many are built on Byzantine foundations.

About 100m downhill from the Mahmut Paşa Hamamı there is an arched gateway on the left side of the street; this is the entrance to the Kürkçü Hanı, the Han of the Furriers. This, too, is a benefaction of Mahmut Paşa and was built at about the same time as his mosque, making it the oldest surviving han in the city. Originally the han consisted of two large courtyards. The first, nearly square, was 45 by 40m, and had about 45 rooms on each of its two floors. The second courtyard to the north was smaller and very irregularly shaped because of the layout of the adjacent streets. It had about 30 rooms on each floor and must have been very attractive; unfortunately it has now been replaced by modern buildings.

After leaving the Kürkçü Hanı, we continue down Mahmut Pas,a Yokus,u and turn left at the next corner on to Çakmakçılar Yokus,u. Just beyond the first turning on the left there is a massive gateway that leads to another Ottoman han. This is the **Büyük Yeni Han**, the Big New Han, built in 1764 by Mustafa III in the baroque style. The tall and very narrow courtyard, with three storeys of round arched arcades, is over 100m in length, divided nearly in the middle by a transverse wing.

Just beyond the Büyük Yeni Han is a much smaller one of about the same date. This is the **Küçük Yeni Han**, or the Small New Han, also a work of Mustafa III. Looking up at this point, we see a small mosque perched on the roof of the han. This curious little mosque, which bears Sultan Mustafa's name, has an almost Byzantine-looking dome and a pretty minaret. It is much frequented by the merchants and workers in the market quarter.

A little farther up Çakmakçılar Yokuşu, and on the opposite side, is the monumental arched entrance to the grandest and most interesting of all the hans in the city, the *Valide Hanı. This han was built by the Valide Sultan Kösem shortly before her death in 1651, apparently on the site of an older Ottoman palace founded by Cerrah Mehmet Paşa. A great double gateway leads into the first courtyard, which is small and irregularly shaped because of the alignment of the han relative to the street outside. From here another arched passage leads into the main court, a vast square area 55m on a side, surrounded by a two-tiered arcade. Behind the arcade on each floor there are 50 vaulted chambers, most of which are now used as workshops or storerooms. Although the entire han is now in a state of appalling squalor and disrepair, it is still impressive and extremely colourful.

A vaulted tunnel leads from the far left-hand corner of the main courtyard into the inner court, which because of the lie of the land is set at a lower level than the rest of the han. The chambers around the two floors of this court house a weaving-mill. At the back of the courtyard are the remains of a Byzantine tower which is built into the structure of the han. This has traditionally been called the Tower of Eirene and is thought to date from the middle Byzantine period, although the evidence for this is very uncertain. The tower appears as a prominent feature of the city skyline in the drawing made by Melchior Lorichs in 1559; it is much taller in the drawing than it is today. The lower part of the tower is now part of the weaving-mill, while the upper room is fitted out as a mosque with a pretty ribbed dome; unfortunately the mosque is now disaffected and is used as a storeroom.

At a corner of the inner court, on its upper floor, an archway leads to an open area to the rear of the han. Just opposite stands the large **mosque of Ibrahim Paşa**, one of the most ancient in the city. This mosque was founded in 1478 by Çandarlı Ibrahim Paşa, Grand Vezir under Beyazit II, who was killed during the siege of Lepanto in 1499. The mosque was in ruins for many years and was restored in the 1970s. However this restoration was so poorly done that it destroyed all that was original in the structure.

More Market Streets

A path between the han and the mosque leads out to another bustling market street named **Uzun Çarşı Cad.**, the Avenue of the Long Market. This follows the course of the ancient Byzantine street called Makros Embolos, which led from the Forum of Constantine to the Golden Horn, down the valley between the Second and Third Hills. The Greek name means Great Colonnade, and the street was indeed lined with colonnaded porticoes on both sides. But today the street is mean and squalid, although always lively and picturesque. For this is the site of the infamous **Secondhand Clothing Bazaar**, where the poor of the city sell one another clothes.

About 200m down Uzun Çarşı Cad., on the right just past the second cross-street, there is a little mosque known as **Yavaşca Şahin Camii**. This is one of several insignificant but very ancient mosques that are found in this neighbour-hood, which, apparently, was the first Turkish quarter to be established in the city after the Conquest. Yavaşca Şahin Paşa was a captain in the fleet of Mehmet II at the time of the Conquest; he built this mosque soon afterwards, but the exact date is unknown. It was badly damaged in the great fire of 1908 but was restored in 1950.

It is one of a small group of early mosques that form a distinct type: the front porch has only two domed bays, with the entrance portal shifted off centre under the south dome. Within, a square chamber with a blind dome resting on an octagonal drum is supported by a series of triangles making a 16-sided base. It is an odd type but not unattractive; unfortunately the porch was not restored because of the intrusion of an adjacent shop.

Just opposite Yavaşca Şahin Camii a street named Ağzlıkçı Sok. leads steeply uphill. At the first corner on the left is a very ancient mosque that has been restored in recent years. This is **Samanveren Camii**, founded soon after the Conquest by a certain Sinan Ağa, an inspector of straw. (In Turkish, Sinan Ağa's title as inspector of straw was Samanveren, hence the name of his mosque.) It is a quaint and interesting building of brick and stone construction. The present minaret, with its curious arcaded loggia for the müezzin instead of a şerefe, is part of the recent reconstruction.

Directly across from Samanveren Camii we take the street that leads downhill toward the Golden Horn. At the second turning on the left a side street leads to a ruined Ottoman building. This is the **medrese of Siyavuş Paşa**, a very irreg-ular structure wedged in an angle of the hill above. The dershane, unusually, is in a corner immediately to the right of the once-handsome entrance portal. The medrese was constructed some time before his death in 1601 by Siyavuş Paşa, brother-in-law of Murat III and thrice his Grand Vezir.

We now continue down toward the Golden Horn to Kantarcılar Cad., the Street of the Scale-Makers, where we turn right. At the first turning on the left we come to **Timurtaş Camii**, another ancient mosque which has been completely restored in recent years. It is very like Samanveren Camii; it is built over a vaulted ground floor with the same brick and stone construction, and has a large wooden porch in front. Its minaret is unusual; instead of having a balcony it is entirely enclosed, with four small grilled openings toward the top through which the müezzin gives the call to prayer. It is thought that Samanveren Camii originally had the same type of minaret, since they seem to be almost twin mosques. The exact date of these mosques is unknown, but both are believed to date from the reign of Fatih.

At the next corner we turn left on Uzun Çarşı Cad. and come to Hasırcılar Cad., the Street of the Mat-Makers. Just before the intersection we see on our left the entrance to an enormous double bath known as the **Tahtakale Hamamı**, which also dates from the reign of Fatih. The hamam has recently been restored and is being converted into a shopping mall. The most impressive chamber is the camekan, which is almost square in plan, 16.70m by 16.25m, covered by a huge dome on a low drum.

*Rüstem Paşa Camii

At the far corner to the right of the intersection we come to Rüstem Paşa Camii (Pl. 10,2) one of the most beautiful of the smaller mosques of Sinan. This mosque was built in 1561 by Rüstem Pas,a, twice Grand Vezir under Süleyman and husband of the Sultan's favourite daughter, the Princess Mihrimah.

Exterior. The mosque is built on a high terrace over an interesting complex of vaulted shops, the rent from which went to maintain the rest of the külliye. Interior flights of steps lead up from the corners of the platform to a spacious and beautiful courtyard, unique in the city. The mosque is preceded by a curious double porch: first the usual type of porch consisting of five domed bays, and then, projecting from this, a deep and low-slung penthouse roof, its outer edge resting on a row of columns. This arrangement, although unusual, is very pleasant and has a definite architectural unity.

Interior. The plan of the mosque consists of an octagon inscribed in a rectangle. The dome is flanked by four small semidomes in the diagonals of the building. The arches of the dome spring from four octagonal pillars, two on the north, two on the south, and from piers projecting from the east and west walls. To the north and south there are galleries supported by pillars and by small marble columns between them.

Rüstem Paşa Camii is especially famous for the very fine tiles which almost cover the walls, not only on the interior but also on the façade of the porch. You should also climb to the galleries to see the tiles there, which are of a different pattern. Like all the great Turkish tiles, those of Rüstem Paşa came from the kilns of Iznik in its greatest period (c 1555–1620), and they show the tomato-red or 'Armenian bole' which is characteristic of that period. These exquisite tiles, in a wide variety of floral and geometric designs, cover not only the walls, but also the columns, the mihrab, and the mimber. Altogether they make this one of the most beautiful and striking mosque interiors in the city.

Just to the east of Rüstem Paşa Camii, a few steps down Hasırcılar Cad. and on the same side of the street, there is a very ancient han. This is **Hurmalı Han**, the Han for Dates, which has been ascribed to early Byzantine times, perhaps the 6C–7C. The oldest part of the structure is the long and narrow courtyard, which is believed to be part of the original structure, while the remainder of the building probably dates from Ottoman times, with modern reconstructions. There are a great many ancient hans in this neighbourhood, but they are for the most part decayed and cluttered, and almost nothing is known about them except their names.

Continuing east along Hasırcılar Cad., we take the next right and then in the middle of the block we turn left into a large open courtyard. This is **Balkapan Han**, the Han of the Honey-Store, of which there remains only the courtyard and the extensive vaults beneath it. Evliya Çelebi, in his *Narrative of Travels*, writes that in his time this was the storehouse used by the Egyptian honey-dealers, hence the name of the han. Access to the vaults is gained through the small building at the centre of the courtyard, where a flight of steps leads down into the vast Byzantine dungeons below. There you can see the ranks and columns of great rectangular pillars of brick supporting massive brick vaulting in the usual Byzantine herring-bone pattern. Unfortunately, the basement is so cluttered with boxes and crates that only a small part of the total area of some 2000 square metres is visible, but even this is extremely impressive. The vaults undoubtedly belong to one of the many granaries and storage-depots which are known to have existed on this site from as early as the 4C–5C AD.

Returning to the main market street, we continue in the same direction. At the next corner the street comes to the west gate of the Spice Bazaar, from where we can return to the great square in front of Yeni Cami at the Stamboul end of the Galata Bridge.

8 · The Third Hill

The broad summit of the Third Hill comprises the area bounded on the east by Beyazit Meydanı, on the south by Ordu Cad., on the north by Şehzadebaşı Cad., and on the west by Atatürk Blv., which runs along the valley separating the Third and Fourth Hills. This region, and the upper part of the slopes leading down to the Marmara and the Golden Horn, contains more than a score of ancient monuments, including some very impressive structures from the late Roman era as well as the Byzantine and Ottoman periods. The most convenient way to see these monuments is to begin at the southwest corner of Beyazit Meydanı, where Ordu Cad. heads west to its intersection with Atatürk Blv., and then walk around the Third Hill in a great arc so as to return in the end to Beyazit Meydanı.

At the beginning of **Ordu Cad.**, flanking both sides of the avenue as it leaves Beyazit Meydanı, we see huge architectural fragments of the **Forum of**

Theodosius, unearthed when the square was redesigned in the 1950s. The square was built on the site of the ancient Forum Tauri in 393 by Theodosius I, after which it was called the Forum of Theodosius. This was the largest of the great public squares of Byzantine Constantinople. It contained, among other things, a gigantic triumphal arch in the Roman fashion, and a commemorative column with reliefs showing the victories of Theodosius I, like that of Trajan in Rome. Colossal fragments of the triumphal arch can be seen just opposite the hamam of Sultan Beyazit. Notice the columns curiously decorated with the peacock-eye or lopped branch design, also the enormous Corinthian columns.

At the very beginning of Ordu Cad. on the left side, just behind the ruins of the triumphal arch of Theodosius, there are the remains of two Ottoman hans of some interest. The first is called **Şimkeşhane** and was originally built as a mint by Mehmet the Conqueror. The mint was later transferred to Topkapı Sarayı, after which Şimkeşhane was used to house the spinners of silver thread. The han was damaged by fire and then rebuilt by Rabia Gülnuş Ümmetullah, wife of Mehmet IV and mother of Mustafa II and Ahmet III.

Its front half was demolished during the 1950s when the avenue was widened, whereupon it began to fall into ruins. The same fate befell the han next to it, which was built in about 1740 by Seyyit Hasan Paşa, Grand Vezir in the reign of Mahmut I. But in recent years the surviving structures of the two hans have been well restored and both of them are now once again in use housing various shops and offices. You should walk around them to see the astonishing and picturesque irregularity of their design, with great zigzags built out on corbels following the crooked line of the streets.

Some 150m down the left side of Ordu Cad. is the ornate entryway to a small *külliye. This delightful little complex was founded in 1762 by Ragıp Paşa, Grand Vezir in the reign of Mustafa III. The architect seems to have been Mehmet Tahir Ağa, whose masterpiece, Laleli Camii, can be seen farther down the avenue on the other side. Above the entryway there is a room which was once a primary school, and which is now used as a children's library. Across the courtyard, surrounded by an attractive garden, is the main library; this has been restored in recent years and is now once again serving its original purpose. From the courtyard a flight of steps leads to a domed lobby which opens into the reading-room. This is square in plan, and the central space is covered by a dome supported on four columns; between these, beautiful bronze grilles form a kind of cage in which the books and manuscripts are kept. Round the sides of this vaulted and domed room are chairs and tables for reading. The walls are revetted in blue and white tiles, either of European manufacture or Turkish tiles strongly under European influence, but charming nevertheless.

In the garden, which is separated from the courtyard by fine bronze grilles, is the pretty open türbe of the founder. Ragıp Paşa, who was Grand Vezir from 1757 until 1763, is considered to have been the last of the great figures to hold that post, comparable in stature to men like Sokollu Mehmet Paşa and the Köprülüs. Ragıp Paşa was also the best poet of his time, and composed some of the most apt and witty of the chronograms inscribed on the street-fountains in Istanbul. His little külliye, though clearly baroque in detail, has a classic simplicity which recalls that of the Köprülü complex on the Second Hill.

After leaving the library, we continue along Ordu Cad. and take the second turning on the left, just opposite Laleli Camii. We turn right at the next corner, and then at the end of the street we ascend a flight of steps on to a large marble-paved terrace. Just beyond the far left corner of the terrace we see a former Byzantine church known locally as **Bodrum Cami** (Pl. 10.3) or the Subterranean Mosque, because of the crypt that lies beneath it.

> The church and the monastery to which it was attached were founded by Romanus I Lecapenus (919–44). The monastery was known as the Myrelaion, the 'place of the myrrh-oil', an ancient name of unknown origin. Next to the church and monastery Romanus also built a palace on the substructure known as the Rotunda, apparently part of a palatial edifice of the late Roman era. He also built a funerary chapel beneath the church, and when his wife Theodora died in 922 she was buried there. The church was converted into a mosque late in the 15C by Mesih Paşa, a descendant of the Palaeologues, who led the Ottoman forces in their first and unsuccessful attack on Rhodes in 1479. The building was several times gutted by fire, but it has since been restored. A more recent project has restored the substructure of the palace of Romanus and converted it into a covered market.

The church and the Rotunda. Studies have shown that the two superimposed churches were built during the period 919–23, and that both of them were of the same design, namely the four-column type so common in the 10C–11C. The upper church now serves as a mosque once again, but the funerary chapel below is closed to the public. The Rotunda of the palace of Romanus has now been converted into a subterranean shopping mall, with its entrance on the south side of the terrace beside the mosque. The Rotunda was originally designed in the 5C AD as the reception hall of a great palace, which apparently was never finished, to be subsequently roofed over and used as a cistern. The roof was supported by a colonnade of 75 columns, and the palace of Romanus was built on top. The recent restoration was very successful, and the Rotunda makes an extremely interesting and attractive site for a shopping centre.

We now retrace our steps to Ordu Cad., where we cross the avenue to approach *Laleli Camii (Pl. 10.3), the Lily Mosque.
    Laleli Camii is the finest of all the baroque mosques in the city. It was founded by Mustafa III and built between 1759 and 1763 by Mehmet Tahir Ağa, the greatest and most original of the Turkish baroque architects.

Exterior. The mosque is built on a high terrace, beneath which there is a veritable labyrinth of winding passages and vaulted shops. In the centre, directly underneath the mosque, there is a great hall supported by eight enormous piers, with a fountain in the centre and a café and shops round about. It has been suggested that this subterranean arcade is a tour de force of Mehmet Tahir, designed to show that he could support his mosque virtually on thin air.
    The mosque itself is constructed of brick and stone, but the superstructure is of stone only; and the two parts do not appear to fit together very well. Along the sides there are amusing but pointless galleries, with the arcades formed of round arches; a similar arcade covers the ramp leading to the imperial loge.

Interior. The plan of the interior is an octagon inscribed in a rectangle. All but the west pair of supporting columns are engaged in the walls; those at the west support a gallery along the west wall. All the walls are heavily revetted in variegated marbles—yellow, red, blue and other colours—which give a gay if somewhat gaudy effect. In the west wall of the gallery there are medallions of opus sectile which incorporate not only rare marbles but also semi-precious stones such as onyx, jasper and lapis lazuli. A rectangular apse contains the mihrab, which is made of sumptuous marbles. The mimber is fashioned from the same materials, while the Kuran kursu is a rich work of carved wood heavily inlaid with mother-of-pearl.

Mosque precincts. Like all of the other imperial mosques, Laleli Camii was surrounded by the many attendant buildings of a civic centre, some of which, unfortunately, have disappeared, notably the medrese and the hamam. On Ordu Cad. there still remains the pretty **sebil** with bronze grilles, and the somewhat sombre octagonal **türbe** in which are buried Mustafa III and his son, the unfortunate Selim III. On the terrace inside the enclosure is the **imaret**, an attractive little building with a very unusual plan.

The street just to the east of the mosque, Fethi Bey Cad., leads at the second turning on the left to a fascinating han that probably belongs to the Laleli complex. This was formerly known as Çukur Çeşme Hanı, the Han of the Sunken Fountain, but now it is called **Büyük Taş Hanı**, the Big Stone Han. You enter through a very long vaulted passage, with rooms and a small court leading from it; it emerges into a large courtyard, in the middle of which a ramp descends into what were once the stables. Around this porticoed courtyard open rooms of most irregular shape, and other passages lead to two additional small courts with even more irregular chambers. You seem to detect in this the ingenious but perverse mind of Mehmet Tahir Ağa. The han has recently been very well restored and now houses shops, cafés and a restaurant.

After leaving the han, we continue in the same direction along the side street and take the first turning on the left; then at the next corner we turn right on to Selim Paşa Sok. This soon reaches the rear of the huge office building that houses the **Belediye**, or Municipality, the headquarters of the civil government of Istanbul.

Just behind the Belediye stands the quaint little **medrese of the Şeyh-ül Islam Ankaravı Mehmet Efendi**, founded in 1707. This has recently been restored and is now used as a research centre by the Economics Faculty of Istanbul University. It is a small and attractively irregular building, chiefly of red brick, with a long narrow courtyard, at the far end of which is the lecture-hall, reached by a flight of steps.

After walking around the Belediye to the left, we find ourself at the intersection of Atatürk Blv. and Şehzadebaşı Cad., with splendid views of the Fatih Camii to the left, the Valens Aqueduct straight ahead, and Şehzade Camii to the right.

On the northeast side of the intersection we see a pretty little mosque just to the west. of the Şehzade Camii precincts. This is **Burmalı Cami**, built c 1550 by the Kadı (Judge) of Egypt, Emin Nurettin Osman Efendi. Although of the very simplest type—a square room with a flat wooden ceiling—it has several peculiarities that give it a cachet of its own. Most noticeable is the brick minaret with spiral ribs, from which the mosque gets its name (in Turkish, burmalı means spiral); this is unique in Istanbul and is a late survival of an older tradition, of which a few examples survive in Anatolia. The porch is also unique: its roof, which is pitched, not domed, is supported by four columns with Byzantine Corinthian capitals. Finally, the entrance portal is not in the middle but on the right-hand side. This is usual in mosques with porches supported by only three columns—to prevent the door from being blocked by the central column—but here there seems to be no reason for it. The interior of the mosque has no special features.

**Şehzade Camii

After leaving Burmalı Cami we return to Şehzadebaşı Cad. and walk down the avenue to the left for about 100m. This brings us to the main entrance of the precincts of Şehzade Camii (Pl. 10,3).

Şehzade Camii, the Mosque of the Prince, was built by Süleyman in memory of his eldest son, Prince Mehmet, who died of smallpox in 1543, when he was only 21 years old. Süleyman was heartbroken at the death of his beloved son, and he sat beside Mehmet's body for three days before he would permit burial to take place. When Süleyman recovered from his grief he decided to erect a great mosque complex dedicated to the memory of Şehzade Mehmet. Sinan was commissioned to design and build the külliye, which was completed in 1548. Sinan himself called this his 'apprentice work', but it was the work of an apprentice of genius, his first imperial mosque on a truly monumental scale.

Exterior. The Şehzade complex is surrounded by an outer courtyard wall, enclosing the mosque and the other institutions of the külliye, which includes a medrese, a tabhane or hospice, a public kitchen, a primary school, and several splendid türbes.

Şehzade Camii is preceded by a handsome inner **courtyard** whose area is equal to that of the mosque itself, with the monumental entrance portal at the centre of the west side. The courtyard is bordered by a portico with five domed bays of equal height on each side, counting corner bays twice, with the voussoirs of the arches in alternating pink and white marble. At the centre of the courtyard there is a **şadırvan** which, according to Evliya Çelebi, was a gift of Murat IV. The two **minarets** are exceptionally beautiful: notice the elaborate geometrical sculpture in low relief, the intricate tracery of their two şerefes, and the use of occasional terracotta inlay. The cluster of **domes** and **semidomes**, many of them with fretted cornices and bold ribbing, crowns the building in an arrangement of repetition and contrast that is nowhere surpassed. It was in this mosque that Sinan first adopted the brilliant expedient of placing colonnaded **galleries** along the entire length of the north and south façades in order to conceal the buttresses. This is certainly one of the very finest exteriors that Sinan ever created; one wonders why he later abandoned, or at least greatly restrained, these decorative effects.

Interior. Sinan wanted a centralised plan and so he adopted an expedient, extending the area not by two but by four semidomes. Although this is the most obvious and logical way of both increasing the space and of centralising the plan, the identical symmetry along both axes has a repetitive effect that tends toward dullness. Furthermore, the four great **piers** that support the dome are stranded and isolated in the midst of the vast space and their inevitably large size is unduly emphasised. These drawbacks were obvious to Sinan once he had tried the experiment, and he never repeated it.

The vast and empty interior is very unusual among the imperial mosques; it has not a single column, nor are there any galleries. Sinan succeeded in minimising the size of the great piers by making them very irregular in shape: contrast their not unpleasing appearance with the gross 'elephant's feet' columns in the Blue Mosque. The general effect of the interior is of an austere simplicity that is not without charm.

The Şehzade türbes. Behind the mosque there is the usual walled garden of türbes. These türbes are quite extraordinary, for they constitute a veritable museum of the two best periods of Turkish tiles, the first from the time of the Conquest up until about 1555, the second and greatest from 1555 to 1620. The türbes in the precincts of Haghia Sophia are larger and grander than those at the Şehzade, but their tiles, magnificent as they are, are all much of the same date and style, as are those at the Süleymaniye. Here, on the other hand, the buildings are of quite different dates and span the whole of the great age of the Iznik kilns, together with a few of those produced at a later period at Tekfursarayı. (Unfortunately, the Sehzade türbes are not open to the public.)

The first and largest türbe in the centre of the garden is that of the ****Şehzade Mehmet** himself. It is octagonal, the faces separated by slender engaged columns; the stonework is polychrome, panels of verd antique being inset here and there in the façades, while the window frames and arches are picked out in terracotta. The dome, which is double and carried on a fluted drum, is itself fluted. The small entrance porch has a fine pavement of opus sectile. Altogether it is a very handsome building in the ornately decorated style of the mosque itself.

The inscription in Persian verse over the entrance portal, which gives the date of the Prince's death, suggests that the interior of the türbe is like a garden in Paradise. It is sheathed in tiles from the floor to the cornice of the dome, all apple-green and vivid lemon-yellow. These are almost the last and by far the most beautiful flowering of the middle period of Iznik tiles, done in the cuerda seca technique. Tiles in this technique and in these colours are extremely rare. They were first manufactured at Iznik in about 1514, when Selim I brought back a group of Persian craftsmen after his conquest of Tabriz, while the latest known examples date from 1555. Thus the türbe of the Şehzade contains the most extensive and beautiful collection of tiles of this rare and beautiful type. The beauty of the türbe is not limited to its tiles, for the upper row of windows contains some of the most perfect examples of Turkish stained glass in rich and brilliant colours.

Just to the left and behind the türbe of the Şehzade is that of Rüstem Paşa, another work of Sinan, completed soon after the Grand Vezir's death in 1561.

Just opposite the southwest precinct gate we see the ***türbe** of the Grand Vezir **Ibrahim Paşa**, son-in-law of Murat III. Ibrahim Paşa died in 1601 and his türbe was completed early in 1603, designed and built by the architect Dalgıç

Şehzade Camii, a drawing by William Bartlett c 1838

Ahmet Çavuş. This türbe almost equals that of the Şehzade in splendour and perfection. It is octagonal and fairly plain on the exterior, though two marble panels on either side of the entrance portal, carved with elaborate floral and arabesque designs in low relief, are unusual and lovely.

There are three other türbes in the garden: those of **Prince Mahmut**, son of Mehmet III; **Hatice Sultan**, daughter of Murat III; and **Fatma Sultan**, grand-daughter of Prince Mehmet, but these are unadorned. There is, however, one more remarkable türbe well worth a visit; this is outside the türbe garden by the main entrance to the mosque precincts. The türbe is that of **Destarı Mustafa Paşa**, dated by an inscription to 1611. It has the unusual form of a rectangle, and is roofed with a low central dome flanked at each end by a shallow cradle-vault. The effect is very pretty. The walls between the windows are revetted with tiles which, though still of the best period, are perhaps not quite so stunning as those in Ibrahim Paşa's türbe; but they do contain a great deal of Armenian bole at its most brilliant.

The mosque precincts. The **medrese** of the Şehzade complex is at the far side of the precincts, near the northwest corner of the outer courtyard wall. It is a handsome building of the usual form. The south side, facing the mosque, has a portico but no cells. Opposite the entrance, instead of the usual dershane, there is an open loggia. The lecture-hall itself stands in the centre of the east side. The building has been well restored and is now a residence for university students.

In line with the medrese but farther east is the **tabhane**, which now serves as a science laboratory for the adjacent secondary school, Vefa Lisesi. This building is probably not by Sinan, although it is obviously contemporary with the rest of the complex. The structure is L-shaped, with the bottom stroke of the L consisting of a long, wide hall, roofed with eight domes supported on three columns down its length; perpendicular to this is a block of eight cubicles, with two spacious halls providing access to them. This interesting building is in good condition.

A gate in the east wall of the türbe garden of the Şehzade leads out into a side street, Dede Efendi Cad. Across this street to the left are the **primary school and public kitchen** of the complex. The primary school is of the usual type. The public kitchen consists of a spacious courtyard, on one side of which there are three double kitchens and a small refectory, its four domes supported on three columns. This is a charmingly proportioned and gracious building. It is now used as a storage place; but the fabric of the structure is in good condition and one hopes that a more worthy use will be found for it.

Turning back towards the main street, we see on the left opposite a very pretty **medrese** with a sebil at the corner. This was built by the Grand Vezir Nevşehirli Ibrahim Paşa, son-in-law of Ahmet III. It is dated by its inscription to 1720 and thus comes just between the end of the classical period and the beginning of the baroque, so that it has pleasing characteristics of both eras. At the ends of the façade stand two large domed chambers surrounded by an attractive raised portico, with the entrance portal in the centre between them. The chamber to the left served as the library, that to the right was the lecture-hall of the Dar-ül Hadis, or School of Sacred Tradition, the study of which was the main function of the medrese. Later, the lecture-hall was turned into a mescit, or small mosque, and a minaret was added. The far sides of the courtyard are partly lined with porticoes with cells beyond them; these are irregularly placed after the baroque fashion. The building is in good condition, and part of it is now used as a clinic.

Outside, at the street corner, is the extremely handsome **sebil**, a favourite among painters and etchers; it was still in use up until recent years, but now it serves as a fruit-seller's shop. Behind the sebil there is a pretty little graveyard in which the founder of this fine small külliye is buried. Ibrahim Paşa served as Grand Vezir under Ahmet III from 1718 until 1730, during the golden years of the Tulip Period. That delightful epoch ended on 20 September 1730, when the Janissaries deposed the Tulip King and strangled Ibrahim Paşa.

Farther on down Dede Efendi Cad., just past the precinct wall of the Şehzade complex, is the **Vefa Lisesi**, built during the 1920s by the architect Kemalettin Bey. In its precincts are two ancient buildings, one of which, the Şehzade tabhane, has already been described. The other is the library of Damat Şehit Ali Paşa, built early in the 18C. The founder, Ali Paşa, was called Damat (son-in-law) because he married Fatma Sultan, a daughter of Ahmet III, and Şehit (martyr), because he was killed in the battle of Peterwaredin in 1716. Fatma did not grieve long for Ali; shortly after she received news of his death she married Nevşehirli Ibrahim Paşa. Ali Paşa's library is raised on a high superstructure and approached by a long flight of steps; it consists of only two rooms, the larger one domed. At present it is not in use.

At the far left-hand corner of the next cross-street, Cemal Yenertosyalı Cad., there is another ancient Ottoman building. This is the handsome **medrese** built sometime before his death, in 1618, by Ekmekçizade Ahmet Paşa, son of an Edirne baker, who rose to the rank of Defterdar (First Lord of the Treasury) and Vezir, and died one of the richest men in the Empire. The right side of the courtyard of the medrese is occupied by the usual dershane, next to which, however, is a türbe of the same size, undoubtedly that of the founder. This is a unique arrangement, but it gives the courtyard a somewhat lopsided appearance. Both the dershane and the türbe still preserve remnants of rather good painted decoration in their domes and pendentives, a rich red with deep green meander patterns.

We now turn left on Cemal Yenertosyalı Cad. and then right at the next corner on Kâtip Çelebi Cad. At the corner to the left is the famous **Vefa Bozahanesi**. (Boza is a drink made from fermented millet, once a favourite of the Janissaries.) Notice the silver cup in a glass case on the wall inside the shop; it is preserved there because Atatürk once drank from it.

Just beyond the Vefa Bozahanesi, on the same side of the street, there is a little mosque called **Mimar Mehmet Ağa Mescidi**. This was built in 1514 by a certain Revani Şuccağ Efendi, who was Sürre Emini, or official escort of the annual embassy to Mecca. It is a small, square building of brick with a dome; it is of no great interest, but it has a pretty minaret. The mosque was well restored in 1960.

At the next corner the street divides, with the right branch taking the name of Vefa Cad. A short way along on the left we come to **Vefa Camii**, the mosque from which the street and the surrounding neighbourhood take their name. This is a brand new mosque erected on the site of the original Vefa Camii, founded in the late 15C. All that is left from the original mosque is the türbe of the founder, Şeyh Muslihiddin Vefa, who died in 1491. His türbe is a popular place of pilgrimage, for he has been one of the most popular Turkish folk-saints in Istanbul for more than five centuries.

Just beyond Vefa Camii, and on the same side of the street we come to the *Library of Atıf Efendi (Pl. 10,1). This is the most charming and original of all the Ottoman public libraries in the city.

The library, founded in 1741–42, is constructed of stone and brick in the baroque style. The building consists of two parts, a block of houses for the staff and the library itself. The former faces the street and its upper storey projects *en cremaillère*, that is, in five zigzags supported on corbels. Three small doors lead to the lodgings, while a large gate in the middle opens into a courtyard, on the other side of which stands the library. This consists of an entrance lobby, a room for book storage, and a large reading-room of astonishing shape. This oblong area, cross-vaulted like the other rooms, is surrounded at one end by a series of five deep bays arranged like a fan. A triple arcade supported on two columns divides the two parts of the room; on the exterior this fan-like arrangement presents seven faces. Displayed near the entrance to the reading-room is the entire vakfiye, or deed of foundation, inscribed on a marble plaque.

The street just opposite the library entrance is called Tirendaz Sok., the Street of the Archer. At the far end of this street, on the left, there is a handsome Byzantine church with a fluted minaret. This is known in Turkish as *Kilise

Cami (Pl. 10,1), literally Church Mosque, a linguistic amalgamation of Christianity and Islam.

This was identified by Gyllius as the church of St. Theodore, but nothing is known of its history other than the fact that it was converted into a mosque soon after the Conquest. The most attractive part of the building is the outer narthex with its façade. Constructed of stone, brick and marble, its elaborate design and decoration identify it at once as belonging to the last great flowering of Byzantine architecture in the early 14C. In the south dome of the outer narthex there were some fine mosaics which have now disappeared except for one or two faded fragments. The inner narthex and the church itself, which is of the four-column type, are dated to some time between the 12C and 14C, when this style was predominant. The narthexes contain some handsome columns, capitals and door-frames which appear to be re-used material from an earlier sanctuary, probably of the 6C.

**Kalenderhane Camii*

To reach the next stop on the itinerary we will follow a rather tricky but quite picturesque route. At the end of Tirendaz Sok. we turn right and then follow a winding cobbled lane that eventually leads to the rear of the medrese of Ekmekçizade Ahmet Paşa. Returning to the corner of Dede Efendi Cad. and Cemal Yenertosyalı Sok., we turn left onto the latter street and follow it for about 200m before turning right on the first through street. This leads through a picturesque arched gateway under the Valens Aqueduct and out onto a large open area on the other side. There to the right we see a large and handsome Byzantine church known in Turkish as Kalenderhane Camii (Pl. 10,3).

> The church was converted into a mosque by Fatih soon after the Conquest; since it was used as a tekke by the dervishes of the Kalender order it came to be known as Kalenderhane Camii. It was once identified as the Church of St. Mary Diaconissa, more recently as that of St. Saviour Akataleptos, but now it has been positively identified as the Church of the Theotokos (St. Mary, the Mother of God) Kyriotissa (an unusual attribute of the Virgin, meaning Her Ladyship); this identification and the detailed architectural study of the building were the work of the Dumbarton Oaks Society and Istanbul Technical University, directed by Professor C. Lee Striker of the Pennsylvania State University. The church was formerly thought to date from the 9C, but Professor Striker's work has shown that the present structure dates from the late 12C, built on the ruins of earlier Byzantine and late Roman structures.

Interior. The church is cruciform in plan, with deep barrel vaults over the arms of the cross and a dome with 16 ribs over the centre. It originally had side aisles communicating with the nave, and galleries over the exonarthex and narthex. The building still preserves its elaborate and beautiful marble revetment and sculptured decoration, making it one of the most attractive Byzantine churches in the city, now once again serving as a mosque.

During the restoration of the church a series of **wall-paintings** were discovered in a small chapel to the right of the apse. These proved to be a fresco cycle of the life of St. Francis of Assisi painted during the Latin occupation of

Constantinople. It is believed that the frescoes were done c 1250, which dates them just a quarter of a century after the life of St. Francis, who died in 1226. This is the earliest fresco cycle of St. Francis in existence, and it is also the only work of art that has survived in situ from the Latin occupation of Constantinople.

The cycle shows the standing figure of the saint with ten scenes from his life, anticipating in many elements the frescoes of the Upper Church at Assisi. Other discoveries include a mosaic of the 'Presentation of the Christ Child in the Temple', dated to the 7C, the only pre-Iconoclastic figurative mosaic ever found in the city. Finally, a late Byzantine mosaic of the Theotokos Kyriotissa came to light over the main door to the narthex (this has been removed for preservation), thus settling the much disputed dedication of the church; another much earlier fresco of the Kyriotissa was soon afterwards found in the side chapel. The paintings and mosaics are now in the Istanbul Archaeological Museum (see p 75).

Precincts. Excavations under and to the north of the church have revealed a series of earlier structures on the site. The earliest are the remains of a Roman bath of the late 4C or early 5C, including a trilobed room, a circular chamber, and evidence of a hypocaust. This was succeeded in the mid 6C by a Byzantine basilica built up against the Valens Aqueduct and utilising the arches thereof as its north aisle. Finally, at some time prior to the Iconoclastic Period, which begain in 743, another church was built on the site, part of its sanctuary and apse being later incorporated into the present church.

After leaving the church, we walk out to Şehzadebaşı Cad. and turn left, crossing over to the other side at the next intersection. There we come upon a **medrese** built into a triangular plot at the angle of two streets. This elegant little complex was built in 1606 by Kuyucu Murat Paşa, Grand Vezir in the reign of Ahmet I. (Murat Paşa received his nickname of kuyucu, or the pit-digger, from his favourite occupation of supervising the digging of trenches for the mass burial of the rebels he had slaughtered.) The apex of the triangle is formed by the columned sebil, a fine work with simple classical lines. Facing the street is an arcade of shops in the middle of which a doorway leads to the courtyard of the medrese. Entering, you find the türbe of the founder in the acute angle behind the sebil, and at the other end the dershane, which, as so often, also served as a small mosque. This building has recently been taken over and restored by Istanbul University; the courtyard has been roofed in and is used as a small museum, while the dershane contains a library.

Continuing along and passing the new University annex, we turn right and soon come on our left to another medrese complex, now the Istanbul University **Institute of Turkology**. This is a baroque building founded in 1745 by the Grand Vezir Seyyit Hasan Paşa, who built the han at the southwest corner of Beyazit Meydanı. It is curiously irregular in design and is raised on a high platform, so that on entering you mount a flight of steps to the courtyard, now roofed in and used as a library. In one corner is the dershane-mescit, which has become the office of the Director of the Institute of Turkology; in another is a room designed as a primary school; and this and other cells of the medrese are used for special library collections or as offices. Outside in the street at the corner of the building is a fine rococo sebil with a çeşme beside it.

After leaving the medrese, we continue walking along the street, which soon veers left and ends in a flight of steps beside the hamam of Sultan Beyazit. This brings us back to the southwest corner of Beyazit Meydanı, the point where this itinerary began.

9 · **The Süleymaniye

We begin this itinerary in Beyazit Meydanı, in front of the monumental entryway to Istanbul University. From there we take the walkway that leads around the southwest corner of the university to Besim Ömer Paşa Cad., where we turn right. This leads us along the west side of the university grounds to Prof. Sıddık Sami Onar Cad., where we turn left along the south side of the Süleymaniye (Pl. 10,2), the great mosque complex of Süleyman the Magnificent.

The Süleymaniye is the second largest but by far the finest and most magnificent of the imperial mosque complexes in the city. It is a fitting monument to its founder, Süleyman the Magnificent, and a masterwork of the greatest of Ottoman architects, the incomparable Sinan.

The construction of the Süleymaniye began in 1550 and the mosque itself was completed in 1557, but it was some years before all the buildings of the külliye were finished. The mosque stands in the centre of a vast outer courtyard surrounded on three sides by a wall with grilled windows. On the north side, where the land slopes sharply down to the Golden Horn, the courtyard is supported by an elaborate vaulted substructure; from the terrace there is a superb view of the Golden Horn. Around this courtyard on three sides the other buildings of the külliye are arranged with as much symmetry as the nature of the site would permit. Nearly all of these pious foundations have been well restored, and some of them are once again serving the people of Istanbul as they did in the days of Süleyman.

The mosque. The mosque is preceded by the usual **avlu**, a porticoed courtyard of exceptional grandeur, with columns of the richest porphyry, marble and granite. The west portal of the court is flanked by a great pylon containing two storeys of chambers; according to Evliya Çelebi, these served as the house and workshop of the mosque astronomer. At the four corners of the courtyard rise the four great **minarets**. The four minarets are traditionally said to signify that Süleyman was the fourth sultan to rule in Istanbul, while the ten şerefes denote that he was the tenth monarch of the imperial Ottoman line.

Entering the mosque, we find ourselves in a vast room, almost square in plan, surmounted by a huge and lofty dome. The **interior** is approximately 58.5m by 57.5m, while the diameter of the dome is 27.5m and the height of its crown above the floor is 47m. To east and west the dome is flanked by semidomes, and to north and south by arches with tympana filled with windows. The dome arches rise from four great irregularly shaped piers. Up to this point the plan follows that of Haghia Sophia, but beyond this—as at the Beyazidiye—all is different. Between the piers, to the north and south, triple arcades on two enormous porphyry monoliths support the tympana of the arches. There are no galleries here, nor can there really be said to be aisles, since the great porphyry

The Süleymaniye rises above the rooftops of the city

columns are so high and so far apart that they do not in any way form a barrier between the central area and the walls. Thus the immense space is not cut up into sections, as at Haghia Sophia, but is centralised and continuous.

The method used by Sinan to mask the huge buttresses required to support the four central piers is very ingenious, and here he has turned what is generally a liability in such a building into an asset. On the north and south he incorporated the buttresses into the walls of the building, allowing them to project about equally within and without. He then proceeded to mask this projection on both sides by building galleries with arcades of columns between the buttresses. On the outside the gallery is double, with twice the number of columns in its upper storey as in its lower; on the inside there is a single gallery only. In both cases—especially on the outside—the device is extremely successful, and is indeed one of the features that give the exterior its interesting and beautiful distinction.

On the east and west façades the buttresses are smaller, for here the weight of the dome is distributed by the semidomes. On the east face, therefore, Sinan merely placed the buttresses wholly outside the building, where their moderate projection gives emphasis and variety to that façade. On the west side Sinan was not so successful. Here, in order to preserve the unity of the courtyard and the grandeur of the west façade, he chose to place the buttresses wholly within the building. Again he masked them with galleries, but in this case the device was inadequate. The great west portal, instead of being as impressive as it ought to be, seems squeezed by the deep projection of the buttresses, which, moreover, not only throw it into impenetrable shadow, but also abut in an unpleasing way on the two small domes on which the west semidome reposes. Sinan was rarely

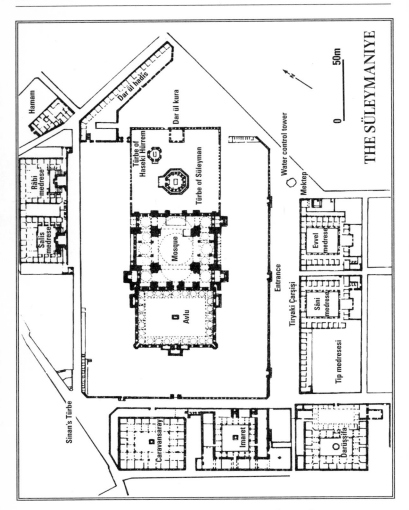

THE SÜLEYMANIYE

completely successful with the interior of his west walls; in almost every case, even in his smaller mosques, there is a tendency to squeeze the main portal. Nevertheless, his solution of the main problem was masterly.

The general effect of the interior is of a severely simple grandeur. Only the east wall is enlivened by some touches of colour: here the lovely **stained glass windows** are by the glazier known as Sarhoş (the Drunkard) Ibrahim. The **tiles**, used with great restraint, are the earliest known examples of the new techniques of the Iznik kilns, leaf and flower motifs in turquoise, deep blue and red on a pure white ground. The mihrab and mimber in Proconnesian marble are of great simplicity and distinction, as is also the woodwork, inlaid with ivory and mother-of-pearl, of the doors, window shutters, and the preacher's chair.

Throughout the building the inscriptions are by the most famous of Ottoman calligraphers, Ahmet Karahisarı and his pupil Hasan Çelebi.

The türbes. The türbes of Süleyman and his wife Haseki Hürrem, better known in the West as Roxelana, are in the walled garden behind the mosque. **Süleyman's *türbe**, as is fitting, is the largest and grandest of Sinan's mausoleums, although not quite the most beau-

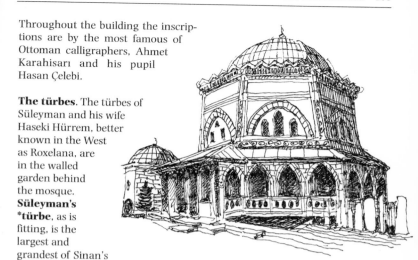

The türbe of Süleyman

tiful. Octagonal in form, it is surrounded by a pretty porch on columns. This türbe, like those at Haghia Sophia and elsewhere, has a double dome, with the inner dome supported by columns in the interior. This inner dome preserves its gorgeous painting in wine-red, black and gold. The walls of the interior are covered with Iznik tiles, twice as many in this small room as in all the vastness of the mosque itself. However, the grand effect has been marred, for the interior of the türbe is dark and overcrowded with cenotaphs; besides that of Süleyman there are also those of his favourite daughter, the Princess Mihrimah, and two later sultans, Süleyman II and Ahmet II. Nevertheless, this remains one of the most impressive monuments of its kind in the city. It is dated 1566, the year of Süleyman's death.

The ***türbe of Haseki Hürrem** stands just to the east of Süleyman's; although this is smaller and simpler than the Sultan's tomb, it is decorated with even finer Iznik tiles. In this türbe the cylindrical base of the dome, slightly recessed from the octagonal cornice of the building itself, is decorated with a long inscription forming a kind of sculptured frieze. This, and the türbe of the princes at the mosque of Selim I (see p 168), are the only ones to use this form and these decorations. For some reason this türbe is not included in the 'Tezkere', the list of Sinan's works, but it is almost certainly his creation. The türbe is dated 1558, the year of Haseki Hürrem's death.

The dar-ül hadis. Farther east along the north terrace, and beyond the wall of the türbe garden, stands the dar-ül hadis, or school of tradition, which runs off at an angle to the line of the terrace, following the direction of the street below. This is a medrese of most unusual form. It consists of 22 cells in a long straight line, rather than around a courtyard; opposite them is a plain wall with grilled openings enclosing a long, narrow garden. At the end of the line of cells nearest the mosque a staircase leads up to a sort of open loggia above, which appears to have served as the dershane. It was for summer use only since it would have been too cold in winter. Unfortunately, this unique and once charming building has been very badly restored.

The arasta. From the outer edge of the terrace you can look down onto the street that borders the north wall of the outer precincts of the Süleymaniye. This was once an attractive arasta, or market street, with shops built into the retaining wall of the terrace and also opposite. The shops still serve the purpose for which they were designed four centuries ago, but they are now rather badly battered.

The Salis and Rabi medreses. Just across the street there are two medreses of the Süleymaniye külliye; these are presently closed to the public and can best be viewed from the terrace. They are by far the most elaborate, original and picturesque of all Sinan's medreses. The one to the west, farther down the street, is called Salis (Third), while that to the east is known as Rabi (Fourth). The two medreses form a group with another pair that stand opposite them on the south side of the külliye; these are called Evvel (First) and Sani (Second); each of them serving as a college in one of the four orthodox schools of Islamic law. There is still another medrese, the Mülazimler (Preparatory Students), which lies beneath the Salis and Rabi medreses.

These three medreses were built on the steep northern slope of the Third Hill, and in order to use this almost precipitous site two expedients were necessary. The north side of the courtyard was raised on high superstructures, beneath which lies the Mülazimler medrese. Even so, the courtyard itself slopes downhill fairly sharply, and the cells along the sides are built on five different levels connected by four flights of six shallow steps each under the portico. On each level outside the cells there is a verandah with a low parapet. The dershane occupies most of the upper (south) side of the courtyard, but since it is at the highest level it is entered from the sides rather than from the façade on the court.

Salis and Rabi are absolutely identical; between them there is a small court from whose lower level two staircases lead to the courtyard of the Mülazimler medrese. This medrese consists of 18 cells with barrel-vaults under the north side of the upper medreses. As a display of architectural virtuosity these medreses surely have no rival; their effortless charm and simple distinction show that they were no empty vaunting of ingenuity, but a genuine inspiration by a master architect. It is to be hoped that they will one day be opened to the public, for they are unique and interesting monuments of Ottoman architecture.

The hamam. At the end of the street, just below the dar-ül hadis, there is a building that was originally the hamam of the Süleymaniye külliye. This fine building, of an original design and once elegantly decorated, has been restored in recent years, and it may soon be open to the public.

The dar-ül kura. The far eastern end of the terrace, the area behind the türbe garden, is a large open area, triangular in shape because of the direction of the streets below. This was known in early Ottoman times as the Iron Wrestling Ground, because weekly wrestling matches were held there. (Wrestling has always been an honoured sport in Islam, and one with religious significance, particularly because the Prophet himself enjoyed wrestling with his companions.) At the western end of the area, set into the middle of the türbe garden wall, there is a handsome building that once served as the dar-ül kura, or school for the study of the Kuran. Such schools appear to have always been small buildings, rather like mekteps or the dershanes of medreses. Sometimes they were directly attached to a mosque and without accompanying living-quarters for students, since the course in Kuran reading was naturally ancillary to more general studies. The school consists of a large domed chamber of very lovely proportions; beneath it there is a small Byzantine cistern with four columns.

Tiryaki Çarşışı. On the south side of the mosque, outside the precinct walls, there stretches a long and broad esplanade lined with institutions belonging to the Süleymaniye külliye. This attractive avenue is called Tiryaki Çarşışı, the Market of the Addicts, because in Ottoman times the cafés which stood outside the medreses here used to serve opium to their customers in addition to tea, coffee and tobacco.

The mektep. At the east end of the esplanade stands the former primary school of the külliye, where the children of the clergy, faculty and staff of the Süleymaniye received their elementary education. This little building, whose entrance is around the corner, has recently been restored and is now in use as a very charming children's library.

The Evvel and Sani medreses. The next two institutions along the esplanade are the Evvel and Sani medreses, forming a group with the other two schools of Islamic law on the north side of the mosque. The entrance to these twin medreses is at the far end of the narrow alley that separates them. The two medreses now house the celebrated Süleymaniye library; this is one of the most important in the city, with more than 32,000 manuscripts. The buildings are mirror-images of one another, and although the arrangement is typical enough—cells around a porticoed courtyard—there are interesting variations. For example, there is no portico on the north side, but, instead, the three cells are open, forming a kind of loggia; the portico on the south side is cut by the dershane. All of the porticoes have been glassed-in to accommodate the library; this has been done well and attractively, and there is a charming garden in the courtyard itself.

The Tip Medresesi. Just beyond the Sani medrese is the building that was originally the Tip Medresesi, or Medical College, once the foremost in the Empire. Unfortunately, all that remains of it now is the row of cells along the Tiryaki Çarşışı; the other three sides have long since disappeared. In their place a modern concrete structure has been built, and the building now serves as a maternity clinic.

The hospital. Across the street from this to the west is the vast darüşşifa,or hospital, now a military printing-house and closed to the public. Like most of the larger Ottoman hospitals, that of the Süleymaniye had a special section for the care of the insane. Foreign travellers to Istanbul were much impressed by these establishments and praised their number and size, charity and organisation.

The imaret. The first building on the street bordering the west end of the mosque courtyard is the imaret, or public kitchen. The imaret is enormous, as well it might be, for it had to supply food not only for the poor of the district but also for the several thousand people directly dependent on the Süleymaniye: the clergy of the mosque, the faculty and students of the several medreses, the staff and patients of the hospital, and the travellers staying at the caravansarai. The courtyard itself is charming, with its ancient plane trees and young palms and a lovely marble fountain in the centre. The imaret now houses the Darüzziyafe, an outstanding restaurant specialising in Ottoman cuisine.

The caravansarai. Next beyond the imaret is the building that was once the caravansarai of the Süleymaniye. This included a kitchen, bakery, olive press, sleeping-quarters for travellers, stables for their horses and camels, and storage-rooms for their belongings. According to ancient Turkish tradition, all accredited travellers to the city were given free food and shelter for three days at this and other caravansarais in the Empire.

The türbe of Sinan. The türbe of Sinan, the architect of the Süleymaniye, stands in a little triangular garden at the northeast corner of the complex, just beyond the caravansarai. Sinan apparently built a house here when he began construction of the Süleymaniye, and he lived in it until his death in 1588; he was then buried in his garden, in a türbe that he had designed and built himself. At the apex of the triangle is a sebil with six grilled openings and covered by a little dome with projecting eaves. From this radiate the garden walls, inside which stands the marble türbe. An arcade with six ogive arches supports a marble roof which has a tiny dome over Sinan's marble sarcophagus, with a turbaned tombstone at its head.

Around the türbe there are other tombstones, presumably marking the graves of members of Sinan's family, but there are no inscriptions to identify them. On the south wall of the türbe garden there is a long inscription by Sinan's friend, the poet Mustafa Sa'i, which commemorates the architect's accomplishments. There could be no more appropriate place for Sinan's tomb, looking out toward the great mosque complex that he created, the crowning glory of Süleyman's golden age.

10 · The Galata Bridge to Şehzadebaşı

This itinerary follows a route that runs first along the Golden Horn between the two bridges, then turns up the valley between the Third and Fourth Hills to visit monuments on the slopes of both eminences, and finally ends at Şehzadebaşı, on the crest of the ridge between the Golden Horn and the Marmara.

We begin this itinerary on the Stamboul shore of the Golden Horn, on the upstream side of the Galata Bridge. From there we walk up the shore of the Golden Horn to the large building just beyond the entrance to the parking lot. This is the **Zindan Han**, a commercial building erected in the late 19C. The han took its name from the ancient tower behind it, which in both Byzantine and

Ottoman times served as a prison (in Turkish, zindan). The tower was originally part of the Byzantine defence walls along the Golden Horn, most notably Zindan Kapı, the ancient market quarter just upstream from the Galata Bridge.

The tower was restored together with Zindan Han in 1990, and its ground floor is now open to the public. There we find the türbe of a Muslim saint named Cafer Baba, whose grave has been a place of pilgrimage since the time of the Conquest. According to tradition, he came to Constantinople as the envoy of Haroun al-Rashid but was imprisoned here and died. His grave was rediscovered and restored after the Conquest, along with that of his former gaoler, Zindancı Ali Baba, a Greek who was executed after he was converted to Islam by Cafer Baba. The tower is known in Turkish as the Cafer Baba Kulesi.

Just beyond the tower there are the shattered remains of an arched gateway dating from the medieval Byzantine period. This is known in Turkish as **Zindan Kapı**, the prison gate, because of its proximity to the prison tower of Cafer Baba. In times past the quarter on this part of the Golden Horn shore was also known as Zindan Kapı. The Byzantine name of this gate is uncertain, but in early Ottoman times local Greeks referred to it as the Porta Caravion, the Gate of the Caravels, because of the large number of ships that docked at the pier nearby, the ancient Scala de Drongario. This was the pier used by the Venetians in the late Byzantine period, when they and other Italian merchants had concessions along the Golden Horn. In Ottoman times it was called Yemiş Iskelesi, the Fruit Pier, and Evliya Çelebi gives a vivid description of the tumultuous and colourful scene here in the mid 17C. This continued to be the principal fish and produce market up until the 1980s, when the Istanbul Municipality demolished the entire Zindan Kapı quarter in a grandiose programme to beautify the shores of the Golden Horn, destroying one of the most historic and colourful quarters in the city.

A short distance beyond the tower and gateway there is an ancient mosque known as **Ahi Çelebi Camii**. This mosque was founded in the early 16C by Ahi Çelebi ibni Kemal, who was Chief Physician at the hospital attached to the külliye of Fatih Camii; he died in 1523 while returning from a pilgrimage to Mecca and the mosque can thus be dated to before that time. The mosque is of little interest except for the fact that it was restored at one point by Sinan. The mosque was abandoned after the destruction of the Zindan Kapı quarter and it is now falling into ruins. Ahi Çelebi Camii figures prominently in the life of Evliya Çelebi, for in a dream he had on his twenty-first birthday, 25 February 1632, he was transported to this mosque and met the Prophet Mohammed, who assured him that he would become a great traveller and would write a chronicle of his times, as he did indeed in his *Narrative of Travels*.

Three Little Mosques

We now cross the shore highway and begin walking towards the Atatürk Bridge. As we do so we pass, in turn, three little mosques which are among the very oldest in Istanbul, all of them built just after the Conquest. The first of these is about 250m along. This is **Kantarcılar Mescidi**, the Mosque of the Scale-Makers, named after the guild whose artisans have had their workshops in this neighbourhood for centuries. This mosque was founded during the reign of the Conqueror by one Sarı Demirci Mevlana Mehmet Muhittin. It has been reconstructed several times and is of little interest except for its great age.

The second of these ancient mosques, which is about 250m beyond the first, is called **Kazancılar Camii**, the Mosque of the Cauldron-Makers, here again named after one of the ancient neighbourhood guilds. It is also known as Üç Mihrablı Cami (literally the mosque with the three mihrabs). Founded by a certain Hoca Hayrettin Efendi in 1475, it was enlarged first by the Conqueror himself and then by Hayrettin's daughter-in-law, who added her own house to the mosque, so that it came to have three mihrabs—the east end of each new building forming a new mihrab—and hence the name.

The main body of the building, which appears to be original in form though heavily restored, consists of a square room covered by a dome resting on a high blind drum; this is worked in the form of a series of triangles so as to dispense with squinches or pendentives. In the dome there are some rather curious arabesque designs; these are not in the grand manner of the 16C–17C nor yet in the degenerate Italian taste of the 19C; their date is uncertain but they are unique in the city and quite attractive both in design and colour. The deep porch has three domes only, the arches are supported at each end by rectangular piers and in the centre by a single marble column. The door is not in the middle, where it would have been blocked by the column, but on the right-hand side; this arrangement was common in the pre-classical period, but there are very few examples in the city.

To the south of the main building there is a rectangular annex with a flat ceiling and two mihrabs, and it is through here that you enter the mosque today. One authority has suggested that this might be the house added to Hayrettin's house by his daughter-in-law; if true, this would be one of the oldest dwelling-places in the city.

The third mosque is found about 150m farther along, a short distance before the Atatürk Bridge. This is **Sağrıcılar Camii**, the Mosque of the Leather-Workers, named after another guild that has long had its workshops in this quarter. This building is of the simplest type, a square room covered by a dome, the walls of stone. It was restored in 1960 with only modest success. But although the mosque is of little interest architecturally, its historical background is fascinating. This is probably the oldest mosque in the city, founded in 1455 by Yavuz Ersinan, standard-bearer in the Conqueror's army during the final siege of Constantinople by the Turks. He was an ancestor of Evliya Çelebi and his family remained in possession of the mosque for at least two centuries, living in a house just beside it. Evliya Çelebi was born in this house in 1611, and 21 years later he began to write his *Narrative of Travels* there, much of it devoted to a description of Istanbul and its daily life in the mid 17C.

The founder is buried in the little graveyard beside the mosque. Beside him is buried one of his comrades-in-arms, Horoz Dede, one of the fabulous folk-saints of Istanbul. Horoz Dede, or Grandfather Rooster, received his name during the siege of Constantinople in 1453, when he made his rounds each morning and woke the troops of the Conqueror's army with his loud rooster call. Horoz Dede was killed in the final assault on the walls, and after the city fell he was buried here, with the Conqueror himself among the mourners.

Atatürk Blv. begins at the Atatürk Bridge and runs uphill along the valley between the Third and Fourth Hills. About 300m up the avenue and on the left side there is a handsome baroque mosque, **Şebsafa Kadın Camii**. This was founded in 1787 by Fatma Şebsafa Kadın, one of the women in the harem of Abdül Hamit I. It is of brick and stone; the porch has an upper storey with a cradle-vault, and inside there is a sort of narthex, also of two storeys, covered with three small domes. These upper storeys form a deep and attractive gallery overlooking the central area of the mosque, which is covered by a high dome resting on the walls. To the north of the mosque there is a long mektep with a pretty cradle-vaulted roof.

We now cross Atatürk Blv., after which we turn right on a steep road leading from the avenue to the heights of the Fourth Hill. A short distance uphill we take the second turning on the left. At the corner on the left we see a small Ottoman primary school in a walled garden, the **mektep of Zenbelli Ali Baba**. The founder was the Şeyh-ül Islam Ali bin Ahmet Efendi, better known as Zenbelli Ali Baba. Ali Baba died in 1525, so his mektep can be dated to some time prior to that year. The mektep has recently been restored and is now used as a children's library; it is a very pleasing example of the minor Ottoman architecture of the early 16C. The founder is buried beneath a marble sarcophagus in the garden.

*Church of the Pantocrator

Continuing up the street past the mektep, we soon come to a small square dominated by the former church of the Pantocrator (Pl. 10,1), known locally as Zeyrek Camii.

The Pantocrator is a composite building that originally consisted of a monastery with two churches and a chapel between them; the whole complex was built within the period 1120–36. The monastery and the south church were founded by the Empress Eirene, wife of John II Comnenus, and dedicated to St. Saviour Pantocrator, Christ the Almighty. After Eirene's death in 1124 John erected another church a short distance to the north of hers; this was dedicated to the Virgin Eleousa, the Merciful or Charitable. When this was finished John decided to join the two churches by another church, dedicated to the Archangel Michael. This was designed to serve as a mortuary chapel for the imperial Comneni dynasty, beginning with the Empress Eirene, who was reburied there after its completion. John II was interred in the chapel after his death in 1143, and his son and successor, Manuel I was buried there in 1180, thus bringing to a close an illustrious century of rule by the Comneni family.

During the first half of the 15C the chapel served as a mortuary for the imperial Palaeologus family, the last dynasty to rule Byzantium. Two of the last three Emperors of Byzantium were buried here: Manuel II in 1425 and John VIII in 1448. Buried alongside John was his wife, Maria of Trebizond, the last Empress of Byzantium, who had died a few years earlier. (Constantine XI Dragases, the last Emperor, was a widower when he succeeded to the throne, and he did not marry again.)

The monastery to which these churches belonged was one of the most renowned in Byzantium. It was a very extensive foundation, including a hospice for old men, an insane asylum, and a famous hospital. All of these have long since disappeared, doubtless the source of the widespread ruins and substructures in the neighbourhood of the Pantocrator.

During the period of Latin rule in Constantinople, 1204–61, the Pantocrator was taken over by the Roman Catholic clergy of the Venetians. Immediately after the recapture of the city by the Byzantines, on 25 July 1261, the Genoese crossed over from Galata and stormed the Pantocrator, where some of the Venetians were still holding out, and in the course of the fighting the monastery burned to the ground. The monastery was soon afterwards rebuilt, and during the latter Byzantine period it resumed its role as one of the most important religious centres in the city.

The most famous resident of the monastery during the last years of Byzantine rule was George Scholarius, better known as Gennadius. Gennadius accompanied John VIII Palaeologus and the Patriarch Joseph to the Council of Ferrara-Florence in 1438, when the Greek and Roman churches were officially reconciled. Gennadius bitterly opposed the union, however, and when he returned to Constantinople he vehemently denounced it; his view was shared by most people in the capital. After that Gennadius retired to his cell in the Pantocrator, emerging only after the city fell to the Turks. Shortly after the Conquest Gennadius was invited to meet Mehmet II, and after several cordial conversations the Sultan appointed him Patriarch, a post which, under Turkish rule, made him head of the entire Greek Orthodox population in the Ottoman Empire.

Interior. In plan the south **church** erected by the Empress Eirene is of the four-column type, with a central dome, a triple apse, and a narthex with a gallery overlooking the nave. (The columns were removed in Ottoman times and replaced by piers.) This church preserves a good deal of its original decoration, including the marble pavement, the handsome door-frames of the narthex, and the almost complete marble revetment of the apse. Recent work by the Byzantine Institute has brought to light again the magnificent opus sectile floor of the church itself, arranged in great squares and circles of coloured marbles with figures in the borders. Notice also the curious Turkish mimber made from fragments of Byzantine sculpture, including the canopy of a ciborium. The investigations of the Byzantine Institute also discovered fragments of stained glass from the east window, which seems to show that the art of stained glass was a Byzantine rather than a western European creation.

The north **church,** erected by the Emperor John, is somewhat smaller than Eirene's but of essentially the same type and plan; here again the columns have been replaced by piers. Unfortunately, it has preserved none of its original decoration and is now in an appalling condition. When this church was finished, the idea seems to have struck the Emperor to join the two churches by building a **chapel** between them. This is a structure without aisles and with only one apse, covered by two domes; it is highly irregular in form in order to make it fit between the two churches, which were not of exactly the same size. Parts of the walls of the churches were demolished so that all three sections opened widely into one another. John also added an outer narthex which must once have extended in front of all three structures, but which now ends awkwardly in the middle of the chapel.

Presently the three churches have been divided from each other by wooden partitions, so that it is quite impossible to form any idea of how the whole building appeared in its original state. At the moment of writing there are defi-

Church of the Pantocrator

nite plans to study and restore the Pantocrator, and in the interim the building is closed to the public.

After leaving the Pantocrator we take Ibadethane Sok., the street that leads westward from the church. At the first intersection we turn left and then left again on Atpazarı Sok., the Street of the Horse Market. There we see on our left an ancient building known as **Şeyh Süleyman Mescidi**. This building is obviously Byzantine in construction and may possibly have been one of the institutions associated with the Pantocrator monastery, perhaps a library or a funerary chapel. On the exterior this is square below and octagonal above; within it is altogether octagonal, with shallow niches in the cross-axes; below there is a crypt. This strange and interesting building has never been seriously investigated, so that neither its identity nor its date are known.

We now retrace our steps to the intersection, after which we turn into Hacı Hasan Sok. We then take the first turning on the left, which brings us on our left to a tiny mosque with a quaint and pretty minaret. The mosque is known as **Eğri Minare** (Pl. 5,8), the Crooked Minaret, for obvious reasons. The minaret has a stone base at the top of which there is a curious rope-like moulding. The shaft is of brick and stone arranged to form a criss-cross or chequerboard design, unique in Istanbul. The şerefe has an elaborate stalactite corbel and a fine balustrade, partly broken; but the scale seems a little too big for the minaret. The mosque itself is rectangular, built of squared stones and with a wooden roof; in its present condition it is without interest. The founder was the Kazasker (Judge) Hacı Hasanzade Mehmet Efendi, who died in 1505; therefore the mosque must be dated no later than that year.

We now turn right at the next corner on to Küçük Mektepli Sok., at the end of which we see a handsome Byzantine church known as **Eski Imaret Camii** (Pl. 5,8).

This has been identified with virtual certainty as the church of *St. Saviour Pantepoptes, Christ the All-Seeing, one of the more important Byzantine churches in the city. The church was founded c 1185 by the Empress Anna Dalassena, mother of Alexius I Comnenus (1081–1118) and founder of the dynasty which ruled so brilliantly over Byzantium in the 11C–12C. Anna was the power behind the throne for the first two decades of her son's reign. She retired in 1100 to the convent of the Pantepoptes and spent the rest of her life there, and on her death in 1105 she was buried in the church that she had founded.

The church was converted into a mosque almost immediately after the Conquest. For a time it served as the imaret of the nearby Fatih Camii, and thus afterwards it was known as Eski Imaret Camii.

Exterior. The exterior is very charming and the fabric is in good condition, though it is closely hemmed in by the surrounding houses. It is a very characteristic Byzantine church of the 11C, with its 12-sided dome, and its decorative brickwork in the form of blind niches and bands of Greek-key and swastika motifs, along with rose-like medallions.

Interior. The Pantepoptes is a quite perfect example of an 11C church of the four-column type, with three apses and a double narthex, where many of the doors retain their magnificent frames of red marble. Over the inner narthex there is a gallery that opens into the nave by a charming triple arcade on two rose-coloured marble columns. The church itself has retained most of its original characteristics, though the four columns have as usual been replaced by piers, and the windows of the central apse have been altered. The side apses, however, preserve their windows and their beautiful marble cornice. The dome, which has 12 windows between which 12 deep ribs taper out toward the crown, rests on a cornice which still preserves its original decoration, a meander pattern of palmettes and flowers.

The northern slope of the Fourth Hill in this area is rather thickly dotted with small mosques, many of them ancient but few of much interest. Some are in a state of ruin or near ruin; others have been restored, often quite badly. Two of these are in the vicinity of the Pantepoptes, but it should be understood that they are of relatively minor interest.

Aşık Paşa Camii and Yarhisar Camii

The first of these mosques is reached by taking Şair Baki Sok. (named after a Turkish poet of the 17C), the continuation of Küçük Mektepli Sok. The mosque is two blocks along on the right, at the corner of Esrar Dede Sok. This mosque, constructed of alternate rows of brick and stone, was built in 1564. It is called **Aşık Paşa Camii**, after a Turkish poet of the early 14C; it was built for the peace of his soul by one of the poet's descendants, Şeyh Ahmet Efendi. Beside it is a tekke, also named after Aşık Paşa; this was built somewhat earlier than the mosque, c 1522, by a man called Seyyidi-Velayet Efendi, but is in the same general style. Opposite the mosque is the grand türbe of Şeyh Ahmet Efendi. Although not actually planned as a külliye, these buildings in their walled garden nevertheless have an attractive unity.

Returning to the Pantepoptes, turn right off Küçük Mektepli Sok. immediately after passing the church. We follow this street past the intersection and for two more blocks beyond; this brings us to an ancient mosque at the corner of Kadı Çeşme Sok. and Sebnem Sok. This is **Yarhisar Camii**, one of the oldest mosques in the city. According to the register of pious foundations ('Hayrat Kaydi'), this mosque was built in 1461; its founder was Musliheddin Mustafa Efendi, Chief Judge of Istanbul during the reign of Fatih. It was once a handsome edifice, built entirely of ashlar; it consists of a square chamber covered by a dome on pendentives, preceded by a porch with two domes and three columns. It was burned in the great fire of 1917, which destroyed much of this district, but even in its ruined state it was a fine and dignified structure. In 1954–56 the building was restored, with a thin veneer of brick and stone, a la Byzantine, covering the original structure, and the interior was redecorated. The restoration was not a success; it obscures what is still attractive in the mosque and it is not true to the spirit of the original structure.

After returning to the Pantepoptes, we retrace the route back past Şeyh Süleyman Mescidi and then turn right at the next corner. A short way along on the left is an old hamam of considerable interest. This is *Çinili Hamam (Pl. 5,8), the Tiled Bath, an early work of Sinan. The hamam was built c 1545 for Süleyman's great admiral Hayrettin Paşa, better known in the West as Barbarossa. It is a double bath, the men's and women's sections standing side-by-side and with their entrances in the same façade, a rather unusual feature; the plans of the two parts are almost identical. In the centre of the great camekan is an elaborate and beautiful marble fountain with goldfish swimming in it. The narrow soğukluk with two little semidomes at each end leads to the cruciform hararet, where the open arms of the cross are covered with tiny domes; the rooms in the corners each have a larger dome.

Here and there on the walls there are small panels of faience, and the floor is paved in opus sectile. In the camekan fragments of a more elaborate wall revetment of tiles of a later period may be seen. A half century ago this fine hamam was abandoned and fell into a state of decay, but in recent years it has been restored and is now once again in use.

Beyond the hamam the avenue, **Itfaiye Cad.**, widens and becomes quite pretty, with a double row of plane trees shading the open stalls of a gay and colourful fruit and vegetable market. We follow Itfaiye Cad. as far as Kovacılar Cad., the last street before the aqueduct, and turn left. At the right on the next corner, where the street intersects Atatürk Blv., there is a small classical külliye built up against the aqueduct. This is the *medrese of Gazanfer Ağa (Pl. 10,1), which now serves as the **Caricature Museum** (Karikatür Müzesi).

■ **Admission**. The museum is open every day 09.00–17.00.

The külliye was founded in 1599 by Gazanfer Ağa, Chief of the White Eunuchs in Topkapı Sarayı, succeeding his brother Cafer Ağa in that post. Gazanfer Ağa was the last of the Chief White Eunuchs to head the civil hierarchy in the Inner Palace, for after his time the Chief Black Eunuch became the dominant figure. Gazanfer was executed in 1603, after having involved himself too deeply in the politics of the Harem.

The külliye includes a small medrese, a charming sebil with handsome grilled windows, and the türbe of the founder, in the form of a marble sarcophagus. The külliye was restored in 1945 and now serves as the Caricature Museum,

The Aqueduct of Valens, a drawing by J.C. Bentley

with exhibitions of work by leading Turkish artists and cartoonists in this field.

The Aqueduct of Valens

After leaving the museum we might take the opportunity to examine more closely the Aqueduct of Valens (Pl. 5,8; 10,1/3), which has been dramatically in view throughout the whole of this and other itineraries.

The aqueduct was built by the Emperor Valens in about AD 375 as part of the new water-supply system that he constructed during his reign. The water, tapped from various streams and lakes outside the city, appears to have entered through subterranean pipes near the Adrianople Gate and to have passed through a large underground pipe along the ridges of the Sixth, Fifth and Fourth Hills to a point near the present site of Fatih Camii (see p 149). From there the water was carried by the aqueduct across the deep valley that divides the Fourth from the Third Hill.

On the Third Hill, near the present site of Beyazit Meyanı, the water was received in a huge cistern, the *nymphaeum maximum*, from which it was distributed to the various parts of the city. This ancient cistern seems to have been near the present *taksim*, the modern water-distribution centre, which is supplied from Lake Terkoz, some 60km northwest of Istanbul, near the Black Sea. The aqueduct was damaged at various times but was kept in good repair by both the Byzantine emperors and the Ottoman sultans, the last important restoration being that of Mustafa II in 1697. The aqueduct continued in use until the late 19C, when it was replaced by the modern water-distribution system.

The length of the aqueduct was originally about 1000m, of which some 625m remain standing; its maximum height, where it crosses Atatürk Blv., is 18.5m.

It consists of two superimposed series of arches; a portion of the eastern side of this was demolished by Süleyman to give a clear view of the Şehzade mosque after it was built. The two tiers of arches marching across the valley gives an imperial Roman aspect to t∫he skyline of the old city when viewed from the Golden Horn. The aqueduct has recently been restored as is now in good condition.

After passing through the aqueduct, we turn right in the park beyond and walk over to Itfaiye Cad., where we see the Headquarters of the Istanbul Fire Department. One of the buildings there has been converted into the **Itfaiye Müzesi** (Fire Brigade Museum), which is open 09.30–17.00, closed Mon.

After leaving the museum we continue to the intersection of Atatürk Blv. and Şehzadebaşı Cad. This brings us to the crest of the ridge between the Third and Fourth Hills, where the present itinerary ends and the next one begins.

11 · The Fourth Hill

The area where Atatürk Blv. and Şehzadebaşı Cad. intersect coincides with the site of the ancient Forum Amastrianum, one of the main squares in Byzantine Constantinople. At this point the Mese, which ran along the same route as Şehzadebaşı Cad., divided into two branches, one of which continued in the same direction along what is now Macarkardeşler Cad. (the continuation of Şehzadebaşı Cad.), while the other branch ran south along the present route of Atatürk Blv. to the Forum Bovis, the modern Aksaray.

When the ground was being cleared for the **Atatürk Blv.** underpass in the mid 1960s the extensive remains of an ancient church were discovered, and its ruins are visible in the open area to the right of the boulevard. An excavation was taken in hand by Dumbarton Oaks under the supervision of Martin Harrison, who identified the church as that of **St. Polyeuktos** (Pl. 9,2).

The church was built between 524 and 527 for the Princess Anicia Juliana, who dedicated it to St. Polyeuktos, and is thus one of the earliest sanctuaries erected in Justinian's reign. It was an enormous building, some 52m on a side (compare the Süleymaniye mosque, which is about 58m on a side); it was essentially basilical in form, but very probably domed. The fragments of columns, capitals, elaborately carved entablature, and parts of a long and beautifully written inscription, by which the building was identified, are very impressive indeed.

Just to the west of the ruins of St. Polyeuktos is the fine *****küllatiye of Amcazade Hüseyin Paşa** (Pl. 9,2). This is one of the most elaborate and picturesque of the smaller classical complexes, another foundation of the illustrious Köprülü family.

Hüseyin Paşa, the founder, was a cousin (in Turkish, amcazade) of Fazil Ahmet Paşa, and was the fourth member of the Köprülü family to serve as Grand Vezir. He held that post from 1697–1702, during which time he founded this külliye. In recent years it has been restored and now houses the

Museum of Turkish Architectural Works and Construction Elements. (The museum is normally not open to the public, but the custodian can sometimes be persuaded to allow you in.)

The külliye. The complex includes an octagonal dershane, which also served as a mosque; a medrese; a library; a large primary school over a row of shops; two little graveyards with open türbes; a şadirvan; a sebil; and a çeşme; all arranged with an almost romantic disorder.

The street façade consists first of the open walls of the small graveyards, divided by the projecting curve of the sebil. All of these have fine brass grilles, those of the türbe nearest the entrance being quite exceptionally beautiful specimens of early 17C grillework. Next comes the entrance gate with an Arabic inscription giving the date 1698. The **çeşme** just beyond it, with its reservoir behind, is a somewhat later addition, for its inscription records that it was built in 1739 for the Şeyh-ül Islam Mustafa Efendi. Finally there is a row of four shops, with an entrance between them leading to the two large rooms of the mektep on the upper floor.

On entering the courtyard, the first of the open türbes—with the exceptionally handsome grilles—is on the left; notice the columned portico of the mosque, which runs around seven of the eight sides of the building and frames it in a rectangle. The mosque itself is without a minaret, and its primary purpose was clearly as the lecture-hall for the medrese. It is severely simple; its dome adorned only with some rather pale stencilled designs probably later than the building itself.

The far side of the courtyard is formed by the 17 cells of the medrese, with their domed and colonnaded portico. Occupying the main part of the right-hand side is the library building. There are two storeys, but the lower floor serves chiefly as a water reservoir; the upper floor is reached by a flight of outside steps around the side and back of the building, leading to a little domed entrance porch on the first floor. The medallion inscription on the front of the library records a restoration in 1755 by Hüseyin Paşa's daughter.

The right-hand corner of the courtyard is occupied by the shops of the külliye and the mektep above them: note the amusing little dovecotes in the form of miniature mosques on the façade overlooking the entrance gate. A columned şadirvan stands in the middle of the courtyard. This charmingly irregular complex is made still more picturesque by the warm red of the brickwork alternating with buff-coloured limestone, and not least by the venerable trees—cypresses, locusts, and two enormous terebinths—that grow out of the open türbes and in the courtyard.

The museum. On exhibition in the külliye are various architectural fragments, sculptured stonework, calligraphic inscriptions, and old tombstones. Many of these were formerly stored in the Second Court of Topkapı Sarayı, where they had been placed for safekeeping after the buildings to which they belonged were either ruined or demolished. One particularly interesting object is the top of one of the minarets of Fatih Camii, toppled by an earthquake in 1894.

Continuing along the avenue on the left side, you pass an ancient but not very interesting little mosque called **Dülgerzade Camii**; this was built by one of Fatih's officials, Şemsettin Habib Efendi, some time before his death in 1482.

The side street to the left beyond the mosque leads to a monument known locally as **Kız Tası**, the Maiden's Column (Pl. 9,2). This is actually the ancient *Column of Marcian, one of three late Roman honorific columns that still stand in the city.

> This column, though known to Evliya Çelebi and described by him in his *Narrative of Travels*, escaped even the penetrating eyes of Gyllius and remained unknown to the West until rediscovered in 1675 by Spon and Wheler. The reason for its obscurity was that it stood in the garden of a tall house, which, together with its neighbours, hid it from view. However, in 1908 a fire destroyed the houses and opened up the column to view, and now it stands in the centre of a small square.

The base is formed by a marble pedestal on three steps; above this stands a monolithic column of Syenitic granite 10m high, surmounted by a battered Corinthian capital and a plinth with eagles at the corners; this once supported a seated statue of the Emperor Marcian (450–57). On the base fragments of sculpture remain, including a Nike, or Winged Victory, in high relief. There is also on the base an elegiac couplet in Latin which records that the column was erected by the Prefect Tatianus in honour of the Emperor Marcian. The Turkish name of the column is undoubtedly due to the figure of the Nike on the base. This has led travellers to confuse this column with the famous Column of Venus, which also stood in this neighbourhood, and which reputedly possessed the power of being able to distinguish true virgins from false ones.

Two blocks farther along Macarkardeşler Cad. and on the same side is another little külliye. This is the medrese founded in 1700 by the Şeyh-ül Islam Feyzullah Efendi, a great scholar and one of the most enlightened men of his time; it now serves as the **People's Library of Istanbul**. The cells of the medrese surround two sides of the courtyard, in the centre of which a şadırvan stands in the midst of a pretty garden.

The street side of the courtyard is wholly occupied by a most elaborate and original dershane building: a flight of steps leads up to a porch covered by nine domes of very different patterns; the arches of these are supported on four columns. The effect of this porch has been somewhat impaired by glazing-in a part of it, but its usefulness has doubtless been increased. To the right and left of the porch are the large domed lecture-rooms of the medrese, now used as library reading-rooms. The medrese was restored and converted into a library by Ali Emiri Efendi, a famous bibliophile who died in 1924; he donated to the people of Istanbul his valuable collection of books and manuscripts.

**Fatih Camii

This brings you to the enormous mosque complex of Mehmet the Conqueror (Pl. 5,8), known in Turkish as Fatih Camii. The massive walls along the right side of the avenue here are the backs of the medreses attached to the mosque complex; its main entrance is reached by taking the first turning on the right onto Islambol Cad., the street bordering the west side of the outer precinct wall. There you are confronted by the imposing edifice of Fatih Camii, flanked on either side by the great medreses and the other institutions of the külliye.

The huge mosque complex built by Fatih was the most extensive and elaborate in Istanbul, and indeed in the whole of the Ottoman Empire. An inscription records that the architect was Atik Sinan, and that the complex was built in the period 1463–70. The identity of the architect is uncertain but he is believed to have been a Greek, from the European provinces of the Empire, who had been taken up in the devşirme, the annual levy of subject youths, and trained in an Ottoman school of architecture. In addition to the great mosque itself, the külliye consisted of eight medreses and their annexes, along with a hospice, public kitchen, hospital, caravansarai, primary school, public bath, and a graveyard with two türbes.

The complex was laid out over a vast, almost square area—about 325m on a side—with almost rigid symmetry. The complex stood on the site of the famous Church of the Holy Apostles, in whose funerary chapel most of the earlier Emperors of Byzantium were buried, and which was exceeded in size in Constantinople only by Haghia Sophia. The church and its attendant buildings, which were already in ruins at the time of the last siege, served as a quarry to supply building material for the Conqueror's mosque complex, and today not a trace of them remains.

The original mosque built by Fatih was completely destroyed by an earthquake on 22 May 1766. Mustafa III immediately undertook its reconstruction, and the present mosque, designed on a wholly different plan, was completed in 1771. What remains of the original mosque complex of the Conqueror is, most probably, the courtyard, the main entrance portal of the mosque, the mihrab, the minarets up to the first şerefe, the south wall of the graveyard and the adjoining gate. All of the other buildings in the külliye were badly damaged in the earthquake but were restored by Mustafa III, presumably in their original form.

There has been considerable speculation about the original plan of Fatih Camii, the first imperial Ottoman mosque to be erected in Istanbul. It is believed that Fatih's mosque had a very large central dome, some 26m in diameter (compare Haghia Sophia, where the diameter is 31m), with a semidome of the same diameter to the east; these were supported by two great rectangular piers on the east and by two enormous porphyry columns toward the west. The two porphyry columns also supported a double arcade below the tympanum walls of the great dome arches, while to north and south there were side aisles, each of which were covered with three small domes. Those who saw and described the mosque before it was destroyed, Turks and foreigners alike, compared it to Haghia Sophia. There is a curious tradition, repeated by Evliya Çelebi and other writers, that the architect was executed by the Conqueror soon after Fatih Camii was completed, because the Sultan was enraged that the dome of his mosque was smaller than that of the Great Church.

The mosque courtyard. Approaching the mosque from the west end of the outer courtyard, we find that part of the west wall of the precinct has been demolished, together with the small library and primary school that once stood outside it. Trees and wooden houses have intruded but they make a picturesque enclave in this corner. Still visible are the remains of one of the original gateways to the outer courtyard; this is **Boyacı Kapısı**, the Painter's Gate. There was

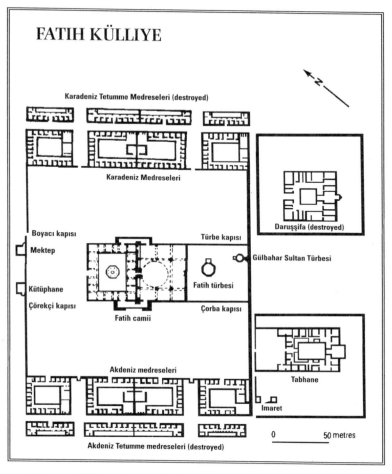

FATIH KÜLLIYE

Karadeniz Tetumme Medreseleri (destroyed)

Karadeniz Medreseleri

Daruşşifa (destroyed)

Boyacı kapısı

Mektep

Türbe kapısı

Gülbahar Sultan Türbesi

Kütüphane

Fatih türbesi

Çörekçi kapısı

Çorba kapısı

Fatih camii

Akdeniz medreseleri

Tabhane

Imaret

0   50 metres

Akdeniz Tetumme medreseleri (destroyed)

a similar portal 75m to the south of this called **Çörekçi Kapısı**, the Gate of the Muffin-Maker; these two gates flanked the mektep (to the north) and the library (kütüphane) (to the south).

The inner courtyard of the mosque begins some 75m to the east; this, with its monumental entrance portal, is original. In the lunettes of the six west windows of the courtyard wall there are some of the most remarkable **inscriptions** in the city: the first Surah of the Kuran is written in white marble letters on a ground of verd antique. The effect is extremely lovely, and one wonders why this fascinating technique of calligraphy should occur only here. The calligrapher was Yahya Sufi, and it was his son Ali who wrote the inscriptions over the main portal of the mosque and also over the Bab-ı Hümayun at Topkapı Sarayı. The dignified but simple portal has rather curious engaged columns at the corners.

Fatih Camii

The convex flutes or ribs of their shafts become interlaced at top and bottom to form an intertwined snake pattern, while the columns end in a sort of hourglass-shaped capital and base. This treatment is found elsewhere in the külliye, but otherwise it is unique in Ottoman architecture.

In the centre of this picturesque courtyard stands the **şadırvan**, with a gay witch's cap conical roof resting on eight marble columns and surrounded by tall cypress trees. In essentials it is original, even to the cypresses, which are constantly mentioned by travellers, though doubtless replanted from time to time. The antique marble columns of the portico have stalactite capitals of fine, bold workmanship. At either end of the mosque porch there are two more exquisite lunette inscriptions, this time in faience, showing a vivid yellow combined with blue, green and white in the cuerda seca technique typical of this early period. Similar panels are to be seen in the mosque of Selim I (see below, p 168), the türbe of the Şehzade Mehmet, and a few other early buildings.

The west façade of the mosque itself belongs to the baroque reconstruction, except for the entrance portal. On the exterior it has the same engaged columns as the gate to the courtyard, and is surmounted by a stalactite canopy enclosed in a series of projecting frames that give depth and emphasis. On the sides and over the door are written in bold calligraphy the historical inscriptions, giving the names of the founder and the architect and the date of completion of the mosque. But the interior side of the portal is even more remarkable; its canopy is a finely carved scallop shell supported on a double cornice of stalactites. Unfortunately, it is masked by a later baroque balcony built in front of it.

The mosque interior. The interior is of little interest. It is a copy of the type in which the central dome is flanked by four semidomes on the axes, invented by Sinan for the Şehzade and used again for the Blue Mosque and Yeni Cami. Here the exterior lines are still reasonably classical and pleasing, but the interior is at once weak and heavy. The painted decoration is fussy in detail and dull in colour; the lower part of the walls is sheathed in common white tiles of such inferior make that they have become discoloured with damp. In the right-hand corner is a curious **fountain** for drinking-water, the only one of its kind in the city, with an old-fashioned bronze pump and silver drinking-mugs; the water is cool and delicious.

The **mihrab**, which is from the original building, resembles in style the entrance portal, though the gilt-framed panels in the lower part are perhaps a baroque addition. Certainly baroque but equally handsome is the mimber, an elaborate structure of polychrome marble. The sultan's loge is also baroque; its antechambers are now being used to house a school for imams. The window shutters in these rooms are fine examples of baroque intarsia work, while the small dome over the loge itself is gaily painted with trompe l'oeil windows.

The *türbes. In the graveyard behind the mosque stand the türbes of Mehmet II and his wife Gülbahar, the mother of Beyazit II. Both of these türbes were completely reconstructed after the earthquake, though on the old foundations. The Conqueror's türbe is very baroque and its interior extremely sumptuous in the Empire style. The türbe of Gülbahar is simple and classical and must resemble the original quite closely. The little library in the southwest corner of the graveyard beside the mosque was built by Mahmut I and dates from 1742.

The medreses. To north and south of the precinct are the eight great medreses; those to the north were known as the Karadeniz Medreseleri, the Medreses of the Black Sea, while those to the south were called the Akdeniz Medreseleri, the Medreses of the White Sea, i.e.the Mediterranean. These buildings, which date from Fatih's original construction, are severely symmetrical and are almost identical in plan. Each contains 19 cells for students and a dershane. The entrance to the dershanes is from the side, and beside each entrance is a tiny garden planted with trees; an effect as rare as it is pretty. Behind each medrese there was originally an annex about half as large; these have totally disappeared.

Altogether there must have been about 255 hücres, or students' rooms, each housing perhaps four youths. Thus the establishment must have provided for about a thousand students in all, making it a university on a big scale. These fine buildings have recently been restored and are now again being used as residences by university students.

The hospice. The **tabhane**, or hospice, stands outside the southeast corner of the mosque precincts. It is approached by a gateway just beside that corner of the mosque graveyard; this is called **Çorba Kapısı**, the Soup Gate, because of the proximity of the imaret. Çorba Kapısı is part of the Conqueror's original külliye; notice the elaborate and most unusual designs in porphyry and verd antique let into the stonework of the canopy, and also the 'panache' at the top in verd antique.

After passing through this gate you come to what is perhaps the finest building of the külliye, the tabhane, or hospice for travelling dervishes. It has a very beautiful courtyard and is in general an astonishing, indeed unique, building. The 20 domes of the courtyard are supported on 16 exceptionally beautiful columns of verd antique and Syenitic granite, doubtless from the Church of the Holy Apostles. At the east end a large square room (which has unfortunately lost its dome) originally served as the mescit-zaviye, the room where the dervish ceremonies were performed. On each side of this there are two spacious rooms opening out into two unenclosed eyvans. These are very interesting: each has two domes supported on a rectangular pillar that at first sight appears to be baroque. However, closer examination shows the same engaged ribbed columns ending in intertwined designs and an hour-glass capital and base as those seen earlier on the entrance portals of the mosque itself. The rosettes too, and even the very baroque-looking mouldings can be paralleled in this and other buildings of Fatih's time. It is thought that the two open eyvans were used for meetings and prayers in summer, the two rooms adjoining the mescit zaviye for the same purpose in winter, and the two farther rooms in the corner as depositories for the guests' baggage.

The two rooms at the west ends of the north and south sides do not communicate with the rest of the building in any way, but have their own entrances from the west forecourt; they were used as kitchens and bakehouses and doubtless depended on the adjacent imaret. This leaves only 10, or possibly 12, rooms for guests, for in the middle of the south side a passage leads through a small arched entryway to the area where the caravansarai and imaret stood; an adjacent staircase leads to a room with a cradle-vault above. Opposite on the north side a similar area was occupied by the lavatories; but here the dome and outer wall have fallen, and a very poor repair makes it difficult to see what was the original arrangement.

The caravansarai. The great vacant lot to the south, now used as a playing-field by the children of the (modern) Fatih school, was the site of the caravansarai (to the east) and the imaret (to the west). Two fragments of the latter—small domed rooms, but ruinous now—remain in the southwest corner. Evliya Çelebi writes that it had 70 domes; this would imply that it was a third again as big as the tabhane, which had 46 domes, but one can quite believe it. As it had to supply two meals a day to the thousand students of the medreses, along with the vast corps of clergy and professors of the foundation, the patients and staff of the hospital, the guests at the tabhane and the caravansarai, as well as the poor of the district, it is clear that the imaret must have been enormous. The caravansarai has wholly disappeared, but it too must have been very big, even if one discounts Evliya Çelebi's statement that it could hold 3000 horses and mules.

This whole area to the south should be excavated; it is clear that the ground has risen considerably, presumably with the rubble of fallen buildings, and it should be possible to determine at least the extent and plan of the imaret and caravansarai. Another building of the külliye that has disappeared is the darüşşifa, or hospital. This was placed symmetrically with the tabhane on the north side of the graveyard; a street-name still recalls its site and bits of its wall may be seen built into the modern houses there.

The türbe of Nakşidil. Opposite the tabhane is the türbe complex built in 1817–18 for the Valide Sultan Nakşidil, wife of Abdül Hamit I and mother of

Mahmut II. Nakşidil's türbe is a very gay one in its baroque-Empire way, forming a pleasant contrast with the austerity of the classical structures of the Conqueror's külliye. At the corner stands the enormous türbe, which has 14 sides; of its two rows of windows the upper ones are oval, a unique and pretty feature. The 14 faces are divided from one another by very slender columns which bear, on top of their capitals at the first cornice level, tall, flame-like acanthus leaves carved almost in the round, giving a fine bravura effect. Nakşidil's türbe is altogether a very original and entertaining building.

The wall stretching along the street opposite the tabhane contains a gate and a grand sebil in the same flamboyant style as the türbe. The gate leads into an attractive courtyard from which you enter Nakşidil's türbe, whose interior decoration is rather elegant and restrained. Diagonally opposite at the far end of the courtyard is another türbe, round and severely plain. In this türbe are interred the Valide Sultan Gülüstü, wife of Abdül Mecit I and mother of Mehmet VI Vahdettin, the last Sultan of the Ottoman Empire, along with other members of the imperial family. Outside, the wall along the street running north ends in a building at the next corner which was once a sibyan mektebi and is now used as a sewing-school. Both the wall and the mektep building, constructed of brick and stone, seem to belong to an older tradition than Nakşidil's türbe, but the recurrence here and there of the flame-like acanthus motif shows that they are part of the same complex.

To Fenari Isa Camii

The street that runs along the east side of the mosque complex is called Aslanhane Sok., the Street of the Lion House, which suggests that the Conqueror may have had a menagerie near his külliye. After crossing the avenue, which is here called Fevzi Paşa Cad., the street takes on the more conventional name of Feyzullah Efendi Sok., after the library at the corner to the left.

At the second intersection after the avenue we turn right on to Sarıgüzel Cad. and continue for two blocks to come on the left to an ancient mosque, **Iskender Paşa Camii**. The mosque is dated by an inscription to 1505, but the identity of the founder is uncertain; he is thought to have been a vezir of Beyazit II who was governor of Bosnia. It is a simple dignified building with a blind dome on pendentives resting on the walls; the three small domes of the porch are supported on ancient columns with rather worn Byzantine capitals. The şerefe of the minaret has an elaborately stalactited corbel, but the curious decoration on top of the minaret probably belongs to an 18C restoration.

After leaving the mosque, we continue along Sarigüzel Cad. for another block and then turn left into Halıcılar Cad. After a walk of c 450m we come to the wide Adnan Menderes Cad., where at the corner to the left there stands the large and handsome Byzantine church of Constantine Lips (Pl. 9,1), known in Turkish as *Fenari Isa Camii** (Pl. 9,1), the Mosque of the Lamp of Jesus.

> This complicated building, the various parts of which were constructed at different dates, consists of two churches, along with a double narthex and a side chapel; its original structure was altered in Ottoman times, when it was converted into a mosque. The first church on the site, the one to the north, was built in 907 by Constantine Lips, a high official in the reigns of Leo VI and Constantine VII Porphyrogenitus. This sanctuary was dedicated

to the Theotokos Panachrantos, the Immaculate Mother of God, and served the monastery that Constantine Lips founded at the same time. The establishment apparently fell into disuse during the Latin Occupation of 1204–61, for soon after the recapture of the city by the Byzantines the monastery was refounded by the Empress Theodora, wife of Michael VIII Palaeologus. At the same time the Empress also added another church to the south, an outer narthex for both churches, and a chapel to the south of her new church dedicated to St. John the Baptist.

The chapel of St. John was designed as a funerary chapel, and several members of the imperial Palaeologus family were interred there during the course of the next two centuries, beginning with the Empress Theodora herself in 1304. Other members of the family buried there include Theodora's sons, Prince Constantine and the Emperor Andronicus II (1282–1328), as well as the Princess Irene of Brunswick, first wife of Andronicus III (1328–41), and the Princess Anna, first wife of John VIII (1428–48). Neither Irene nor Anna lived to become Empress of Byzantium, for they died before their husbands were raised to the throne. Chronicles of the time tell how Anna was buried in the church in the dead of night, in a city terrified by the Black Death.

The church was converted into a mosque in 1496, and at that time the monastery was given over to a community of dervishes. The first head of this dervish tekke was called Isa, which is the Muslim name for Jesus, and the mosque thereafter was known as Fenari Isa Camii. The mosque was abandoned at the beginning of the present century after having been badly damaged in a fire, which utterly destroyed the monastery. The building has since been completely restored by the Byzantine Institute of America, and its structure is now in excellent condition. After the restoration it was rededicated as a mosque, and in recent years it has also been used to house a Kuran school.

Interior. The original north church constructed by Constantine Lips was of the four-column type (the columns were replaced by arches in the Ottoman period), but quite unusually it had five apses, the extra ones to north and south projecting beyond the rest of the building. The northern apse is now demolished, while the southern one is incorporated into the south church. Another unusual, perhaps unique, feature is that there are four little chapels on the roof, grouped around the main dome.

The south church erected by the Empress Theodora was of the ambulatory type; that is, its nave was divided from the aisles by a triple arcade to north, west, and south, with each arcade supported by two columns. (All this was removed in Ottoman times, but the bases of some of the columns still remain and you can see the narrow arches of the arcades above, embedded in the Turkish masonry.) Of its three apses, the northern one was the southern supernumerary apse of the older church. Thus there were in all seven apses, six of which remain and make the eastern façade of the building exceedingly attractive. On the interior walls a certain amount of good sculptured decoration survives in cornices and window frames, especially in the north church.

Yeni Bahçe

Menderes Cad. runs along the ancient course of the Lycus River through a district called Yeni Bahçe, the New Garden. Until recently this was mostly garden land, and a certain number of vegetable gardens still survive, but now the district is rapidly being covered with apartment buildings.

West of the monastery church of Constantine Lips, on the other side of Menderes Cad., there is a large and handsome **medrese**, founded in 1562–63 by Süleyman and dedicated to the memory of his father, Selim I; the architect was Sinan. The 20 cells of the students occupy three sides of the courtyard; on the fourth side stands the large and handsome lecture-hall, which was at some point turned into a mosque. The original entrance, through a small domed porch, is behind the dershane and at an odd angle to it; the wall that encloses this whole side is irregular in a way that is hard to account for. Nevertheless, the building is very attractive, and once inside you do not notice its curious dissymmetry.

Just west of this medrese across a side street there is a small **külliye** consisting of a mektep and a türbe in a walled garden. The entrance to the gaily planted garden is through a gate in the north wall; on the left is the octagonal türbe, that of Şah Huban Kadın, a daughter of Selim I, who died in 1572. While there is nothing remarkable about the türbe the mektep is a grand one. It is double: that is, it consists of two spacious square rooms, each covered by a dome and containing an elegant ocak, or fireplace. The wooden roof and column of the porch are modern, part of a recent restoration. Both the mektep and the türbe are works of Sinan, and they are dated to the year of Şah Huban's death. The mektep now serves as an out-patient clinic for mental illnesses.

Recrossing Menderes Cad., we take the street just opposite, Akdeniz Cad.,and walk uphill as far as the fourth turning on the left, Hüsrev Paşa Sok. One block down this street, at the far corner to the left, is a handsome and elaborate türbe. This is the **tomb of Hüsrev Paşa** (Pl. 5,7), built by Sinan and dated by an inscription to 1545–46.

> Hüsrev Paşa was a grandson of Beyazit II and had been one of the leading generals in the great Ottoman victory of Mohacs in 1526, when the fate of Hungary was decided in less than two hours. After that victory Hüsrev Paşa governed Bosnia for a decade with great pomp and luxury, but also with severe justice. Later he became governor of Syria, and in 1536–37 he commissioned Sinan to build a mosque for him in Aleppo; this is the earliest dated building by the great architect and it is still in existence. While governor of Rumelia in 1544 Hüsrev Paşa fell into disgrace through his complicity in a plot against the Grand Vezir Süleyman Paşa. Despairing because of his fall from power, he took his own life soon afterwards by literally starving himself to death, one of the very rare incidents of suicide among the Ottomans.

The türbe of Hüsrev Paşa is octagonal in form. The eight faces are separated from one another by slender columns that run up to the first cornice, which is elaborately carved with stalactites; the dome is set back a short distance and has another cornice of its own, also carved. At the moment the türbe is made more picturesque by the bushes that grow out of the cornice, but they are destroying the fabric of the structure, and a careful restoration is in order.

Two blocks north on the side street that passes the türbe we come on our right to **Bali Paşa Camii**. An inscription over the portal records that the mosque was built in 1504 by Huma Hatun, daughter of Beyazit II, in memory of her late husband, Bali Paşa, who had died in 1495. Since this mosque appears in the 'Tezkere', the listing of Sinan's works, it appears that Sinan must have built Bali Paşa Camii some time later, though whether on its old plan or a new one it is impossible to say.

The plan of the mosque is simple and to a certain extent resembles that of Iskender Paşa Camii, visited earlier on this walk. The chief difference between these two mosques is that in Bali Paşa Camii the dome arches to north, west, and south are very deep, almost barrel vaults; thus room is left, on the north and south, for shallow bays with galleries above. The mosque was severely damaged in the earthquake of 1894 and again in the fire of 1917; it was partially restored in 1935 and more thoroughly in recent years.

After leaving the mosque we return to Hüsrev Paşa Sok. and continue on in the same direction. We then take the second turning on the left, Akşemsettin Cad., and walk one block downhill. There, at the corner to the left, we come to **Mimar Sinan Camii**, a little mosque that Sinan himself endowed and built in 1573. The original mosque itself was rather irregular, consisting of two rectangular rooms with a wooden roof. The present mosque is a modern structure, the only original element remaining being the minaret. This is of a very rare type, perhaps the only one of its kind that Sinan ever built. It is octagonal and without a şerefe; instead, at the top, a decorated window in each of the eight faces allowed the müezzin to give the call to prayer, a function now performed by a tape-recorder and microphones.

We now walk back uphill along Akşemsettin Cad. for about 250m to a square dominated to the left by a fine classical mosque. This is **Mesih Paşa Camii**, built by an unknown architect in 1585. (The mosque is popularly attributed to Sinan, but without any evidence.) The founder was the eunuch Mesih Mehmet Paşa, infamous for his cruelty as Governor of Egypt, who became Grand Vezir for a short time at the age of 90 in the reign of Murat III. The courtyard of the mosque is attractive but rather sombre. It consists of the usual domed porticoes under which, rather unusually, are the ablution fountains; this is because the usual place of the şadırvan in the centre of the courtyard has been taken up by the picturesque open türbe of the founder.

The mosque is preceded by a double porch, but the wooden roof of the second porch has disappeared, leaving nothing for the arcades to support; the inner porch has the usual five bays. In plan the building is an octagon inscribed in a square with semidomes as squinches in the diagonals; to north and south are galleries. But the odd feature is that whereas in most mosques of this form aisles are under the galleries here they are turned into porches. That is, where one would expect an arcade of columns, one finds a wall with windows opening onto an exterior gallery which, in turn, opens to the outside by enormous arches, now glazed in. The mihrab and mimber are very fine works in marble, as are the grilles above the windows. Tiles of the best period complete the decoration of this interesting building.

The south side of the mosque opens onto a road that winds uphill, soon leading you to a mosque of a very different style indeed. This is **Hirka-i Şerif Camii**, the Mosque of the Holy Mantle, built in 1851 by Sultan Abdül Mecit I to house the second of the two mantles of the Prophet that are among Mohammed's chief relics in Istanbul. (The other is in its own treasury in Topkapı Sarayı; see p 56.) The mosque is in the purest Empire style and just misses being a great success, as do most buildings in that style; nevertheless it is very entertaining. A monumental gateway leads to a spacious paved courtyard, at the corners of which are the two tall minarets; these are extremely slender and have balconies in the form of Corinthian capitals.

The façade is a little forbidding, more like a palace than a mosque, but the interior is very gay; it is in the form of an octagon with an outside gallery. The walls and dome, of a greenish brown, are covered with plaster mouldings of garlands and vines in buff, done with a certain bravura but also with elegance. The mihrab, mimber, and Kuran kursu, elaborately carved, are of a deep purple conglomerate marble flecked with grey, green, blue, black and yellow, all highly polished. Part of the decoration consists of elegant inscriptions by the famous calligrapher, Mustafa İzzet Efendi; others are by Sultan Abdül Mecit I, who was himself an able calligrapher. This is a building which should not be missed by anyone who delights in the follies and oddities of architecture as long as they have a certain verve and charm.

Hürrem Çavuş Camii

Hirka-i Şerif Camii is built on a high terrace, partly artificial, to the south of which a long staircase leads to a lower monumental gateway opening on to the street below, Keçiciler Cad., the Avenue of the Goatherders. About 500m to the right down this street we find on the left a small mosque that is of little interest save that its architect was Sinan. According to an inscription, the mosque was founded in 1560 by one Hürrem Çavuş, who was a messenger in Topkapı Sarayı. The mosque is of the rectangular type with wooden roof and porch. Other inscriptions record restorations to the mosque in 1844 and 1901. A much more recent restoration has destroyed whatever charm the mosque might once have possessed.

12 · The Fifth and Sixth Hills

This Route leads from the Fatih Camii on a circuit around the Fifth and Sixth Hills of the old city. The walk begins at the west side of the outer courtyard of the mosque, where Darüşşafaka Cad. leads off to the north, passing through the lively market quarter of Çarşamba.

Çarşamba, which in Turkish means Wednesday, is named after the picturesque street market that throngs its streets on that day each week, as it has for centuries past. This is a travelling market that sets up its stalls and barrows in various parts of the city on different days; thus there are neighbourhoods in Istanbul named after all the days of the week except Saturday and Sunday, the Muslim and Christian days of rest.

About 500m beyond Fatih Camii (Pl. 5,8) Darüşşafaka Cad. intersects Yavuz Selim Cad.; we turn left here and 150m farther along we turn right at the first through street. A short way along this street on the left is a mosque known as **Kumrulu Mescit**, the Little Mosque of the Turtle-Dove. The mosque takes its name from a fragment of Byzantine sculpture used in the adjoining çeşme, in which a relief represents two turtle-doves drinking from the Fountain of Life. This mosque is of interest principally because its founder and builder was Atik Sinan, the architect of the original Mosque of the Conqueror. Atik Sinan's tombstone is to be seen in the mosque garden, with an inscription recording that he was executed by the Conqueror in 1471; the mosque, therefore, is dated prior to that year.

Continuing along the same street, we soon see on the left the beautiful *mosque of Nişancı Mehmet Paşa Camii (Pl. 5,5).

> This mosque is popularly ascribed to Sinan, but it does not appear in the best texts of the 'Tezkere', the list of his works; therefore it is probably not by him. The mosque was built between 1584 and 1588 for Mehmet Paşa, who was Keeper of the Seal (in Turkish, Nişancı) in the reign of Murat III.

Exterior. Even from a distance the elegance of line and the masterly arrangement of the upper structure of the mosque can be seen: the great dome surrounded by the eight little weight-turrets (the continuation of the columns that support the dome arches), the eight semidomes of two sizes, and the minaret unusually close to the dome base: an excellently proportioned distribution of curves and verticals. You enter through a very charming courtyard, where the arches are of the ogive type; under the porch of five bays an inscription with the imperial monogram of Mustafa III records a restoration in 1766, presumably after the very severe earthquake of that year.

Interior. The plan of the mosque is an interesting variation of the octagon inscribed in a square. Eight partly engaged columns support the dome arches; in the axes there are four semidomes, while in the diagonals four smaller semidomes serve as squinches instead of pendentives. The eastern semidome covers a projecting apse for the mihrab, while those to north and south also cover projections from the square. The western corners of the cross so formed are filled with small independent chambers; above on three sides there are galleries. The whole arrangement is original and masterly; and there are interesting details.

In the corners of the east wall there are two charming little platforms, which can be reached by staircases built into the thickness of the wall from the recesses. In the voussoirs and balustrades of these platforms, in the window frames, and elsewhere throughout the mosque, an interesting conglomerate marble of pale violet and grey is used. For the columns that support both platforms and galleries there is another conglomerate marble of tawny brown flecked with yellow, grey, black and green. The arches of the galleries, like those of the courtyard, are of the ogive type. As a whole, the mosque is a masterpiece; it is as if the unknown architect, in the extreme old age of Sinan, had decided to play variations on themes invented by Sinan himself and to show that he could do them as well as the Master. In the little graveyard behind the mosque is the small and unpretentious türbe of Nişancı Mehmet Paşa.

Leaving the mosque and continuing in the same direction, we soon come to a small square called Üç Baş Meydanı, literally the Square of the Three Heads. The square takes its name from **Üç Baş Mescidı**, the tiny mosque to the right, an early and minor work of the great Sinan.

Evliya Çelebi writes that the mosque received this odd name 'because it was built by a barber who shaved three heads for a single copper coin, and, not-withstanding, grew so rich that he was enabled to build this mosque, which is small but particularly sanctified'. A more prosaic explanation is given in the 'Hadika', the comprehensive description of the mosques of Istanbul written in 1780; there it is recorded that the founder of this mosque, Nurettin Hamza ben Atallah, came from a village in Anatolia called Üç Baş. An inscription over the gate gives the date of foundation as 1530–31. This is the earliest building that can definitely be ascribed to Sinan, though all that remains of the original mosque are the mineret and the inscribed portal.

Opposite the mosque there is a ruined medrese founded in 1575 by a certain Halil Efendi. In the centre of the square there is an ancient **çeşme**, with a beau-tifully written inscription recording that it was founded in 1681 by a man called Mustafa Ağa.

Continuing on in the same direction, we take the next turning on the left to come to a little mosque called **Zincirli Kuyu Camii**. This was built in about 1500 by Atik Ali Paşa, Grand Vezir of Beyazit II, whose larger and better-known mosque stands next to Constantine's Column. Zincirli Kuyu Camii is a small rectangular building of brick and stone, covered by six equal domes in two rows of three supported by two massive rectangular pillars; its original porch of three bays has disappeared, and the present porch is a poor reconstruction.

The mosque is interesting as being a tiny example of the so-called Ulu Cami type borrowed from Selçuk architecture, which was fairly common during the period when the Ottoman capital was still in Bursa. The type consists of a square or rectangular space covered by a multiplicity of equal domes supported by pillars or columns; it can be very large and impressive, as in the Ulu Cami of Bursa with its 20 domes. On the very small scale of Zincirli Kuyu Camii it is rather heavy and oppressive.

Opposite the mosque there is a small late baroque **türbe** dated by an inscrip-tion to 1825. Here is buried the famous calligrapher Hattat Rakım Efendi who designed the beautiful inscriptions on the türbe and sebil of the Valide Sultan Nakşidil (*see* Fatih Camii, see p 154).

Beyond the türbe on the main street there is an attractive **medrese** of the clas-sical period, which has recently been restored and converted into a children's clinic. This medrese, also called Zincirli Kuyu (the name of the quarter), was founded by Semiz (the Fat) Ali Paşa, Grand Vezir in the reign of Süleyman the Magnificent. Ali Paşa was born of a Christian family in Dalmatia, and after having been taken up in the devşirme he was educated in the Palace School in Tozpkapı Sarayı. He rose rapidly in the Ottoman hierarchy, becoming in turn Ağa of the Janissaries, governor of Rumelia, Second Vezir, and finally Grand Vezir. Since he died in office in 1564, the medrese must have been built before that time. It is a work of Sinan, but presents no special features except the two symmetrical entrances on either side of the dershane.

About 100m past the medrese along the main avenue, Fevzi Paşa Cad., is a huge open cistern now used as a **football stadium**. This is one of the three Roman reservoirs in the city; its attribution was long in doubt but it has been identified with great probability as the reservoir constructed c 421 by Aetios, Prefect of Constantinople in the reign of Theodosius II. Huge as it is, it is yet the smallest of the three Roman cisterns that still survive in the city, measuring 224m by 85m; its original depth was probably about 15m. Like the others, it was already dry in later Byzantine times and was used as a kitchen garden, but now it has been converted into a stadium.

We descend the flight of steps at the southeast end of the stadium and continue ahead on Kelebek Sok. At the end of the street we turn left on Kurtağa Çeşme Cad., after which we take the third turning on the right on to Dolmuş Kuyu Sok., which descends steeply into the valley below. At the end of the street we turn right on Draman Cad., which after about 50m brings us on our right to a Byzantine building now known as **Kefevi Camii**, formerly called Kefeli Camii.

The building is in fairly good condition and is still in use as a mosque. It is a long narrow structure with two rows of windows and a wooden roof; the entrance is now in the middle of the west wall. The identification of this building is uncertain; it may have belonged to the Monastery of the Prodromos (St. John the Baptist) in Petra, which is known to have been located in this area; but the building here was probably a refectory, not a church, since it has only one apse and is oriented north instead of east. It has been dated variously from the 9C to the 12C.

A short way farther along Draman Cad. we turn left into the yard of a ramshackle group of auto repair shops. At the back of the yard a gate leads into the yard of a tyre repair shop, where we see the fragmentary apse of a tiny Byzantine building. This is known as **Boğdan Saray**, the Moldavian Palace, because from the 16C to the 18C it served as a private chapel attached to the palace of the Hospodars of Moldavia. It is thought to have been a funerary chapel dedicated to St. Nicholas, and it appears to date from the 12C–13C. At the beginning of the present century it had an upper storey with a dome, but the owner of the property used it as a quarry for building material and now all that remains is part of the apse, which is almost buried under the tyres in the yard.

About 200m along Draman Cad. past Kefevi Camii we see on the right a small mosque on a high terrace reached by a double staircase. This is **Draman Camii**, a minor work of Sinan.

> Inscriptions show that the külliye was founded in 1541 by Yunus Bey, the famous interpreter (in Turkish, drağman, or dragoman) of Süleyman the Magnificent. According to Bassano da Zara, Venetian ambassador to the Sublime Porte, Yunus Bey was a Greek from Modon and 'possessed the Turkish, Greek, and Italian languages to perfection'. In collaboration with Alviso Gritti, bastard son of the Doge of Venice, he wrote in the Venetian dialect a brief but very important account of the organisation of the Ottoman government. He also seems to have served on at least two occasions as the representative of the Grand Vezir Ibrahim Paşa to the Venetian Republic.

The mosque. Unfortunately, the mosque has been badly restored and has lost any interest it might have had. It was of the rectangular type, covered by a wooden roof and preceded by a wooden porch, now hideously rebuilt in concrete. Originally the mosque was the centre of a small complex consisting of a medrese and a mektep, both presumably by Sinan. The medrese has perished but the mektep remains, though in ruins; it is the fine domed building to the northeast of the mosque. Although the mosque itself is disappointing, the high terrace, the mektep, and the wild garden and graveyard are attractive.

**Fethiye Camii

We continue in the same direction along the main avenue, whose name here changes to Fethiye Cad. About 200m past Draman Camii, just before the main avenue makes a sharp turn to the right, a short street named Fethiyekapısı Sok. leads off to the left. A few steps further we come to Fethiye Camii (Pl. 5,5), the former church of the Theotokos Pammakaristos, the Joyous Mother of God.

■ **Admission**. Permission to visit the church must be obtained from the Haghia Sophia Museum.

This complicated building consists of a central bay with a narthex; a small chapel, or pareeclesion, on the south; and a curious perambulatory forming a side aisle on the north; with an outer narthex on the west; and two bays of an aisle on the south in front of the pareeclesion. Each of these three sections was radically altered when the building was converted into a mosque. The work of the Byzantine Institute of America has at last cleared up many of the puzzles arising from the various periods of construction and transformation. It now appears that the main church was built in the 12C by an otherwise unknown John Comnenus and his wife Anna Doukaina, whose names indicate that they were related to the royal family. In form this church was of the ambulatory type, a triple arcade in the north, west, and south dividing the central domed area from the ambulatory; at the east end there were the usual three apses, and at the west a single narthex.

Toward the end of the 13C the church was reconstructed by a prominent general named Michael Doukas Glabas Tarchaniotes. Then, in about 1310, a pareeclesion was added on the south side of the church by Michael's widow, Maria Doukaina Comnena Palaeologina Blachena, as a funerary chapel for her husband. This chapel was of the four-column type and was preceded by a two-storeyed narthex covered by a tiny dome. In the second half of the 14C the north, west, and south sides were surrounded by a perambulatory, which ran into and partly obliterated the south chapel.

The church remained in the hands of the Greeks after the Conquest, and in 1456 it was made the site of the Greek Orthodox Patriarchate after the Patriarch Gennadius abandoned the Church of the Holy Apostles. It was in the pareeclesion of the Pammakaristos that Fatih came to discuss questions on religion and politics with Gennadius. The Pammakaristos continued as the site of the Patriarchate until 1586; five years later Murat III converted it into a mosque. He then called it Fethiye Camii, the Mosque of Victory, to commemorate his conquest of Georgia and Azerbaijan.

When the building was converted into a mosque the main concern seems to have been increasing the available space. Most of the interior walls were demolished, including the arches of the ambulatory; the three apses were replaced by the present domed triangular projection; and the side chapel was made part of the mosque by removing the wall and suppressing the two

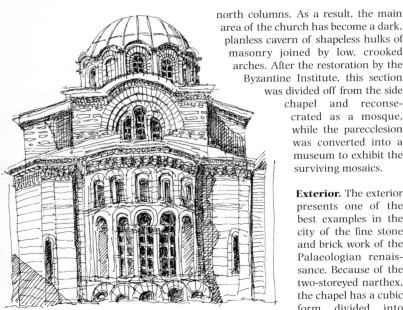

Side chapel of Fethiye Camii

north columns. As a result, the main area of the church has become a dark, planless cavern of shapeless hulks of masonry joined by low, crooked arches. After the restoration by the Byzantine Institute, this section was divided off from the side chapel and reconsecrated as a mosque, while the parecclesion was converted into a museum to exhibit the surviving mosaics.

Exterior. The exterior presents one of the best examples in the city of the fine stone and brick work of the Palaeologian renaissance. Because of the two-storeyed narthex, the chapel has a cubic form divided into three storeys of blind arcades; with a succession of wide and narrow arches, slender niches, and concave roundels.

Interior. The side chapel has been most beautifully restored by the Byzantine Institute, its missing columns replaced, and its surviving mosaics uncovered and cleaned. (In the description that follows, the number in parenthesis before the name of a mosaic is keyed to the Plan.)

The mosaics in the dome were never concealed but now they once again gleam with their former brilliance. In the crown of the dome is (**1**) Christ Pantocrator, surrounded by twelve Prophets: (**2**) Moses; (**3**) Jeremiah; (**4**) Zephaniah; (**5**) Micah; (**6**) Joel; (**7**) Zachariah; (**8**) Obadiah; (**9**) Habakkuk; (**10**) Jonah; (**11**) Malachi; (**12**) Ezekiel; (**13**) Isaiah. In the conch of the apse is (**14**) Christ Hyperagathos, the All-Loving; on the left wall of the bema is (**15**) The Virgin; on the right wall is (**16**) St. John the Baptist; and in the domical vault above there are depicted the four archangels: (**17**) Michael; (**18**) Raphael; (**19**) Gabriel; (**20**) Uriel. In the conch of the side apse to the left is (**34**) St. James, Cousin of Christ; to the left (**35**) St. Clement (?); to the right (**36**) St. Metrophanes of Constantinople. In the conch of the side aisle to the right is (**22**) St. Gregory the Theologian; to the left (**23**) St. Cyril; to the right (**24**) St. Athanasius.

On the soffit of the arch between the northeast pier and the pilaster to its east: (to the east) (**25**) St. Gregory the Miracle-Worker; (to the west) (**26**) St. Gregory of Agrigentum. On the soffit of the arch between the northeast pier and the pilaster to its south: (to the north) (**27**) St. Antipas; (to the south) (**28**) St.

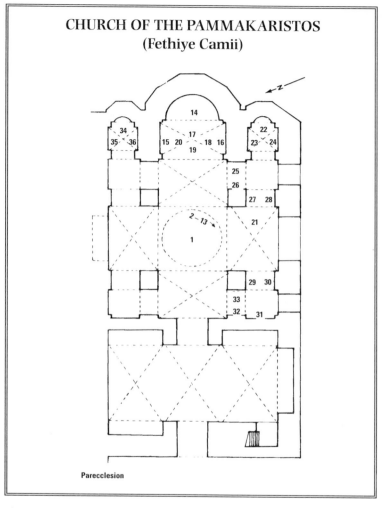

CHURCH OF THE PAMMAKARISTOS
(Fethiye Camii)

Parecclesion

Blasius. The only surviving scene mosaic is on the east section of the domical vault in the south aisle; this depicts (**21**) The Baptism of Christ. On the soffit of the arch between the southeast pier and the pilaster to its south: (to the north) (**29**) St. Sabas; (to the south) (**30**) St. John Climacus. On the soffit of the arch between the southeast pier and the pilaster to its west: (to the west) (**32**) St. Chariton; (to the east) (**33**) St. Arsenius. At the west end of the south aisle: (**31**) St. Euthemius.

Between the marble facing on the lower part of the south wall and the mosaics on the upper part there is a long inscription in gold letters on a blue ground. This is a threnody written by the Byzantine poet Philes to commemorate the love which Maria, the founder of the funerary chapel, bore for her departed husband Michael Tarchaniotes.

The mosaics in the Pammakaristos are dated to the early 14C, and they are thus contemporary with those at Kariye Camii. Though the mosaics here are far fewer in number and less various than those at Kariye Camii, they are, nevertheless, an extremely precious addition to our knowledge of the art of the last Byzantine renaissance.

We return to the main avenue, which now changes its name to **Manyaszade Cad.**, we follow it as it bends to the right and then take the first turning on the right. A short distance ahead is a tiny Byzantine church in the angle between two streets; this is the former church of St. John in Trullo, known locally as **Ahmet Paşa Mescidi** (Pl. 5,5).

Nothing whatever is known of the history of this church in Byzantine times. In 1456, when Gennadius transferred the Patriarchate to the Pammakaristos, he turned out the few nuns who still remained there and gave them this church instead. There were nuns in residence here until about 1586, when the church was converted into a mosque by Hirami Ahmet Paşa, from whom it takes its Turkish name.

The church. This little building is a characteristic example of the four-column type of church with a narthex and three semicircular apses, evidently of the 11C–12C. Until a few years ago it was ruined and dilapidated, but still showed signs of frescoes under its faded and blotched whitewash. Recently it underwent a partial and badly botched restoration, which utterly destroyed whatever remained of the underlying frescoes. The original four columns, long since purloined, were replaced with poor columns and awkward capitals, and the restored brickwork is also wrong.

Returning to the main avenue, we take the first street to the right. At the end of the block to the left we see a small mosque in its walled garden; this is **Mehmet Ağa Camii**, part of a small külliye that includes the mosque, a türbe, and a hamam.

Though of modest dimensions, this is a pretty mosque and interesting because it is one of the relatively few that can be confidently attributed to Davut Ağa, Sinan's colleague and his successor as Chief Architect to the Sultan. Over one of the gates to the courtyard there is an inscription naming Davut Ağa as architect and giving the date 1585, at which time Sinan was still alive. The founder, Mehmet Ağa, was Chief of the Black Eunuchs in the reign of Murat III.

In plan the mosque is of the simplest type: a square room covered by a dome, with a projecting apse for the mihrab and an entrance porch with five bays. But unlike most mosques of this simple type, the dome does not rest directly on the walls but on arches supported by pillars and columns engaged in the walls; instead of pendentives there are four semidomes in the diagonals. Thus the effect is that of an inscribed octagon, as in several of Sinan's mosques, but in this case without side aisles. The effect is unusual but not unattractive. The interior is adorned with faience inscriptions and other tile panels of the best Iznik period; but the painted decoration is tasteless; fortunately it is growing dim with damp. Mehmet Ağa's türbe is in the garden to the left; it is a rather large square building of little interest.

Just to the south outside the precincts stands a handsome **double bath**; this is part of Mehmet Ağa's külliye and presumably was also built by Davut Ağa. In the men's bath there is a large camekan whose dome is supported on squinches in the form of conches, and a cruciform hararet with cubicles in the corners of the cross. However, the lower arm of the cross has been cut off and turned into a small soğukluk which leads through the right-hand cubicle into the hararet. In the cubicles there are very small private washrooms separated by low marble partitions, a unique disposition. As far as one can judge from the outside, the women's section seems to be a duplicate of the men's.

Returning once again to the main avenue, we continue along in the same direction and take the next left. Halfway down the block on the right side there is a handsome old Ottoman building standing in an extensive and very pretty walled garden. This is the ***library of Murat Molla** (Pl. 5,5), founded in 1775 by a distinguished judge and scholar. The library is a large square building of brick and stone built on Byzantine substructures, fragments of which may be seen in the garden. The central area of the main reading-room is covered by a dome supported by four columns with re-used Byzantine capitals; the corners of the room also have domes with barrel-vaults over them. It is a very typical and very attractive example of an 18C Ottoman library, to be compared with those of Ragıp Paşa and Atif Efendi, seen on previous tours; like these, it is constantly in use.

Head back to Manyasizade Cad., and at the next corner on the left we come to a mosque known as **Ismail Efendi Camii** (Pl. 5,5). This is a quaint and entertaining example of a building in a transitional style between the classical and baroque, founded in 1724 by the Şeyh-ül Islam Ismail Efendi. The vaulted substructure contains shops, with the mosque standing on a terrace above them; according to the 'Hadika', this was done in order to have the structure resemble the sacred Kaaba at Mecca. Above the main entrance to the courtyard there is a very characteristic sibyan mektebi of one room. To the right a long double staircase leads up to the mosque: the porch has been tastelessly reconstructed in detail but the general effect is pleasing except for the glazed-in portico. On the interior there is a very pretty—perhaps unique—triple arcade in two storeys of superposed columns repeated on the south, west, and north sides and supporting galleries, giving the dome an unusually high appearance.

At the back of the courtyard there is a small dar-ül hadis, or school of tradition. It has been greatly altered and walled-in, so that it has little resemblance to the original structure. Nevertheless, it is once again being used for something like its original purpose, for it now houses a Kuran kursu, a school for reading the Kuran. All-in-all this little külliye is quite charming, with its warm polychrome of brick and stone masonry; it was, on the whole, fairly well restored from near ruin in 1952.

Returning once again to Manyasizade Cad., we walk one block and turn left onto Yavuz Selim Cad. There we see the imperial mosque of Sultan Selim I standing in its walled garden at the far end of an enormous Roman reservoir. The reservoir has been identified as the ***Cistern of Aspar** (Pl. 5,6), constructed by a Gothic general put to death in 471 by the Emperor Leo I. This is the second largest of the three Roman cisterns in the city, exceeded in size only by the Mocius Cistern on the Seventh Hill; it is square, 152m on a side, and was originally 10m deep. Until recently you could still see its original construction in courses of stone and brick, with shallow arches on its interior surface. Up until the late 1970s the cistern was the site of an exceedingly picturesque village, whose house-tops and trees barely reached the level of the surrounding streets. But then all of the village, except for the mosque, was demolished to make way for a parking area, destroying yet another of Istanbul's ancient beauty-spots.

**The mosque of Selim I

The cistern is an appropriately grand foreground for the mosque of Selim I (Pl. 5,6), which stands on a high terrace overlooking the Golden Horn.

> The mosque was finished in 1522 under Süleyman the Magnificent, but it may have been begun two or three years earlier by Selim himself, as the Arabic inscription over the entrance portal would seem to imply. Although the mosque is very often ascribed to Sinan, even by otherwise reliable authorities, it is certainly not so: it is too early, and is not listed in the 'Tezkere.' Unfortunately, the identity of the actual architect has not been established.

Exterior. The mosque, with its great shallow dome and cluster of little domes on either side, is impressive and worthy of the site. The courtyard is one of the most charming and vivid in the city, with its columns of various marbles and granites, the polychrome voussoirs of the arches, the very beautiful tiles of the earliest Iznik period in the lunettes above the windows—turquoise, deep blue, and yellow—and the pretty şadırvan surrounded by tapering cypress trees.

Interior. The plan of the mosque is quite simple: a square room, 24.5m on a side, covered by a shallow dome 32.5m in height under the crown, with the cornice resting on the outer walls through smooth pendentives. The dome, like that of Haghia Sophia, but unlike that of most Ottoman mosques, is significantly less than a hemisphere. This gives a very spacious and grand effect, recalling to a certain extent the beautiful shallow dome of the Roman Pantheon. The room itself is vast and empty, but saved from dullness by its perfect proportions and by the exquisite colour of the Iznik tiles in the lunettes of the windows. The mosque furniture, though sparse, is quite fine, particularly the mihrab, mimber, and sultan's loge.

The border of the ceiling under the loge is a quite exceptionally beautiful example of the painted and gilded woodwork of the early 16C; notice the deep, rich colours and the varieties of floral and leaf motifs in the five separate borders, like an Oriental rug, only here picked out in gold. To north and south of the great central room of the mosque are annexes consisting of a domed cruciform passage giving access to four small domed rooms. These, as in other early mosques elsewhere in the city, served as hospices for travelling dervishes.

The türbes. In the garden behind the mosque is the grand **türbe of Selim I**, externally octagonal. In the porch on either side of the door are two beautiful panels of tilework, presumably from Iznik but unique in colour and design. The interior has unfortunately lost its original decoration, but it is still impressive in its solitude, with the huge catafalque of the Sultan standing alone in the centre of the tomb, covered with a sheet of embroidered velvet and with Selim's enormous turban at its head.

Facing Selim's türbe is another in which four children of Süleyman the Magnificent are buried. This, too, has a pretty and unique feature: the circular drum of the dome, set back a little from the octagon of the building itself, is adorned with a long inscription carved in the stonework. The porch also has panels of faience, hexagonal tiles with stylised floral motifs set separately on the stone. This türbe was built in 1556, probably by Sinan.

Standing in the garden near Selim's türbe is that of **Sultan Abdül Mecit I**, built some time before his death in 1861; for a building of this late date it is simple and has good lines. Abdül Mecit chose this spot for his türbe because of his admiration for his great warrior-ancestor, who in his time was called Selim the Grim.

The mosque of Selim I was formerly surrounded by the usual buildings of a külliye, which in this case included a public kitchen, a medrese, and a primary school. Of these only the last remains, a little domed building at the southwest corner of the outer courtyard.

After leaving the mosque we turn left and then right at the next corner into Yavuz Selim Cad., the street that borders the Cistern of Aspar to the south. As we approach the far end of the cistern we make a short detour left into Ali Naki Sok., where we stop at the second building from the corner on the right, an ancient structure with barred windows. If you peer through the windows it will be found that this is a superb **Roman basement**, with a colonnade of marble columns consisting of four rows of seven monoliths topped with Corinthian capitals and imposts. The date and identity of this structure are uncertain, although there is some reason to believe that it was built by the Empress Pulcheria, sister of Theodosius II (408–50) and wife of the Emperor Marcian (450–57).

We now continue along Yavuz Selim Cad. as far as Darüşşafaka Cad., which leads back to the outer courtyard of Fatih Camii at the end of our itinerary.

13 · **Kariye Camii

From Fatih Camii we take Fevzi Paşa Cad. out almost as far as the Edirne Gate. We turn right there on to Hoca Çakır Cad., the street that runs just inside the Theodosian walls, and then take the third right into Nester Sok., which leads directly to Kariye Camii.

■ **Admission**. Kariye Camii is open 09.30–16.30; closed Tue.

■ (Note: the present description of Kariye Camii is based almost entirely on the great publications by Paul A. Underwood, in particular the following: Paul A.

Kariye Camii (Pl. 5,3), the former church of St. Saviour in Chora, is, after Haghia Sophia, the most interesting Byzantine church in the city. This is not due to the building itself, pretty as it is, but because of the superb mosaics and frescoes that it contains, a magnificent heritage of Byzantine art that has no equal in the world.

The name of the church 'in Chora' means 'in the country', because the original church and monastery on this site were outside the walls of Constantine. Later, when it was included within the Theodosian walls the name remained (compare St. Martin in the Fields, London) but was given a symbolic sense: Christ as the 'country' or 'land' of the Living, and the Blessed Virgin as the 'dwelling-place' of the Uncontainable, as they are referred to in inscriptions on mosaics in the church.

No trace remains of the original ancient church, nor is anything certain known about its origin. The present building in its first form dates only from the late 11C. This church was founded by Maria Doukaina, mother-in-law of Alexius I Comnenus, between the years 1077 and 1081; it was probably of the four-column type so popular at that time. However, this church did not last long in its original form; the foundations at the east end appear to have slipped, causing the apses to fall in, and so the opportunity was taken to remodel the building. At the east the present wide central apse with its deep barrel-vault was erected; the walls of the nave were retained, but the piers were added in the corners as supports for the arches of a much larger dome. A narrow side passage was added to the south, traces of which remain in the passages and gallery between the nave and the present parecclesion, which dates from a still later reconstruction. This elaborate remodelling was apparently carried out early in the 12C by Maria Doukaina's grandson, the Sebastocrator Isaac Comnenus, third son of Alexius I Comnenus.

A third period of building activity some two centuries later created the present church. At this time the nave area was left essentially unchanged except for redecoration. But the inner narthex was rebuilt, the outer narthex and the parecclesion were added, the small side apses reconstructed and the northern passage with its gallery was built in its present form. In addition to all these structural alterations, the church was completely redecorated, and the interior was adorned with the superb marble revetment, mosaics and frescoes that we see today. All of this rebuilding and decoration was carried out in the period 1315–21.

The man responsible for all of this was Theodore Metochites, who served as both Prime Minister and First Lord of the Treasury during the reign of Andronicus II Palaeologus. Metochites was one of the greatest men of the age: a diplomat and high government official, theologian, philosopher, astronomer, poet and patron of the arts, a leader in the artistic and intellectual renaissance of the late Byzantine era. The peak of his career came in

1321, when he was appointed as Grand Logothete, the highest-ranking official in the Byzantine Empire, an honour which was accorded him just weeks after he presided at the opening of the newly restored and redecorated church of St. Saviour in Chora. But his career ended just seven years later, when Andronicus III usurped the throne; Metochites was stripped of his power and possessions and sent into exile, along with most other officials of the old regime. He was allowed to return to the capital in 1330, on condition that he retire as a monk in the monastery of the Chora, where he died on 13 March 1332. Toward the end of his life Metochites wrote of his hope that the church of St. Saviour in Chora would secure for him 'a glorious memory among posterity till the end of the world'.

At the time of the last siege the Chora's proximity to the Theodosian walls placed it virtually in the front line. At that time the Chora was used to house the famous icon of the Virgin Hodegetria, the Guide, or Teacher. This icon, which according to tradition was painted by St. Luke, was the legendary protectress of the city, and during times of siege it was carried in procession along the Theodosian walls. When the Turks broke through the walls on the morning of 29 May 1453 the Chora was pillaged and the icon of the Hodegetria disappeared, never to be seen again.

Early in the 16C the Chora was converted into a mosque by the eunuch Atik Ali Pasa, Grand Vezir in the reign of Beyazit II. The mosaics and frescoes were never wholly obliterated, though in the course of time most were obscured by plaster, paint and dirt, and many were shaken down by earthquakes. The church and its extraordinary works of art were unknown to the scholarly world until 1860, when the Greek architect Pelopidas Kouppas brought it to the attention of Byzantinists in the West. In 1948 the Byzantine Institute of America, under the direction of Paul A. Underwood, began a project to uncover the surviving mosaics and frescoes and to restore them and the fabric of the church to their original condition. After a series of eleven annual campaigns the project was carried through to completion in 1958, and today the church of St. Saviour in Chora stands as one of the greatest monuments of Byzantine art in existence.

Exterior. The church is preceded by an exonarthex and a narthex, with the parecclesion to the right and the two-storeyed northern passageway to the left. The archways in the bays of the exonarthex, where the main entrance is located, were walled up in Ottoman times, when the minaret was erected at the southwest corner of the building. The central area of the church is covered on a dome carried on a high drum. There are two smaller domes carried on lower drums above the first and fourth (numbering from left to right) bays of the narthex, as well as one above the westernmost bay of the parecclesion, with still smaller domes above the prothesis and diaconicon, the apsidal chambers that flank the main apse to north and south, respectively. (These latter domes are visible only from the rear of the church, where you can also see the large buttress supporting the apse and the earlier substructures of the building.)

The narthexes. The exonarthex and narthex were entirely new constructions of Metochites. In the vertical walls and lunettes the masonry consists of bands of four courses of brickwork alternating with four courses of roughly dressed stone. The masonry in the arches and vaults is entirely of brick. The walls of both narthexes were faced with decorative slabs of Proconnesian marble and verd antique, but most of this revetment was stripped from the exonarthex in Ottoman times. Above the cornice in both narthexes all surfaces were covered with mosaics, including the arches, vaults and lunettes. The floor of the inner narthex, like that of the nave, is paved in marble, but that of the exonarthex also vanished in Ottoman times and has been replaced by a modern pavement.

The outer narthex extends across the entire width of the church in six bays, with a seventh bay extending at right angles to the east, so as to go around the south end of the inner narthex and open into the west end of the parecclesion. The third bay in the exonarthex, through which you pass into the narthex and then the nave, is square in plan and covered with a domical vault, as are the sixth and seventh bays, the two largest. The two pairs of bays on either side of the entryway are oblong in shape; thus to cover them with domical vaults it was necessary to reduce them to squares by constructing arches against the east and west walls, an expedient that was also necessary in the second and third bays of the inner narthex.

In order to provide illumination for the inner narthex, the two end bays, the first and fourth, were covered by domes carried on high drums, the sides of which were pierced by circlets of windows. This was not necessary in the exonarthex, for that was illuminated by semicircular windows at the top of the arches of the bays to the west (these originally had marble balustrades below), while the seventh bay at the end of the parecclesion had a triple-arched window in its south wall. At some later time, slightly pointed reinforcing arches of roughly dressed stone were added within the original transverse arches of the sixth bay; these rest on squat granite shafts without bases and detract somewhat from the general appearance of the exonarthex.

The nave. In Theodore Metochites's own description of the Chora, he states that little if any reconstruction was required in the nave. However, during the restoration it was discovered that Metochites had in fact rebuilt the dome and its supporting drum, along with parts of the pendentives and the crown of the west arch. The drum is supported on four huge pilasters that stand at the corners of the nave; four great arches spring from these and pendentives make the transition from them to the cornice. The present dome is Turkish, made of wood and covered with plaster, but the drum is from the reconstruction of 1315–21. The drum has 16 flutes, each pierced by a window.

There are also great triple-arched windows in the apse and in the three tympanum walls, though those to the north have been blocked because of the intrusion of the upper floor of the north annexe. Nothing now survives of the liturgical furnishings of the bema; i.e. the altar, ciborium, and the iconostasis. However, excavations in the apse revealed the emplacement for the altar and the foundations for the columns of the ciborium. Of the mosque furnishings of Kariye Camii, all that remains is the mihrab, which is rotated somewhat with respect to the axis of the church.

As mentioned earlier, the apse was flanked to north and south, respectively, by two domed apsidal chambers that served as the prothesis and the diaconicon. In Byzantine churches the **prothesis**, which was generally, as here, to the left of the bema, was used for the preparation and storage of the species of the Eucharist, while the diaconicon served as the sacristy. In the 12C church of the Chora both of these chambers were connected to the apse by short passageways. The prothesis is still connected in this way but in the 14C restorations a passage was opened from it into the bema of the pareccles-ion. From the time of this alter-ation the prothesis apparently served as the sacristy for the main church and the **diaconicon** was used for the same purpose in the side chapel. There is also a passageway in the south wall of the nave leading to the west bay of the parecclesion. In the walls of this passageway doors open on either side into small

The nave of Kariye Camii

enclosures which were apparently used as oratories.

The parecclesion. The parecclesion was also a construction of Metochites, designed to serve as a funerary chapel. It lies parallel to the south side of the nave; the principal entryway is at its west end, where it is separated from the seventh bay of the exonarthex by two columns bearing a tympanum pierced by arches. The chapel consists of two square bays and at the east end a bema with a semicircular apse covered with a conch. The west bay is covered by a ribbed dome carried on a drum pierced by a circlet of windows; on the east and west the dome is carried on transverse arches. The east bay is covered by a domical vault. There are triple-arched windows in the conch of the apse and also in the south tympanum walls of the two bays.

Around the walls of the parecclesion, at the springing level of the arches, there runs a cornice. The north and south walls below this cornice are articulated into bays by pilasters that receive the three transverse arches. Four recessed niches (arcosolia) are built within the thickness of the walls, one on each side of each of the two bays; these were designed to serve as sepulchral monuments for Metochites and other important persons.

The north annexe. Another structure built by Metochites is the two-storeyed annexe adjoining the north side of the nave and parallel to it. At the east end of the lower floor this annexe connected with the prothesis, and at its west end with the first bay of the inner narthex. The lower floor of this annexe is believed to have served as the skeuophylakion, or treasury, where all the precious objects and sacred relics of the church were stored for safekeeping. It has been suggested

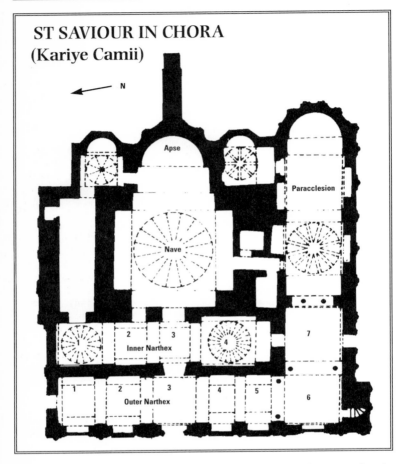

ST SAVIOUR IN CHORA (Kariye Camii)

N

Apse

Paracclesion

Nave

Inner Narthex

2   3

4

1

7

Outer Narthex

1   2   3   4   5   6

that the second floor of the annexe was used to house Theodore Metochites's celebrated collection of books and manuscripts.

**The mosaics

The mosaics and frescoes in the Chora are by far the most important and extensive series of Byzantine paintings in the city and among the most interesting in the world. They are of almost exactly the same date as the work of Giotto in Italy, and though quite unlike Giotto's work in detail they seem to breathe the same spirit of life and reality, so typical of the dawn of the Renaissance.

To view the mosaics intelligently, as the artist intended them to be seen, you must follow their iconographic order. They fall into seven quite distinct groups: **I**: Six large dedicatory and devotional panels, in the outer and inner narthexes; **II**: The Ancestry of Christ, in the two domes of the inner narthex; **III**: The Cycle of the Life of the Blessed Virgin, in the first three bays of the inner narthex; **IV**:

The Cycle of the Infancy of Christ, in the lunettes of the outer narthex; **V**: The Cycle of Christ's Ministry, in the vaults of the outer narthex and the fourth bay of the inner narthex; **VI**: Portraits of Saints; **VII**: The Mosaics in the Nave.

The genealogy in the domes serves as a prelude to the narrative cycles of the lives of the Blessed Virgin and Christ, which comprise the major elements in the programme. These mosaic cycles are closely linked together and form one continuous narrative, for the cycle in the outer narthex takes up the account at the precise point in Mary's life, as it is narrated in the apocryphal Protoevangelium of James; where the Gospel accounts begin, they supersede the apocryphal account as the authority. However, while the mosaics depicting the Infancy of Christ are based upon the Gospels and quote their texts in inscriptions, at many points they illustrate events derived from the Protoevangelium. In the account that follows the mosaics will be described in the order in which they occur in the seven groups, with each subject identified by a parenthetical number keyed to the plans.

I. Dedicatory and Devotional Panels. (**1**) Christ Pantocrator (in lunette over door to inner narthex): The inscription reads: 'Jesus Christ, the Land of the Living', with a play on the name of the church and a reference to Psalm 116–19: 'I will walk before the Lord in the Land of the Living'. (**2**) The Virgin Blachernitissa and Angels (opposite the above, over entrance door to the building). The prominent position of this mosaic, facing that of Christ, indicates that the church was dedicated to the Virgin as well as to her Son. Here she is shown praying in an attitude characteristic of the type known as the Blachernitissa, or the Theotokos of the Blachernae, who was venerated at a sacred spring near the Palace of Blachernae. The inscription reads: 'The Mother of God, the Dwelling-Place of the Uncontainable', with the same play on the name of the church and a reference to the mystery of the Incarnation.

(**3**) The Enthroned Christ with the Donor (inner narthex in lunette over door to nave): Metochites offers a model of his church to the enthroned Christ. He is dressed in his official robes, wearing an extraordinary turban-like hat called a skiadon, literally a sunshade. Christ has the same inscription as in the outer narthex, while the figure of the Donor is thus identified: 'The Founder, Logothete of the Genikon (First Lord of the Treasury) Theodore Metochites'. (**4**) St. Peter and (**5**) St. Paul (to the left and right of the door leading into the nave): the two saints are represented here in standing, full-length poses as the two 'Princes of the Apostles'; in this context they too, as it were, assume the character of 'founders', in as much as they, more than any of the other Apostles, were most influential in bringing Christ's church into existence.

(**6**) The Deesis (right of the door in east wall of south bay): (a Deesis is a representation of Christ with his Mother on his right and—usually, though not here—St. John the Baptist on his left). Here Christ is of the type known as Chalkites, from the famous icon over the main gate to the Great Palace of Byzantium. Below are the figures of two donors (very unusual in a deesis). At the Virgin's right stands 'The son of the most high Emperor Alexius Comnenus, Isaac Porphyrogenitus'; this is Isaac Comnenus, third son of Alexius I, who was probably responsible for the rebuilding of the church in the 12C. The inscription of the other figure is partly lost; what remains reads: '...of Andronicus Palaeologus, the Lady of the Mongols, Melane the nun'. This was either Maria,

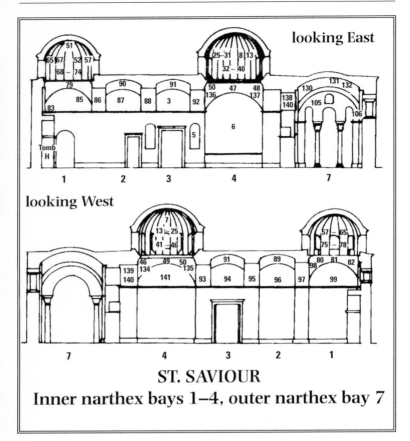

ST. SAVIOUR
Inner narthex bays 1–4, outer narthex bay 7

half-sister of Andronicus II, known as the Despoina of the Mongols, who founded the still-extant church of St. Mary of the Mongols; or else another Maria, an illegitimate daughter of Andronicus II, who also married a Mongol Khan. To add to the confusion, both of these women took the name of Melane when they became nuns, making it impossible to say which of them is represented in the mosaic.

II. The Geneaology of Christ. These mosaics are contained in the two domes of the inner narthex. In the crown of the south dome there is a medallion of Christ Pantocrator and in the flutes two rows of his ancestors, from Adam to Jacob in the upper zone, and in the lower the 12 sons of Jacob and some others. In the crown of the north dome there is a medallion of the Blessed Virgin with the Christ Child; below, in the upper zone 16 kings of the House of David, in the lower 11 figures representing 'other ancestors in the genealogy'.

South dome (medallion): (**7**) Christ Pantocrator. south dome, upper zone; from Adam to Jacob: (**8**) Adam; (**9**) Seth; (**10**) Noah; (**11**) Cainan; (**12**) Maleleel;

(13) Jared; (14) Lamech; (15) Sem; (16) Japeth; (17) Arphaxad; (18) Sala; (19) Heber; (20) Saruch; (21) Nachor; (22) Thara; (23) Abraham; (24) Isaac; (25) Jacob; (26) Phalec; (27) Ragau; (28) Mathusala; (29) Enoch; (30) Enos; (31) Abel. South dome, lower zone; the Sons of Jacob: (32) Reuben; (33) Simeon; (34) Levi; (35) Judah; (36) Zebulun; (37) Issachar; (38) Dan; (39) Gad; (40) Asher; (41) Naphtali; (42) Joseph; (43) Benjamin; (44) Pharez; (45) Zareh; (46) Esrom.

North dome (medallion): (51) The Theotokos, the Mother of God. North dome, upper zone; Kings of the House of David, David to Salathiel: (52) David; (53) Solomon; (54) Roboam; (55) Abia; (56) Asa; (57) Josophat; (58) Joram; (59) Ozias; (60) Joatham; (61) Achaz; (62) Ezekias; (63) Manasses; (64) Amon; (65) Josias; (66) Jechonias; (67) Salathiel. North dome, lower zone: 'Other ancestors outside the geneaology'. (68) Hananiah; (69) Azariah; (70) Mishael; (71) Daniel; (72) Joshua; (73) Moses; (74) Aaron; (75) Hur; (76) Samuel; (77) Job; (78) Melchizedek.

III. The Cycle of the Life of The Blessed Virgin. These mosaics are located in the first three bays of the inner narthex. The Cycle of the Life of the Virgin is based mainly on the Apocryphal Gospel of St. James, better known as the Protoevangelium, which dates back to at least the 2C. This gives an account of her birth and life from the rejection of the offerings of Joachim, her father, to the birth of Jesus. It was very popular in the Middle Ages and is the source of many cycles of pictures both in the East and the West. The most notable is Giotto's fresco cycle in the Arena Chapel at Padua, painted at a slightly earlier date and representing many of the same scenes. Here in Kariye Camii there were 20 scenes, of which 19 are either completely or partially preserved.

(82) Joachim's Offerings Rejected (first bay, northwest pendentive of dome): Zacharias, the High Priest before the altar, raises his hands in a gesture of refusal. (The rest of the scene in the northeast pendentive is lost; it must have shown Joachim and his wife Anne bearing offerings. Their offerings were rejected because they had no children.) (83) Fragmentary Scene (in lunette of north wall): probably Joachim and Anne returning home; only a maid looking out of a doorway is preserved. (84) Joachim in the Wilderness (in southeast pendentive): ashamed at the rejection of his offerings, Joachim goes into the wilderness to pray for offspring. (85) The Annunciation of St. Anne (in lunette of east wall, left half of scene lost): the right half of the scene shows the angel of the Lord announcing to Anne that her prayer for a child has been heard. (86) The Meeting of Joachim and Anne (in east soffit of arch between first and second bays): Anne informs Joachim on his return from the wilderness of the annunciation of the angel. The scene is inscribed: 'The conception of the Theotokos'.

(87) The Birth of the Blessed Virgin (in east lunette of second bay). (88) The First Seven Steps of the Virgin (in east soffit of arch between second and third bays): she took her first seven steps when she was six months old. (89) The Virgin Blessed by the Priests (west side of domical vault in first bay). (90) The Virgin Caressed by her Parents (east side of domical vault in first bay). Note the two magnificent peacocks, representing incorruptibility, in the two pendentives. (91) The Presentation of the Virgin in the Temple (in domical vault of third bay): the scene is inscribed 'The Holy of Holies'. At the age of three the Virgin was

presented as an attendant at the Temple, where she remained until she was about twelve.

(**92**) The Virgin Receiving Bread from an Angel (in east soffit of arch between third and fourth bays): while the Virgin remained in the Temple she was miraculously fed by an angel. (**93**) The Instruction of the Virgin in the Temple (in west soffit of arch between third and fourth bays): the central figures of the scene, unfortunately, have been destroyed. (**94**) The Virgin Receiving the Skein of Purple Wool (in lunette above door from outer narthex): the priests decided to have the attendant maidens weave a veil for the Temple; the royal colours, purple, blue and scarlet, fell to Mary by lot. (**95**) Zacharias Praying before the Rods of the Suitors (in west soffit of arch between second and third bays): when the time came for the Virgin to be married, the High Priest Zacharias called all the widowers together and placed their rods on the altar, praying for a sign showing to whom she should be given.

(**96**) The Virgin Entrusted to Joseph (in west lunette of second bay): when the rods were returned to the widowers, Joseph's rod began to sprout with green leaves and the Virgin was awarded to him. (**97**) Joseph taking the Virgin to his House (in west soffit of arch between first and second bays): here they are just leaving the Temple; the youth is one of Joseph's sons by his former wife. (**98**) The Annunciation to the Virgin at the Well (in southwest pendentive of dome in first bay). (**99**) Joseph taking leave of the Virgin; Joseph reproaching the Virgin (two scenes in west lunette of first bay): Joseph had to go away for six months on business; when he returned he found the Virgin pregnant and was angry (until reassured by a dream, as in the first scene of the next cycle).

IV. The Cycle of the Infancy of Christ. Each of the 13 extant or partly extant Infancy scenes occupies a lunette of the outer narthex, proceeding clockwise round all seven bays. In the soffits of the arches are saints, while in the domical vaults are the scenes of Christ's Ministry, which will be described later. The Infancy Cycle is largely based on the canonical Gospels, and most of the scenes are inscribed with quotations which sufficiently identify them.

(**100**) Joseph Dreaming; The Virgin with Two Companions; The Journey to Bethlehem (three scenes in north lunette of first bay): first scene inscribed: 'Behold, the angel of the Lord appeared to him in a dream, saying: "Joseph, thou son of David, fear not to take unto thee Mary thy wife: for that which is conceived in her is of the Holy Ghost"'. (Matt. 1:20); second scene uninscribed; third scene inscribed: 'And Joseph also went up from Galilee, unto the city of David, which is called Bethlehem...' (Luke 2:4). (**101**) The Enrolment for Taxation (in east lunette of first bay): inscription: '...(because he was of the House of David) to be taxed with Mary, his espoused wife, being great with child'. (Luke 2:4–5, continued from above).

(**102**) The Nativity (in east lunette of second bay): inscription is simply the title 'The Birth of Christ'. To the shepherds the angel says: 'Fear not; for behold, I bring you tidings of great joy, which shall be to all people'. (Luke 2:10). (**103**) The Journey of the Magi; the Magi before Herod (two scenes in east lunette of fourth bay): inscription: 'And behold, there came wise men from the East to Jerusalem, saying: "Where is he that is born King of the Jews?"' (Matt. 1:12). The second scene in the lunette is out of its proper chronological order, for, according to the texts, Herod consulted his priests and scribes (an incident illustrated in mosaic

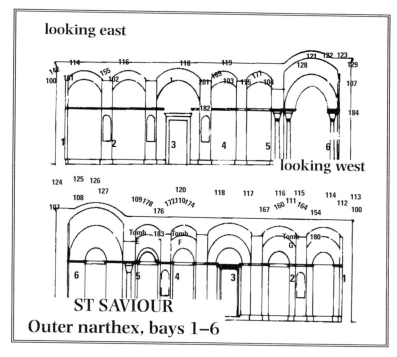

looking east

looking west

ST SAVIOUR
Outer narthex, bays 1–6

(104) in the next lunette) before consulting the Magi for information regarding the birthplace of Christ, whom he secretly wished to destroy. (**104**) Herod enquiring of the Priests and Scribes (in east lunette of fifth bay): partly destroyed; inscription (mutilated): 'And when he had gathered all the priests and scribes together he demanded of them where Christ should be born'. (Matt. 2:4).

Now turn the corner into the seventh bay. The lunette above the door to the inner narthex, now blank, probably contained the Adoration of the Magi. The lunette above the columns and arches that led to the parecclesion retains traces of (**105**) The Return of the Magi to the East. (**106**) The Flight into Egypt (in south lunette of seventh bay): main scene destroyed, only title remaining. On right of window scene of Fall of Idols from the Walls of an Egyptian Town as the Holy Family passes by (from an apocryphal source).

The mosaics in the west lunette of the sixth bay depict the Massacre of the Innocents. (**107**) (to the left): Herod Orders the Massacre; inscription: 'Then Herod, when he saw that he was mocked of the Wise Men, was exceeding wroth, and sent forth and slew all the children that were in Bethlehem, and in all the coasts thereof, from two years and under'. (Matt. 2:16). (**108**) (to the right) The Soldiers go forth to Slay the Children: central part and inscription destroyed. (**109**) Mothers Mourning their Children (in west lunette of fifth bay): inscription: 'In Rama was there a voice heard, lamentation and weeping, and great mourning'. (Matt. 2:18).

(**110**) The Flight of Elizabeth (in west lunette of fourth bay): inscription is the

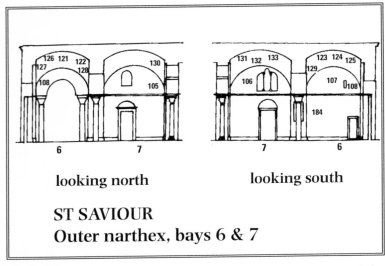

looking north   looking south

ST SAVIOUR
Outer narthex, bays 6 & 7

title. The scene, from the Protoevangelium 22:3, depicts Elizabeth with her baby son, John the Baptist, born about the same time as Christ, seeking refuge from the massacre in the mountains which open up to receive her. (**111**) Joseph Dreaming; The Return of the Holy Family from Egypt (in west lunette of second bay): inscription: 'Being warned of God in a dream, he (Joseph) turned aside into the parts of Galilee: and he came and dwelt in a city called Nazareth'. (Matt. 2:22–23). (**112**) Christ Taken to Jerusalem for the Passover (in west lunette of first bay): inscription: 'Now his parents went to Jerusalem every year at the Passover'. (Luke 2:41).**V. The Cycle of Christ's Ministry**. This cycle occupies the domical vaults of all seven bays of the outer narthex as well as parts of the south bay of the inner narthex. Unfortunately, all but one of the vaults in the outer narthex are very badly damaged, many scenes being lost or reduced to mere fragments. The series begins in the vault of the first bay.

(**113**) Christ among the Doctors (in vault of first bay, north side, fragments only). (**114**) John the Baptist bearing witness of Christ I (in vault of first bay, south side, fragments only). (**115**) John the Baptist bearing witness of Christ II (in vault of second bay, north side): inscription: 'This was he of whom I spake, he that cometh after me is preferred before me: for he was before me'. (John 1:15). (**116**) The Temptation of Christ (in vault of second bay, south side).

The four scenes of the Temptation are accompanied by a running dialogue between Christ and the Devil (from Matt. 4:3–10): 1. Devil: 'If thou be the Son of God, command that these stones be made bread'. Christ: 'It is written, Man shall not live by bread alone, but by every word that proceedeth out of the mouth of God'. 2. Devil: 'All these things will I give thee, if thou wilt fall down and worship me'. Christ: 'Get thee behind me, Satan' (the Devil has offered 'all the kingdoms of the world', represented by six kings in a walled town). 3. 'Then the Devil taketh him up to the holy city (and setteth him on a pinnacle of the temple)'. 4. Devil: 'If thou be the Son of God, cast thyself down'. Christ: 'It is written, thou shalt not tempt the Lord thy God'.

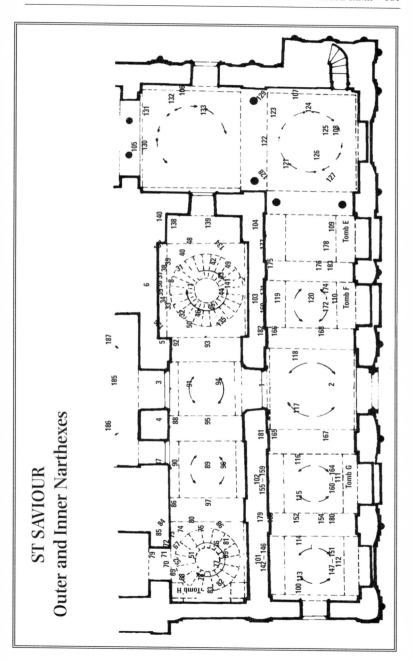

ST SAVIOUR
Outer and Inner Narthexes

(117) The Miracle at Cana (in vault of third bay, north side, badly ruined). (118) The Multiplication of the Loaves (in vault of third bay, south side, badly ruined). (119) Christ Healing a Leper (in vault of fourth bay, east side, fragments only). (120) Christ walking on the Water (in vault of fourth bay, west side, fragments only).

The fifth vault is completely empty. The vault of the sixth bay contains fragments of the following nine scenes, the identification of some of which are uncertain, at best: (121) Christ Healing the Paralytic at the Pool at Bethesda; (122) an unidentified scene showing the fragmentary figures of two disciples; (123) Christ Healing the Dropsical Man; (124) Christ Healing the Paralytic at Capernaum; (125) an unidentified scene, showing the fragmentary figures of nine disciples; (126) fragment showing the lower part of a barefooted figure; thought to be either the healing of the Gadarene Demoniac or the Healing of the Blind and Dumb Demoniac of Capernaum; (127) Christ and the Samaritan Woman at the Well (in the northwest pendentive); (128) the Paralytic Carrying off his Bed (in the northeast pendentive); (129) Christ Healing the Blind Born (in the southeast pendentive).

In the seventh bay there are fragments of four scenes, three of which (130, 131, and 133) are so meagre that they cannot be identified; the fourth (132) has been identified as a representation of Christ calling Zacchaeus from the Sycamore Tree, with part of the inscription saying, 'Zacchaeus, make haste and come down'.

Now re-enter the inner narthex to see the eight scenes of Christ's Ministry, almost all of which are well preserved; these are to be found in the pendentives, vaults and lunettes under the southern dome. The inscriptions in this series are merely the titles of the scenes.

(134) Christ Healing the Blind and Dumb Man (in southwest pendentive); (135) Christ Healing the two Blind Men (in northwest pendentive); (136) Christ Healing Peter's Mother-in-Law (in northeast pendentive); (137) Christ healing the Woman with the Issue of Blood (in southeast pendentive); (138) Christ healing the Man with the Withered Hand (in soffit of south arch, east side); (139) Christ Healing the Leper (in soffit of south arch, west side); (140) an unidentified scene, showing a miracle of healing (in south lunette, inscription and half of the mosaic lost); (141) Christ Healing a Multitude Afflicted with Various Diseases (in the west lunette).

VI. Portraits of Saints. The soffits of the arches in the outer narthex are decorated with the portraits of martyr-saints; there were originally 50, of which 37 still exist in whole or in part. The portraits were of two kinds: busts in medallions, and full-length standing figures. In addition to these there were also a dozen portraits of saints on the pilasters that receive the transverse arches in the outer narthex, of which only battered fragments of six have survived.

Martyrs in the arches: First bay, east arch, medallions (left to right, facing east): (142) St. Mardarius of Sebaste; (143) St. Auxentius of Sebaste; (144) St. Eustratius of Sebaste; (145) St. Eugenius of Sebaste; (146) St. Orestes of Sebaste. First bay, west arch, medallions (left to right facing west): (147) St. Anempodistus of Persia; (148) St. Elpidephorus of Persia; (149) St. Acindynus of Persia; (150) St. Aphthonius of Persia; (151) St. Pegasius of Persia. First bay, south transverse arch, one medallion and two full-length figures: (152) medallion of unidentified martyr, perhaps St. Probus of Cilicia; (**153**) St. Andronicus of Cilicia; (**154**) St. Tarachus of Cilicia.

Second bay, east arch, medallions (left to right facing east): (**155**) St. Philemon of Egypt; (**156**) St. Leucius of Nicomedia; (**157**) St. Agathonicus of Nicomedia; (**158**) St. Thyrsus of Nicomedia; (**159**) St. Apollonius of Egypt. Second bay, west arch, medallions (left to right facing west): (**160**) St. Laurus of Illyria; (**161**) St. Florus of Illyria; (**162**) St. Menas of Phrygia; (**163**) St. Victor; (**164**) probably St. Vincentius. Second bay, south transverse arch, east side, full length figure: (**165**) probably St. George of Cappadocia.

Third bay, south transverse arch, east side, full-length picture: (**166**) probably St. Demetrius of Thessalonica. Second bay, south transverse arch, west side, full-length figure: (**167**) an unidentified martyr. Third bay, south transverse arch, west side, full-length picture: (**168**) an unidentified martyr. Fourth bay east arch, medallions (left to right facing east): (**169**) St. Abibus of Edessa; (**170**) St. Gurius of Edessa; (**171**) St. Samonas of Edessa; (**172**) St. Eugraphus of Alexandria; (**173**) St. Menas of Alexandria; (**174**) St. Hermogenes of Alexandria. Fourth bay, south transverse arch, full-length figures: (**175**), (**176**) unidentified martyrs. Fifth bay, east arch, medallion (left side of arch): an unidentified martyr. Fifth bay, west arch, medallion (right side of arch): St. Sergius or St. Bacchus.

Saints in the wall panels. The six panels in the first, second and third bays would seem to have been devoted to portraits of those who, by divine intervention, were precursors of the Incarnation. Facing one another across the exonarthex between the first and second bays are (**179**) (to the east) St. Anne, with the infant Mary in her arms; and (**180**) (to the west) her husband Joachim. Between the second and third is (**181**) (to the east) the Virgin Mary and the Christ Child; facing this (to the west) there was in all probability the figure of Joseph, but this has been entirely destroyed. On the east pilaster between the third and fourth bays is a small fragment of (**182**) St. John the Baptist; across from this there would have been a portrait of either John's father Zacharias or his mother Elizabeth, but this too has disappeared.

The panels on the other six pilasters undoubtedly also bore portraits of saints; of these only two fragments remain: (**183**) an unidentified military saint (on the west pilaster between the fourth and fifth bays); and (**184**) St. Euthymius, the Palestinian hermit (on the south pilaster between the sixth and seventh bays).

VII. The Panels in the Nave. (**185**) The Dormition (Koimesis) of the Virgin (over the central door from the narthex). Here the Virgin is shown laid out on her bier. Behind her Christ stands holding her soul, represented as a babe in swaddling clothes, while over his head hovers a six-winged seraph. Around the bier there stand apostles, evangelists and early bishops. The theme is taken from an apocryphal work, Concerning the Koimesis of the Holy Mother of God, ascribed to St. John the Divine. (**186**) Christ (in panel at left of bema), with an inscription reading: 'Jesus Christ, the dwelling-place of the Living'. Christ holds the Gospels open to Matthew 11:28: 'Come unto me, all ye that labour and are heavy laden, and I will give you rest'. (**187**) The Virgin Hodegetria (in panel at right of bema), with an inscription reading: 'The Mother of God, the dwelling-place of the Uncontainable'.

The Parecclesion: **the frescoes

The superb fresco decoration of the parecclesion was the last part of Theodore Metochites's work of redecoration to be carried out, probably in 1320–21. The great but unknown master artist of these frescoes also, probably, created the mosaics in the rest of the church. The decoration of the chapel is designed to illustrate its purpose as a place of burial. Above the level of the cornice the paintings represent the Resurrection and the Life, the Last Judgement, Heaven and Hell, and The Mother of God as the Bridge between Earth and Heaven. Below the cornice there is a procession of saints and martyrs, interrupted here and there by tombs. The following account will deal first with the upper series of frescoes, beginning at the east, then with the portraits of the saints below cornice level, and finally with the tombs.

I. **Scenes of Resurrection. (**201**) The Anastasis (Resurrection). This scene, called Anastasis in Greek, is better known in English as the Harrowing of Hell. The central figure in this scene is Christ, who has just broken down the gates of Hell, which lie beneath his feet, while Satan lies bound before him. With his right hand Christ pulls Adam out of his tomb; behind Adam stand St. John the Baptist, David, Solomon, and other righteous kings. With his left hand he pulls Eve out of her tomb; standing in it is Abel and behind him another group of the righteous. This is surely one of the greatest paintings in the world, and the apogee of Byzantine art in its last renaissance. (**202**) Christ raising the Widow's Son (north side of bema arch). (**203**) Christ raising the Daughter of Jairus (south side of bema arch).

II. The Last Judgement: Heaven and Hell. (**204**) The Second Coming of Christ (in vault of east bay). This vast scene occupies the whole domical vault; the title is inscribed at the centre. It represents the Doctrine of the Last Things: death, judgement, immortality in Heaven or damnation in Hell. In the crown is the Scroll of Heaven (Apocalypse 6:14). In the east half sits Christ in Judgement. To the souls of the saved on his right he says: 'Come, ye blessed of my Father, inherit the kingdom prepared for you from the foundation of the world'. (Matt. 25:34). To the condemned souls on his left he says: 'Depart from me, ye cursed, into everlasting fire, prepared for the Devil and his angels'. (Matt. 25:41). Below to the left a River of Fire broadens into a lake in which are the damned. Below Christ is the Hetoimasia, the empty throne prepared for the Second Coming, with Adam and Eve prostrate before it. Below this is depicted the Weighing and Condemnation of Souls.

The west half of the vault is occupied by the Choirs of the Elect in clouds. (**205**) The Land and the Sea giving up their Dead (in southwest pendentive). (**206**) An Angel conducts the Soul of Lazarus to Heaven (northwest pendentive). (**207**) Lazarus the Beggar in Abraham's Bosom (northeast pendentive). (**208**) The Rich Man in Hell (southeast pendentive). (**209**) The Torments of the Damned (in lunette of south wall, east half). This scene consists of four rectangular panels, identified as: (upper left) The Gnashing of Teeth; (upper right) The Outer Darkness; (lower left) The Worm that Sleepeth Not; (lower right) The Unquenchable Fire. (**210**) The Entry of the Elect into Paradise (in lunette of north wall). The Elect are led by St. Peter toward the Gate of Paradise, guarded by a Cherub; the Good Thief welcomes them and points to the enthroned Mother of God.

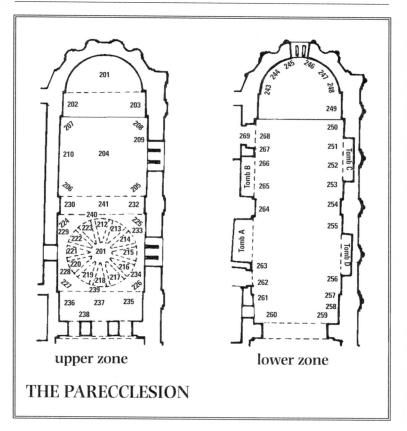

upper zone   lower zone

THE PARECCLESION

III. The Mother of God and her Prefigurations. This cycle, in the west dome and bay, represents the Blessed Virgin in a series of five episodes from the Old Testament, which came to be symbolically interpreted as prefigurations or 'types' of the Mother of God and the Incarnation. (**211–223**) The Virgin and Child (211) in the crown, surrounded by the heavenly court of angels (212–223) in the spaces between the ribs. (**224–227**) Four Hymnographers (in the pendentives of the dome). These poets were chosen because in their hymns, verses of which are inscribed on their scrolls, they referred to the prefigurations of the Virgin depicted below: (**224**) St. John Damascene (northeast); (**225**) St. Cosmas the Poet (southeast); (**226**) St. Joseph the Poet (southwest); St. Theophanes (northwest).

(**228**) Jacob's Ladder; Jacob wrestling with the Angel (in west half of north lunette). This symbolises the ladder or bridge to heaven as a prefiguration of the Virgin. The inscription reads: 'And Jacob took one of the stones of the place, and put it at his head, and dreamed; and behold, a ladder fixed on the earth, whose top reached to heaven, and the angels of God ascended and descended on it. And the Lord stood upon it.' (Genesis 28: 11–13). Note that the Lord, here and else-

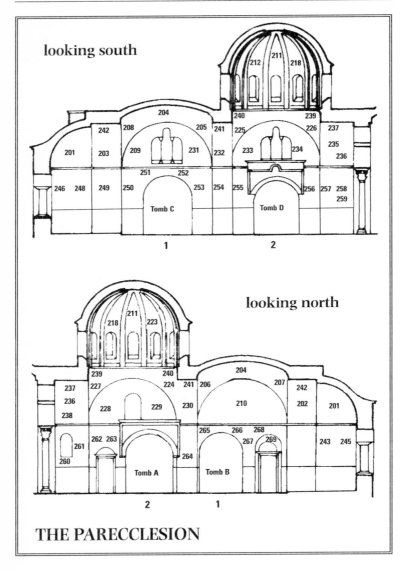

looking south

looking north

THE PARECCLESION

where, is represented by the Virgin and Child. The story of Moses and the
Burning Bush is represented in two scenes in the east half of the north lunette
and on the soffit of the adjacent arch: (**229**) Moses before the Bush; Moses
removes his sandals; (**230**) Moses hides his Face. The burning bush that was not
consumed was another prefiguration of the Virgin. The first scene is inscribed:
'Now Moses came to the mountain of God, even to Choreb. And the angel of the

Lord appeared to him in a flame of fire out of the bush ... saying "Put off thy shoes from off thy feet, for the place whereon thou standest is holy ground".' (Exodus 3:1–2,5). The second scene, on the arch, is inscribed: 'And Moses hid his face; for he was afraid to look upon God' . (Exodus 3:6).

Four scenes on the south wall depict the Dedication of Solomon's Temple: (**231**) The Bearing of the Ark of the Covenant; (**232**) The Bearing of the Sacred Vessels; (**233**) Solomon and all Israel; (**234**) The Installation of the Ark in the Holy of Holies. The Ark of the Covenant is here symbolised as a prefiguration of the Virgin. The first scene, in the west half of the south lunette, is inscribed: 'And it came to pass when Solomon was finished building the house of the Lord, that he assembled all the elders of Israel in Sion, to bring the Ark of the Covenant of the Lord out of the City of David, that is Sion, and the priests took up the Ark of the Covenant and the tabernacle of the testimony'. (I Kings 8:1–4). The inscription on the second scene, on the soffit of the arch, is lost, but it was probably a continuation of verse 4: 'and the holy vessels that were in the tabernacle of testimony'. The third scene, on the east half of the south lunette, is inscribed: 'And the King and all Israel were assembled before the Ark.' (v.5). The fourth scene, on the west half of the south lunette, is inscribed: 'And the priests bring in the Ark of the Covenant into its place, into the oracle of the house, even into the holy of holies, under the wings of the cherubim.' (I Kings 8:6).

(**235**) Isaiah Prophesying; The Angels Smiting the Assyrians before Jerusalem (in south soffit of west arch). Here the inviolable city is a prefiguration of the Virgin. The inscription on Isaiah's scroll is almost illegible, but probably reads: 'Thus saith the Lord concerning the King of Assyria: "He shall not come into this city."' (Isaiah 37:33). (**236**) Aaron and his Sons before the altar (in the north soffit of the west arch). Here the altar is a prefiguration of the Virgin. The inscription, almost illegible, is perhaps: 'They draw nigh to the altar and offer their sin-offerings and their whole burnt-offerings.' (Leviticus 9:7). (**237, 238**) The Souls of the Righteous in the Hand of God (in crown of west arch). This scene is almost entirely lost, but you can make out part of the hand of God holding the souls of the righteous, represented as infants in swaddling bands.

Medallion Portraits in the Arches. The only portraits on the vaults still to be described are the four medallion portraits in the crowns of the transverse arches. (**239**) Melchizedek the Righteous (at the centre of the vertical face of the west arch, in the narrow space below the dome cornice, head missing in its entirety). (**240**) Jesus Christ (facing **239** in the corresponding position on the arch at the east side of the dome; the head is damaged but the essential features remain). These two portraits were placed in confrontation to illustrate that Melchizedek the Righteous, King of Salem and priest of the most high God, who offered bread and wine to Abraham and blessed him (Gen. 14: 18–19), was the foreshadowing of Christ. A second medallion portrait of Christ (**241**) is found on the same arch as (**240**), on the horizontal surface in the centre of the soffit.

The fourth medallion portrait (242) is a bust of the Archangel Michael at the centre of the bema arch; this is larger than the other three medallions and is in a much better state of preservation. The large scale and prominent position of this portrait have led some scholars to suggest that Theodore Metochites may have dedicated the funerary chapel to the Archangel Michael.

Portraits on the Walls. A long frieze of portraits encircles the chapel on the walls below the cornice. In the apse there are the full-length figures of six Church Fathers; they are, from left to right: (**243**) Fragments of an unidentified bishop; (**244**) St. Athanasius; (**245**) St. John Chrysostom; (**246**) St. Basil; (**247**) St. Gregory the Theologian; (**248**) St. Cyril of Alexandria. In the rectangular panel on the pier to the south side of the bema arch there is a life-size portrait (**249**) of the Virgin and Christ Child. The portrait of the Virgin is of the type called Eleousa, the Merciful or Compassionate. There was originally a portrait of Christ on the opposite panel on the north side of the bema arch, but this has entirely disappeared.

Outside the bema, the frieze in the lower zone of the parecclesion consists mainly of portraits of martyrs and warrior-saints, the most prominent of them full-length military figures dressed in full armour. South wall, east bay: (**250**) St. George of Cappadocia; (**251**) St. Florus (medallion); (**252**) St. Laurus (medallion); (**253**) St. Demetrius of Thessalonica. South wall, pier between east and west bays: (**254**) St. Theodore Tiro. South wall, west bay: (**255**) St. Theodore Stratelates; (**256**) St. Mercurius. South wall, west pier: (**257**) St. Procopius; (**258**) St. Sabas Stratelates. West wall, south pier: (**259**) an unidentified saint. West wall, north pier: (**260**) St. David of Thessalonica. North wall, west pier: (**261**) St. Eustathius Plakidas.

North wall, west bay: (**262**) St. Samonas of Edessa; (**263**) St. Gurias of Edessa. North wall, pier between west and east bays (**264**) inscription lost; either St. Artemius or St. Nicetas. North wall, east bay: (**265**) St. Bacchus (medallion); (**266**) St. Sergius (medallion); (**267**) an unidentified military saint; (**268**) an unidentified saint (medallion). North wall, soffit of arch: (**269**) an unidentified stylite saint (a stylite is one who lives out his life perched on a pillar).

The tombs. There were four tombs in the parecclesion, each in a deep niche which originally held a sarcophagus with mosaics or frescoes above; some fragments of this decoration still exist. Tomb A, the first in the north wall, has lost its identifying inscription. Nevertheless, it is almost certainly that of Theodore Metochites himself; it has an elaborately carved and decorated archivolt above. Tomb B is entirely bare, and there is no evidence to identify who was buried there. Tomb C has well-preserved paintings of a man and woman in princely dress, but there is no inscription to identify them. Tomb D is that of Michael Tornikes, a general who was a close friend of Metochites. The deceased is identified by a long inscription above the archivolt, which is even more elaborately carved than that of Metochites himself. Fragments of the mosaic and fresco decoration still exist.

Tomb E, in the fifth bay of the outer narthex, is that of the Princess Eirene Raoulaina Palaeologina, a connection by marriage of Metochites; it preserves a good deal of its fresco decoration. Tomb F, in the fourth bay of the outer narthex, is that of a member of the imperial Palaeologus family; however, it cannot be more definitely identified. Part of the fresco decoration of the tomb survives, showing the lower halves of a couple dressed in colourful princely costumes. Tomb G, in the second bay of the outer narthex, is the latest in the church, dating to the very last years before the Turkish Conquest, with fresco decoration showing strong influence of the Italian Renaissance. Unfortunately, the inscription has vanished and the identity of the deceased is unknown.

Tomb H, in the north wall of the inner narthex, is that of the Despot Demetrius Doukas Angelus Palaeologus, youngest son of the Emperor Andronicus II, who died c 1340. Only a small part of the mosaic decoration has survived, and the only intact figure is that of the Virgin. Beneath her a fragmentary inscription reads: 'Thou art the Fount of Life, Mother of God the Word, and I, Demetrius, am thy slave in love'.

The Turkish Touring and Automobile Club has restored some of the old Ottoman houses in the little square in front of Kariye Cami, converting one of them into a hotel and another into a café. The café is modelled on an old-fashioned Turkish confectionary, and it is a pleasant place to relax and have a drink after a visit to Kariye Camii.

14 · The Stamboul Shore of the Golden Horn

The region along the Stamboul shore of the Golden Horn above the two bridges is one which few tourists ever see. This is a pity, for it has a distinctive atmosphere which is quite unlike that of any other part of the city. Some of its quarters, particularly Fener and Balat, are very picturesque and preserve aspects of the life of old Stamboul which have all but vanished elsewhere in the modern city.

This is the second of two strolls along the Stamboul shore of the Golden Horn above the Galata Bridge. This stroll starts at the Atatürk Bridge and follows the shoreline as far as the point where the ancient Byzantine land-walls come down to the Golden Horn, with occasional detours into the labyrinth of narrow, winding streets in the old quarters of this very picturesque part of Stamboul. The parks along the Golden Horn afford views of the old city that were not open to pedestrians in times past. The creation of this parkland involved the demolition of several old quarters along the shore of the Golden Horn, although the few buildings of historic value there have been preserved. Among these are the massive stone and brick structures known as 'meta-Byzantine', i.e. erected after the Conquest in the Byzantine style, a few of which have been restored along the inner side of the park.

Here and there along the way you see some stretches of the **Byzantine sea-walls** that once extended along the Golden Horn from Saray Burnu out to the land-walls, along with a few of their ancient towers and gateways.

The sea-walls along the Golden Horn began on the shore below the acropolis on the First Hill, there joining the maritime defence-walls along the Marmara, and stretched out to meet the Theodosian land-walls at the northwest corner of Constantinople. The walls along the Golden Horn were repaired and reconstructed many times during the Byzantine period, particularly by the Emperor Theophilus in the 9C. These fortifications consisted for the most part of a single line of walls 10m high and 5km long, studded by a total of 110 defence towers placed at regular intervals.

Considerable stretches of this wall still remain, although almost all of it is in ruins. Much of this ruination was brought about in the last great sieges of Constantinople, by the Crusaders in 1203–04 and by the Turks in 1453. In both instances the besiegers lined up their warships against the sea-walls along the Golden Horn and repeatedly assaulted them. And the destruction wrought by these sieges and subsequent centuries of decay is now being rapidly completed by the encroachment of modern highways and factories.

The sea-walls along the Golden Horn were pierced by about a score of gates and posterns, many of them famous in the history of Byzantine Constantinople. Of these only one or two remain, although the location of the others can easily be determined, since the streets of the modern town still converge where these ancient gates once opened, following the same routes that they have for many centuries.

The first part of our stroll up the Golden Horn takes us past the quarter known as **Cıbalı**. The huge building that towers above the shore road to our left is the former Cıbalı Tobacco Factory, one of the first factories in the Ottoman Empire, built in 1884.

After passing the factory we come to one of the surviving gates of the Byzantine sea-wall, the Porta Puteae, known in Turkish as **Cıbalı Kapı** (Pl. 6,7). A Turkish inscription beside the gate commemorates the fact that it was breached on 29 May 1453, the day on which Constantinople fell to the Turks. This gate also marks the point which stood opposite the extreme left wing of the Venetian fleet in their final assault on 12 April 1204.

About 250m past Cıbalı Kapı we see on our left the Greek church of **Haghios Nikolaos** (St. Nicholas), housed in a pink-walled meta-Byzantine building. The earliest recorded mention of this church is 1573 by the German traveller Stefan Gerlach, though the present structure dates from a rebuilding in 1837. It was originally a metochion, or dependency, of the Vathopedi Monastery on Mount Athos. The corbelled stone structure in which the church is housed is one of the few Ottoman buildings of its type still to be seen along the Golden Horn, most of them dating from the 17C–18C. Built into a wall of the courtyard there is an ancient Graeco-Roman tombstone with a relief of the deceased bidding farewell to his wife. Notice also in the narthex of the church the model of an ancient galleon hanging from the ceiling. Ship models such as this are to be found in many of the waterfront churches of the city, placed there by Greek sailors in gratitude for salvation from the perils of the sea. In the exonarthex there is an ayazma, or holy well, dedicated to Haghios Charalambos (St. Charalambos). The courtyard behind the church is partly enclosed by a well-preserved stretch of the ancient Byzantine sea-walls.

Just beyond the church the shore road passes **Aya Kapı** (Pl. 6,5), the Holy Gate, a small portal in the sea-walls. This was known in Byzantium as the Gate of St. Theodosia, since it led to a famous church of that name. After passing through the gate, we walk straight ahead for about 50m before taking the second turning on the left; we then proceed for another 50m to find an imposing but sombre Byzantine edifice. This is the former *church of St. Theodosia, known in Turkish as **Gül Camii** (Pl. 6,5).

The church is believed to date from the 12C. It was originally dedicated to St. Euphemia of the Petrion, but when the very popular iconodule, St. Theodosia, was later buried here it came to be known by her name instead.

The church was renowned for its collection of sacred relics, which were carried in procession twice a week and were reputed to have effected many miraculous cures. However, these were all stolen by the Crusaders when they sacked the city in 1204, and many of them still exist in the churches of western Europe.

The church figured prominently in the final hours of Byzantine history, for the Emperor Constantine XI Dragases stopped to pray here after his final visit to Haghia Sophia. The church was adorned with roses to commemorate the feast-day of St. Theodosia, which was celebrated annually on 29 May. When the Emperor arrived, accompanied by the Patriarch and the Senate, he found the church packed with women, children, and old men, all of them praying to Theodosia to intercede with Christ and the Virgin to spare their city. After the Emperor and his entourage left the congregation remained, and they were captured there when the city fell to the Turks the following morning. The Turkish soldiers who stormed the church were evidently moved by the garlands of roses they found festooned there, for the tale became one of the enduring traditions of the Conquest.

After the Conquest the church became a storehouse for the Ottoman navy, because of its proximity to the great arsenal on the Golden Horn (*see* Kasımpaşa, p 235). Then, in the first decade of the 17C, it was converted into a house of Islamic worship, known since then as Gül Camii, the Mosque of the Rose.

Exterior. The upper parts of the church were considerably altered in Ottoman times, a reconstruction that gave it the appearance of a medieval fortress. The two side apses, nonetheless, are worthy of note, with their three tiers of blind niches and their elaborate brick corbels. Among the more pleasing aspects of the exterior is the minaret, which is handsomely proportioned and clearly belongs to the classical period of Ottoman architecture, when the church was converted into a mosque.

Interior. The building is a cross-domed structure with side aisles surmounted by galleries; the piers supporting the dome are disengaged from the walls, and the corners behind them form alcoves of two storeys. The central dome and the arches that support it are Ottoman reconstructions, as are most of the windows.

After leaving Gül Camii we turn left, and then at the second turning turn left again. A short distance down the left side of the street there stands one of the oldest and grandest Turkish baths still in use in the city. It is now called **Küçük** (Little) **Mustafa Paşa Hamamı** (Pl. 6,5), but it seems actually to have been founded by Koca Mustafa Paşa, Grand Vezir to Beyazit II, who built it some time before his death in 1512. The plan of the hamam and the incredibly varied and intricate structure of its domes would entirely bear out that early date. The camekan, about 14.5m on a side, is among the largest in the city, so that the later wooden galleries around it do not detract from its grandeur. The soğukluk, typically, is merely carved out of the hararet, consisting of its right-hand cubicle and the bottom arm of the cross. The hararet itself is very splendid, covered by a central dome with a deep cornice of elaborately carved stalactites.

Each of the three remaining cross-arms is covered with a vault of utterly different structure; the prettiest is perhaps that on the right, which has a semi-dome in the form of a deeply ribbed shell. The two corner cubicles at the back have domes supported on a cornice of juxtaposed triangles, while the third cubicle has a very beautiful opus sectile pavement in a variety of brilliant coloured marbles. This delightful bath was in disuse half a century ago, but has since been restored and is in use once again.

After leaving the hamam we retrace our steps to Aya Kapı, after which we continue walking up the Golden Horn. A short distance beyond we come to another gateway in the sea-walls known as **Yeni Aya Kapı**. This portal is not one of the original gateways in the Byzantine sea-walls, but was constructed in 1582 by Sinan. The local residents had petitioned the government to open a gate there so that they could more easily make their way to a new bath which had been constructed outside the walls at that point. This bath, the **Havuzlu Hamam**, is probably also a work of Sinan, built by him for Nur Banu, wife of Selim II and mother of Murat III. Unfortunately, the hamam is now in a state of advanced decay.

About 100m beyond this gate Sadrazam Ali Paşa Cad. branches off at a slight angle to the left from the shore road along the Golden Horn. This was the site of the **Gate of the Petrion**, one of the portals in the Byzantine sea-walls. The quarter for which it was named was a walled enclave that comprised the lower slope of the Fifth Hill leading down to the Golden Horn.

> The **Petrion** figured prominently in the assaults upon the sea-walls by the Crusaders and the Turks. On 13 July 1203 the Venetian galleys under Doge Dandalo pushed their prows up against the sea-walls of the Petrion and captured 25 defence towers. Though the Doge was nearly 90 years old and almost totally blind, he personally commanded the attack, carrying the banner of St. Mark as his men helped him from his galleon onto the ramparts.
>
> In the final Crusader assault upon the city on 12 April 1204 the Petrion was once again the centre of the action. It was here that two brave Crusader knights jumped from the flying-bridge of the galleon Pelegrine onto a defence tower, and from there led the charge that breached the walls and brought about the capture of the city. On 29 May 1453 the Petrion with-stood a sustained attack by the Turkish fleet, and the defenders surrendered only when they heard that the land walls were breached and that the city had fallen. Since the Petrion had surrendered rather than being taken by assault, Fatih decreed that the houses and churches in the quarter would be spared in the general sack of the city.

Leaving the main road and veering left along Sadrazam Ali Paşa Cad., we soon come to the entrance to the *Greek Orthodox Patriarchate** (Pl. 5,6). On entering notice that the main gate is welded shut and painted black; this is the famous **Orta Kapı**, the Central Gate, which has become a symbol of Greek–Turkish intransigence: it was here that Gregory V, Patriarch of Constantinople, was hanged for treason on 22 April 1821, at the outbreak of the Greek War of Independence.

The Greek Orthodox Patriarchate has been on this site since 1601. Within the enclosure are the patriarchal church of Haghios Georgios (St. George) and the administrative offices of the Greek Orthodox Patriarchate. During the Ottoman period the Ecumenical Patriarch of Constantinople, under the suzerainty of the Sultan, was the religious leader of all Christians in the Empire. The first Greek Orthodox Patriarch after the Conquest was Gennadius, who with Fatih's approval established his headquarters at the church of the Pammakaristos (see p 163). The Patriarchate remained there until 1586, after which it was moved to several other places before being established on its present site.

The church. Like almost all of the post-Conquest sanctuaries in the city, the patriarchal church of St. George is a small basilica. This form was adopted partly because of its simplicity, but largely because the Christians in Istanbul were forbidden to build churches with domes or masonry roofs, so that the basilica with its timbered roof, a traditional Christian edifice, was the obvious solution. The earlier church of St. George, first mentioned in 1573 by Stefan Gerlach, seems to have had the same form, for an Italian traveller who saw it in 1615 described it as 'of moderate size, long in form, and with several aisles'.

Among the many relics in the church are the bodies of St. Omonia, St. Theophano, and St. Euphemia of Chalcedon, whose remains were brought here after her martyrium near the Hippodrome was destroyed c 1524 (see p 88). On the right side of the central aisle is the patriarchal throne, which is thought to date from the late Byzantine period. The church also contains a beautiful portative mosaic of the Blessed Virgin dating from the 11C.

Precincts. Across the courtyard from the church are the other buildings of the Patriarchate. With the exception of the library and an ayazma dedicated to St. Charalambos, these are all modern structures erected after the disastrous fire of 1951, which gutted most of the buildings on this side of the courtyard. It was fortunate that the library was spared, because it houses an important collection of Byzantine manuscripts and documents.

Fener

After leaving the Patriarchate, we continue along Sadrazam Ali Paşa Cad. for a few paces to the next intersection. Just to the right, at this point, is the site of the famous **Fener Kapısı** (Pl. 5,4), the ancient Porta Phanari, or the Gate of the Lighthouse. This gate, now vanished, long ago gave its name to the adjacent quarter, the **Fener**, so famous in the history of Istanbul during the Ottoman period.

Beginning in the early 16C, Greeks of this quarter, the Feneriotes, amassed considerable wealth in trade and commerce under the protective mantle of the Ottoman Sultan. Many Feneriotes achieved positions of great eminence in the Empire, and several families between them even gained control of the trans-Danubian principalities of Moldavia and Wallachia, client states of the Ottomans. The Feneriotes ruled there as Hospodars, or Princes, a position that allowed them to acquire enormous wealth. Much of this wealth was brought back to the Fener, where the Hospodars and other members of their family and court built magnificent mansions and palaces. The palaces of the Feneriotes have all vanished, but a few of their mansions have survived, although in very dilapidated condition. They can be seen here and there along the Golden Horn road, identified by their massive stone walls and their upper storeys projecting out on corbels.

Continuing along in the same direction for a few steps past the site of Fener Kapısı, take the first left and then almost immediately turn right into the next street, Vodina Cad. At the next corner turn left and then right at the next turning. At the end of this street we come to a stepped lane that leads up past a high wall that encloses a large open area extending up the side of the hill. This area is the metochion of the Greek Orthodox Patriarchate of Jerusalem, and within it are two churches of some historic interest. They can be seen only with the permission of the Patriarchate.

The first of these is the **church of Haghios Georgios Metochi** (Pl. 5,4), founded in the 12C. The first mention of it after the Turkish Conquest is by Tryphon Karabeinikov, who in 1583 came to Istanbul as a representative of Czar Ivan IV, the Terrible. Since the middle of the 17C this has been the Metochion of the Jerusalem Patriarchate. In 1906 a careful study of the manuscripts in the church was made by the German scholar Heiberg, who discovered in palimpsest a perfect and complete copy made in the 10C of a lost work of Archimedes. This is his 'Method of Treating Mechanical Problems, Dedicated to Eratosthenes', written in Alexandria c 250 BC.

The second church within the walled enclosure is the **Panaghia Paramithias (St. Mary the Consoler)**, which dates from the mid 16C. It served as the Patriarchal church from 1586 until 1596, after the Patriarchate had been moved from the Pammakaristos. Unfortunately, the church was gutted in a disastrous fire in 1976 and has not been rebuilt. It is known in Turkish as Vlach Saray, since it stood within the precincts of the palace of the Princes of Wallachia, Feneriote Greeks who ruled that trans-Danubian principality under the aegis of the Sultan.

Halfway up the stepped path we come to the locked gate of the enclosure. Beside the gate there is a plaque with a portrait relief of Demetrius Cantemir, a Feneriote Greek who in 1710 became Prince of Wallachia, residing here in Vlach Saray. He is noted as the author of 'The history of the growth and decay of the Othman Empire', published in 1727. He also composed a work dedicated to Ahmet III, the 'Book of the Science of Music as Explained in Letters', in which he transcribed 351 Turkish, Persian and Arabic tunes according to his own system of notation.

At the top of the steps we turn left, and then at the upper end of the street we come to a rose-red Byzantine church with an unusually high drum. This is the church dedicated to the Theotokos Panaghiotissa, the All-Holy Mother of God, but it is more generally called the *Panaghia Mouchliotissa, or St. Mary of the Mongols. This building has little to recommend it architecturally, but it is interesting historically as the only Byzantine sanctuary continuously in the hands of the Greeks since before the Turkish Conquest.

This church was either founded or rebuilt c 1282 by the Princess Maria Palaeologina, an illegitimate daughter of the Emperor Michael VIII

Palaeologus. In 1265 Maria was sent off by her father as a bride to Hulagu, the Great Khan of the Mongols. However, Hulagu died before Maria arrived at the Mongol court, so she was married instead to his son and successor Abagu. Maria lived at the Mongol court in Persia for about 15 years, and through her influence the Khan and many of his court became Christians. But then, in 1281, Abagu was assassinated by his brother Ahmet and Maria was forced to return to Constantinople. After Maria's return her father offered her as bride to another Khan of the Mongols, Charabanda, but this time she refused. At about this time she founded the present church, together with a convent, and dedicated it to the Virgin, the protectress of the Christian Mongols. Maria, the Despoina of the Mongols, as she was then known, became a nun and spent her last years in retirement in her convent. After the Conquest Fatih, at the request of his Greek architect Christodoulos (who may be Atik Sinan, the architect of the original Fatih Camii), issued a firman, or imperial decree, confirming the right of the local Greeks to keep this church. The Greeks remain in possession of the church to this day, and copies of Fatih's firman and those of several of his successors are displayed on the rear wall.

Interior. The plan of the church was originally quatrefoil internally and trefoil externally. That is, the small central dome on a high drum was surrounded by four semidomes along the axes, all but the western one resting on the outer walls of the building, which thus formed exedrae, with a narthex of three bays preceding the church to the west. But the entire southern side of the church was swept away in modern times and replaced by a squarish narthex, which is in every direction out of line with the original building. The effect is most disconcerting; nevertheless, the church is very pretty, particularly when its lights are turned on and its candles lit for a service, illuminating the blackened old paintings on its iconostasis.

We now walk back around the church to the huge structure that dominates the skyline in this part of the city, an ugly red-brick building completed in 1881. This is the **Megali Scholi**, the Great School, a secular institution of higher education for Greeks founded c 1840. Prior to that time the Patriarchate had operated a school of higher learning on this site that offered both religious and secular studies, one of the very few such institutions in the Ottoman Empire. Here many of the Greek Voivodes (Governors) and Hospodars of Moldavia and Wallachia were educated, as well as most of the chief interpreters, who often wielded great influence at the Sublime Porte. This latter group includes men with the illustrious names of the Byzantine aristocracy: Palaeologus, Cantacuzenos, Cantemir, Mavrocordato and Ypsilanti. The school was closed by the Turkish government in 1971, but it has since reopened, though with a very small enrolment.

We now retrace our route to Fener Kapısı, after which we continue walking up the shore of the Golden Horn.

Some 125m beyond Fener Kapısı we come to a restored meta-Byzantine building that now houses the **Kadın Eserleri Kütüphanesi ve Bilgi Merkezi** (Women's Library and Cultural Centre).

■ **Admission.** The library is open Sat, Sun, & Mon, 13.00–19.00; Tue, Thu, Fri, 10.00–19.00; closed Wed. (Address: Fener Mahallesi, Haliç -34220, Istanbul; tel. 534-9550; fax 523-7408).

The library. The library, which opened in 1990, is the first institution of its type in Turkey. Its collection includes works by and about women, including a complete collection of all the women's magazines and periodicals published in Turkey in the 19C–20C. It is a research centre for women's studies, and one of its aims is to encourage the women of the Fener quarter and elsewhere to make use of its resources.

After another 150m we come to the **church of St. Stephen of the Bulgars**. This was erected in 1896, at a time when the Bulgarian Church was asserting its independence from the Greek Orthodox Patriarchate of Constantinople. The astonishing thing about the church is that it is constructed entirely of cast iron, not only the structure itself but all of its interior decorations, and all is in the neo-Gothic style. The church was prefabricated in Vienna and shipped down the Danube and across the Black Sea in sections, after which it was erected here on the Stamboul shore of the Golden Horn. The church is actually rather handsome, both inside and out, and it is kept in excellent repair by the small community of Bulgarians who worship here. The church is surrounded by a pretty and well-tended garden in which several metropolitans of the Bulgarian Orthodox Church are buried.

About 250m farther along we come one of the oldest and grandest of the former **Feneriote mansions**, still impressive though it is in a very dilapidated condition. This is the finest extant example of a Greek residence in Istanbul of the Ottoman period, the type known as meta-Byzantine. Its walls are constructed of alternate courses of stone and brick; the upper storey projects out over the street, corbelled out on elaborate consoles; with the cornice under the roof consisting of courses of brick in saw-tooth design. The mansion is very stoutly built, with massive walls and iron doors and window-shutters, more like a fortress than a dwelling-place.

> The mansion is part of the Metochion of the monastery of St. Catherine on Mount Sinai. St. Catherine's was founded by Justinian, and since Byzantine times it has been under the aegis of the Patriarchate of Alexandria. The monastery, like many others, has always been represented in Constantinople by one of its archimandrites, who are mentioned as having been in residence in this mansion as early as 1686. The mansion was badly damaged during an anti-Greek riot in 1955, and then a decade later it was closed by the Turkish government. It has been abandoned since then and is now rapidly falling into ruins.

Just beyond the mansion a gateway leads into the courtyard of the **Greek church of Haghios Ioannis Prodromos** (St. John the Baptist) **Metoki**, which is also part of the metochion of St. Catherine. The church is Byzantine in foundation, referred to in historical sources as early as 1334, the first mention of it after the Conquest being by Tryphon in 1583. The present church dates from a rebuilding in 1830; it was abandoned after being badly damaged in the 1955 riot, but it has since been restored and is open for occasional services.

About 150m farther along we come to the site of **Balat Kapısı**, another of the Byzantine sea-gates along the Golden Horn, of which only fragments now remain. This has been identified variously as the Gate of Haghios Ioannis Prodromos or that of Haghios Ioannis Kynegos (St. John the Hunter). The Turkish name is a corruption of Palation or Palace, because of its proximity to the Byzantine Palace of Blachernae, the ruins of which stand just inside the Theodosian walls (see below). Although the gate has now all but disappeared, its name survives in that of the surrounding quarter, the picturesque and venerable Balat.

Balat has been for many centuries one of the principal Jewish quarters of the city. Many of the people of the quarter were Greek-speaking Jews who had resided here since the Byzantine period, but these were later absorbed by the Sephardim who emigrated from Spain in 1492 and took up residence in the Ottoman Empire at the invitation of Beyazit II. There are still half-a-dozen ancient synagogues in the quarter, at least one of them dating in foundation from Byzantine times, although most of the present structures date from no earlier than the first half of the 19C. Although many in the Jewish community have now moved to more modern neighbourhoods in Istanbul or emigrated to Israel, some still remain in their old quarter in Balat, continuing to speak the medieval Ladino of their Spanish ancestors. There were also many Greeks and Armenians in Balat, as evidenced by the number of their churches in the quarter, though their numbers too have greatly diminished in recent years.

There are a few monuments of some interest in the immediate vicinity of Balat Kapısı. The first of these is on the second street in from the Golden Horn road and somewhat to the left of the gate. (Although the gate no longer exists, there is no mistaking its former location, for all the local streets converge on it.) This is the Armenian church of Surp Reşdagabet (Holy Archangels), which stands on the site of a Byzantine church of the 13C–14C, apparently rebuilt in the second quarter of the 19C. The church originally belonged to the Greeks, but the Armenian community took possession in 1629 and retain it to the present day. Beneath the church there is a crypt with an ayazma, evidently a very old one, as evidenced by the ancient Greek funerary stelae set into its walls.

To the right of Balat Kapısı and on the same street as the church there is a small **mosque** which is a minor work of Sinan. A long and handsomely written inscription, in Arabic, over the fine entrance portal, states that the mosque was built in 1562–63 by Ferruh Ağa, Kethüda (Steward) of the Grand Vezir Semiz Ali Paşa. The mosque is of the simple rectangular type; it probably once had a wooden ceiling with a little dome, but this has been replaced in a recent restoration by a flat concrete ceiling. The building is very long and narrow, with a shallow apse for the mihrab, which is adorned with tiles from the Tekfursarayı period. A wooden balcony runs along the west wall, but this is clearly not like the original, for it obstructs the windows in an awkward way.

A deep porch precedes the mosque: this originally had a colonnade of eight columns, but these were removed so as to glaze in the porch. All the same, the porch is attractive, with its marble portal, two handsome niches with pretty conch tops, and at each end a curious sort of anta or projection of the mosque

wall with windows above and below. This is the handsomest and most interesting of Sinan's many mosques of this simple type.

Close to the mosque there is an ancient Turkish bath called **Çavuş Hamamı**.
This has been attributed to Sinan, but wrongly; it is not in the 'Tezkere', and
furthermore it appears much earlier in a vakfiye, or deed of a pious foundation,
of Fatih himself. However, it is not very impressive and is hardly worth a visit.

The oldest and most historic synagogue in Balat is a short way to the south on
Kürkçü Çeşme Sok. This is the **Ahrida Synagogue**, which dates back to the first
half of the 15C, the only synagogue in the city that can definitely be dated to the
Byzantine period. The synagogue has been reconstructed recently and is now
open as a museum, although permission to visit must be obtained from the office
of the Chief Rabbinate (see above, p 24). The synagogue is noted for its association with Sabbattai Sevi, the so-called False Messiah, who in 1667 gave a sermon
here to proclaim that he was the long-awaited Saviour.

We now retrace our steps to Ferruh Kethüda Camii and continue up the
Golden Horn along the street that runs by the north side of the mosque. About
150m beyond the mosque on the left we come to the Greek **church of the
Panaghia Balinou**. The first mention of this church is in Tryphon's list of
1583, while the present structure dates from a rebuilding in 1833. In the
narthex there is a fine marble relief in the Byzantine style of the Dormition of
the Virgin, dated 1833.

About 100m farther along, just to the right past a bend in the road, there is
another Greek church, that of **Haghios Demetrius** (St. Demetrius) **Kanabou**.

> The church of St. Demetrius Kanabu is also included in Tryphon's list of
> 1583, although the present structure dates from a rebuilding in 1730. The
> origins of St. Demetrius go back to Byzantine times, for a church of that
> name is known to have existed on this site as early as 1334. It is suggested
> that the church may have been founded by the family of Nicholas Kanabou,
> who became emperor for a few days in April 1204, in the brief interval
> between the deposition of the co-emperors Alexius IV and Isaac II and the
> later usurpation by Alexius V. (The rule of Nicholas Kanabou was so brief
> that he is not included among the list of Byzantine emperors.) St. Demetrius
> served as the Patriarchal church from 1597 until 1601, the period just
> before the Patriarchate was shifted to its present site.

The very pretty garden of the church is built up against a section of the medieval
Byzantine sea-walls, from where you can look out over the Golden Horn. There
we see the old Galata Bridge, which after its demolition in 1992 was moved here
and reconstructed in 1994, spanning the Golden Horn between Ayvansaray
and Hasköy.

Beyond the church we bear right and continue up the Golden Horn on the first
street in from the coastal highway, Mustafapaşa Bostani Sok. We take the first
turning toward the highway, and then on our right we come to a Byzantine
church converted into a mosque known as **Atik Mustafa Paşa Camii** (Pl. 5,1).
This has been identified tentatively as the church of SS. Peter and Mark. It is a
domed-cross church dated to the 9C. The wooden porch, the dome and its drum,
and probably some of the roofs and many of the windows, are Turkish restora-

tions. For the rest, the church preserves its original plan, which is simple and, for a Byzantine structure, regular. A dome, doubtless originally on a fairly high drum with windows, covers the centre of the cross. The arms of the cross are barrel-vaulted, as are the four small rooms beyond the dome piers that fill up the corners of the cross: these are entered through high, narrow arches. The three apses, semicircular within, have three faces on the exterior. It must once have been an attractive little church, and it still has a faded charm.

After returning to the street by which the church was first approached, we continue in the same direction as before. At the next corner on the left we come to the entrance to the famous **ayazma of Blachernae**, a sacred spring enclosed by a little shrine surrounded by a garden.

> This ayazma has been venerated since the early Byzantine period, since its waters are believed to possess healing powers. The ayazma at Blachernae was one of the most popular in the city and even the Emperor and Empress came here to partake of the life-giving waters. In 451 a great church was built over the spring by the Empress Pulcheria, wife of the Emperor Marcian. A few years later the church served to house the celebrated robe and mantle of the Virgin. These garments, which had been stolen from a Jewess in Jerusalem by two Byzantine pilgrims, were considered to be the most sacred relics in Constantinople, 'the palladium of the city and the disperser of all warlike foes'. The Blachernitissa, as the Virgin was here called, was revered as the protectress of the city; according to tradition, she appeared on the walls to disperse the Avars when they almost broke into the city near the Golden Horn in 626.
>
> The ancient church of the Blachernae was destroyed by fire in 1434, and it was subsequently rebuilt several times, most recently in the 1960s. The shrine is still a popular place of pilgrimage among the Greeks of the city; and each year, on the anniversary of the repulse of the Avars, they gather here to give thanks to the Blachernitissa in a very moving liturgy known as the Akathisthos.

After leaving the ayazma we turn left and then right at the next corner on to Dervişzade Sok., the Street of the Dervish's Son, which winds uphill to a broad terrace just inside the ancient Byzantine land-walls. At the north end of the terrace, standing close to the ramparts, there is a very attractive mosque called ***Ivaz Efendi Camii** (Pl. 5,1).

> Some scholars have attributed the mosque to Sinan, but it does not appear in the 'Tezkere' and there seems to be no definite evidence to identify the architect. There is no historical inscription, and the date of construction is given variously as 1581 or 1586, the latter being the year when Ivaz Efendi died. The founder had been Chief Judge of Istanbul in the reign of Murat III.

Exterior. The west façade of the mosque is most unusual: instead of a central entrance-portal there are double doors at each end of the façade, the rest of it being filled in with windows, producing a very pretty effect. Another odd, indeed unique, feature is that the minaret is at the southeast corner of the building.

Originally there was a porch, evidently with a sloping roof supported by columns, which ran around three sides of the building.

Interior. The mosque is almost square in plan; the dome rests on four semi-domes with stalactite cornices, while the mihrab, in a projecting apse, is decorated with Iznik tiles of the best period. The centre of the west wall is occupied by a gallery in two storeys supported on slender marble columns. There are also wooden galleries to north and south, but these are probably not original, certainly not in their present form. The interior is very elegant and gives a great sense of light: there are many windows in all its walls.

The terrace on which Ivaz Efendi Camii stands is the site of the famous ***Palace of Blachernae** (Pl. 5,1), the imperial residence during the last centuries of Byzantine rule. Only a tower and some substructures of the palace remain; nevertheless, it is one of the most romantic and historic sights in the city.

> The first palace on this site was built by the Emperor Anastasius I (491–518). The palace was thenceforth used by the imperial family whenever they came to visit the nearby shrine of the Blachernitissa. Over the centuries the Palace of Blachernae was rebuilt and enlarged several times, particularly during the reign of the Comneni dynasty in the 11C–12C. From that time on Blachernae became the favourite residence of the imperial family, gradually supplanting the Great Palace on the First Hill.
>
> After the Latin Occupation of 1204–61 the Great Palace on the Marmara was abandoned altogether, and for the remainder of the Byzantine period the imperial family lived exclusively at Blachernae. They were still in residence here when the city fell to the Turks on 29 May 1453. Because of its close proximity to the defence-walls, the palace suffered grievously during this campaign.

The tower just behind Ivaz Efendi Camii is a part of the palace. It is traditionally called the **Tower of Isaac Angelus**, after Isaac II Angelus (1185–95, 1203–04, who was imprisoned here in the years between his two reigns. The tower was probably built by Isaac II during his first reign; it was perhaps designed as a private palace with its upper level serving as a belvedere. Certainly the upper storey of the tower, on a level with the terrace, commands a superb view of the Golden Horn and the surrounding countryside; notice outside the windows the shafts of columns that once supported a balcony.

A modern concrete stairway in the terrace leads down to the substructures of the palace. These are quite impressive, but visitors must be equipped with a flashlight. The penetralia consist of two nearly parallel walls some 60m long; the space between, which varies from 2–12m in width, is divided by arched cross-walls into three storeys of compartments, 42 in all. Since the wooden floors have long since decayed, these vast dungeons give an impression of immense height. This passage leads to the Tower of Isaac Angelus from where a ramp leads down to a small entrance at the foot of the wall.

After leaving the palace, return along Dervişzade Sok. to the main road along the Golden Horn. A short distance along to the left is the last stretch of the maritime fortifications along the Golden Horn, a massive wall and the impressive ruins of three defence towers. Just beyond that stretch the sea-walls on this side of the city came to an end, joining the great land-walls after their long march across the Thracian downs from the Sea of Marmara to the Golden Horn.

15 · The Seventh Hill

The first six hills of the city march in an almost straight line above the right bank of the Golden Horn. The Seventh Hill stands by itself toward the Marmara shore, comprising most of the southwest area of the old city. One of its two peaks is at the Gate of Romanus (Top Kapı), whence it slopes down to the north toward the valley of the Lycus, which divides it from the Sixth, Fifth and Fourth Hills. To the south it approaches the Marmara, leaving sometimes a wide, sometimes a narrow, plain along the shore.

This walk goes along the Marmara slopes of the Seventh Hill, through one of the most pleasant and picturesque parts of the city. This region preserves something of the flavour of Ottoman Stamboul, with its winding cobbled streets lined with old wooden houses, its vine-shaded teahouses sitting under venerable plane trees, and its ancient mosque courtyards still serving as communal centres as they did in centuries past.

Our route begins in **Aksaray Square** (Pl. 9,4), at the intersection of Ordu Cad. and Atatürk Blv. Like Beyazıt Square, Aksaray occupies the site of an ancient Roman forum, in this case the Forum Bovis. At the Forum Bovis the ancient Mese (middle way) once again divided into two branches, one leading off to the northwest along the route of the modern Millet Cad., the other going to the southwest, following approximately the course of Cerrah Paşa Cad. In times past Aksaray was a lively, colourful market square, but it has been utterly destroyed by a massive clover-leaf intersection.

Just to the north of the overpass stands **Valide Sultan Camii**, the last imperial mosque to be erected in Istanbul. It is generally ascribed to the Italian architect Montani, and was built in 1871 for Pertevniyal Valide Sultan, mother of Sultan Abdül Aziz. The foundress was a veritable Cinderella, for she was elevated in a single day from the palace kitchens to the bed of Sultan Abdül Mecit. She was not so fortunate in her mosque, a tasteless structure that combines elements of Moorish, Turkish, Gothic, Renaissance and Empire styles in a garish rococo hodgepodge. One authority on the monuments of Istanbul has described Valide Sultan Camii as the bitter end of Ottoman architecture.

At the west of the overpass, and to the left down the first cross street, there is a handsome **sıbyan mektebi**. This was founded in 1723–24 by Ebu Bekir Paşa; it has recently been restored and is now in use as a children's library, like so many other old Ottoman one-room schoolhouses of its type.

Beyond the west end of the overpass two modern highways meet in an acute angle; the southern one, Millet Cad., runs up the back of the Seventh Hill to Top Kapı, one of the ancient gateways in the Theodosian walls; the northern one, Menderes Cad., follows the ancient course of the Lycus River, which is canalised beneath it. In the angle between these two avenues stands ***Murat Paşa Camii** (Pl. 9,4), one of the oldest and most attractive vezirial mosques in the city.

The founder, Murat Paşa, was a convert to Islam from the imperial Palaeologus family; he became one of the Conqueror's vezirs and died in battle as a relatively young man. The date of construction of his mosque is given, in an intricate inscription in Arabic over the main door, as 1469. (The calligraphy in this inscription is exceptionally beautiful and is probably by Ali Sufi, who carved the fine inscription over the Imperial Gate to Topkapı Sarayı.)

The mosque. Murat Paşa Camii is the second in date of the two mosques of the 'Bursa type' that still survive in Istanbul, built seven years after Mahmut Paşa Camii. Murat Paşa's mosque is smaller and less elaborate than that of Mahmut Paşa; nevertheless, it resembles it in general plan. A long rectangular room is divided by an arch into two squares each covered by a dome, with two small side chambers to north and south forming hostels for travelling dervishes. Of the two large domes the eastern one rests on pendentives, but the western one has the same curious arrangement of triangles seen on the smaller domes at Mahmut Paşa. The porch has five domed bays with six very handsome ancient columns, two of Syenitic granite, four of verd antique. The capitals are of three different kinds, arranged symmetrically, two types of stalactite and the lozenge capital. The walls of the building are in alternating courses of brick and stone. The pious foundation originally included a medrese and a large double hamam, but unfortunately these perished during the widening of the adjacent streets.

Just behind Murat Paşa Camii a large ancient **catacomb** was discovered in 1972 during excavations for a new sewer. A cursory exploration at that time revealed that there were eight vaulted chambers extending over an area roughly 30m on a side. It is thought that there is a second storey of comparable size beneath the first, but this has not yet been explored. The catacomb is believed to date from the 6C AD; unfortunately, it is not open to the public.

A little farther up Millet Cad., on the same side of the avenue, is an interesting **mosque** which has recently been reconstructed here. It was founded by Selçuk Hatun, daughter of Sultan Mehmet I (1413–21) and an aunt of Mehmet the Conqueror. Selçuk Hatun died in 1485, therefore her mosque must be dated no later than that. In the 17C the mosque was partially destroyed in a fire and was later reconstructed by the Chief Black Eunuch Abbas Ağa. In 1956, when Millet Cad. was widened, the mosque was demolished and re-erected not far from its original site. How far the reconstructed building follows the original plan is not clear; at all events the mosque is rather attractive and the rebuilding at least adequate.

Now cross Millet Cad. and continue south for a short distance as far as Cerrah Paşa Cad., which leads westward parallel to the Marmara shore. A short way along on the left you come to an imposing mosque surrounded by a walled garden. This is *Cerrah Paşa Camii (Pl. 9,3), the fine mosque after which the avenue and the surrounding neighbourhood are named.

The founder, Cerrah Mehmet Paşa, served as Grand Vezir for a short time during the reign of Mehmet III (1595–1603). He had originally been a barber and surgeon (cerrah), and rose in the favour of Murat III after having performed the circumcision of the crown prince, the future Mehmet III. The latter in 1598 appointed him Grand Vezir and wrote him a letter warning that he would be drawn and quartered if he did not do his duty. But he was dismissed after about six months, without being drawn and quartered, after the failure of a military campaign that he led against Hungary.

Interior. An Arabic inscription over the door of the mosque gives the date as 1593; the architect was Davut Ağa, Sinan's successor as Chief Architect of the Empire. Historians of Ottoman architecture generally rank Cerrah Paşa Camii among the half-dozen most successful of the vezirial mosques. Its plan presents an interesting modification of the hexagon-in-rectangle type. The four domes that flank the central dome at the corners, instead of being oriented along the diagonals of the rectangle, are parallel with the cross axis. This plan has the advantage that, for any hexagon, the width of the building can be increased without limit. Such a plan was never used by Sinan, and is seen elsewhere only in Hekimoğlu Ali Paşa Camii, which is a little farther west on the Seventh Hill (see below).

The mihrab is in a rectangular apse which projects from the east wall. The galleries, which run around three sides of the building, are supported by pretty ogive arches with polychrome voussoirs of white stone and red conglomerate marble; in some of the spandrels there are very charming rosettes. In short, the interior is elegant in detail and gives a sense of spaciousness and light.

Exterior. The exterior, too, is impressive in its proportions, despite the ruined state of the porch and the unfortunate restoration of the domes and semidomes. The porch originally had seven bays; its handsome antique columns are still standing: four of Proconnesian marble, two of Theban granite, and two of Syenitic granite. The **türbe** of the founder, a simple octagonal building, is in front of the mosque beside the entrance gate. Nearby there is a ruined şadırvan, and outside in the corner of the precinct wall there is set a pretty çeşme. The külliye originally included an interesting hamam, but unfortunately this has vanished.

Immediately across the street there is an interesting **medrese** which is not a part of Cerrah Paşa's foundation. This was built in the second half of the 16C by Gevher Sultan, daughter of Selim II and wife of the great admiral Piyale Paşa. This medrese, recently restored, has the standard form of a rectangular porticoed courtyard with cells beyond.

Continue along Cerrah Paşa Cad. for another 100m and take the second turning on the right, Haseki Kadın Sok. A short distance up the street, on the right, are the shapeless remains of a massive column base wedged tightly between two houses. It is nearly as tall as the houses and is covered with ivy. This is all that is left of the famous *Column of Arcadius** (Pl. 9,3), erected by that emperor in 402 to commemorate his military triumphs. It stood in the centre of the Forum of Arcadius and was decorated with spiral bands of sculpture in bas relief representing the Emperor's victories, like Trajan's column in Rome. At the top of the column, which was more than 50m high, there was an enormous statue of Arcadius, placed there in 421 by his son and successor, Theodosius II. This statue was eventually toppled from the column and destroyed during an earthquake in 704.

The column itself remained standing for more than another thousand years until it was deliberately demolished in 1715, when it appeared to be in imminent danger of collapsing on the neighbouring houses. Now all that remains are the mutilated base and some fragments of sculpture from the column that are on display in the Archaeological Museum. It is possible to enter the interior of the base through a side door in the house to the left. Inside the base, there is a stairway to the top of the ruin; there you see a short stump of the column, with barely discernible remnants of the sculptured decoration.

After leaving the column, continue along Haseki Kadın Sok. to the end of the street. There you find the **külliye of Bayram Paşa**, which is divided by the street itself; on the right are the medrese and mektep, and on the left the mescit, tekke, türbe, and sebil. An inscription on the sebil gives the date of construction of the külliye as 1634. At that time Bayram Paşa was Kaymakam, or Governor, of Istanbul; two years later he became Grand Vezir under Murat IV and soon afterwards he died on the Sultan's expedition against Baghdad.

At the corner to the left is the handsome sebil, with five grilled openings; behind it is the really palatial türbe of the founder, looking rather like a small mosque. (It is said to be revetted inside with fine and original tiles; unfortunately it is shut up and inaccessible.) At the far end of the enclosed garden and grave-yard stands the mescit, which is flanked on two sides by the porticoed cells of the dervish tekke. The mescit is a large octagonal building which served also as the room where the dervishes performed their mystical ceremonies, with music and dancing. The whole complex is finely built of ashlar in the high classical manner, and the very irregularity of its design makes it singularly attractive.

*The Külliye of Haseki Hürrem

Turning left at the corner and passing the külliye of Bayram Paşa, you come immediately to the külliye of Haseki Hürrem (Pl. 9,3), which is contiguous with it to the west. This is the third largest and most magnificent mosque complex in the old city, surpassed only by those of the Conqueror and Süleyman the Magnificent.

This külliye was built by Süleyman for his wife, Haseki Hürrem, the famous Roxelana. The mosque and its dependencies were designed by Sinan and completed by him in 1539, making this the earliest known külliye by the great architect in Istanbul. According to tradition, Süleyman kept the project secret from Roxelana while the külliye was being built, and brought her to the site only on the day the mosque complex was completed and dedicated in her honour.

The mosque. The mosque itself is disappointing, especially as it is a work of Sinan. Originally it consisted of a small square room covered by a dome on stalactited pendentives, preceded by a rather pretentious porch of five bays that overlapped the building at both ends. It may perhaps have had a certain elegance of form and detail in its original design. But in 1612 a second and iden-tical room was added on the north: the north wall was removed and replaced with a great arch supported on two columns. The mihrab was then moved to the middle of the new extended east wall, so that it stands squeezed behind one of the columns. The result is distinctly unpleasing.

The pious foundations. The other buildings of the mosque complex are magnificent; comprising a medrese, primary school, public kitchen, and hospital. Moreover, most of the complex has been well restored. The **medrese** is immediately across the street from the mosque. It is of the usual type: a porticoed courtyard surrounded by the cells of the students and the larger domed dershane; but apart from its truly imperial size, it is singularly well-proportioned and excellent in detail. Its 20 columns are of granite, Proconnesian marble, and verd antique; their lozenge capitals are decorated with small rosettes and medallions of various elegant designs, as well as here and there a sort of snaky garland motif—a unique design. Also unique are the two pairs of lotus flower capitals, their leaves spreading out at the top to support a sort of abacus; though soft and featureless, they make a not unattractive variation from the almost equally characterless lozenge.

Two carved hemispherical bosses in the spandrils of the arcade call attention to the **dershane**, a monumental square room with a dome. The great charm of this courtyard must have been still greater when the faience panels with inscriptions were still in place in the lunettes of the windows; many years ago, when the building was abandoned and dilapidated, they were removed to the museum and are now on display at the Çinili Köşk (see p 81). Next to the medrese is the large and very oddly shaped **sibyan mektebi**, which is in two storeys with wide projecting eaves.

The **imaret**, which is beyond the mektep, is entered through a monumental portal that leads to an alleyway. At the end of this you enter the long rectangular courtyard of the imaret, shaded with trees. Vast kitchens with large domes and enormous chimneys (better seen from outside at the back) line three sides of the courtyard.

Haseki Hürrem's **hospital** is behind the medrese and entered from the street behind the külliye to the north. It is a building of most unusual form: the court is octagonal but without a columned portico. The two large corner-rooms at the back, whose great domes have stalactited pendentives coming far down the walls, originally opened to the courtyard through huge arches, now glassed-in; with these open rooms or eyvans all the other wards and chambers of the hospital communicated. Opposite the eyvans on one side is the entrance portal; this is approached through an irregular vestibule, like that found so often in Persian mosques. On the other side are the lavatories, also irregular in shape, while the eighth side of the courtyard forms the façade on the street with grilled windows. This building too has recently been well restored and is once again in use as a hospital.

Returning to the street outside Haseki Hürrem Camii, we continue in the same direction for about 400m. Then on the left, set back from the road and partly concealed by trees and houses, we come to the fine old mosque that has given its name to this quarter. This is *Davut Paşa Camii (Pl. 8,4), dated by an inscription over the door to 1485. Davut Paşa, the founder, was Grand Vezir under Beyazit II.

Interior. In plan the mosque is of the simplest type: just a square chamber covered by a large blind dome. However, the mihrab is in a five-sided apse projecting from the east wall, and to north and south there are small rooms, two on each side, once used as hostels for travelling dervishes. What gives the building its distinction and harmony is the beautiful shallow dome, quite obviously less than half a hemisphere. The pendentives of the dome are an unusually magnificent example of the stalactite form, here boldly incised and brought far down the corners of the walls.

Behind the mosque a delightfully topsy-turvy graveyard surrounds the founder's türbe, octagonal in form and with an odd dome in eight triangular segments. Across the narrow street to the north stands the medrese of the külliye, almost completely surrounded and concealed by houses. The courtyard is extremely handsome, with its re-used Byzantine columns and capitals, but it is in an advanced state of ruin and urgently needs restoration to something like its original form. The külliye also once had an imaret and a mektep, but these have completely disappeared.

Some 200m beyond Davut Paşa Camii and on the same side of the street we come to a grand and interesting mosque, ***Hekimoğlu Ali Paşa Camii** (Pl. 8,4).

> The founder of the mosque, Ali Paşa, was an Ottoman nobleman who was the son (oğlu) of the court physician (hekim), and was himself Grand Vezir for 15 years under Mahmut I. A long inscription in Turkish verse over the door to the mosque gives the date of construction as 1734–35; the architect was Ömer Aga.

Exterior. You can consider this complex to be either the last of the great classical buildings or the first in the new baroque style, for it has characteristics of both. At the corner of the precinct wall beside the north entrance is a very beautiful **sebil** of marble with five bronze grilles. Above this is an elaborate frieze with a long inscription and fine carvings of vines, flowers and rosettes in the new rococo style that had recently been introduced from France.

The façade of the **türbe** along the street is faced in marble, corbelled out toward the top and with a çeşme at the far end. It is a large rectangular building with two domes dividing it into two equal square areas. This form was not unknown in the classical period (compare Sinan's Pertev Paşa türbe at Eyüp, see chapter 17) but it was rare, and the use of it here seems to indicate a willingness to experiment with new forms.

Farther along the precinct wall stands the monumental gateway with a domed chamber above; this was the **library** of the foundation. Though the manuscripts have been transferred elsewhere, it still contains the painted wooden cages with grilles in which they were stored; an elegant floral frieze runs around the top of the walls and floral medallions adorn the dome. From the columned porch at the top of the steps leading to the library there is a good view of the whole complex, with its singularly attractive garden full of tall cypresses and aged plane trees, and opposite the stately porch and very slender minaret of the mosque.

Interior. The **mosque** itself, raised on a substructure containing a cistern, is purely classical in form. Indeed, its plan is almost an exact replica of that at Cerrah Paşa, seen earlier on this itinerary. In contrast to Cerrah Paşa, the present building is perhaps a little weak; there is a certain blurring of forms and enervating of structural distinctions, an effect not mitigated by the pale colour of the tile revetment. The tiles are still Turkish, not manufactured at Iznik as formerly, but at the recently established kilns at Tekfursarayı (see p 231) in Istanbul. All the same, the general impression of the interior is charming if not exactly powerful.

There is a further hint of the new baroque style in one of its less pleasing traits in some of the capitals of the columns, both in the porch and beneath the sultan's loge. The traditional stalactite and lozenge capitals have been abandoned there in favour of a very weak and characterless form like an impost capital, which seems quite out of scale and out of place.

Precincts. The whole complex within the precinct wall has been well restored. Outside the precinct, across the street to the northeast, stands the **tekke** of the foundation, but little is left of it save a very ruinous zaviye, or room for the dervish ceremonies.

We now walk back to the intersection we passed just before we reached the mosque. There we turn into Yaprağı Sok, which after the first intersection becomes Sırrı Paşa Sok. Just before the next turning on the left we come to a Greek Orthodox church surrounded by a garden. This is the **church of the Panaghia Gorgoepikoos**, the 'Virgin who answers petitions quickly'. The church is referred to as early as 1342, and the first mention of it after the Conquest is in Tryphon's list of 1583. The epithet Panaghia Gorgoepikoos seems to be a survival of the ancient cult of Athena. Ancient architectural fragments found in a nearby construction project some years ago indicate that a temple of Herakles or Zeus may have stood here.

We turn left at the corner beyond the church, and then after the first intersection we see on our right the ruins of a once handsome **medrese**. It was built by Sinan for Nişancı Mehmet Bey, who served as Keeper of the Royal Seal (Nişancı) in the reign of Süleyman the Magnificent. The medrese was built before 1566, when Nişancı Mehmet Bay died on hearing the news of Süleyman's death.

At the corner beyond the medrese we turn right on Köprülüzade Sok., which after three blocks brings us to the southwest corner of an enormous open reservoir at one of the two summits of the Seventh Hill, an eminence known in Byzantine times as Xerolophos, the Dry Hill. This the third of the city's three surviving open Roman reservoirs, known in Turkish as **Altı Mermer**, the Six Marbles; in Byzantium it was called the Cistern of St. Mocius, from a famous church of that name which stood in its vicinity. The cistern was constructed during the reign of Anastasius I (491–518); like the two other surviving Roman reservoirs, it fell into disuse in the later Byzantine period. It has recently been converted into a playground known as the **Fatih Educational Park**.

The cistern is a vast rectangle measuring 170m by 147m on the inside, with walls 6m thick; the present depth is about 10–15m. On the east and south sides the wall emerges, between 2m and 4m, from the surrounding earth. The walls are of good late Roman construction, they are composed of brick, alternating both inside and out with beds of dressed stone, 15cm to 20cm high. The interior of the cistern is most easily reached on the north side.

We now retrace our steps to the intersection just east of Hekimoğlu Ali Paşa Camii, after which we head south on Ese Kapısı Sok., following this to its intersection with Koca Mustafa Paşa Cad. (the continuation of Cerrah Paşa Cad.). We then take the street opposite and slightly to the left, Tekkesi Sok. On the opposite side of the street, within the grounds of a government building, there are the remains of an interesting monument that is partly Byzantine and partly Ottoman.

This complex, known in Turkish as **Ese Kapı Mescidi**, consists of two walls of a Byzantine church and the wreck of a medrese by Sinan. Of the church only the south and east walls remain. It was of the simplest kind: an oblong room without aisles ending at the east in a large projecting apse and two tiny side apses. The church is thought to date from the beginning of the 14C, but nothing is known of its history nor even the name of the saint to whom it was dedicated. In about 1560 the church was converted into a mosque by Hadım (the Eunuch) Ibrahim Paşa, who at that time was Süleyman's Grand Vezir, and who added to it a handsome medrese designed by Sinan. Both mosque and medrese were destroyed by the great earthquake of 1894, and they have remained abandoned ever since.

The ruins of the medrese, which is unusual in plan, are rather fine; its large dershane still retains traces of plaster decoration around the dome, and the narrow courtyard beyond must have been very attractive. In the southern side apse there could be seen up until recent years the traces of frescoes, but these have now disappeared. The name Ese is a corruption of Isa, or Christ. Thus Ese Kapı means the Gate of Christ, and some scholars have suggested that it preserves the memory of one of the gates in the city walls built by Constantine the Great, which are thought to have been close by. This is possible, but the evidence is inconclusive.

We continue along Tekkesi Sok. to the first turning on the right, Gümrükçü Sok; we follow this for one block and then turn left on Sancaktarlar Tekkesi Sok.

After a few turnings this takes us to an octagonal Byzantine building known as **Sancaktar Mescidi** (Pl. 8,6). This has been tentatively identified, on very slender evidence, as one of the buildings of the Monastery of Gastria. The legend is that this monastery was founded in the 4C by St. Helena, mother of Constantine the Great, and that it derives its name of Gastria, which means 'vases', from the vases of flowers she brought back from Calvary, where she had discovered a fragment of the True Cross. This story has been refuted by the French scholar Janin, who shows that there is no trace of the existence of the monastery before the 9C.

The present little building has the form of an octagon on the exterior with a projecting apse at the east end; the interior takes the form of a domed cross. It is thought that it was once a funerary chapel, and has been dated variously from the 11C to the 14C. The building was for long an abandoned ruin, but it has now been restored and is once again serving as a mosque.

Leaving Sancaktar Mescidi, we walk straight ahead for a few paces to the next intersection and then turn right on to Marmara Cad. This leads back to Koca Mustafa Paş̧a Cad.; we turn left there and then take the second right onto Ramazan Efendi Cad. A short way along on the right we come to a small but charming mosque with a pretty garden courtyard in front; this is ***Ramazan Efendi Camii**, a work of Sinan (Pl. 8,4).

The mosque was founded by an official in the Ottoman court named Hoca Hüsref, but it soon took the name of Ramazan Efendi Camii, after the first şeyh of the dervish tekke that was part of the original külliye. The mosque was designed and built by Sinan, and a long inscription over the inner door by his friend, the poet Mustafa Sa'i, gives the date as 1586; thus this is undoubtedly the last mosque erected by the great architect, completed when he was well into his nineties.

The mosque. The mosque is a structure of the simplest type: a small rectangular room with a wooden roof and porch. It is thought that it was originally covered by a wooden dome and that it had a porch with three domed bays supported by four marble columns; the present wooden porch and flat wooden ceiling are botched restorations after an earthquake. The minaret is an elegant structure both in proportion and detail, while the small şadırvan in the courtyard is exquisitely carved. The great fame of the mosque comes from the magnificent panels of faience with which it is adorned. These are from the Iznik kilns at the height of their artistic production, and are thus some of the finest tiles in existence; the borders of 'tomato-red' or Armenian bole are especially celebrated.

After leaving the mosque, we return to Koca Mustafa Paşa Cad. and continue in the same direction as before. A short way along the avenue forks to the right and soon comes to a square shaded with trees and lined with teahouses. At the left side of the square is the entrance to the outer courtyard of ***Koca Mustafa Paşa Camii** (Pl. 8,4), the mosque after which the avenue and the surrounding neighbourhood are named.

The central building of this picturesque complex is Koca Mustafa Pasa Camii, which was originally a Byzantine church tentatively identified as St. Andrew in Krisei. The identification and history of this church are, however, very obscure and much disputed. The opinions of Byzantinists may be summarised as follows: Koca Mustafa Pasa may have been one of the churches in this region dedicated to a St. Andrew; if it is, it is probably that dedicated to St. Andrew of Crete in c 1284 by the Princess Theodora Raoulaina. Also, the present building was almost certainly of the ambulatory type; it may have been built on the foundations of an earlier church dedicated to St. Andrew the Apostle; and it certainly re-used 6C materials, especially capitals. In any event, the church was converted into a mosque by Koca Mustafa Pasa, Grand Vezir in the reign of Selim I (1512–20).

Interior. When the church was converted into a mosque the interior arrangements were re-oriented by ninety degrees because of the direction in which the building was laid out. Thus the mihrab and mimber are under the semidome against the south wall; and the entrance is in the north wall, in front of which a wooden porch has been added. You enter through a door at the west end of the north aisle into the narthex, from where you should proceed at once to the central bay of the narthex. This bay has a small dome supported by columns with beautiful 6C capitals of the pseudo-Ionic type. From here the central portal opens into a sort of inner narthex or aisle, separated from the nave by only two verd antique columns; this aisle is regrettably obstructed by a large wooden gallery.

From this point the whole interior of the former church is visible; it now has a trefoil shape but was probably originally ambulatory: that is, there would have been a triple arcade supported by two columns to north and south, like the one that still exists on the west. To the east the conch of the apse is preceded by a deep barrel-vault; to the north and south the two later Ottoman semidomes open out. Even in its greatly altered form it is an extremely attractive building.

Precincts. The dependencies of the mosque include a medrese, a tekke, a mektep, and two türbes; what survive of these are of a much later date than the conversion of the church into a mosque. The mosque is one of the most popular Muslim religious shrines in the city, for in one of the türbes in the courtyard the famous Istanbul folk-saint Sümbül (Hyacinth) Efendi is buried. Sümbül Efendi was the first şeyh of the dervish tekke established here in the early 16C, and in the centuries since then he has been prayed to by the people of the city for help in solving their problems. In the other türbe Sümbül Efendi's daughter Rahine is buried; she is generally prayed to by young women looking for husbands. The ancient tree tottering above her türbe is also said to possess miraculous powers.

After leaving the mosque precincts, we return along Koca Mustafa Paşa Cad. as far as the first right after the fork in the road. This street, Müdafayi Milliye Cad., leads down the slope of the Seventh Hill towards the Marmara shore. About 250m along turn left on Marmara Cad., a wide avenue that runs along the heights parallel to the sea. A short way along we see, on the right, the large Armenian **church of Surp Kevork** (St. George), known in Turkish as **Sulu Monastir**.

> The present church is built on the site of the ancient Byzantine monastery of St. Mary Peribleptos, the All-Seeing, of which nothing but substructures remain. It was founded by the Emperor Romanus III Argyrus (1028–34), and after the recapture of Constantinople by the Byzantines in 1261 it was restored by Michael VIII Palaeologus (1259–82). It remained in the hands of the Greeks after the Conquest, but then in 1458 Fatih gave it over to the Armenians. The church served as the Patriarchate of the Armenian Gregorian Church until 1643–44, when it was supplanted by the church of Surp Asdvadzadzin in Kumkapı (see below).

Once past the church we turn right on Canbaziye Sok., which leads steeply downhill towards the Marmara. As we do so we see below us and to the left the domes of a large double bath known as **Ağa Hamamı**, a work of Sinan, now disaffected and used for commercial purposes, part of it in ruins.

At the lower end of the street we turn right on Orgeneral Abdurrahman Nafiz Gürman Cad., formerly known as Samatya Cad. This avenue skirts the foot of the Seventh Hill not far from the sea, following the branch of the ancient Mese that led to the Golden Gate.

After the first intersection we see on our left the courtyard wall of the Greek **church of Haghios Georgios Kyparissas**, St. George of the Cypresses. The original church on this site is believed to have been founded in the medieval Byzantine period. The first reference to it after the Conquest is by Stefan Gerlach in 1573. The present church dates from a rebuilding in 1834.

A little farther along the avenue, on the right, we see on the heights above the tall campanile of a modern Greek church, **Haghios Menas** (St. Menas). The earliest mention of the church is in Tryphon's list of 1583. The present church dates to a rebuilding in 1833.

Beneath the church, but in no way connected with it, there are some very important and ancient substructures. They are entered from the main avenue and are presently used as a carpentry shop. These substructures, discovered only in 1935, have been identified as the crypt of the *__Martyrium of SS. Karpos and Papylos__ (Pl. 8,6), dedicated to two martyrs who perished during the Decian persecutions in 250–51. The crypt is a large circular domed chamber reminiscent of the tholos tombs at Mycenae, only constructed of brick rather than stone, in the excellent late Roman technique of the 4C–5C AD. At the east end is a deep apse, while completely round the chamber runs a vaulted passage, also of brick.

About 150m farther along, after crossing Hacı Kadın Çeşmesi Sok., we come on our right to the Armenian Catholic church of __Surp Nikogos__ (St. Nicholas), a modern structure of little interest.

The side street directly opposite leads to two interesting old Greek Orthodox churches just inside the Marmara sea-walls. The first of these that we come to is __Haghios Nikolaos__. This is mentioned in Tryphon's list of 1583, the present church dating from a reconstruction in 1830. A short way beyond it toward the Marmara we come to the __church of Christos Analepsis__ (the Resurrection of Christ), first referred to in 1573 by Stefan Gerlach, with the present building dating from a reconstruction in 1832. Many consider this to be the most beautiful of the post-Conquest Greek churches in Istanbul, particularly because it retains its original wooden colonnade and iconostasis.

We now continue on the main avenue, and after about 350m we come on our right to the Greek __church of Haghioi Konstantinos kai Eleni__, dedicated to Constantine the Great and his mother Helena. It is believed that the church dates back to the early 15C, shortly before the Conquest. After the Conquest it was used by the Turkish-speaking Christians from Anatolia known as the Karamanlı. The earliest recorded reference to this church is by Petrus Gyllius in 1547, while the present building dates from a reconstruction in 1833. On the outer wall of the church near the entryway there is a relief showing Constantine and Helena holding between them the True Cross, a representation patterned on the statue that stood on top of the Milion at the beginning of the ancient Mese (see p 201).

**St. John the Baptist of Studius

The second street to the left past SS. Constantine and Helena leads to the walled courtyard of a ruined but extremely impressive Byzantine church. This is the former monastic church of St. John the Baptist of Studius, known in Turkish as İmrahor Camii (Pl. 8,6). This is the oldest surviving Christian sanctuary in the city, and though in ruins it is still one of the greatest monuments of architecture remaining from the days of Byzantium.

The church of St. John the Baptist was completed in 463 and its associated monastery was founded shortly afterwards. The church and monastery were benefactions of the Roman patrician Studius, who served as consul during the reign of the Emperor Marcian (450–57). The first monks in the Studion, as the monastery was called, were from an order known as the Akoimati, receiving this name because they perpetuated the divine service day and night throughout the year, praying in shifts around the clock and calendar.

In its early years the Studion housed a full thousand monks, and was one of the richest and most populous monasteries in Byzantium. Later, however, during the Iconoclastic Period, the Studion and all other monasteries in the Empire were suppressed and then finally shut down altogether in 754 by Constantine V. They remained closed for the next generation but were reopened in 787, after the first restoration of icons by the Empress Eirene, mother of Constantine VI.

The golden age in the history of the Studion began in 799, when the great abbot Theodore arrived to take direction of the monastery. During the following generation Theodore made the Studion the most powerful and influential monastery in the Empire. He was a leader in the struggle to restore icon veneration, which was proscribed again in 815 during the reign of the iconoclast Leo V. Theodore was also an outspoken critic of court morals, an activity that brought him into conflict with four successive emperors in the first quarter of the 9C. Although he was reviled, beaten, deposed and exiled by each of them in turn, he held firm to his stern principles to the grave. Theodore died in exile on the isle of Prinkipo in the Marmara on 11 November 826, but in 843 he was reburied in the garden of the Studion, after the final restoration of icons under Michael III. Today he is venerated in the Greek Orthodox Church as St. Theodore of Studion.

Under the direction of St. Theodore, and his successors, the Studion flourished and became a centre for the first cultural and artistic renaissance of Byzantium in the early 9C. Many monks of the Studion won renown as composers of sacred hymns, painters of icons, and illuminators of manuscripts. The monastery was also noted for its scholarship and was one of the centres for the preservation and copying of ancient manuscripts, many of which would be carried to Europe by Byzantine scholars during the Western renaissance in the 14C–15C.

The most momentous hour in the long history of the Studion occurred on 15 August 1261, when Byzantium was officially restored in its ancient capital after the recapture of the city from the Latins. On that day Michael VIII Palaeologus entered in triumph through the Golden Gate and walked in procession to the Studion, following the sacred icon of the Hodegetria, which was being carried before the populace in a chariot. After reaching the Studion the icon was placed on the main altar of the church, and the Emperor joined the Patriarch in a ceremony of thanksgiving. Then the Emperor left the church and mounted his white charger in the square outside, after which he and his entourage rode off to Haghia Sophia for his formal recoronation.

The Studion continued as one of the spiritual and intellectual centres of the Empire right up to the Conquest. During the first half of the 15C the University of Constantinople was located at the Studion, and during that period some of the greatest scholars in the history of Byzantium taught and studied there, men who would later be influential figures in the Italian renaissance of the 15C. The Studion survived the fall of Byzantium and continued to function for nearly half a century after the Conquest, celebrating its millennium in 1463.

But then at the close of the 15C the church of St. John was converted into a mosque, and the few monks that were still resident in the monastery were forced to seek shelter elsewhere. The founder of the mosque was Ilyas Bey, Master of the Horse (Imrahor) under Beyazit II, and so it came to be called Imrahor Camii. What was left of the monastery in modern times was utterly destroyed in the earthquake of 1894. The church itself was badly damaged in the earthquake, and from that time on it was abandoned and allowed to fall into ruins. Although several cursory studies have been made of the building, it still awaits a thorough archaeological and architectural investigation.

The church. The church was preceded by an atrium, or courtyard, whose site is now occupied by the walled garden through which the building is approached. The narthex is divided into three bays; the wider central bay has a very beautiful portal consisting of four columns in antis, with magnificent Corinthian capitals supporting an elaborate entablature with richly sculptured architrave, frieze and cornice. Two of the marble door-frames still stand between the columns. From the narthex five doors lead into the church. In form the church was a pure basilica, with a nave flanked by side aisles separated from the sanctuary by two rows of seven columns each. Six of these on the north side still stand; they are of verd antique, with capitals and entablature as in the narthex.

The nave ends in a single semicircular apse where tiers of seats once rose, for the clergy, with the altar in front of them. Originally there was a second row of columns, above the entablature of the aisle colonnades, which supported the wooden roof. The interior was revetted with marble and the upper parts decorated with mosaics. The floor was also of mosaic in opus sectile design, and of this some portions may still be seen, although they are fast disappearing.

Leaving the church, we turn left and follow the winding path that leads around to the southwest corner of its outer precincts. Here, at the edge of a vacant lot, there is a small shed that gives access to a covered **cistern** that was once part of the Studion. It is quite impressive, containing 23 granite columns with handsome Corinthian capitals. The cistern is usually accessible, being used as a sort of iron-shop and storage-place for bedsteads. Beside it there is a holy well with two ancient columns, the identity of which is unknown.

After leaving the cistern, we continue on in the same direction as far as the railway line. There turn left and follow the railway as far as the first underpass, from where a path leads out to the sea-walls. At this point turn right to come to an ancient portal called **Narlı Kapı**, the Pomegranate Gate, from where a path leads out to the Marmara highway.

In Byzantine times this gateway was used by the Emperor when he went from the Great Palace to the Studion by sea. According to the Book of Ceremonies, the imperial visit to the Studion occurred annually on 28 August, the feast day of the Decapitation of St. John. The Emperor landed at a quay before the gateway, he was received by the Abbot of the Studion, and the two led the procession to the church, walking between two long files of chanting monks holding lighted tapers. At the end of the service the Emperor was served refreshments in the monastery gardens, after which he returned in procession to the royal barge, passing once again through the portal which even then was known as the Pomegranate Gate.

From Narlı Kapı you can walk westward along the shore road to the city walls, where the next itinerary begins. Those who wish to follow that itinerary on another day can return to town by walking back along the shore road. This is a pleasant stroll on a fine day, and along the way stretches of the ancient Byzantine sea-walls and the remains of some of the massive defence towers can be seen. The walls and towers along this part of the Marmara shore were built by the Emperor Theophilus (829–42), at a time when the city was threatened by an Arab invasion fleet. But the fleet never appeared before the city at that time, undoubtedly because the Arabs were deterred by the great walls that ringed it both by land and by sea.

Outside Narlı Kapı we come to a church built up against the Marmara sea-walls. This is the Armenian Catholic church of **Surp Mıgırdıç** (St. John the Baptist). It has been suggested that the original church here was Byzantine in foundation, and that it was a dependency of the Studion monastery.

We now start walking back along the Marmara shore. Much of this is now flanked with parks, so that you can to some extent escape the noise and fumes of the traffic on the coastal highway. This highway was laid out on filled-in land and was completed in 1959. Before that time the sea came right up to the Byzantine sea-walls along the Marmara shore. Considerable stretches of these walls have survived and we see them paralleling the railway line as we stroll along the Marmara shore.

About 2km past Narlı Kapı we come to the site of the ancient **Harbour of Theodosius**. This was originally created during the reign of Constantine the Great by a certain Eleutherios, by whose name it is sometimes known. Theodosius I (379–95) dredged the harbour and surrounded it with massive defence walls, of which those on the seaward side are now being rebuilt. The area inside the sea walls here is called **Vlanga**, a name that goes back to Byzantine times. Vlanga has always been an area given over to kitchen gardens, and it still remains so to a certain extent, despite the enormous amount of building that has gone on around it in recent years. The soil of these gardens is alluvial earth deposited by the Lycus River, which still flows into the sea here after flowing underground through the city.

Another 1.5km or so brings us to the site of the ancient Kontoskalion Harbour, now known as **Kumkapı** (Pl. 10,6), the Sand Gate. This was originally built by the Emperor Julian (361–63), and it was dredged and its fortifications strengthened and repaired by several later emperors. After the reconquest of the city from the Latins in 1261, Michael VIII Palaeologus made the Kontoskalion the main base for the Byzantine navy. The harbour silted up in Ottoman times and was no longer used. A new harbour has been created here in recent years for the local fishing fleet, which sells its catch in a market around the port. Kumkapi is the largest and busiest fishing-port in the city, and is used by the local fishermen who sail from here out into the Marmara, up the Bosphorus, and along the coasts of the Black Sea. The port is always filled with picturesque caiques and the quayside is often carpeted with brilliantly dyed fishing-nets spread there to be dried and mended by the fishermen and their families. The fish-market is one of the most colourful in the city, as the fishmongers shout out in Turkish, Greek, Armenian, and even Laz, the language of the Caucasian people who live along the eastern coast of the Black Sea in Turkey,

We now enter the city via an underpass that takes us beneath the railway line. This takes us through the site of the ancient **Porta Kontaskalion**, one of the principal gateways in the Byzantine sea-walls along the Marmara.

At the first intersection we come **Kumkapı Meydanı**, an extremely lively and picturesque market square lined with some of the best fish-restaurants in the city. This is the principal Armenian quarter of the city, and in times past a large number of Greeks lived here as well, their numbers now much diminished.

The Armenian Patriarchate is a short way to the west of the square in the precinct of the Gregorian church of **Surp Asdvadzadzin** (The Immaculate Conception). This was originally a Greek church given over to the Armenians after the Turkish Conquest, becoming the cathedral of the Armenian Patriarchate in 1641. The present church dates to a rebuilding in 1828 after a fire that destroyed the earlier building. Beneath the church there is an ayazma dedicated to St. Theodoros.

There are two Greek churches a short way to the east of the square. The first of these that we come to is the **Panaghia Elpida**. The earliest mention of a church of this name is in 1400, and the first reference to it after the Conquest is by Stefan Gerlach in 1576. The present church dates from a complete rebuilding in 1895. A crypt beneath the church contains an ayazma dedicated to St. George.

The second of the two Greek churches is that of **Haghia Kyriaki** (St. Kyriaki). The earliest reference to this church is Tryphon's list of 1583. The present church is also due to a rebuilding in 1895. A crypt beneath the church contains the ayazma of St. Basil.

There are also two old mosques in Kumkapı, though both have been almost completely rebuilt. Close to the western side of the square is **Tavası Süleyman Ağa Camii**, founded early in the 17C and rebuilt in the 19C. The founder, Süleyman Ağa, was a tavası, or black slave,who was castrated and sold to Topkapı Sarayı, where he rose to the rank of Chief Black Eunuch. The only part of the mosque remaining from the original foundation is the wooden minaret, a very interesting example of Ottoman wood-carving.

The second of the mosques, **Nişancı Mehmet Paşa Camii**, is some distance to the northwest of the square. This was founded in 1475 by Karamanlı Mehmet Paşa, one of Fatih's Grand Vezirs. The two-storied wooden building that serves as the outer prayer-room of the mosque dates from a late Ottoman reconstruction. Behind the mosque is the double bath of this little külliye; this is the Nisancı Hamamı, which is still in use today.

We leave Kumkapı Meydanı via Ördekli Bakkal Sok. and then Büyük Kömürcü Sok. This takes us to Tiyatro Cad. which leads up the southern slope of the Third Hill to Beyazit Square, where this long itinerary comes to an end.

16 · Along the Land Walls

This itinerary begins at the Sea of Marmara and follows the land-walls to the Golden Horn, with several detours to visit places of interest inside and outside the ancient fortifications. For the most part, no specific directions will be given for walking this chapter, for in some stretches it is more convenient to walk inside the walls, in others outside, and sometimes you can stroll along the walls themselves.

See main Atlas pages 8, 4 and 5, plus sectional plans (Land-Walls I, II, III) within this walks.

The ****Byzantine** (or **Theodosian**) **land-walls** extend from the Sea of Marmara to the Golden Horn, a distance of about 6.5km. These walls protected Byzantium from its enemies for more than a thousand years, and in that way had a profound effect on the history of medieval Europe. Although they are now in ruins, the walls of Byzantium are still a splendid and even awesome sight, with towers and battlements marching across the hills and valleys of Thrace.

The land-walls were, for the most part, constructed in the first half of the 5C, during the reign of Theodosius II (408–50). The first phase of the Theodosian wall was completed in 413 under the direction of Anthemius, Prefect of the East. This consisted of a single wall studded with defence towers at regular intervals. However, in 447 a violent earthquake destroyed much of this wall, throwing down 57 towers. This happened at a very critical time, for Attila the Hun was then advancing on Constantinople. Reconstruction of the fortifications began immediately under the direction of the then Prefect of the East, Constantine.

The circus factions of the Hippodrome all worked together in the project, each of them assigned a certain stretch of the circuit, and within two months the walls had been rebuilt and were far stronger than they had been before the earthquake. In addition to restoring and strengthening the original wall, Constantine added an outer wall and a moat, making the city virtually impregnable to assault by land. The new walls saved the city from Attila, the Scourge of God, who redirected his invasion against the western regions of the Roman Empire.

Plans of the walls. Even though large stretches of the fortifications are in ruins, enough remains of the Theodosian walls to reconstruct their original plan. The main element in the defence system was the inner wall, which was about 5m thick at the base and rose to a height of 12m above the city. This wall was guarded by 96 towers, 18m to 20m high, at an average interval of 55m; these were mostly square but some were polygonal. Each tower was generally divided into two floors, which did not communicate with one another. The lower storeys were used either for storage or for guard-houses, and were entered from inside the city. The upper rooms were entered from the parapet walk, which was connected by staircases to the ground and to the tops of the towers, where engines were placed for hurling missiles or the terrible incendiary mixture known as Greek Fire.

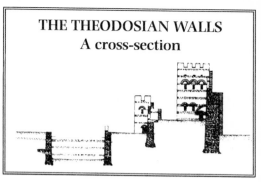

THE THEODOSIAN WALLS
A cross-section

Between the inner and outer walls there was a terrace, called the peribolos, which varied from 15m to 20m in breadth, and stood at about 5m above the level of the inner city. The outer wall, the protichisma, was about 2m thick and 8.5m in height. This wall also had 96 towers, alternating in position with those of the inner wall; in general these were either square or crescent-shaped in turn. Beyond this there was an outer terrace called the parateichion, bounded on the outside by the counterscarp of the moat, which was a battlement nearly 2m high.

The moat itself was originally about 10m deep and 20m wide, and was flooded when the city was threatened by invaders. Altogether it was a most formidable system of fortification, perhaps the most elaborate and unassailable ever devised in the medieval world.

Most of the inner wall and nearly all of its huge towers are still standing, although sieges, earthquakes, and the ravages of time have left their scars. While a few of the towers are still intact, most of them are split or cracked, or have half-tumbled to the ground. The outer walls have been almost completely obliterated in many places, and the fragmentary remains of only about half of the towers can still be seen. But in recent years large sections of the walls have been reconstructed, particularly in the stretch midway between the Marmara and the Golden Horn, where you can see the whole cross-section of the defence-works from the inner ramparts through the outer works, including the ditch that extended along their outer periphery.

The Marble Tower to Yedikule (c 620m)

The sea-walls along the Marmara joined the land-walls at the southwest corner of the city; they are anchored by the **Marble Tower**, the handsome structure standing on a little promontory by the sea. This tower, 13m on a side, at its base, and 30m high, with its lower half faced in marble, is unlike any other structure in the whole defence system. It is thought that it may have been designed as an imperial sea-pavilion, a pied-à-terre for the Emperor and his party when they came by sea from the Great Palace to visit the shrine of Zoodochos Pege, which was outside the Theodosian walls. The tower also seems to have served, for a time, as a prison, and you can still see the chute down which the bodies of those executed were thrown into the sea.

A short way in from the shore highway, immediately to the north of the first tower of the inner wall, there is one of the ancient gateways of the city; this is called the **Gate of Christ** because of the laurate monogram XP (the first two Greek letters in his name) above it.

Entryways

In the long line of the Theodosian walls there were only ten gates and a few small posterns. Five of the ten gates were public entryways and five were used exclusively by the military, such as the Gate of Christ (this was also called the **First Military Gate**. The distinction was not so much in their structure as in the fact that the public gates had bridges leading over the moat to the country beyond, while the military gates gave access only to the fortifications. Until the end of the last century Stamboul was still a walled town and these gates were the only entrances to the city from Thrace. However, in recent times the walls have been breached in several places to permit the passage of the railway and modern highways. Nevertheless, nearly all the ancient gates continue in use, as they have now for more than fifteen centuries.

The first stretch of the Theodosian walls is rather difficult to inspect because of the impedance of the railway line. Those able to make the effort will find that the wall around the Gate of Christ is in a remarkably good state of preservation, with hardly a stone out of place. The first small tower of the protichisma bears an inscription of John VIII Palaeologus (1425–48); the fourth tower in the inner wall (counting from the Marmara) has an inscription of Romanus I Lecapenus (919–44); and the seventh inner tower has one with the names of Leo III (717–41) and his son Constantine V (741–75); all of them recording repairs to the walls. There are still 30 legible inscriptions recording imperial repairs on the towers, gates and ramparts that remain standing between the Marmara and the Golden Horn; they range over a period of more than a thousand years, evidence of how carefully the Byzantines maintained the great walls that stood between them and their enemies.

The railway cuts through the walls between the seventh and eighth towers of the inner wall. The eighth tower of the inner wall forms the southwest corner of **Yedikule**, the Castle of the Seven Towers, while the ninth and tenth towers are marble pylons flanking the famous Golden Gate; these towers are also part of Yedikule, as is the eleventh and last tower in this first stretch of the Theodosian walls. Immediately beyond this last tower is **Yedikule Kapı**, a small portal which was the public entryway to this part of the city in Byzantine times, the Golden Gate being reserved for ceremonial occasions. In the interior above the arch of this gate there is the figure of an imperial Byzantine eagle represented in white marble. After passing through the gate we walk a short distance along the main avenue, Yedikule Cad., after which we bear right to walk around the walls of the fortress to its entrance.

**Yedikule and the Golden Gate

Yedikule (Pl. 8,7) is a curious structure, partly Byzantine and partly Turkish. The seven eponymous towers consist of four in the Theodosian wall itself, plus three additional towers built inside the walls by Fatih. The three inner towers are connected together and joined to the Theodosian walls by four heavy curtain-walls, forming a five-sided enclosure. As has been seen, the two central towers in the Theodosian wall are marble pylons flanking the Golden Gate, and are actually older than the walls themselves. Yedikule was never used as a castle in the usual sense, but two of the towers served in Ottoman times as prisons; the others were used as storage places for a part of the State treasure.

The main entrance to Yedikule (open 09.30–17.00; closed Mon) is by a gate near the east tower; once inside the grounds we turn left to enter the tower itself. This is sometimes called the Tower of the Ambass-adors, since in Ottoman times foreign envoys were often im-prisoned here. Many of these unfortunates have carved their names and dates and tales of woe upon the walls of the tower in half adozen languages. An in-scription in French gives this advice in verse; 'Prisoners, who in your misery groan in this sad place, offer your sorrows with a good heart to God and you will find them light-ened'. The floors of the tower have fallen out, but a staircase in the thickness of the wall leads up to the top. When at the top it is worth

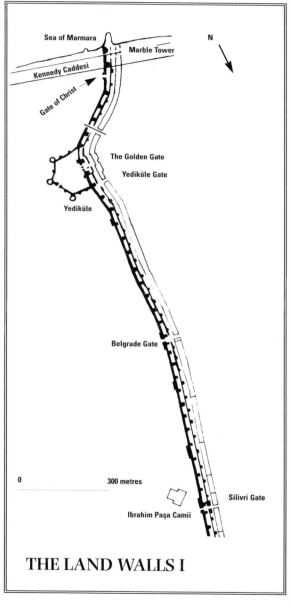

while walking around the chemin de ronde as far as the Golden Gate, for there is a fine view of the castle and of the Theodosian walls down to the sea.

The pylon to the left of the Golden Gate was also used as a prison in Ottoman times, and it was one of the principal places of execution in the city. On exhibition are the instruments of torture and execution that were used here in Ottoman times, as well as the infamous 'well of blood', down which the heads of those executed in the tower were supposed to have been thrown to be flushed into the sea. Sultan Osman II was one of the many executed here, strangled by the bowstring after he was deposed on 22 May 1622, when he was only 17 years old.

The much celebrated ****Golden Gate** between the pylons was actually a Roman triumphal arch erected in about 390 by Theodosius I, the Great. At that time the present city walls had not yet been built and the triumphal arch, as was customary, stood by itself on the Via Egnatia, about 2km outside the walls of Constantine. The arch was of the usual Roman form, with a triple arcade consisting of a large central archway flanked by two smaller ones. The outlines of the arches can still be seen clearly although the openings were bricked up in later Byzantine times. The gates themselves were covered with gold plate—hence the name—and the façade was decorated with sculptures, the most famous of which was a group of four elephants, placed there to commemorate the triumphal entry of Thedosius the Great after his victory over Maxentius.

When Theodosius II decided to extend the city walls two decades later, he incorporated the Golden Gate within his new land-walls. It was presumably in connection with this new wall that he built the small marble gate outside the triumphal arch; the arch itself would have had no gates, except for ornamental iron or bronze grilles, and would have been indefensible. The outer gateway is part of the general system of defence; together with the curtain walls that join it to the city walls near the polygonal towers, it forms a small courtyard in front of the Golden Gate.

> After the time of Theodosius the Great, the Golden Gate was, on many occasions, the scene of triumphal entries by Byzantine emperors: Heraclius in 629 after he saved the Empire by defeating the Persians; Constantine V, Basil I, and Basil II after their victories over the Bulgars; John I Tzimisces after his defeat of the Russians; Theophilus and his son Michael III after their victories over the Arabs. Perhaps the most emotional of all these triumphal entries was that of 15 August 1261, when Michael VIII Palaeologus rode through the Golden Gate on a white charger after Constantinople was recaptured from the Latins. This was also the last time an Emperor of Byzantium rode in triumph through the Golden Gate. In its last two centuries the history of the Empire was one of continuing defeat, and by that time the Golden Gate had been walled up for defence, never again to open.

There is an interesting old mosque a short distance to the north. of Yedikule, approached from Yedikule Cad. along Hacı Evhat Sok. This brings us to **Hacı Evhat Camii**, built by Sinan in 1585. The mosque was heavily restored in 1945 after having been destroyed by a fire in 1920. The only singular feature of the mosque is its minaret, which rises from over the door in the centre of the entrance façade.

Yedikule to Belgrad Kapı (c 620m)

From Yedikule to the next town gate, Belgrad Kapı, it is possible to walk either on top of the great wall or on the terrace below, for the fortifications along this stretch are in quite good condition. All of the 11 towers that guard the wall along this line are still standing, as are all but one of those in the outer wall. An inscription on the eighth tower of the inner wall records repairs by Leo III and Constantine V in the years 720 to 741, and one on the tenth tower of the outer wall states that it was restored in 1434 by John VIII Palaeologus.

Belgrad Kapı was known in Byzantium as the Second Military Gate. It was also called Porta tou Deuterou, because it led to the military quarter of Deuteros, where the Gothic soldiers had their barracks during the early Byzantine period. This was the largest of all the military gates and it may also have been used in Byzantium by the public, as indeed it has been since. The gate came by its Turkish name because Süleyman settled in its vicinity many of the artisans he brought back with him from Belgrade after his capture of that city in 1521.

There are two minor but interesting monuments, inside the gate, approached by walking in along Hacı Hamza Mektebi Sok.

The first that we come to is the Greek **church of the Koimisis tis Theotokou**, the Dormition of the Virgin. The earliest reference to this church is in 1521, and it also appears in Tryphon's list of 1583. Within the precincts there is an ayazma dedicated to the Virgin, who here is also called Our Lady of Belgrad, because of the proximity of the church to the Belgrad Gate.

A little farther along we come to the **külliye of Küçük Efendi**, a baroque complex dating from 1825, but reconstructed after being badly damaged by a fire in 1957. The külliye consists of a mosque, dervish tekke, library, fountain, cistern and graveyard. The tekke is to the left as you enter, with the graveyard beyond to the left of the mosque. The mosque is actually the former semahane, the room where the dervishes performed their mystical whirling dance. The prayer room of the mosque is oval, the plan of many semahanes; its domed central area is enclosed by a colonnade of piers and columns, with a gallery above. Above the entrance foyer there is a screened loge built for Mahmut II.

On the opposite side of the prayer room is an apse with a recessed mihrab flanked by a pair of facing mimbers. Behind the mihrab there is a small room with a window at its rear and a side door leading into the garden. A corridor on the northeast side of the prayer room leads into the library, whose outer hall is approached from the garden by a twin flight of steps. The short minaret rises from the junction of the mosque and the north wall of the library, its şerefe barely rising above the eaves of the tile roof. The minaret is surmounted by a tapering onion-shaped cupola unique in Ottoman architecture. The precinct wall beyond the library bows out in a baroque çeşme.

Belgrad Kapı to Silivri Kapı (c 680m)

The stretch of walls from Belgrad Kapı to the next town gate, Silivri Kapı, is also in good condition, with all 13 towers still standing in the inner wall and only one missing in the outer. The third and fourth towers of the inner walls both bear inscriptions of Leo III and Constantine V; while the fifth, tenth, and twelfth towers of the protichisma have inscriptions of John VIII, the first dated 1440 and the second and third 1434.

Silivri Kapı was known in Byzantium as the Porta tou Pege because it was near the famous shrine of Zoodochus Pege (see below). Like all of the larger gates, it is double, with entryways through both the inner and outer walls. On the south tower beside the gate there is an inscription dated 1438, recording a repair by Manuel Bryennius, a nobleman in the reign of John VIII, and on the north tower there is an inscription of Basil II (976–1025) and his brother Constantine VIII (1025–28).

The most memorable day in the history of this gate was 25 July 1261. On that day a small body of Greek troops led by Alexius Strategopoulos overpowered the Latin guards at the gate and forced their way inside, thus opening the way to the recapture of Constantinople and the restoration of the Byzantine Empire in its ancient capital.

Excavations just outside the gate in 1988 unearthed a hypogeum, or burial chamber, dating from the 4C–5C. The reliefs found in the hypogeum are now in the Archaeological Museum (see p 75).

The ancient shrine of **Zoodochos Pege** (Pl. 8,3), the Life-Giving Spring, is some 500m outside the walls in the vicinity of the Silivri Gate. It is approached by walking out from the gate along Seyitnizam Cad. for a short distance and veering right along Silivrikapı Balıklı Cad. The shrine stands to the left of this road just before the first crossroads; it is known locally as Balıklı Kilesi, the Church of the Fish, a name it acquired because of the fish that have swum in the sacred spring since Byzantine times.

> According to the Byzantine chronicler Nicephorus Caliste, the spring was first enclosed within a Christian shrine by the Emperor Leo I (457–74). Tradition has it that Justinian, while hunting on the Thracian downs one day, came upon a crowd of women at the sacred spring, who told him that its waters had been given therapeutic powers by the Blessed Virgin. Soon afterwards Justinian built a larger sanctuary to enclose the spring, using in its construction surplus materials from Haghia Sophia. This church was destroyed and rebuilt several times during the Byzantine period, and it remained in the hands of the Greeks after the Conquest. The first mention of the church after the Conquest is by Petrus Gyllius in 1547. The church was rebuilt again during the Ottoman period, and the present structure dates only from 1833.

The shrine. The outer courtyard is particularly interesting because it is paved with old tombstones, many of which have inscriptions in the curious Karamanlı script, i.e. Turkish written in the Greek alphabet. This was the script used by Turkish-speaking Anatolian Christians, whose clergy used Greek only in the liturgy. Many of the tombstones are carved with emblems representing the trade of the deceased: scissors for a tailor, scales for a grocer, a barrel for a tavern-keeper, etc. The inner courtyard has several elaborate tombs of bishops and patriarchs of the Greek Orthodox Church.

The entrance to the shrine is in the corner between the inner and outer courtyards. From there a long flight of steps leads down to a small chapel enclosing the sacred spring. The fish that swim in the ayazma pool are the subject of legend. It seems that during the siege of Constantinople a monk was frying fish here when he was told that the city had fallen to the Turks. Thereupon the half-fried fish jumped back into the pool, browned on one side and still gold on the other, though the fish that swim here today have reverted to their normal colour.

Just inside Silivrı Kapi there is a fairly large and charming mosque, *Ibrahim Paşa Camii for Hadım Ibrahim Paşa, who at that time was Grand Vezir under Süleyman the Magnificent. The mosque has a fine porch with five domed bays and a portal surmounted by an elaborate stalactited baldachino. In form it is an octagon inscribed in a rectangle with galleries on each side; it has no columns, but in the angles of the octagon pretty pendentives in the form of shells support the dome. The marble mimber and sultan's loge are of admirable workmanship, as are the inlaid ivory panels of the door. Over the mihrab are tiles with inscriptions; these must be a subsequent addition, for they appear to be from the very latest Iznik period or perhaps even from the 18C potteries of Tekfursarayı. In the mosque garden there is the attractive open türbe of the founder with a marble sarcophagus. The pious foundation, whose date is given in calligraphic inscriptions over the garden gates, originally included a mektep and a hamam, but these have perished.

Silivri Kapı to Yeni Mevlevihane Kapı (c 900m)

All of the original 15 towers are still standing in the stretch of wall between these two gates, but neither they nor the walls themselves are as well preserved as those closer to the Marmara. Between the fifth and seventh towers there is a curious indentation in the wall; this is known as the **Sigma** because its shape resembles the uncial form of that Greek letter, which is like the letter C. Just beyond the Sigma is the **Third Military Gate**, now walled up. Over this little gate there once stood a statue of Theodosius II, builder of these walls; this did not disappear until the 14C. The second tower of the inner wall bears an inscription of Leo III and Constantine V, and on the tenth tower is one with the names of Leo IV (775–80), Constantine VI (780–97), and the Empress Eirene (797–802). Two of the towers in the outer wall, the first before the Sigma and the second beyond it, bear inscriptions of John VIII, dated respectively 1439 and 1438.

Yeni Mevlevihane Kapı takes its Turkish name from a tekke of Mevlevi dervishes that once stood outside the gate. In Byzantium it was called the Gate of Rhegium, and sometimes also the Gate of the Reds, after the circus faction that built it. The gateway is remarkable for the number of inscriptions preserved upon it. One inscription mentions the Red faction and is, undoubtedly, of 447, when the final phase of the Theodosian walls was completed by Constantine, Prefect of the East. This great feat is commemorated in two inscriptions on the south corbel of the outer gate, one in Greek and the other in Latin. The Greek inscription merely gives the facts; the Latin one is more boastful, reading: 'By the command of Theodosius, Constantine erected these strong walls in less than two months. Scarcely could Pallas herself have built so strong a citadel in so short a span'.

There is also an inscription on the lintel of the outer gate recording a restoration by Justin II (565–78), his wife Sophia, and Narses. Narses was a eunuch who succeeded Belisarius as commander of the Byzantine army, and was the last

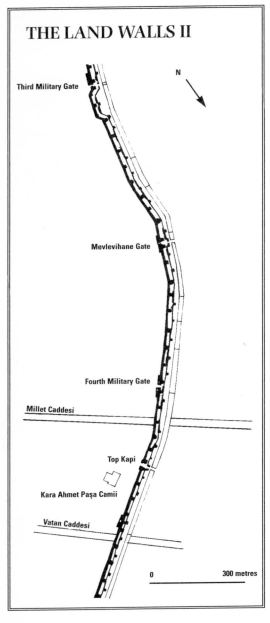

THE LAND WALLS II

Third Military Gate

N

Mevlevihane Gate

Fourth Military Gate

Millet Caddesi

Top Kapi

Kara Ahmet Paşa Camii

Vatan Caddesi

0   300 metres

Byzantine Exarch of Italy before its conquest by the Lombards. Another inscription bears the names of Basil II (976–1025) and Constantine VIII (1025–28).

There is an interesting Muslim shrine outside the gate, approached by turning off from Yeni Mevlevihane Kapı to the right on Merkez Efendi Cad. This brings us to the **Merkez Efendi Tekkesi**, a 16C dervish lodge. The tekke was founded by Şeyh Muslihiddin Merkez Musa Efendi, whose monumental türbe was reconstructed in 1837 by Şah Sultan, daughter of Selim III. According to Evliya Çelebi, Merkez Efendi built the tekke after he discovered here a miraculous ayazma, which is still a popular shrine.

There are two minor Ottoman monuments in-side the gate, approached along Mevlanakapı Cad. At the end of this street on the left we come to **Mimar Acem Camii**. The mosque was built in 1523 by Acem Ali, who had been brought from Iran by Selim II and appointed Chief of the Imperial Arch-itects. Nearby is the **Örüm-ceksiz Dede Türbesi**, named for a local Muslim holy man who was buried here in the late 15C, according to tradition, although it has been suggested that this is actually the tomb of Acem Ali.

Yeni Mevlevihane Kapı to Top Kapı (c 900m)

The stretch between these two gates forms the centre of the long arc of walls extending from the Marmara to the Golden Horn. All but one of the 15 towers in the inner wall are still standing, along with all 14 towers of the protichisma. The seventh tower of the inner wall bears the names of Leo III and Constantine V, along with this inscription: 'Oh Christ, God, preserve thy city undisturbed and free from war. Conquer the wrath of our enemies'. Between the ninth and tenth towers the inner wall is pierced by the **Fourth Military Gate**, now closed up. On the first tower of the protichisma north of this gate there is an inscription mentioning a certain Georgius. This is believed to have been removed from a nearby church and placed in the walls during the restoration by John VIII in 1438–39, evidence that many buildings near the walls were torn down to strengthen them against the impending siege by the Turks.

A short distance to the north of the Fourth Military Gate the walls have been breached to permit the passage of Millet Cad. Some 300m down Millet Cad. and on the right is a minor monument, perhaps of interest only to Byzantinists; this is the tiny Byzantine church, known locally as **Monastir Mescidi**, located just inside the entrance to a vast bus depot. Its Byzantine name and history are unknown; various identifications have been proposed, but none is at all convincing. The church is of the very simplest form: a long rectangular chamber ending at the east with the usual three projecting apses, and preceded at the west by a small narthex; a date between the 13C and 14C seems most likely.

Opposite Monastir Mescidi on the north side of Millet Cad. is an equally insignificant little mosque called **Kürkçübaşı Camii**. This was founded by one Ahmet Bey, who was Kürkçübaşı, or Chief of the Guild of Furriers, during the reign of Süleyman the Magnificent. The mosque is rectangular in form and has a wooden roof. It once had a fine porch, of which only the columns now remain; they are Byzantine, with crosses on the shaft and interesting Corinthian capitals.

After starting back on Millet Cad., we take the first left on to Topkapı Cad. At the end of this street on the left there is another small mosque, which is of little interest except for its great age. This is **Beyazit Ağa Camii**, which dates from the reign of the Conqueror. It is of the same type as Kürkçübaşı Camii; that is, rectangular with a wooden roof, and it appears to be built on top of an ancient cistern.

Just opposite the end of Topkapı Cad. is a very impressive mosque complex a short distance inside the Theodosian walls; this is ***Kara Ahmet Paşa Camii** (Pl. 4,7), one of the loveliest and most masterful of Sinan's works. Sinan built this mosque complex in 1554 for Kara Ahmet Paşa, who at that time served as Grand Vezir under Süleyman the Magnificent.

Exterior. You enter through a gate in the south wall of the complex, passing into a spacious and charming courtyard shaded by plane trees. The court is formed by the cells of the medrese; to the left stands the large dershane with pretty shell-shaped pendentives under the dome; beside it a passage leads to the lavatories. The porch of the mosque has unusually wide and attractive arches supporting its five domes. Over the niches of the porch there are some exceptional tiles, decorated, predominantly, in apple-green and vivid yellow in the old cuerda seca technique. They are the latest recorded examples of the second period of the Iznik potteries, the only other important examples being those in the türbe of the Şehzade and the fine series of panels in the mosque of Selim I.

A few more of these panels, but with blue and white inscriptions, will be found inside the mosque on the east wall. The marble revetment around the entrance portal evidently belongs to a restoration carried out in 1896; fortunately, though very Empire in style, it is restrained and does not clash badly with the rest.

Interior. The internal plan of the mosque is a hexagon inscribed in a rectangle. The four semidomes lie along the diagonals of the building and each rests on two small conches; six great columns support the arches, and there are galleries on three sides. The proportions of the building are unusually fine, as are many of the details; for example, the polychrome voussoirs of the arches and the elegant mihrab and mimber.

The wooden ceilings under the west galleries, painted with elaborate arabesques in rich reds, dark blue, gold and black, are most original features. This is perhaps the most extensive and best-preserved example of this kind of painting in the city; it is singularly rich and beautiful. Unfortunately, the ceiling on the left has recently been spoiled by an attempt at restoration, but the one on the right still retains its sombre brilliance.

Precincts. Outside the courtyard wall, towards the west, is the türbe of the founder, a simple octagonal building; unfortunately it is ruined inside. Beyond it stands the large double mektep, of a very interesting design: a long rectangular building with a wooden roof. It is still in use as a primary school, one of the very few Ottoman mekteps that continues to serve its original purpose.

Top Kapı, the Cannon Gate, was known in Byzantium as the Gate of St. Romanus, because of its proximity to a church of that name. Its Turkish name stems from the siege in 1453 when the gate faced the largest cannon in the Turkish arsenal, the famous Urban. This enormous weapon was named after the Hungarian engineer who made it for Mehmet II; it was 8m long, 20cm in diameter, and could fire a 1200-pound cannon ball a distance of one mile. This cannon caused considerable damage during the final days of the siege, which was principally directed against the stretch of walls between the Sixth and Seventh Hills.

Just inside the gate, to the north on Sulukule Cad. we come to the Greek Orthodox **church of Haghios Nikolaos**. The earliest reference to the church is in Tryphon's list of 1583. The floor of the nave has a number of old tombstones dating back to the 16C.

A short distance outside Top Kapı there is an unusual and interesting mosque that is well worth a detour. This is approached by taking Topkapı Davut Paşa Cad., the road that leads off from the gate; it stands about 500m along on the left. This is ****Takkeci Ibrahim Ağa Camii** (Pl. 4,7), recognisable immediately by its unique wooden porch and dome.

The mosque was founded in 1592 by a certain Ibrahim Ağa, who was a maker of the felt hats called takke, the most distinctive of which were the tall conical headdresses worn by the dervishes. (In Turkish, a maker of such hats would be called a takkeci.) Takkeci Ibrahim Ağa Camii is the only ancient wooden mosque in the city to have retained its porch and dome, spared by its remote location outside the walls from the many fires that destroyed or badly damaged all of the other structures of its type that once stood in the city.

Exterior. A stone wall with grilles and the remains of a fine sebil at the corner surrounds a very dirty and unkempt yard; one can scarcely call it a garden. The deeply projecting tiled roof of the porch is supported by a double row of wooden pillars. Since the porch extends halfway round both sides of the mosque, the pillars give the effect of a little copse of trees, the more so since the paint has long since worn off. The roof itself has three dashing gables along the façade; a very quaint and pretty arrangement. On the right rises the fine minaret with a beautiful stalactited şerefe. Handsome but rather heavy inscriptions adorn the spaces above the door and windows.

Interior. Within, a wooden balcony runs around the west wall and half of the side walls; it has a cornice that preserves the original arabesque painting, such as that just seen at Kara Ahmet Paşa Camii. The ceiling is of wood painted dark green and in the centre is a wooden dome on an octagonal cornice. Here you see how greatly the dome adds to the charm of the interior, and what a disaster it is when these ceilings are reconstructed flat. Two rows of windows admit light; the tiny one over the mihrab preserves some ancient and brilliant stained glass. Beneath the upper row of windows the walls are revetted, entirely, with tiles of the greatest Iznik period in large panels with vases of leaves and flowers. These are celebrated, and are as fine as those seen on the previous itinerary at Ramazan Efendi Camii.

Top Kapı to Edirne Kapı (c 1250m)
The stretch of fortifications between these two gates was known in Byzantium as the Mesoteichion. This part of the walls was the most vulnerable in the whole defence system, since here the fortifications descend into the valley of the Lycus, which entered the city midway between the two gates. During the last siege the defenders on the Mesoteichion were at a serious disadvantage, being below the level of the Turkish guns on either side of the valley. For that reason, the walls in the Lycus valley are the most badly damaged in the whole length of the fortifications, and most of the defence towers are mere piles of rubble or great shapeless hulks of masonry.

It was this section of the walls that was finally breached by the Turks on the morning of 29 May 1453. The final charge was led by a giant Janissary named Hasan, who fought his way up onto one of the towers of the outer wall. Hasan himself was slain, but his companions then forced their way across the peribolos and over the inner wall into the city, and within hours Constantinople had fallen to the Turks.

The course of the ancient river Lycus is today marked by the broad Adnan Menderes Cad., formerly known as Vatan Cad., which breaches the walls

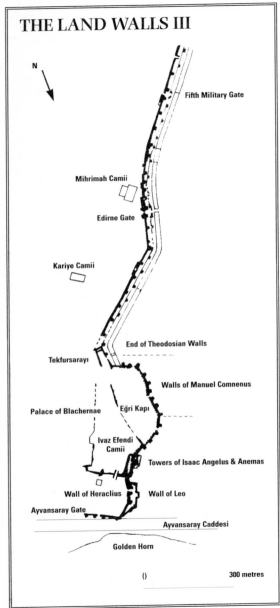

THE LAND WALLS III

N

Fifth Military Gate

Mihrimah Camii

Edirne Gate

Kariye Camii

End of Theodosian Walls

Tekfursarayı

Walls of Manuel Comnenus

Palace of Blachernae   Eğri Kapı

Ivaz Efendi
Camii

Towers of Isaac Angelus & Anemas

Wall of Heraclius   Wall of Leo

Ayvansaray Gate

Ayvansaray Caddesi

Golden Horn

0   300 metres

midway between Top Kapı and Edirne Kapı. Just inside the walls between this breach and the Fifth Military Gate, about 400m to the north, is the area called Sulukule. Since late Byzantine times this has been the Gypsy quarter of the city, and, despite frequent attempts by the authorities to evict them, the Gypsies still live here, in ramshackle wooden houses built right up against the The-odosian walls.

The section of walls in the area that is now called Sulukule was originally known as the Murus Bacchatureus; according to tradition this is where Constantine XI had his command post during the last siege. He was last seen there just before the walls were breached, fighting valiantly beside his cousins Theophilus Palaeologus and Don Francisco of Toledo and his faithful comrade John Dalmata, none of whom survived. The Fifth Military Gate is known in Turkish as Hücum Kapısı, the Gate of the Assault, preserving the memory of that last battle. On the outer lintel of the gate there is an inscription recording a repair by one Pusaeus, dated to the 5C. On the eighth tower of the protichisma there is an inscription of John VIII dated 1433 and another by one Manuel Iagari, in the reign of Constantine XI (1449–53). The latter inscription is the latest record of a repair to the walls, and it was probably placed there at the time of the preparations for the final siege in 1453.

Edirne Kapı stands at the peak of the Sixth Hill and is thus at the highest point in the old city, 77m above sea-level. This gate has preserved in Turkish form one of its ancient names, Porta Adrianopoleos, as this was the beginning of the main road to Adrianople, Turkish Edirne. It was also known in Byzantium as the Gate of Charisius, or sometimes as the Porta Polyandriou, the Gate of the Cemetery. This latter name came from the large necropolis outside the walls in this area; this still exists with large Turkish, Greek, and Armenian burial-grounds.

It was through Edirne Kapı that Mehmet II made his triumphal entry after his capture of Constantinople, early in the afternoon of 29 May 1453, and a plaque on the south side of the gate commemorates that historic event.

Mihrimah Sultan Camii

Just inside Edirne Kapı, to the south, stands the splendid Mihrimah Sultan Camii (Pl. 4,6), one of the great imperial mosques of Istanbul. Built on the peak of the Sixth Hill, it adorns the view from all parts of the old city and is one of the most prominent landmarks on the skyline of Stamboul.

> Mihrimah Camii is one of the architectural masterpieces of Sinan, built by him for the Princess Mihrimah, the favourite daughter of Süleyman the Magnificent. The külliye was built between 1562 and 1565 and includes, besides the mosque, a medrese, mektep, türbe, double hamam, and a long row of shops in the substructure of the terrace on which it was built. Unfortunately, the complex has been very severely damaged by earthquakes at least twice, in 1766 and 1894. Each time the mosque itself was restored, but the attendant buildings were for the most part neglected; in recent years some not altogether satisfactory reconstruction has been carried out.

Exterior. From the exterior the building is strong and dominant, as befits its position at the highest point of the city. The square of the dome base with its multi-windowed tympana, identical on all sides, is given solidity and boldness by the four great weight-towers at the corners, prolongations of the piers that support the dome arches. Above this square rises the dome itself on a circular drum pierced by windows.

The mosque is approached from the main street through a gate giving access to a short flight of steps leading up to the terrace. On the right is the great courtyard, around three sides of which are the porticoes and cells of the medrese. The west side, which stands opposite the Theodosian walls with only a narrow road between, has only had its portico restored, and it is difficult to be sure how many cells there would have been along this side and whether the dershane had stood there, as one might expect. In the centre of the courtyard there is an attractive şadırvan.

The mosque is preceded by an imposing porch of seven domed bays supported by eight marble and granite columns. This was originally preceded by another porch, doubtless with a sloping wooden roof supported on 12 columns, the bases of which may be seen on the ground. This type of double porch was a favourite of Sinan's; he used it in an earlier mosque built for Mihrimah (see Iskele Camii, p 287) and in many others.

Interior. The central area of the interior is square, covered by a great dome 20m in diameter and 37m high under the crown, resting on smooth pendentives. To north and south high triple arcades supported on granite columns open into side aisles with galleries above; each of these has three domed bays, reaching only to the springing of the dome arches. The tympana of all four dome arches are filled with three rows of windows, flooding the mosque with light.

Unfortunately, the interior stencil decoration is modern, insipid in colour and characterless in design. The mimber, however, is a fine original work of white marble with a beautiful medallion perforated like an iron grille. The voussoirs of the gallery arches are fretted polychrome of verd antique and Proconnesian marble. Altogether Mihrimah Camii is one of the very finest mosques in the city and must be counted as one of Sinan's masterpieces.

Precincts. To the south of the mosque is a small graveyard, at the end of which stands an unusually large sibyan mektebi with a central dome flanked by two cradle-vaults. Beyond this, and entered through the mosque, is the ruined **türbe** of the Grand Vezir Semiz Ali Paşa, Mihrimah's son-in-law. (Mihrimah herself is buried in her father's türbe at the Süleymaniye.) Ali Paşa's türbe is like only one other built by Sinan, that of Pertev Paşa at Eyüp (see p 244). It is rectangular, more than twice as long as it is wide; its roof has fallen in but you can see that it was originally covered by a large dome and two cradle-vaults. The türbe contains a large number of sarcophagi of members of Princess Mihrimah's family, many of them children.

On the northeast side of the mosque, entered from the main street, are the remains of the double **hamam** of the foundation. The camekan of the women's bath is a complete ruin, while that on the men's side now has a wooden roof supported by wooden columns; originally both undoubtedly had masonry domes. The soğukluk and the hararet of both sides are still structurally intact, though in poor condition and mostly stripped of their marble fittings. There is nothing unusual about the plan of this hamam: the eyvans of the hararet have semidomes; the domes of the cells are on simple pendentives; and the entrance is, as so often, off-centre through one of the cells. This must once have been an elegant example of a Sinan bath, and it is urgent that it should be restored before it is too late. At the corner of the hamam there is a simple but well-designed çeşme.

There are two Greek Orthodox churches in the immediate vicinity of Mihrimah Camii, one to its south and the other to its north.

The first of these churches is approached via the street just to the south of Mihrimah Camii, Muhtar Muhiddin Sok., which leads to Prof. Naci Sensoy Cad. This brings us to the church of Sarmaşık Haghios Demetrius, **St. Demetrius of**

the Vines. Haghios Demetrius dates in foundation to the Byzantine period, for there is record of an imperial decree issued by Fatih allowing the Greeks to retain possession of the church after the Conquest. The earliest reference to the church is dated 1604, while the present edifice dates from a rebuilding in 1834. In the south wall of the courtyard there is an ancient Greek tombstone with a relief showing the deceased bidding farewell to his wife and two children. Adjoining the church there is an ayazma dedicated to St. Basil.

The second church is approached via Hocaçakır Cad., the street that leads north from Mihrimah Camii just inside the walls. This is the church of Haghios Georgios Adrianopoleos, **St. George of Adrianople**, the latter name coming from its proximity to the Adrianople Gate. The original church of St. George by the Adrianople Gate was built by Constantine V (741–75) on the present site of Mihrimah Camii, and there is a reference to this church as late as 1438. This building was demolished in 1562 to make way for Mihrimah Camii, after which an imperial edict was issued giving the Greeks a plot of land on which they could build a new church of St. George, which is noted in Tryphon's list of 1583. The present church was built in 1836 and restored in 1922–24.

Edirne Kapı to Tekfursarayı (c 650m)

Just beyond Edirne Kapı the walls are breached by the broad Fevzi Paşa Cad. The Theodosian walls continue on for about 600m beyond Edirne Kapı, at which point they give way to a stretch of walls constructed in later times. The inner wall in this stretch is well preserved and has nine towers that are more or less intact.

At the end of the existing Theodosian walls we come to the exceptionally well preserved remains of an imperial Byzantine palace of great grandeur. The Turkish name of the building is *Tekfursarayı (Pl. 5,3), the Palace of the Sovereign, better known in English as the **Palace of the Porphyrogenitus**.

The palace was probably built in the latter part of the 13C or early in the 14C and served as one of the imperial residences during the last two centuries of Byzantium; it was perhaps an annexe of the nearby Palace of Blachernae. Its close proximity to the walls caused the palace to be badly damaged in the last siege, but after the Conquest it was repaired and used for a variety of purposes. During the 16C–17C it served as an imperial menagerie, particularly for larger and tamer animals such as elephants and giraffes. (The latter particularly amazed European travellers to the city.)

Before the end of the 17C the animals were moved elsewhere and the palace served for a while as a brothel. But it was soon redeemed from this misuse, for in 1719 the famous Tekfursarayı pottery was set up here. The Tekfursarayı tiles were inferior to those of Iznik and beginning to show European influence, but nevertheless quite charming. The project, however, was short-lived, and by the second half of the 18C the palace was in full decline and eventually lost its roof and floors. During the first half of the 19C Tekfursarayı served as a poorhouse for Jews and in the present century it housed a bottle works before being abandoned altogether. Today the palace is a mere shell, but in recent years its structure has been well restored.

The palace. Tekfursarayı is a large three-storeyed building originally wedged in between the inner and outer fortifications of the last stretch of the Theodosian walls. On the ground floor an arcade, with four wide arches, opens on to the courtyard, which is overlooked on the first floor by five large windows. The top floor, which projects above the walls, has windows on all sides, seven overlooking the courtyard, a curious bow-like apse on the opposite side, and a window with the remains of a balcony to the east. The roof and all of the floors have disappeared. The whole palace, but especially the façade on the court, is elaborately decorated with geometrical designs in red brick and white marble, so typical of the later period of Byzantine architecture.

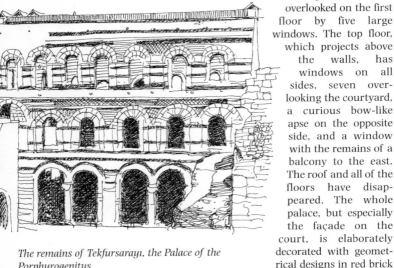

The remains of Tekfursarayı, the Palace of the Porphyrogenitus

There is an interesting old Greek church a short way to the southwest of Tekfursarayı, approached by turning in from Hocaçakir Cad. along Yeni Usul Sok. This brings us to the **church of the Panaghia Hançerli**, Our Lady with the Dagger. The latter name comes from an ancient Byzantine icon in the church, which has affixed to it a sheath holding a small dagger. The church dates back to the Iconoclastic Period of the Byzantine era, 8C–9C. The earliest post-Conquest reference to the church is in 1652, with the present building dating from a rebuilding in 1837. Behind the church is an ayazma dedicated to St. Paraskevi which is supposed to date back to the Byzantine era.

Tekfursarayı to Eğri Kapı (c 220m)

Just beyond Tekfursarayı the Theodosian walls come to an abrupt end and the fortifications are continued by walls of later construction. There has been much discussion about the original course of the Theodosian walls from Tekfursarayı down to the Golden Horn. It would appear that they turned almost due north at Tekfursarayı and from there followed a more-or-less straight line down to the Horn, whereas the present walls are bent in an arc farther out into Thrace. Stretches of what are undoubtedly the original Theodosian walls can be seen at Tekfursarayı and also along Mumhane Cad., which can be reached by turning right in the little square beyond the palace and then taking the first left. The ruined walls along this street are quite impressive and picturesque.

The present stretch of walls from Tekfursarayi to the Golden Horn is quite different from the Theodosian fortifications. It is a single bulwark without a moat; to make up for this deficiency it is thicker and more massive than the main Theodosian wall, and its towers are stronger, higher and placed closer together. The part of it that encloses the western bulge between Tekfursarayı and the Blachernae terrace can best be seen by following the street just inside the wall and walking along the garden paths of the intervening houses.

Eğri Kapı to the Golden Horn (c 650m)

The first part of this section of the walls was built by Manuel I Comnenus (1143–80). This wall begins just beyond Tekfursarayı, where it starts westward almost at right angles to the last fragment of the Theodosian wall, then turning north at the third tower. The Wall of Manuel Comnenus is an admirably constructed fortification consisting of high arches closed on the outer face; it contains nine towers and one public gate, now called Eğri Kapı.

Most authorities identify **Eğri Kapı** with the ancient Gate of the Kaligaria. It was here that Constantine XI Dragases was last seen alive by his friend George Sphrantzes, who would later write a history of the fall of Byzantium. On the night of 28 May 1453 the Emperor, accompanied by Sphrantzes, stopped briefly at the Palace of Blachernae after returning from his last visit to Haghia Sophia. According to Sphrantzes, Constantine assembled the members of his household and said goodbye to each of them in turn, asking their forgiveness for any unkindness he might ever have shown them. 'Who could describe the tears and groans in the palace?' Sphrantzes wrote, 'Even a man of wood or stone could not help weeping'. The Emperor then left the Palace and rode with Sphrantzes down to the Gate of the Kaligaria. They dismounted there and Sphrantzes waited while Constantine ascended one of the towers nearby, from where he could hear the Turkish army preparing for the final assault. Soon after he returned and mounted his horse once again. Sphrantzes then said goodbye to Constantine for the last time and watched as the Emperor rode off to his command post on the Murus Bacchatureus, never to be seen again.

Eğri Kapı, the Crooked Gate, is so called because the narrow lane that leaves the city here must detour around a türbe that stands almost directly in front of the portal. This is the supposed **tomb of Hazret Hafız**, a companion of the Prophet, who, according to tradition, was killed on this spot during the first Arab siege of the city in 674–78. Several sainted Arab heroes of that campaign are buried in the vicinity, all having been dispatched to Paradise by the defenders on the walls of Byzantium. The burial-place of Hazret Hafız was only 'discovered' in the 18C by the Chief Black Eunuch Beşir Ağa, who thereupon built this türbe.

From Eğri Kapı we continue along the path just inside the walls to see the remainder of the wall of Manuel Comnenus, which ends at the third tower past the gate. The rest of this section of wall, from the third tower to where it joins the retaining wall of the Blachernae terrace, appears to be of later construction. The workmanship here is much inferior to that in the wall of Manuel Comnenus; this can clearly be seen where the two join without bonding, just beyond the third tower from Eğri Kapı. This section is guarded by four towers, all square and also much inferior to those in the previous section. The wall of Manuel Comnenus bears no dated inscriptions; the later northern one has three: one dated 1188 by Isaac II Angelus; another in 1317 by Andronicus II Palaeologus; and the third in 1441 by John VIII Palaeologus. There is also in this northern section a postern, now walled up, which is thought to be the ancient **Gyrolimne Gate**. This was an entrance to the Palace of Blachernae, whose outer retaining wall continues the line of fortifications in this area (see p 200).

The fortifications from the north corner of the Blachernae terrace to the Golden Horn consist of two parallel walls joined at their two ends to form a kind of citadel. The inner wall was built by the Emperor Heraclius in 626 in an attempt to strengthen the defences in this area, for the city was at that time being attacked by both the Avars and the Persians. The three hexagonal defence towers in this short stretch of wall are perhaps the finest in the whole system. In 813, when the city was threatened by Krum of the Bulgars, Leo V decided to strengthen the defences in this vulnerable area by building an outer wall with four small towers, a fortification thinner than the older one behind it and much inferior in construction. These walls were pierced by a single entryway, the **Gate of the Blachernae**; that part of the gate which passed through the wall of Leo has now collapsed, but it is still open through the Heraclian wall, passing between the first and second towers.

The citadel between the walls of Leo and Heraclius is quite fascinating. At one end of the citadel there is a small Muslim **cemetery** that contains the graves of Ebu Seybet ül-Hudri and Hamd ül-Ensari, two other martyred companions of the Prophet. At the northern end of the citadel the walls of Leo and Heraclius come together and link up with the sea-walls along the Golden Horn.

After leaving the citadel we turn left on Toklu Dede Sok., named after a Muslim saint who is buried within the citadel. At the first corner on the right there was in times past a mescit dedicated to Toklu Dede. This mescit had originally been a Byzantine church dedicated to St. Thecla, founded in the second half of the 11C. But then in the early 1980s the building was demolished and not a trace of it now remains.

At the end of the street we turn left and pass through the site of the Ayvansaray Gate in the Byzantine sea-walls. This brings us out on to the shore road along the Golden Horn, ending our long stroll along the ancient land-walls of Byzantium.

17 · Up the Golden Horn to Eyüp

This itinerary will take us up the Golden Horn to the great Muslim shrine of Eyüp, a journey of c 5km.

The **Golden Horn** is a scimitar-shaped inlet of the Bosphorus, joining the strait just before it flows into the Marmara. The modern English name for the inlet is a direct translation of its ancient Greek name, Chrysokeras, the linguistic derivation of which is obscure. The Horn (in Turkish, Haliç) is some 7.5km long; at its broadest part, near Kasımpaşa, it is 750m in width; and reaches a maximum depth of 35m where it joins the Bosphorus to flow into the Sea of Marmara.

The trip begins at the iskele, or ferry-landing, on the Stamboul shore of the Golden Horn above the Galata Bridge. On the first stage of the itinerary we will take a ferry across the Golden Horn to Kasımpaşa, the first stop on the opposite shore, just above the Atatürk Bridge.

As the ferry approaches the Kasımpaşa iskele we pass on our right the huge ship-yard just above the Atatürk Bridge. This is the site of the famous **Tersane**, or Ottoman Naval Arsenal, founded by Fatih soon after the Conquest. In the 16C–17C the Tersane made a great impression on foreign travellers, for it could accommodate 120 ships at one time. Today the Tersane is one of the largest shipyards in Turkey, extending well up the Golden Horn from the Atatürk Bridge.

Kasımpaşa. Just upstream from the Kasımpaşa ferry-landing, we see on the water's edge a pretty little neoclassical Ottoman palace called **Bahriye Nezareti**; this is on the grounds of Taşkızak Tersanesi and is used as the head-quarters of the naval commandant. The first palace on this site was built by Ahmet I (1603–17), while the present edifice dates from the reign of Abdül Aziz (1861–76).

Just downstream from the iskele there is a **park** named for Cezayirli (the Algerian) Gazi (Warrior for the Faith) Hasan Paşa, Grand Admiral of the Ottoman Navy under Mustafa III (1757–74) and then Grand Vezir under Abdül Hamit I (1774–89). At the centre of the park there is a bronze statue of Hasan Paşa, who is shown with the pet lion that he led on a leash when he strolled around the Tersane.

Across the avenue from the park we see the south side of **Kalyoncu Kışlası**, the Barracks of the Galley-Men. This was built by Cezayirli Gazi Hasan Paşa in 1785 as a barracks for the marines of the Ottoman Navy. The mosque at the centre of the barracks square was also erected at that time by Hasan Paşa.

The principal monument in the vicinity of Kasımpaşa is *Piyali Paşa Camii (Pl. 6,2), one of the most interesting and enigmatic of the classical mosques. The mosque is some 2km up the valley from the Kasımpaşa iskele, approached by going up Bahriye Cad. to its end and then turning left on Dolapdere Cad., which changes its name to Piyale Paşa Blv. The mosque is to the left of the highway in a picturesque grove of cypresses and plane trees.

> The mosque was completed in 1573 by an unknown follower of Sinan. Piyali Paşa, the founder, began life as a Christian, the son of a Croatian shoemaker; he was taken up in the devşirme, educated in the Palace School, and eventually rose to the rank of Grand Admiral. While in command of the Ottoman fleet he terrorised the eastern Mediterranean, raiding as far as the coast of southern Italy, and captured a number of Aegean isles, including Chios. He was a favourite of Selim II (1566–74), and capped his career by marrying one of the Sultan's daughters, Hace Guheri Mülük Sultan.

Exterior. Piyali Paşa Camii is unique in the classical period in more than one respect. In the first place, it is the only classical mosque to revert to the Ulu Cami or multi-domed type common in the Selçuk and early Ottoman periods. Its six ample and equal domes in two rows of three each are supported by two great red granite columns. Thus far the plan follows the earlier type, but all else is different. Round three sides of the building there is a deep porch whose vaults are supported by stout rectangular pillars. Above the side porches are galleries with sloping roofs supported on small columns, while in front of the main western porch there was another lower porch with 22 columns.

Unfortunately, the roofs of this and the upper galleries on the sides have vanished, but from old prints and photographs of the mosque you can see how fascinating this unique arrangement was. The founder's türbe behind the mosque also had a colonnaded porch, but this too has gone. In the centre of the west wall there is a small balcony supported on six columns; behind this rises the single minaret, which is thus in the very unusual position of being in the middle of the west façade. The entrance portals are to the right and left of the balcony.

Interior. The mosque is lighted by numerous windows; many of the upper ones are round, oeils-de-boeuf. Between the second and third tier of windows a wide frieze of faience has inscriptions from the Kuran in white on a blue ground; these are from the hand of the famous calligrapher Karahisarı, who wrote the inscriptions in the Süleymaniye. The mihrab is also a very beautiful work, with Iznik tiles of the best period. The whole interior is not only unusual but exceptionally charming.

Kasımpaşa to Hasköy

We now return to Kasımpaşa and begin walking up the Golden Horn along the shore road, which changes its name several times en route.

After passing the palace of Bahriye Nezareti we see on our right the **Istanbul Naval Hospital**, distinguished by its central tower. This was built in 1785 and is still used by the Turkish Navy. The road then passes through the southern end of **Kulaksız Mezarlığı**, the Cemetery of Those Without Ears, a curious name of unknown origin. We then come to the entrance of *Aynalıkavak Kasrı, the Palace of the Mirroring Poplars.

■ **Admission.** The palace is open 09.00–17.00; closed Mon, Thu.

The original imperial building on this site was a pavilion erected by Ahmet I (1603–17), who used it as a pied-à-terre when he came to practice his archery on the Okmeydanı, or Archery Field, on the hill above Hasköy, as did his successors. The palace was rebuilt on a larger scale and elegantly decorated by Ahmet III (1703–30), who used Aynalıkavak as one of the sites for his famous Tulip Festivals.

The palace was extensively repaired by the Grand Vezir Koca Yusuf Pasa during the reign of Abdül Hamit I (1774–89). During his reign the palace gave its name to the Treaty of Aynalıkavak. which was signed here on 9 January 1784 by representatives of Russia and the Ottoman Empire. The palace took on its present form under Selim III (1789–1807), who used to stay here when he was composing and performing his works in Turkish classical music. The palace was restored in the Republican era, and on 26 July 1984 it was officially opened as a museum by President Kenan Evren.

The palace. Aynalıkavak is surrounded by particularly beautiful gardens, shaded by a grave of venerable trees, including a magnificent larch. The pavilion is in two storeys on the side facing the Golden Horn and on one storey to the rear, an arrangement dictated by the natural slope of the site. Aynalıkavak is celebrated for its many windows, with those in the upper course delicately fringed in stained glass. The furniture and décor are from the period of Selim III, including many original works. The elaborate inscriptions are from poems by Şeyh Galip and Enderunlu Fazıl, as well as the tuğra, or imperial monogram, of Selim III, all inscribed by the calligrapher Yesarı.

The principal rooms are the Arz Odası, or imperial audience-chamber, the Divanhane, or council hall, the Mother-of-Pearl Room, named after the inlaid suite there, and the Composition Room, so called became Selim III is thought to have composed music there. The palace also houses the **Turkish Musical Research Centre** and **Musical Instruments Museum**, where concerts are given from time to time. The museum has an extraordinary collection of the instruments used in Turkish classical music, with illustrations from miniatures showing their use in Ottoman times.

We now continue up the Golden Horn to the Hasköy iskele, which is just above the eastern end of the reconstructed Galata Bridge.

Hasköy

Just beyond the Hasköy iskele we turn right into Baçtar Sok., which at the first intersection brings us to the Greek church of Haghia Paraskevi (**St. Paraskevi**). The original church on this site dates back to the Byzantine period, and in the post-Conquest period it is first mentioned in 1547 by Petrus Gyllius. The church was rebuilt in 1692 by Constantine Brankovanos, Prince of Wallachia, and in 1833 it was restored and took on its present appearance. Within the picturesque courtyard there are a number of interesting old tombstones, as well as a relief with the Emperor Constantius Chlorus (305–06) and his wife Helena, parents of Constantine the Great (324–37), who are shown holding between them the True Cross.

Continuing up Baçtar Sok. to the next corner, we turn right on Mezarlık Üstü Sok. and follow this to its intersection with Mahlul Sok. and Harap Çeşme Sok., in the vicinity of which there are two synagogues.

Hasköy in times past had a large Jewish community, but only these two **synagogues** are still functioning; their congregations have much diminished and they are now used only infrequently. There are also a Jewish home for the aged and a cemetery. The Jewish community in Hasköy included members of the Karaite sect, who were moved here from their original quarter in Eminönü early in the 17C when Yeni Cami was built. The Orthodox Jews worship at the Mualem Synagogue on Harap Çeşme Sok., while the Karaites use the Bnai Mikra Synagogue at 3 Mahlul Sok. The Orthodox synagogue has a dedicatory inscription on its entryway dated 1734, while that of the Karaites is undated The Jewish cemetery on the hill above Hasköy has sections for both the Orthodox and Karaite communities.

We now retrace our steps to the shore road, where we turn right and continue walking up the Golden Horn. After some 250m we come to the *****Rahmi M. Koç Industrial Museum** (Pl. 5,2) (open 10.00–17.00; closed Mon). This recently opened museum is housed in a beautifully restored Ottoman Lengerhane, or forge for making ship's chains and anchors, a structure dating from the reign of Ahmet III (1703–30). The exhibits are mostly engines, machines and scientific instruments, as well as model automobiles, steam locomotives, aeroplanes and ships, including a model of a ship's bridge that can be operated by visitors, all attractively and imaginatively displayed. At the entrance to the museum there are a number of ancient Greek tombstones found at various sites in the city. One of the buildings of the Lengerhane has been converted into a very attractive restaurant called the Café du Levant.

We now retrace our steps to the reconstructed Galata Bridge, where we cross to the opposite shore of the Golden Horn. There we turn right to continue walking up the Golden Horn, passing along the seaward side of the Ayvansaray quarter. As we do so we pass on our right the Jewish hospital, **Or-Ahayim**, founded in 1889. The road then takes us out beyond the ancient land-walls of the city and under **Fatih Köprüsü**, the bridge that carries the ring highway over the Golden Horn. This brings us to the outskirts of Eyüp, the suburb named for the great Muslim shrine at the head of the Golden Horn.

**Eyüp*

Eyüp (off Pl. 4,2, Pl. 12) is the holiest Muslim shrine in Istanbul; indeed, after Mecca and Jerusalem, it is perhaps the third most sacred place of pilgrimage in the Islamic world.

> The shrine is famous as the reputed burial-place of Eyüp (Job) Ensari, the friend and standard-bearer of the Prophet Mohammed. Long after the Prophet's death Eyüp is said to have been among the leaders of the first Arab siege of Constantinople in the years 674–78, when he was killed and buried somewhere outside the walls of the city. According to tradition, the grave of Eyüp was miraculously discovered by the Şeyh-ül Islam Akşemsettin during the Turkish siege in 1453, after which Fatih built a mosque and türbe on the site.
>
> The legend of Akşemsettin's discovery of Eyüp's grave, although repeated in countless guidebooks to the city, is probably apocryphal, because the tomb is known to have been a sacred place in the Byzantine period. Several Muslim historians note that it was made a condition of peace after the first Arab siege that the tomb should be preserved. An Arab traveller during the reign of Manuel I Comnenus (1143–80) mentions it as still existing in his day, while another traveller, Zakariya al-Kazwini (c 1203–83) relates that 'this tomb is now venerated among them [the Byzantines] and they open it when they pray for rain in time of drought, and rain is granted them'. If the tomb was still visible in the 13C, it seems unlikely that it should have disappeared so completely before the Turkish Conquest. Probably Fatih restored the shrine or rebuilt it on a grander scale.
>
> During Ottoman times numerous great men and women of the Empire arranged to be buried here in splendid türbes, many of which were the centres of extensive pious foundations. As a result, Eyüp is a veritable outdoor museum of Ottoman architecture, particularly of sepulchral monuments. Many other Ottomans of lower station chose to be buried on the hill above the shrine, which became one of the most extensive cemeteries in the Turkish world.
>
> Until half a century ago Eyüp had the reputation of being wildly romantic and picturesque. Surrounded on two sides by high hills covered with groves of cypress trees and turbaned tombstones, commanding magnificent views of both shores of the Golden Horn, it was a peaceful backwater devoted to death and religion. Since then the uncontrolled devel-

opment of industry has badly polluted the Golden Horn. But Eyüp itself, because of its sacrosanct status as a religious shrine, has been spared from this decay, and it has retained most of its unique character and charm.

About 250m beyond the bridge we see a small mosque on the left side of the road, which is here called Defterdar Cad. This is **Defterdar Camii**, built in the mid 16C by Nazlı Mahmut Efendi, who served Süleyman the Magnificent as Defterdar, or Lord High Treasurer. The mosque was totally rebuilt in the 18C, and is of little intrinsic interest. In the garden is the founder's curious open türbe, covered by a dome supported on arches with scalloped soffits.

We now continue along the shore road, which here changes its name to Feshane Cad. The name comes from the huge building on the right, the **Feshane**, or Fez Factory. The original Feshane on this site was erected in 1833 to produce the hat known as the 'fez' for the New Army of Mahmut II. The building was redesigned in 1843, and in 1894 it was expanded. After the fez was banned in the clothing reform of 1925, the Feshane was converted to other uses; then in 1986 it was closed and a number of its buildings were demolished during the programme for cleaning up the Golden Horn. The building has recently been restored; it is now used as an exhibition hall, and there are plans to convert it into a museum and art gallery.

At the next corner we turn left, and after a few steps we then turn right on to Zalpaşa Cad. The small mosque at the corner to our right is **Cezri Kasım Paşa Mescidi**, erected in 1515. It has a pretty porch with four handsome antique columns of red granite, and the balcony of the minaret is supported on an unusual zigzag corbel. Most of the tile decoration inside the mosque is of late date and of little merit, but near the mihrab there is a very interesting panel dated 1726 and signed 'Mehmet, son of Osman of Iznik'. This is a very fine tile showing the Kaaba at Mecca with much interesting detail, including large tents in the background; it is one of the earliest products of the kilns at Tekfursarayı.

Continuing up Zalpaşa Cad., we now pass between a pair of mosques. On the left is the small Silahi Mehmet Bey Mescidi, and on the right is Zal Mahmut Paşa Camii.

**Zal Mahmut Paşa Camii is the grandest and most interesting mosque in Eyüp, a mature but unique work of Sinan.

> The date of construction of the mosque is unknown; that usually given, 1551, is at least 20 years too early, and a date in the mid 1570s seems most likely. Zal was a rather unsavoury character; when in 1553 Süleyman decided to execute his son Mustafa it was Zal who finally strangled him. Later he became Grand Vezir and married the Princess Şah Sultan, daughter of Selim II. This was a reward, it was said, for having smoothed Selim's path to the throne by the elimination of his brother. Little is known of Zal's subsequent career, except that in 1580 he and his wife died on the same night, for reasons unknown.

Exterior. A fine view of the south façade of the building may be had from the garden of Silahi Mehmet Bey Mescidi, which is a little higher. With its four tiers of windows and its great height and squareness it looks more like a palace than a mosque. The north façade is even more towering, for the mosque is built on a slope and supported on vaulted substructures in which rooms for the lower medrese have been made. The building is constructed of alternate courses of brick and stone.

Interior. A handsome porch of five bays gives access to the interior. This is a vast rectangular room; the massive dome arches spring on the east from supports in the wall itself, on the west from thick and rather stubby pillars some distance in from the west wall. Round three sides of the mosque a rather heavy arcade supports a gallery; some of the arches are of the ogive type. The walls, which rise in a rectangle to the height of the dome drum, are pierced with many windows, so that despite the width of the galleries the mosque is full of light.

The leaves of the main entrance door are fine inlaid work in wood, as are the mimber and müezzin's pew in carved marble. The only other decoration that survives is some excellent faience in the mihrab. It is possible that some tile work has perished, for Evliya Çelebi writes that 'architectural ornaments and decorations are nowhere lavished in so prodigal a way as here, in this the finest of all the mosques in the Empire built by vezirs'.

The mosque was for many years in a state of near ruin, but recently it has been very well restored. The general effect of the interior is perhaps a little heavy, but nonetheless grand and impressive; there is no other mosque quite like it.

Precincts. The complex includes two **medreses**; like the mosque itself, these are built of brick and stone, one around three sides of the main courtyard, the other on a lower level to the north, enclosing two sides of the türbe garden. They are both extremely picturesque and irregular in design. In the upper medrese most of the south side consists of a building without a portico, which looks rather like an imaret and may perhaps have served as one. The dershane is not in the centre of the west wall, but has been shifted to near the north end, and the last arches of the portico on this side are smaller than the others. There is no obvious reason for any of these abnormalities, but they have a certain charm, enhanced by the ogive arches of the arcade. At the northeast corner a long flight of steps leads down to the garden of the **türbe**, two sides of which are partly enclosed by the lower medrese. It is an octagonal building of the usual type, within which are the catafalques of Zal Mahmut Paşa and his wife.

A door in the east wall of the türbe garden leads to another **külliye** of a very different type, one of the most delightful of the smaller baroque complexes. It consists of an elaborate türbe and mektep, with a sebil on the street and a çeşme in the garden. It was built at the end of the 18C by Şah Sultan, a sister of Selim III. The undulating façades of the türbe and the amusing turned-back staircase of the mektep are very charming.

Silahi Mehmet Bey Mescidi is dated c 1490. This little mosque is of the simplest type, but with an unusual and fascinating minaret. This is hexagonal in shape, built of stone and brick; instead of the usual balcony it has a sort of lantern with six windows and a tall conical cap. There are in the city three or four other minarets with this lantern arrangement but this is much the most striking and pretty.

Eyüp, one of the most sacred places of pilgrimage in the Islamic world

We now continue along Zalpaşa Cad, and on our right, just before the first turning on that side, we see a small mosque known as **Kızıl Mescit**. Built in 1581 by Kiremitçi Süleyman Çelebi, it too is of the simplest type, a rectangular room of stone and brick with a tiled roof and a brick minaret.

Turning right at the corner, we continue straight ahead at the next intersection This brings us to Eyüp Iskele Cad., where across the street we see **Kaptan Paşa Camii**. This mosque was originally built in 1577 by Hacı Mahmut Ağa. It took on its present form in 1903 when it was rebuilt by Kaptan Hasan Hüsnü Paşa, Minister of the Ottoman Navy under Abdül Hamit II.

We now turn left on Camii Kebir Sok. At the corner to the left on the far side of the intersection we see the türbe of **Ferhat Paşa**, an octagonal structure with a richly decorated cornice and polychrome voussoirs and window-frames.

Halfway along Camii Kebir Cad. we come to two classical türbes of great simplicity facing one another across the street. The one on the left is the *türbe of the Grand Vezir **Sokollu Mehmet Paşa**, built by Sinan c 1572 as part of a small külliye. Elegant and well proportioned, it is severely plain. The interior contains some interesting stained glass, partly ancient and partly a modern imitation, but very well done; alternate windows are predominantly blue and green. A little colonnade attaches the türbe to the dershane of the külliye's very fine medrese. Notice the handsome identical doorways of the two buildings; the only difference is that the rich polychrome work of the türbe is in verd antique, while that of the dershane is in red conglomerate marble. The dershane also has stained glass windows; these are of modern manufacture and not as good as those in the türbe. The dome is supported on squinches of very bold stalactites.

The opposite door leads into the medrese courtyard; this is long and narrow, with 10 domes on the long sides of its colonnade, only three at the ends. Recently the building has been well restored and is now used as a children's clinic; it is pretty and charming, with a delightful, well-kept garden. In the little garden of the türbe the family and descendants of Sokollu Mehmet Paşa are buried. Just beyond the graveyard there is a building in the same style as the dershane; this is the dar-ül kura, the school for the study of the Kuran. This little complex as a whole is certainly one of Sinan's most attractive works.

The türbe across the street from Sokollu Mehmet's tomb is that of the Grand Vezir **Siyavus Paşa**. This is again austere, but adorned within by inscriptions and pendentives in excellent Iznik tiles. This türbe is also by Sinan. Siyavus Paşa died in 1601, outliving Sinan by a dozen years; he seems to have had Sinan build this türbe originally for some of his children who died young, and was finally buried here himself.

At the end of the street we come to the main square of Eyüp, with the main entrance to the precincts of ****Eyüp Sultan Camii** on our right.

> The külliye as a whole, including the türbe, mosque, medrese, han, hamam, imaret, and market, was originally built by Fatih in 1458. Here on their accession to the throne the sultans were girded with the sword of Osman, the eponymous founder of the Ottoman (in Turkish, Osmanlı) dynasty, a ceremony equivalent to coronation. By the end of the 18C the mosque had fallen into ruins, perhaps a victim of the great earthquake of 1766 that had destroyed Fatih's own mosque. In 1798 Selim III ordered that the remains of the building be torn down and a new mosque built in its place, a project that was completed in 1800. The mosque that is seen today dates from that time, except for the minarets, which were erected by Ahmet III early in the 18C.

Exterior. The mosque is approached through an exceptionally picturesque outer courtyard: the two great gateways with their undulating baroque forms, the huge old plane trees in whose hollows live lame storks and in whose branches beautiful grey herons build their nests in spring, the flocks of pampered pigeons being fed by the pilgrims. It is the gayest and most delightful courtyard in Istanbul. From here you enter the inner court, shaded by venerable plane trees and with an unusually tall and stately colonnade along three sides.

Interior. In plan the mosque is an octagon inscribed in a rectangle. In spite of its late date the mosque is singularly attractive, with its pale honey-coloured stone, the decorations picked out in gold, the elegant chandelier hanging from the centre of the dome, and the magnificent turquoise carpet that covers the entire floor.

**The türbe. The side of the building opposite the mosque is a blank wall, most of it covered with panels of tiles without an overall pattern and of many different periods, some of them of great individual beauty. A door in the wall leads to the vestibule of the türbe of Eyüp Ensari, an octagonal building, three sides of which project into the vestibule. The latter is itself sheathed in tiles, many of them of the best Iznik period. The türbe is sumptuously decorated, though with work largely of the baroque period.

Precincts. According to Evliya Çelebi, the medrese of the külliye formed the courtyard of the mosque; this was evidently swept away during the rebuilding in 1798–1800. Apparently the imaret was not included in that rebuilding, for it is a total ruin. But of the hamam the soğukluk and hararet still remain and are in use; they have the elaborate and attractive dome structure typical of the early period, along with handsome marble floors. The original camekan has completely disappeared and been replaced by a rather makeshift one largely of wood. (In the Victoria and Albert Museum, London, there is a very fine panel of 24 Iznik tiles of c 1570 from this hamam, very probably from the demolished camekan.)

We leave the precincts of Eyüp Sultan Camii by its north gate, after which we turn right. As we do so we pass between two tombs, with the türbe of **Ayaz Mehmet Paşa** (1539) on the left and that of **Lala Mustafa Paşa** (1580) on the right. We then continue straight ahead on Bostan Iskelesi Sok., which leads to what was once the imperial landing stage on the Golden Horn. When a new Ottoman sultan came to be girded with the sword of Osman he landed at the iskele there, walking this way in procession to the mosque, a scene depicted in a number of old prints.

Most of the left side of this street is occupied by the enormous **külliye of Mihrişah Valide Sultan**, mother of Selim III. Built in 1791, this is one of the largest and most elaborate of all the baroque complexes; it includes the türbe of the foundress, together with a mektep, an imaret, and a splendid sebil and çeşme. The türbe is round, but the undulating façade turns it into a polygon, with the various faces separated by slender columns of red or dark grey marble. The entrance is in a little courtyard filled with tombstones and trees; the columned portico of the mektep runs along one side.

Farther along the street another monumental gateway leads into the vast main courtyard, which is filled with more tombstones and surrounded on three sides by the porticoes of the huge imaret. This is the only imaret in Istanbul that still fulfils its original function as a soup kitchen for the poor of the city; some 1500 people are served free food here daily at 11.00, and are allowed to take away with them enough food for the evening meal. In leaving the imaret do not fail to notice the magnificent sebil at the end of the garden on the street side.

Continuing along the street past the intersection, we pass between the two buildings of a little **külliye** founded in 1839 by Hüsref Paşa, with the founder's türbe on the right and the library on the left. They are both in the Empire style; but the domes of the library reading-rooms contain a good example of that Italianate comic opera painted decoration of garlands, draperies and columns, so distressing when it occurs in classical buildings, but quite appropriate here.

We now return to the intersection and turn left on Boyacı Cad., the street that runs parallel to the Golden Horn. Toward the end of the street we see on our left the neoclassical **türbe of Sultan Mehmet V Reşat** (1909–18). Mehmet V was the penultimate ruler of the Ottoman Empire; oddly enough, he was the only one of all the sultans to be buried in the holy precincts of Eyüp and the last to be interred in his own country. The last Sultan, Mehmet VI (1918–22), died in exile and was buried abroad, as was Abdül Mecit (II) (1922–24), who held only the title of Caliph. It is a rather heavy building, the interior revetted in modern Kütahya tiles predominantly of an overly vivid green.

At the corner we now turn right into a narrow street of tombs called Beybaba Sok. A short way along we see on our right the *türbe of Mehmet Pertev Paşa, built by Sinan in 1572–73. The türbe is of a very unusual design, rectangular in plan, looking more like a house than a tomb; unfortunately it is now in ruins. It was originally divided into two equal areas each covered with a dome exquisitely painted, but these were destroyed through neglect. Inside the türbe there are still to be seen some charming marble sarcophagi of Mehmet Pertev Paşa and his family.

At the end of the street we find ourselves back beside the north gate of Eyüp Sultan Camii. Here we make our way to the path that leads up to the great **cemetery of Eyüp, the last resting-place of many notables from Ottoman times as well as generations of the ordinary people of Istanbul. The path that winds uphill through the cemetery is lined with tombstones in picturesque disarray, the older grave markers of the men topped with turbans, those of the women adorned with reliefs of flowers, occasionally surmounted by the tiara of a princess.

At the top of the hill, above the cemetery, there is a café known as the **Teahouse of Pierre Loti**; this is named after the French novelist who frequented it during his stay in Istanbul. The café commands a superb view of the Golden Horn, particularly in late afternoon and early twilight. Clearly visible are the upper reaches of the Golden Horn and of the two little streams that flow into it at its northern extremity. These are Alibey Suyu on the west and Kağıthane Suyu on the east, the ancient Barbyzes and Cydaris, respectively.

These streams are separated at their mouth by the promontory known in Turkish as **Sivri Tepe**, the Semistra of the Greeks. According to Dionysius of Byzantium, it was on this hill that Io, daughter of Inachus, who had fled here pursued by the gadfly of jealous Hera, gave birth to Cereossa. According to one version of the myth, Byzas, the eponymous founder of Byzantium, was the son of Poseidon and Cereossa.

During Ottoman times the two streams that fed the Golden Horn were known in English as the Sweet Waters of Europe. For centuries the meadows and banks of the Sweet Waters were the site of royal palaces, mansions, gardens and pavilions, and were a favourite holiday resort for the ordinary people of Istanbul. But now these pleasure domes have disappeared and the upper reaches of the Golden Horn are surrounded by the massed apartment houses of the characterless suburbs that have enveloped the imperial city on all sides. Nevertheless the view is still magnificent from Pierre Loti's café, particularly at sunset, when the Golden Horn does indeed take on the colour of molten gold.

18 · Galata and Pera (Beyoğlu)

This itinerary will begin at the northern end of the Galata Bridge in Karaköy, the quarter on the opposite shore of the Golden Horn from Eminönü. Here we are in the heart of old Galata, which in late Byzantine times was an independent city-state governed by the Genoese. From here we will make our way to the heights above the confluence of the Bosphorus and the Golden Horn, the district known in times past as Pera and today as Beyoğlu, and from there we will go on to Taksim Square and the more modern districts to its north.

History

The historic origins of **Galata** and **Pera** are as remote as those of Constantinople itself. From very early times there had been settlements along the northern shores of the Golden Horn; Byzas himself is said to have erected a temple there to the hero Amphiaraus. The most important of these communities, Sykai, the 'Fig Trees', was located on the present site of Galata. As early as the 5C AD, this was included as the VIIIth Region of Constantinople itself, under the name of Regio Sycaena; it had churches, a forum, public baths, a theatre, a harbour, and was surrounded by a defence-wall. In 528 Justinian restored its theatre and defence-walls, grandiloquently renaming it Justinianae, a name which soon fell out of use and was forgotten.

Toward the end of the same century Tiberius II (578–82) is said to have built a fortress at the confluence of the Golden Horn and the Bosphorus, from which a chain could be stretched to the opposite shore to close the Horn to enemy shipping. The name Sykai seems to have continued in use until the 9C, when the name Galata began to supplant it, at first for a small district only, later for the whole region. The derivation of the name Galata is unknown, though that of Pera is quite straightforward. In Greek 'pera' means 'beyond', at first in the general sense of 'on the other side of the Golden Horn', later restricted to medieval Galata, and still later to the heights above.

The town of Galata took its present form chiefly under the Genoese. After the reconquest of Constantinople from the Latins in 1261, the Byzantine emperors granted the district to the Genoese as a semi-independent colony with its own Podesta, or Governor, appointed annually by the senate of Genoa. Although the Genoese were expressly forbidden to fortify the colony, they did so almost immediately and went on expanding its area and fortifications for more than a hundred years. The first fortified area, walled in as early as 1304, was a long, narrow rectangle along the Golden Horn between where the two bridges now begin. In order to defend themselves more adequately on the side of the heights above Galata, the Genoese added a triangular wedge with the Tower of Christ as its highest point. Later still, in 1387 and 1397, they took successive areas to the northwest, and finally, in 1446, they enclosed the eastern slope of the hill leading down to the Bosphorus. The final defence system consisted of six walled enceintes, with the outer wall bordered by a moat. Sections of these walls with a few towers and one postern are still in existence and will be seen on the present itinerary.

After the Turkish Conquest of 1453 the outer walls of Galata were partially destroyed, as the district became the general European quarter of the city. Here the foreign merchants had their houses and shops and the ambassadors of the European powers also built their palatial embassies here. When the Sephardic Jews in Spain were expelled by Ferdinand and Isabella in 1492, Beyazit II invited them to live in the Ottoman Empire and many settled in Galata. Early in the following century a large number of Moorish refugees settled there as well, joining the large number of Greeks and Armenians who had arrived from Anatolia in the century after the Conquest, giving Galata the polyglot flavour that it retained until very recent times.

As time went on the confines of Galata became too crowded for the tastes of the foreign ambassadors and richer merchants, who began to move out, beyond the medieval walls, to the hills and vineyards above. Here the foreign powers built enormous mansions surrounded by spacious gardens; all of them standing along the road that would later be known as the Grande Rue de Pera. Nevertheless, the region must have remained rural until well into the 18C; for in that period you often see references to 'les vignes of Pera'. But as Pera became more and more built up, it fell a prey like the rest of the city to the endemic fires that ravaged it periodically. Two especially devastating fires, in 1831 and 1871, destroyed nearly everything built before those dates. Hence the dearth of anything of much historic or architectural interest in modern Beyoğlu.

We begin our itinerary by walking up the Golden Horn on the left side of the shore highway that extends between the Galata Bridge and the Atatürk Bridge. As we do so we see on the opposite side of the highway the lower entrance to **Tünel**, the underground funicular railway, which in 80 seconds ascends to the heights of Pera. Tünel was built by French engineers in 1875 and was one of the first underground railways in the world.

About 150m from Karaköy Square we turn left into Kardeşim Sok., the Street of My Brother. We then turn right at the next corner into an alleyway that leads into a handsome but dilapidated old commercial building, the **Rüstem Paşa Hanı** (Pl. 6,8). This was built by Sinan for the Grand Vezir Rüstem Paşa shortly before 1550. The date of construction is fixed by Petrus Gyllius, who says that while he was in the city, 1544–50, the Latin church of St. Michael was demolished to make way for the han. A Corinthian capital from the church can be seen to the left of the entryway to the building. The han is built in two storeys around a long, narrow courtyard, from the centre of which a stairway leads to the upper floor, an arrangement as picturesque as it is unique. The lower arcade has round arches, while those of the gallery are ogive.

We now make our way back to the main avenue and continue on in the same direction. After the first side street we come to an ancient and imposing building with nine domes. This is the **Galata Bedesten** (Pl. 6,8), a covered market built by Fatih soon after the Conquest. The building is made of brick and rubble and is nearly square in plan; its nine equal domes are supported by four great rectangular piers, and around the outside is a series of vaulted shops.

We continue to the end of the avenue, passing on our left a short stretch of ancient wall with a series of arches, part of the fortifications of Genoese Galata that was revealed recently when the surrounding houses were demolished.

At the end of the avenue we come to the **Azapkapı Sebili**, one of the most beautiful Ottoman street-fountains in the city. This baroque structure was founded in 1732–33 by Saliha Valide Hatun, mother of Mahmut I. It consists of a projecting sebil with three grilled windows flanked by two large and magnificent çeşmes. The façades of the çeşmes and sebil are entirely covered with floral decorations in low relief and with a little dome. Unfortunately, during a repair the fluted drum of the dome was restored in concrete, spoiling its appearance; nevertheless it remains one of the most attractive of the early 18C baroque fountains in the city.

We now walk over to the handsome mosque on the shore of the Golden Horn beside the Atatürk Bridge. This is *Azapkapı Camii (Pl. 6,8), a work of Sinan.

The mosque was built by Sinan in 1577–78 for the Grand Vezir Sokollu Mehmet Paşa, for whom the architect had six years earlier built another mosque on the First Hill below the Hippodrome.

Exterior. Like Rüstem Paşa Camii across the Golden Horn, the mosque is raised on a high basement in which there were once vaulted shops; the entrance, now rather squeezed in by the approach to the bridge, is by staircases under the enclosed porch. The minaret is unusual both in position and structure. First of all, it is on the left or north side rather than the south; this is doubtless because the sea at that time came up very close to the south wall and the ground there would not have been firm enough to support a minaret. Furthermore, it is detached from the building and placed on a solid foundation of its own, connected with the mosque above porch level by a picturesque arch; this contains a communicating passage so that it can be entered from the porch.

Interior. Internally the plan is an octagon inscribed in a nearly square rectangle. The dome is supported by eight small semidomes, the cupolas in the axes slightly smaller than those in the diagonals, while the eastern semidome covers a rectangular projecting apse with narrow galleries on three sides. The mihrab and mimber are very fine works in carved marble. It appears that the interior was covered with Iznik tiles, like those of Rüstem Paşa's other mosque on the First Hill, but these have been replaced by modern Kütahya tiles. This detracts considerably from the appearance of the interior; nevertheless, Azapkapı Camii is among the more interesting and important of Sinan's buildings.

We now cross Tersane Caddesi, the avenue between the two bridges. There we see the **Yeşildirek Hamam**, a work of Sinan that is no longer operating and is now abandoned.

We turn in to the street just beyond the hamam, Yolcuzade Sok., and then at the next corner we turn right. This brings us to **Yanık Kapı Sok.**, the Street of the Burnt Gate, which takes its name from the ancient portal we now see in front of us. This is the only surviving gateway of Genoese Galata, opening between the fourth and fifth enceintes of the walled city. Above the archway of the gate there is a bronze tablet emblazoned with the Cross of St. George, symbol of Genoa the Superb, between a pair of escutcheons bearing the heraldic arms of the noble houses of Doria and De Merude.

We continue on Yanık Kapı Sok. to the first intersection and turn right, after which we turn left on Galata Mahkemesi Sok. We then come to a very unusual edifice ending in a tall square tower with a pyramidal roof; this is known in Turkish as ***Arap Camii** (Pl. 6,8), one of the surviving Latin churches of Genoese Galata.

> There are many baseless legends concerning the origin and history of the building, some of which are repeated in recent guidebooks. But the evidence indicates that it was constructed by the Dominicans during the years 1323–37 and dedicated to St. Dominic; it seems to have included a chapel of St. Paul, by whose name the church was popularly known. Early in the 16C it was converted into a church and given over to the colony of Moorish refugees who had settled in Galata; hence its Turkish name, the Mosque of the Arabs.

Interior. The building has been partially burned and restored several times; on one occasion it was considerably widened by moving the north wall several metres to the north. Nevertheless, it remains a rather typical medieval Latin church, originally Gothic: a long hall ending in three rectangular apses, and with a belfry (now the minaret) at the east end. The flat wooden roof and the rather pretty wooden galleries date from a restoration in 1913–19. At that time also the original floor was uncovered and large quantities of Genoese tombstones of the late Byzantine period came to light. Some of the tombstones bore the date 1347, the year when the Black Death struck Constantinople before ravaging western Europe; these are now in the Archaeological Museum (see p 75). On the north side of the building there is a picturesque courtyard with a şadırvan.

We continue along Galata Mahkemesi Sok. to the next intersection, where we turn left on **Perşembe Pazarı Cad**. This street is lined with picturesque old houses and hans which used to be identified as Byzantine or Genoese, although in fact they are typical Turkish buildings of the 18C. The most handsome is the one near the next corner on the left, dated by an inscription to 1735–36. The general structure is completely characteristic of Turkish buildings of that period, with the masonry in alternate courses of brick and stone and the pointed arches of the windows. It has three storeys, the upper ones projecting in zigzags held up by corbels, with two zigzags in Perşembe Pazarı Cad. and four in the alley beside it.

At the end of the street we cross Voyvoda Cad., continuing uphill on Galata Kulesi Sok. The building to the right at the beginning of this street is the former Palazzo Communale, also known as the **Podestat**; this was the official residence and headquarters of the Podesta, the Genoese governor of Galata. The building was erected in 1316, and it retained its original appearance until the late 19C, when its façade was rebuilt during the widening of the avenue. The building behind it, on the other side of Kartçınar Sok., is also a Genoese foundation of 1316.

Turning left on to Eski Banka Sok., we see on the right a huge old building known as the **Han of Ste. Pierre**, built in 1771 by the Compte de Saint Priest as the 'lodging-place and bank of the French Nation', as recorded in his bequest. The French poet Andre Chénier was born in an earlier house on this site on 30 October 1762, as noted by a plaque on the façade; next to this are the arms of the Comte de Saint Priest and of the Bourbons.

We now retrace our steps and turn left at the corner into Galata Kulesi Sok. A third of the way up the street on the left is the entrance to another of the surviving medieval Latin churches in Galata. This is the **church of SS. Peter and Paul**, which, with its Dominican convent, was founded in the late 15C by the Genoese. Later it was taken under the protection of France and became the French parochial church in Galata; in more recent times it has been the parish church of the local Maltese community, several of whose tombstones are built into the courtyard wall along with an ancient Greek funerary stele. The present church dates from a rebuilding in 1841 by the Fossati brothers. At the rear of the monastery there is a fairly well-preserved stretch of the ancient Genoese wall that led up to the Galata Tower, with two defence towers still standing.

****The Galata Tower and Galata Mevlevi Tekke**

We continue up the street to the **Galata Tower** (Pl. 7,7), the most prominent landmark on this side of the Golden Horn.

■ **Admission**. The observation deck is open 08.00–21.00 every day, and the Galata Tower Night Club is open until the small hours.

The Galata Tower was the apex of the Genoese fortifications of medieval Galata. Originally known as the Tower of Christ, it was built in 1348 in connection with the first expansion of the Genoese colony. Until the late 1960s the tower was used as a fire observation post, but then it was restored and converted into a tourist attraction.

The tower. The top of the tower is 140m above the Golden Horn; it rises 61m from its foundations, with an internal diameter of 8.95m and walls 3.75m thick. There are eleven floors; with the fifth housing an Oriental Coffee House, the eighth a Genoese tavern, and the eleventh a restaurant and night club, surrounded by an observation deck that commands a magnificent view of the city and its surrounding waters.

In the little square beside the tower, fixed against the remnants of the barbican, is a famous **street-fountain**. In its present form it dates from 1732, but it was originally constructed just after the Conquest. Its founder was Bereketzade Hacı Ali Ağa, the first Turkish governor of the citadel of Galata. The fountain originally stood near Bereketzade's mosque, which was located a short distance away from the tower, but it was moved to its present site in 1950 when that was demolished. Unfortunately, this charming rococo fountain has suffered badly from being painted.

We now walk across the square to Galip Dede Cad., which we ascend to the heights of Pera. Near the upper end of the street we come on our right to the entrance of the ***Galata Mevlevi Tekke** (Pl. 7,5).

■ **Admission**. The tekke, which also houses the Museum of Turkish Court Poetry (Divan Edibiyatı Müzesi), is open 09.30–16.30; closed Mon.

The tekke, or dervish monastery, was founded in the last decade of the 15C by Şeyh Muhammed Semai Sultan Divanı, a descendant of Mevlana Celaleddin Rumi, the great divine and mystic poet who in the 13C founded the religious brotherhood known as the Mevlevi, famous in the West as the 'Whirling Dervishes'. The most famous sheik of the Galata tekke was Galip Dede, whose ornate türbe is on the left side of the path leading into the interior courtyard. The sebil on the right at the entrance is an early 19C work founded by one Halil Efendi.

Interior. At the left rear of the courtyard we come to the heart of the tekke, its semahane, or dancing-room, a beautiful octagonal chamber that was splendidly restored in the early 1970s. The semahane and its adjacent chambers now house the **Divan Edibiyatı Müzesi** (Museum of Turkish Court Poetry), a form inspired by the mystical verses of Mevlana. The collection includes manuscripts of the works of Galip Dede and other mystic poets, as well as examples of Ottoman calligraphy and other memorabilia of the Mevlevi Dervishes who lived here until the mid 1920s, when all of the dervish orders were abolished in Turkey. Performances of the ethereal Mevlevi dance and the hauntingly beautiful music that accompanies it are given here and in Konya each year on his feast day (17 December).

Precincts. The graveyard beside the tekke has some very interesting old tombstones. One of these marks the grave of the famous Count Bonneval, known in Turkish as Kumbaracı Ahmet Paşa. Bonneval was a French officer who enrolled in the Ottoman army during the reign of Mahmut I (1730–54) and was made Commandant of the Corps of Artillery. He became a Muslim, changed his name to Kumbaracı (the Bombardier) Osman Ahmet, and spent the remainder of his life in the Ottoman service, dying in Istanbul in 1747. A French contemporary of Bonneval wrote of him that he was 'a man of great talent for war, intelligent, eloquent with charm and grace, very proud, a lavish spender, extremely debauched, and a great plunderer'.

Istiklal Caddesi

At the top of Galip Dede Cad. we come to the upper end of **Tünel** and the beginning of **Istiklal Caddesi**, the former Grande Rue de Pera. The embassies in this part of old Pera, on or near the Grande Rue, belong to those powers that have had legations here since the early centuries of the Ottoman Empire. Though most of these buildings are relatively modern, the embassies themselves—especially those of Venice, France, Britain, Holland, Sweden and Russia—are of some historical interest.

They were established more or less where they are now in the course of the 16C–18C, generally by grants of land bestowed by the sultans, and each formed the centre of its 'Nation', as it was called; that is, of the community of resident merchants and officials of the various countries. These embassies came to exert a growing influence on the Ottoman Empire as its powers declined, and collectively they dominated the life of Pera until the establishment of the Turkish

The Galata Tower rising above the confluence of the Golden Horn and the Bosphorus

Republic. Near the embassies various churches were established, more or less under their protection, and some of these survive in a modern form. They are all situated along Istiklal Cad. between Tünel and Galatasaray Meydanı, the square midway along the avenue, some of them standing next to the old ministries to whose 'Nation' they once ministered.

The whole length of Istiklal Caddesi is now a pedestrian mall, with an old-fashioned tram running from Tünel to Taksim Meydanı, the square at the upper end of the avenue.

At the first street that leads off Istiklal Caddesi to the right, Şahkule Bostan Sok., we will take a detour downhill. At the lower end of the street we turn left and come to the **Crimean Memorial Church** (Pl. 7,5), by far the largest and most handsome of the western churches in the city. This was built between 1858 and 1868 under the aegis of Lord Stratford de Redcliffe, known to the Turks as Büyük Elçi, or the Great Ambassador, because of the enormous influence he exerted on Turkish affairs during his three terms as Great Britain's Ambassador to the Ottoman Empire during the period 1810–56. The church was designed by C.E. Street, the architect of the London Law Courts; it is built in the neo-Gothic style with a cavernous porch, like the Law Courts themselves. The church was abandoned for a time, but recently it has been well restored and is once again in use.

Retracing our steps, we now head up Istiklal Cad. Almost immediately we see on our right a gateway opening to the grounds of the **Swedish Embassy**. (This is now officially the Swedish Consulate, for all the foreign embassies were relocated in Ankara after that became the capital of the Turkish Republic in 1923; nevertheless, this and the other palatial old ambassadorial residences are still referred to as embassies.). The Embassy of Sweden was established here on its present site in 1755; the present building was erected in 1870 by the Austrian architect Pulgher.

Directly across the street from the Swedish Embassy is the **Narmanlı Han**, which housed the Russian Embassy up until 1845, when it was replaced by another building farther along the avenue. Its most distinctive features are the row of engaged Doric columns along the façade on the avenue and the round-arched portal leading into the interior courtyard. The apartment on the upper floor at the corner facing Tünel was for half a century the residence of Aliye Berger-Boronai (1904–73), one of the greatest painters in modern Turkey.

At the next corner we make a detour to the left along Asmalı Mescit Sok., which at its end brings us to Mesrutiyet Cad. and the quarter known as Tepebaşı. There to our right we see the famous *Pera Palas Hotel, built in the years 1893–95 by the French architect Alexander Vallaury. On our left we see the consulate of the United States of America. This is housed in the **Palazzo Corpi**, built in the years 1873–82 for Ignazio Corpi, a Genoese shipowner. The building was acquired by the US in 1907, the first American diplomatic property in Europe.

We now retrace our steps to Istiklal Cad., where we continue walking up the avenue. Halfway along the next block we see on the right the **Russian Embassy**. This neo-classical edifice was built in the years 1837–45 by Giuseppe Fossati, replacing the earlier building we have just seen.

Farther along the block on the same side we come to to the Franciscan **church of St. Mary Draperis**, down a flight of steps from the street level. The first church on this site was built in 1678 and the present structure dates from 1789. The parish itself, however, is a very ancient one, dating from the beginning of 1453, when the Franciscans built a church near the present site of Sirkeci Station. After the Conquest the Franciscans were forced to leave Constantinople, settling first in Galata and then here in Pera. The Franciscans still preserve in the church a miraculous icon of the Virgin, which they claim to inherit from their first church in Constantinople.

Churches and Embassies

The next turning on the right is Postacılar Sok., which leads to a number of old European embassy buildings and churches.

A short way down and on the left is the entrance to the **Dutch Chapel**. Since 1857 this building has housed the Union Church of Istanbul, an English-speaking congregation from many lands. The chapel dates from the late 17C or the early 18C. The basement rooms of the chapel, now used as a Sunday school, have in the past served as a prison. The building is basically a single massive barrel-vault of heavy masonry; the brickwork of the façade, newly exposed to view, is particularly fine.

A short way below the Dutch Chapel on the right is the former Spanish Embassy, no longer functioning, with only the **chapel** remaining in use. This little church, dedicated to Our Lady of the Seven Sorrows, was originally founded in 1670; the present building dates from 1871.

At the bottom of the street is a small square flanked by two large old buildings. The one to the left, at the top of the square, is the former **French Tribunal of Justice**, a 19C structure in which the legal affairs of the European 'Nations' were handled in late Ottoman times. The handsome old building on the right side of the square is the **Palazzo di Venezia**, now the Italian Embassy. The present building is believed to date from c 1695, though it was completely rebuilt c 1750. In Ottoman times this was the residence of the Venetian bailio, the ambassador of the Serene Republic and one of the most powerful of the foreign legates in the city. We learn from his `Memoirs' that Giacomo Casanova was a guest here in the summer of 1744; in his three months in the city this great lover did not make a single conquest but was himself seduced by one Ismail Efendi.

Returning to Istiklal Caddesi, after a few steps we see on our right the **Dutch Embassy**, a very pretty building that looks rather like a small French château. The original Dutch Embassy, built in 1612, was burned down twice, but parts of the substructure of the earlier buildings were preserved and incorporated into the present Embassy. The present building was designed by the Fossati brothers and completed in 1855; the lower structure, visible from the garden, goes back two centuries or more. The Fossati brothers, of Italian Swiss origin, had been in Moscow for several years as official architects of Czar Nicholas I, who sent them to Istanbul to build his new embassy in Pera. Here they remained for 20 years or so as official architects for the Sultan, restoring Haghia Sophia in 1847–49 and building several other structures, including the Russian and Dutch Embassies and the church of SS. Peter and Paul in Galata.

A few steps farther along we see on our right the French Embassy; it is situated in a fine French garden with views of the Bosphorus and the Marmara. France was the first European nation to establish formal diplomatic relations with the Ottoman Empire, beginning with the envoys sent by François I to Süleyman in 1525. The original embassy was destroyed by fire in 1831, and the present building was erected in the years 1839–47 by Pierre Laurecisque. (It was on this site that the great Turkish astronomer Takiuddin built his observatory in 1570.) The **chapel** connected with the embassy, that of St. Louis of the French, is the oldest in foundation of the Latin churches along the Grande Rue de Pera, dating from 1581; though the present structure also postdates the fire of 1831.

Among the masses celebrated here every Sunday there is one in the Chaldean rite. St. Louis is the local house of worship for the Chaldean Church, an 18C offshoot of the ancient Nestorian Church that is in union with Rome. The members of this Church in Istanbul are all from the Hâkkari region in the far southeast corner of Turkey, descendants of the ancient Chaldean and Assyrian peoples; parts of their mass are still sung in Aramaic, the language of Christ.

After the second turning on the right we come to the Franciscan **church of St. Anthony of Padua**, the largest Roman Catholic sanctuary in the city. The first church of St. Anthony was established on this site in 1725; the present building, a good example of Italian neo-Gothic architecture in red brick, was completed in 1912 by the Istanbul-born Italian architect Giulio Mongeri.

A short way beyond the church we turn left off the avenue into the Hacopulo Pasajı, a picturesque alley reminiscent of Pera of times past. Midway along the passage an alley on the left leads to the Greek **church of Eisodeia tis Theotokou** (the Presentation of the Virgin), also known as Our Lady of Pera, dedicated in 1807 and rebuilt in 1855. On the right side of the iconostasis there is an icon of the Virgin and Christ-Child dating from the 10C.

At the end of the alley we turn right on Meşrutiyet Caddesi, where at the first intersection we see on our right the entrance to the **British Embassy**, a disciple of Sir Charles Barry, architect of the Houses of Parliament in London. At the rear of the Embassy there is a magnificent and very English garden.

Street Markets and Meyhanes

We now turn right at the intersection and return to Istiklal Cad. at Galatasaray Meydanı. The square takes its name from the **Galatasaray Lycée**, whose ornate gateway at the northeast corner of the intersection leads to the extensive grounds of the school. Although the present Lycée building dates only to 1908, Galatasaray traces its origins back to the early Ottoman period in Istanbul. It was founded by Beyazit II (1481–1512) as a school for the imperial pages, ancilliary to the one in Topkapı Sarayı. After a somewhat chequered career, it was reorganised in 1868 under Sultan Abdül Aziz as a modern lycée on the French model, with the instruction partly in Turkish, partly in French. After the University of Istanbul, Galatasaray is the oldest Turkish institution of learning in the city, and it has produced a large number of the statesmen and intellectuals who have shaped modern Turkey.

We now continue up Istiklal Caddesi. At the first turning on the left beyond the square we pass Şahne Sok., which leads downhill through the *Galatasaray street market. This is the most colourful quarter in Beyoğlu, with the street and its tributary alleyways lined with the shops, stalls and barrows of fishmongers, greengrocers and other merchants and itinerant pedlars, along with kerbside eating and drinking places and old-fashioned meyhanes, or Turkish taverns.

Many of these meyhanes are in the *Çiçek Pasajı, or Passage of Flowers, an L-shaped passage that has entrances on both Şahne Sok. and Istiklal Cad. This was originally the 'Cité de Pera', built in 1870 by the Greek businessman Zographos Efendi as a de luxe apartment house with elegant shops along the arcade on the street level. During the 1930s a number of meyhanes were opened in the arcade, along with the flower shops that gave the passage its name, though these have long since been displaced by taverns.

Close to the Çiçek Pasajı and opening off the opposite side of the street is the **Avrupa Pasajı**, which extends from Şahne Sok. to Mesrutiyet Cad. This was built by the architect Pulgher in 1870, modelled on a passage in Paris; it is also called Aynalı Pasaj, or the Mirrored Arcade, because of the mirrors that reflected the light of the gas lamps that once illuminated it in the evening. The passage has recently been restored and is once again functioning as a shopping arcade.

A short way down Şahne Sok. beyond these passages we see on our right the Armenian **church of Üç Horon** (The Holy Trinity). This was first built in wood in 1807; then after being destroyed in a fire it was rebuilt in stone in 1907.

The first turning to the right from Şahne Sok. brings us to **Nevizade Sok.**, a colourful street lined with the best meyhanes in Istanbul.

We now resume our walk up Istiklal Cad., which between Galatasaray and Taksim is lined with shops, eating places and cinemas, the streets leading off from it on either side flanked by bars, restaurants, meyhanes and night clubs, for here we are in the heart of downtown Istanbul. Many of the buildings along the avenue date to the last half century of the Ottoman era, such as Tokatliyan

Hanı, Cercle d'Orient, the Atlas Cinema, and Cité Roumelie. Halfway along this stretch of the avenue we see on our left **Ağa Camii**, the only mosque on Istiklal Cad. The first mosque on this site was founded in 1594–95 by Hüseyin Ağa of the Galatasaray School; this was rebuilt in 1839 and restored in 1936.

At the end of the avenue we pass on our left the old **French Consulate**, originally constructed in 1719 as a hospital for those suffering from the plague. Beyond that is the pretty little octagonal building that has given its name to Taksim Square and the surrounding quarter. This is the **Taksim Meksemi**, or water-distribution centre, built by Mahmut I in 1732.

The last street on the right before the end of the avenue, Meselik Sok., leads to the courtyard entrance of **Haghia Trianda**, the largest Greek Orthodox church in Istanbul, completed in 1880.

Modern Istanbul

We now come to **Taksim Square**, the centre of modern Istanbul. At the centre of the square is the **Independence Monument**, a statue group representing Atatürk and other leaders of the Turkish Nationalist movement, completed in 1928 by the Venetian sculptor Pietro Canonica . The glass-walled building at the far end of the square is the **Ataürk Cultural Centre** (Kültür Merkezi), home of the Instanbul **Opera**; this was completed in 1969, only to burn down the following year, and repairs were not completed until 1978.

Taksim Square is the hub of the modern city, with Siraselviler Cad. heading off to the south, Taki Zafer Cad. (and its continuation, Inönü Cad.) to the west, and Cumhuriyet Cad. to the north, the first two avenues leading down to the Bosphorus and the third to the modern quarters of Harbiye, Nişantaşı, Teşvikiye, and Şişli.

There are two museums of interest to the north of Taksim Square, and we will end this itinerary by visiting both of them. They are both approached along Cumhuriyet Cad., which we follow as it passes Taksim Park, the Hilton Hotel, and Radioevi (the building that houses Radio Istanbul), after which we turn right on Gümüş Sok., following it as it veers left to pass behind the Harbiye Barracks. Then on the left side of the street we come to the *****Askeri Müze** (Military Museum) (Pl. 7,2).

■ **Admission**. The museum is open 09.00–17.00; closed Mon, Tue.

The museum has an extensive and interesting collection of exhibits from all periods of Ottoman military history. Among these are the beautiful cannons captured by the Turks in their campaigns in Europe and the Middle East, all of them arrayed outside the museum. The miniature Janissary costumes include all of those worn by their different ranks and units, a fascinating and colourful collection. Another notable exhibit is the huge and sumptuous imperial tent in which the Sultan lived when he accompanied the army on campaign. There are also performances of Ottoman military music every day except Mon, Tue from 15.00–16.00 by the Mehter Band.

We approach the second museum by retracing our steps to Cumhuriyet Cad., where we cross the avenue and turn right, continuing straight ahead on Halaskargazi Cad. This brings us to the Atatürk Museum, at 25 Halaskargazi Cad.

■ **Admission**. The museum is open 09.30–16.30; closed Thur, Sun.

The museum is housed in the old mansion where Atatürk lived in 1919, just before he went off to Anatolia to organise the Turkish Nationalist movement, an effort that gave rise to the Turkish Republic in 1923. On exhibit are a number of Atatürk's personal effects as well as photographs, documents and memorabilia associated with his residence here.

19 · **The Bosphorus

This itinerary will take us up the European shore of the Bosphorus from the Galata Bridge to the Black Sea, after which we will come back along the Asian shore to our starting point. You can do this Route by successive stages on land and sea, the latter using the Bosphorus ferries, whose various routes take them back and forth between the continents. In the description that follows we will go up the European shore of the Bosphorus on the coastal road as far as Rumeli Kavağı, and the rest of the itinerary will be by sea.

Since antiquity travellers have praised the beauties of the Bosphorus and its verdant shores, for this historic strait is one of the loveliest and most dramatic sights in the world. New parks and promenades, particularly on the European side, have opened up the shores of the Bosphorus to strollers, so that it is now possible to walk for miles without interruption, a pleasure that was not possible just a decade or so ago.

The Bosphorus derives its name from the myth of Io, a priestess of Hera who was seduced by Zeus. Zeus transformed Io into a heifer to conceal her from his jealous wife, but Hera was not deceived and sent a gadfly to torment Io. Pursued by the gadfly, Io plunged into the strait that separates Europe from Asia, and thenceforth it was known as the Bosphorus, or the Ford of the Cow. The Bosphorus also appears in Greek mythology in the legend of Jason and the Argonauts, who travelled up the strait to the Black Sea, the ancient Euxine, in their quest for the Golden Fleece. Many places on the Bosphorus are associated with the adventures of the Argonauts on their way up the strait, an heroic voyage which represents the expansion of the Ionian Greeks along the shores of the Euxine at the beginning of the first millennium BC.

The Bosphorus first appears in Greek literature in the 'Histories' of Herodotus, where he describes the bridge of boats Darius constructed in 512 BC to transport his army across the strait in his campaign against the Scythians. From that time onward it played an important and even decisive role in the history of the city founded at its southern extremity in 667 BC; for as Gyllius eloquently points out, the Bosphorus is 'the first creator of Byzantium, greater and more important than Byzas, the founder of the City'. And he later sums up the predominant importance of this 'Strait that surpasses all straits', by the epigram: 'The Bosphorus with one key opens and closes two worlds, two seas'.

Topography and oceanography

The Bosphorus is a strait some 30km long, running in the general direction north-northeast to south-southeast, and varying greatly in width from about 700m at its narrowest to over 3.5km at its widest. Its average depth at the centre of the channel is between 50m and 75m, but at one point it reaches a depth of over 100m. The predominant surface current flows at a rate of 3–5km per hour from the Black Sea to the Marmara, but, because of the sinuosity of the channel, eddies producing strong reverse currents flow along most of the indentations of the shore. A very strong wind may reverse the main surface current and make it flow toward the Black Sea, in which case the counter-eddies also change their direction. At a depth of about 40m there is a sub-surface current, called kanal in Turkish, which flows from the Marmara to the Black Sea.

Its waters, however, are for the most part prevented from entering the Black Sea by a threshold just beyond the mouth of the Bosphorus; these lower waters, denser and more saline than the fluid above them, are turned back by the threshold, mingle with the upper waters, and are driven back toward the Marmara with the surface current. The lower current is so strong, under certain conditions, that if fishing nets are lowered into it, it may pull the boats toward the Black Sea against the surface current.

Both shores of the Bosphorus are indented with frequent bays and harbours, and in general it will be found that an indentation on one shore corresponds to a cape or promontory on the other. Most of the bays are at the mouths of valleys reaching back into the hills on either side, and a great many of these have streams that flow into the Bosphorus. Almost all of these are insignificant, only the so-called Sweet Waters of Asia has any claim to be called a river, and this is quite small.

Both shores are lined with hills, none of them very high, the most imposing being Büyük Çamlıca (262m) and Yuşa Tepesi (201m), both on the Asian side. Nevertheless, especially on the upper Bosphorus, the hills often seem very high because of the way in which they come down in precipitous cliffs into the sea. In spite of the almost continuous line of villages and the frequent forest fires, both sides of the Bosphorus are well-wooded, especially with cypresses, umbrella-pines, plane trees, horse chest-nuts, terebinths, and judas trees. The pink blossoms of the judas trees in spring, mingled with the mauve flowers of the wisteria and the red and white candles of the chestnuts, make the Bosphorus during that season even more spectacularly beautiful.

Galata Bridge to Tophane (c 1km)

Our itinerary will begin in **Karaköy** (Pl. 7,7), the great square at the northern end of the Galata Bridge. The area along the shore beside the bridge is extremely lively, colourful and picturesque, with fishermen hawking their catch from boats along the shore, and with ferries and water-taxis criss-crossing the Golden Horn in all directions.

From the upstream side of the Galata Bridge the shore road, Rihtim Cad., leads past the large ferry-terminal and towards the docks along the lower Bosphorus. We cross Rihtim Cad. and walk along its left side for about 200m; we then turn left and left again at the next corner, after which we find, on the right, the entrance to ***Yer Altı Cami** (Pl. 7,7), the Underground Mosque, one of the strangest and most fascinating monuments in the city.

> The mosque is housed in the low, vaulted cellar or keep of a Byzantine tower or castle, which some scholars have identified with the ancient Castle of Galata, originally constructed by the Emperor Tiberius II (578–82). This was the place where one end of the famous chain that closed the mouth of the Golden Horn in times of siege was fastened; the other end was fixed somewhere along Saray Point, and the chain was kept afloat by buoys.

Descending into the mosque, you find yourself in a maze of dark, narrow passages between a forest of squat pillars supporting low vaults; six rows of nine each, or 54 in all. Toward the rear of the mosque are two large chambers separated from the rest of the interior by grilles. These are the tombs of two sainted martyrs, Abu Sufyan and Amiri Wahibi, both of whom died in the first Arab siege of Constantinople in 674–78. The site of their graves was revealed in a dream to a Nakşibendi dervish one night in 1640. When Murat IV learned of this he had the graves opened and the saints reinterred in a shrine on the site; later, in 1757, the whole dungeon was converted into a mosque by Köse Mustafa Paşa, who was Grand Vezir under three sultans: Mahmut I, Osman III, and Mustafa III.

Kemeraltı Caddesi

Walking away from the Bosphorus to the main avenue, Kemeraltı Cad., on the far side we see a church with a tall tower. This is the **church of St. Benoit**, founded by the Benedictines in 1427; later it became the royal chapel of the French ambassadors to the Ottoman Empire, several of whom are buried there. After being in the hands of the Jesuits for several centuries, it was given, on the temporary dissolution of that order in 1773, to the Lazarists, to whom it still belongs. In 1804 they established a school next to the church; this is still in operation and continues to be one of the best foreign lycées in the city. Of the original 15C church, only the tower remains, with the rest of the building dating from two later reconstructions: the nave and south aisle in 1732, and the north aisle in 1871.

Turning right on Kemeraltı Cad., we soon see on the right a church built of gleaming white stone. This is the Armenian **church of Surp Kirkor Lusavoriç**, St. Gregory the Illuminator, erected in 1960 after the previous church near the site had been demolished to widen the avenue. The original church was erected in 1431 on land purchased from the Genoese of Galata. The new church was designed by Bedros Zobyan as a replica of the famous church of St. Gregory at Echmiadzin in Armenia, a 7C sanctuary which is one of the masterpieces of medieval Armenian architecture.

The quarter between Kemeraltı Cad. and the Bosphorus, in this area, is a labyrinth of narrow, winding streets in which it is impractical to give specific directions. By wandering through the neighbourhood behind St. Gregory you come upon three Greek churches of some interest. These are the churches of Haghios Nikolaos, Haghios Ioannis Prodromos, and the Panaghia. All three of these sanctuaries currently belong to the so-called Turkish Orthodox Church, whose symbol is a cross with the Turkish star and crescent in the upper right-hand quadrant. This sect was founded in 1924 by a dissident priest from Anatolia known as Papa Eftim, who took his parishioners with him in a schism with the Greek Orthodox Church. The mass in this Church is said in Turkish rather than Greek, as this is the language of the Anatolian Christians known as the Karamanlı. During the half-century from that time until his death, Papa Eftim, who styled himself Patriarch Efthemios I, engaged in a running battle with the Ecumenical Patriarchate that has been continued by his successors, though the congregation has now dwindled to just a handful of followers.

The **church of Haghios Ioannes Prodromos** (St. John the Baptist) is just off Kemeraltı Cad. at Vekilharç Sok. 15. The first reference to the church is by Tryphon in 1583. The original church was destroyed by fire in 1731, and the present building was completed in 1734.

The **church of Haghios Nikolaos** (St Nicholas) is at Hoca Tahsin Sok. 12 and Mumhane Cad. 45. The earliest reference to the church is in Tryphon's list of 1583, while the present church dates from a rebuilding in 1804. The ayazma in the narthex dates from 1867 and is dedicated to St. Anthony.

The **church of the Panaghia** is at Ali Paşa Değirmeni Sok. 2. It is dedicated to the Koimesis tis Theotokou, the Dormition of the Virgin. The church is popularly known as Panaghia Kafatiane, our Lady of Kaffa, because it was founded by Greeks from Kaffa in the Crimea. The first church on this site was built in 1475 on land purchased from the Genoese of Galata. It is mentioned in Tryphon's list of 1583. The present edifice dates from a rebuilding in 1734, and since 1924 it has been the patriarchal seat of the Turkish Orthodox Church. Its most treasured possession is an icon of the Hodegetria known as the Black Virgin, which was brought from Kaffa in 1475.

Continuing along Kemeraltı Cad. and crossing to the left side, we soon come to **Hendek Sok.**, the Street of the Moat. The name stems from the fact that the street follows the course of the moat that once extended around the walls of medieval Galata. In fact, a fragment of the medieval fortifications still survives in the structure of the teahouse at the street corner. This was part of a tower that formed the junction between the walls running along the Bosphorus and those coming down from the heights above.

*Kılıç Ali Paşa Camii

Just across the avenue at this point we see Kılıç Ali Paşa Camii (Pl. 7,5), the most impressive mosque on the European shore of the Bosphorus.

This mosque complex was built by Sinan in 1580 for Kılıç Ali Paşa, one of the great admirals in Ottoman history. Born in Calabria of Italian parents, he was captured in his youth by Algerian pirates and spent 14 years as a galley slave. After regaining his freedom he entered Süleyman's service as a buccaneer, becoming a Muslim and changing his name to Uluç Ali. He distinguished himself in several naval engagements, and as a reward for this he was made an admiral and was also given the post of Governor of Algiers. He was one of the few officers to serve with distinction at the disastrous Ottoman defeat at the battle of Lepanto in 1571. As a result of this Selim II appointed him Kaptan Pasa, the chief of command of the entire Ottoman navy, and renamed him Kılıç Ali, or Ali the Sword.

While serving as Governor of Algiers Kılıç Ali Paşa came into contact with Miguel Cervantes, who had been enslaved there after his capture at the battle of Lepanto. Five years after being brought to Algiers Cervantes managed to escape, but he was recaptured and brought before Kılıç Ali Paşa. Ali Paşa was apparently impressed with Cervantes, for he released him from captivity and gave him enough money to return to Spain. Cervantes paid tribute to the kindness of Ali Paşa in Chapter 32 of *Don Quixote*, where 'The captive relates his life and adventures'.

The climax of Ali Paşa's career came in 1573, when he recaptured Tunis from Don Juan of Austria. Seven years later he retired to Istanbul, when he decided to build his mosque complex. When Ali Paşa asked permission from Murat III to build his mosque, so the story goes, the Sultan sarcastically suggested that he construct it on the sea, since that was the Kaptan Paşa's domain. Ali Paşa proceeded to do just that, and commissioned Sinan to build him a mosque on land he had filled-in along the shore of the Bosphorus in Tophane.

Exterior. Although Sinan had been deeply impressed and inspired by Haghia Sophia, he had always avoided any kind of direct imitation of that edifice. Now in his old age—he was nearly ninety when he built the mosque—he designed a near replica of the Great Church. It is one of his least successful buildings, perhaps because the greatly reduced proportions make the building seem heavy and squat.

The mosque is preceded by a very picturesque double porch. The outer porch has a deeply sloping penthouse roof, supported by 12 columns on the west façade and three on each side, all with lozenge capitals. In the centre of this porch is a monumental marble portal, and there are bronze grilles between the columns. The inner porch is of the usual type, with five domed bays supported by columns capped with stalactite capitals. Above the entrance portal is the historical inscription giving the date of foundation of the mosque, and above this is a text from the Kuran in a fascinating calligraphy, set in a curious projecting marble frame, triangular in shape and adorned with stalactites.

Interior. Sinan's main departures from the plan of Haghia Sophia are these: the provision of only two columns instead of four between each of the piers to north and south, and the suppression of the exedrae at the east and west ends. Both of these departures seem to have been dictated by the reduced scale; had the original disposition been retained the building would certainly have been even heavier and darker. Nevertheless, the absence of the exedrae deprives the mosque of what in Haghia Sophia is one of its main beauties. The mihrab is in a square projecting apse, where there are some Iznik tiles of the best period. At the west there is a kind of pseudo-narthex of five cross-vaulted bays separated from the prayer area by four rectangular pillars.

Precincts. The külliye of Kılıç Ali Paşa Camii is extensive, including a medrese, a hamam, and the türbe of the founder, who died in 1587. (The 19C historian von Hammer thus describes Ali Paşa's death: 'Although ninety years of age, he had not been able to renounce the pleasures of the harem, and he died in the arms of a concubine'.) The **türbe** is in the pretty graveyard behind the mosque; it is a plain but elegant octagonal building with alternately one or two windows in each façade, in two tiers. The medrese, opposite the southeast corner of the mosque, is almost square; like the mosque itself it is a little squat and shut in. This structure is probably not by Sinan, since it does not appear in the 'Tezkere', the list of his works; it is now used as a clinic.

The **hamam,** which is a single bath, is just in front of the medrese. The plan is unique among the extant hamams of Sinan. From the vast camekan, doors lead into two separate soğukluks situated on either side of the hararet, each consisting of three domed rooms of different sizes. From the soğukluk on the right, the only one now being used for its original purpose, a passage leads off to the lavatories; the rooms in the opposite soğukluk are used as semi-private bathing cubicles. The hararet itself, instead of having the usual cruciform plan, is hexagonal, with open bathing places in four of its six arched recesses, the other two giving access from the two soğukluks. The plan of the bath is an interesting variation on the standard one, and broadly similar to one or two of the older hamams at Bursa, the first Ottoman capital.

Across the street north of Kılıç Ali Paşa Camii is one of the most famous of the baroque street-fountains in the city, the **Tophane Çeşmesi**. Built in 1732 by Mahmut I, it has marble walls completely covered with floral designs and arabesques carved in low relief, which were originally painted and gilded. Its charming domed and widely overhanging roof was lacking for many years but has recently been restored.

Directly across the avenue from Kılıç Ali Paşa Camii is a little mosque known as **Karabaş Mescidi**. The mosque was founded in 1530 by Karabaş Mustafa Ağa, who served as Chief Black Eunuch during the reign of Süleyman the Magnificent. It is rectangular in plan with a hipped wooden roof. The building was restored in 1962 and is once again in use.

Tophane

Across the side street from Karabaş Mescidi is the building from which the whole district takes its name; this is Tophane, the Cannon House (Pl. 7,5), which was once the principal military foundry in the Ottoman Empire.

> The original Ottoman foundry was built on this site by Mehmet II soon after the Conquest. It was extended and improved by Beyazit II, but then demolished by Süleyman the Magnificent, who replaced it with a larger and more modern establishment in preparation for his campaigns of conquest. Süleyman's foundry has long since disappeared; the present structure was built by Selim III in 1803, doubtless in connection with his own attempt to reform and modernise the Ottoman army.

Exterior. The foundry is a large rectangular building of brick and stone, with eight great domes supported by three lofty piers. Some years ago a project was begun to restore the building, but sadly it was abandoned halfway through. At present the military are occupying the building and it is closed to the public.

Beyond the foundry itself, along the height overlooking the street, you see a series of ruined substructures, walls and domes; these once formed part of the general complex of Tophane, which included extensive barracks for the artillerymen. Across the street there is a small kiosk in the Empire style that was also part of the Tophane complex; this was built by Abdül Aziz as a pavilion from which he could review parades of his artillery troops.

Tophane to Kabataş (c 1km)

Beyond the kiosk is **Nusretiye Camii**, the Mosque of Victory. This was built between 1822 and 1826 by Mahmut II; it was completed just after the Sultan's extermination of the Janissaries, and its name commemorates that event. The architect was Kirkor Balyan, the founder of the large family of Armenian architects who served the sultans through most of the 19C and who built many of the mosques and palaces that you see today along the shores of the Bosphorus. Kirkor Balyan had studied in Paris and his mosque shows a curious blend of baroque and Empire motifs, highly un-Turkish, but not without charm.

In building the mosque he abandoned the traditional arrangement of a monumental courtyard and substituted an elaborate series of palace-like apartments in two storeys; these form the western façade of the building, a feature which became a characteristic of all the Balyan mosques. Notice the bulbous weight-towers, the jutting dome arches, and the overly slender minarets (they were so slender that they fell down soon after construction and had to be re-erected). Observe also the ornate bronze grilles and inside the abundance of marble garlands in the Empire style. Do not fail to look closely at the mimber, a marvellous baroque creation.

Not far beyond the Nusretiye, on the heights above, we see the dome and minaret of **Cihangir Camii**. The present mosque, which was built for Abdül Hamit II in 1890, is of no interest whatsoever. However, it occupies the site of a mosque built in 1553 by Sinan for Süleyman the Magnificent. The mosque was dedicated to Prince Cihangir, Süleyman's hunchback son, who died in that year of heartbreak, it is said, because of the Sultan's execution of his beloved half-brother, Prince Mustafa. Sinan's mosque was burned down in 1720, as were several other mosques erected successively on the site before the present building.

Beyond Tophane we come to Fındıklı. During the Byzantine era this settlement was known as Argyropolis, the Town of Silver, since it stood opposite Chrysopolis (modern Üsküdar), the City of Gold.

After passing **Mimar Sinan University**, named for the great Ottoman architect, we see a handsome classical mosque on the edge of the sea. This is ***Molla Çelebi Camii** (Pl. 13), built by Sinan in 1561–62; the founder was Mehmet Vusuli, also known as Molla Çelebi, Chief Justice in the reign of Süleyman the Magnificent. The building is hexagonal in plan, covered by a dome supported by pillars engaged in the walls. Between these pillars to north and south there are four small semidomes, with another small semidome covering the rectangular projecting apse in which stands the mihrab.

About 100m farther along we see on the right a street-fountain built in 1732 by Hekimoğlu Ali Paşa, Grand Vezir of Mustafa I. This a beautifully carved work in white marble, with a fountain on its two faces; unfortunately, it has lost its quaint overhanging roof.

Directly across the highway from the fountain there is one of the most beautiful of the baroque **sebils** in the city; this was built in 1787 by Koca Yusuf Paşa, Grand Vezir of Abdül Hamit I. It has a magnificent çeşme in the centre, flanked by the two grilled windows of the sebil. The whole of the sebil is elaborately carved and decorated with encrustations of various marbles, with a long calligraphic inscription forming a frieze above the windows.

We now come to the **iskele of Kabataş**, one of the principal ferry-stops on the lower Bosphorus, with water taxis continually crossing the strait to Üsküdar.

The mosque on the seashore some 300m upstream from the Kabataş iskele is **Dolmabahçe Camii**. This was built in 1853 for the Valide Sultan Bezmialem, mother of Sultan Abdül Mecit; the architect was Nikoğos Balyan, grandson of Kirkor Balyan, builder of Nusretiye Camii. Nikoğos Balyan came at a bad time in the development of late Ottoman architecture and it is only with difficulty that one can admire any of his buildings. The great cartwheel arches of this mosque seem particularly disagreeable; but the two very slender Corinthian minarets, one at each end of the little palace-like structure that precedes the mosque, have a certain charm.

The baroque clock-tower to the north of the mosque was erected by Sarkis Balyan in 1890–95 for Abdül Hamit II; completed in 1854, it is made of cut stone and has a height of 27m. There are clocks in all sides with Arabic numbers; these were made by the French clockmaker Paul Garnir.

Directly across the avenue from Dolmabahçe Camii there is a tiny **külliye** with a sebil as its dominant structure. This was built in 1741 by the Sipahi (cavalry knight) Hacı Mehmet Emin Ağa. The Turkish architectural historian Halil Edhem says rightly that this is 'perhaps the most interesting eighteenth-century sebil in Istanbul'. The five-windowed sebil is flanked symmetrically by a door on one side and by a çeşme on the other; there follow three grilled windows for the members of the sipahi's family, his own tomb, unusually, is in the sebil itself. Beyond the graveyard there is a small mektep that has not been restored. The sebil itself was restored in the mid 1970s and now serves as a very pleasant café.

**Dolmabahçe Sarayı

After passing Inönü Stadium we see on our right the gardens and then the buildings of Dolmabahçe Sarayı (Pl. 13), the principal imperial residence in the late years of the Ottoman Empire. The public entrance to the palace is through the gardens to its south.

■ **Admission.** The palace is open 09.00–16.00; closed Mon, Thu.

The present site of the palace was originally a small harbour on the Bosphorus. On 22 April 1453, during the Ottoman siege of Constantinople, Mehmet II had 70 ships of his fleet anchored here in preparation for the strategem that turned the tide of battle in his favour. After sunset that day he had the ships placed on wheeled platforms and hauled by oxen, pulling them over the heights of Pera and then down to Kasımpaşa on the Golden Horn, thus bypassing the chain with which the Byzantines closed the mouth of the inner harbour. This gave the Turks control of the Horn and set the stage for their final conquest of Constantinople on 29 May of that year.

Shortly after the Conquest Fatih laid out a royal garden on this site, and early in his reign Selim I built a seaside kiosk here. Gyllius writes that in his time this was known as the Little Valley of the Royal Garden. Early in the 17C Ahmet I extended the royal gardens by filling in the seashore in front of them, a project that was completed by his son and successor, Osman II; thenceforth this site was known as Dolmabahçe, the 'filled-in garden'. By the beginning of the 19C there was a large imperial summer residence at Dolmabahçe, and Mahmut II seems to have preferred this to the old palace of Topkapı Sarayı.

His son and successor, Abdül Mecit, decided to move out of Topkapı Sarayı altogether, and in 1844 he commissioned Karabet Balyan (son of Kirkor Balyan) and his son Nikoğos to replace the existing structures at Dolmabahçe with a new palace. The new palace of Dolmabahçe was completed in 1855, whereupon the Sultan and his household moved in there, abandoning the old palace on the First Hill that had been the imperial residence for nearly four centuries. Dolmabahçe served as the principal imperial residence of all but one of the later Ottoman sultans; the exception was Abdül Hamit II, who preferred the more secluded residence that he built for himself a bit farther up the Bosphorus at Yıldız.

After the establishment of the Turkish Republic, Dolmabahçe served as Atatürk's presidential residence whenever he was in Istanbul. Atatürk lived in Dolmabahçe Palace during his last illness, and he died there on 10 November 1938, in a seaside bedroom that is still furnished as it was at the time of his death. The palace has been restored in the past quarter century and it is now open as a museum and as a showplace for the holding of gala official functions.

Main gateway of Dolmabahçe Sarayı

Exterior. The main entrance to Dolmabahçe is through the gardens at its southern end. The most impressive aspect of the palace is its seaside façade of white marble, 284m in length fronting on a quay some 600m long.

Interior. The core of the palace is a great imperial state hall flanked by two main wings containing the state rooms and the royal apartments, with the selamlık on the south side and the harem on the north; the apartment of the Sultan Valide is in a separate wing linked to the Sultan's harem through the apartment of the Crown Prince; in addition there was another harem for the women of the princes, and still another residence at the northwest corner of the palace for the Chief Black Eunuch. The complex also included rooms for those of the palace staff who lived within Dolmabahçe, as well as kitchens, an imaret to feed the staff, an infirmary with a pharmacy, stables, carriage houses, and barracks for the halberdiers who guarded the imperial residence. All in all, there were a total of 285 rooms, including 43 large salons and six hamams, with the Sultan's private bath centred on an alabaster bath tub.

The palace interior was the work of the French decorator Sechan, who designed the Paris Opera, and thus the décor and furniture of Dolmabahçe are strongly reminiscent of French palaces and mansions of a somewhat earlier period. A number of European artists were commissioned to adorn the palace with paintings, the most notable being Boulanger, Gerome, Fromentin, Ayvazovski, and Zonaro; outstanding examples of their work can still be seen in the original rooms for which they were commissioned, and others are displayed in the **Exhibition Hall**, which has a separate entrance on the court-yard off the shore highway. The opulent furnishings of the palace include 4455 sq m of hand-woven Hereke carpets; the fireplaces and chandeliers are of Bohemian glass and Baccarat crystal. The world's largest chandelier hangs in the Muayede Salon, or State Room, comprising 4½ tonnes of Bohemian glass with 750 lights.

A great showpiece is the ornate stairway that leads up from the Hall of the Ambassadors, its balusters made of Baccarat crystal and its upper level framed with monoliths of variegated marble. Other impressive chambers are the Zülveçheyn Salonu, the Kırmızı Oda (Red Room), the Mavi (Blue) Salon, the Pembe (Pink) Salon, the Valide Sultan's apartment, the apartment of Sultan Abdül Aziz, Atatürk's apartment, and the School Room.

Kabataş to Beşiktaş (c 1km)

A short distance beyond Dolmabahçe Sarayı we come to the **Resim ve Heykel Müzesi** (Painting and Sculpture Museum), open 12.00–16.00; closed Mon, Thu, where there are exhibits of modern Turkish works.

A short way farther along we come to the *Deniz Müzesi (Maritime Museum) (Pl. 13). The museum is open 09.30–17.00; closed Mon, Tue. In the garden there are arrayed cannons and other naval armaments, and inside there are exhibits of naval uniforms and models of warships, along with photos, engravings, paintings and other memorabilia ranging from Ottoman to Republican times. The prize exhibit is the map of America made in the first half of the 16C by Piri Reis, the Turkish cartographer. Also of considerable interest are the great imperial caiques used in Ottoman times to row the Sultan to his seaside palaces along the Bosphorus.

The side street just opposite the Maritime Museum, Ortabahçe Cad., which a little farther along changes its name to Ihlamur Deresi Cad., leads to an imperial Ottoman pavilion in a valley of the hills above the Bosphorus. This is **Ihlamur Kasrı**, the Linden Pavilion. The palace takes its name from Ihlamur Deresi, the Valley of the Lindens, the once-lovely vale in which it is set. Ahmet III, the Tulip King, laid out gardens here during the first quarter of the 18C, and these would have been used in his annual Tulip Festivals. Abdül Mecit erected a kiosk here early in his reign, and then in 1849–55 Nikoğos Balyan built for him the pair of kiosks that constitute the present Ihlamur Kasrı. These are Maiyet Köşkü, the Kiosk of the Retinue, and Merasim Köşkü, the Ceremonial Kiosk. The first of these, as its name implies, was used by the Sultan's retinue, including the women of his harem, while the second was used for his guests, including visiting dignitaries. Ihlamur Kasrı has recently been superbly restored, along with its surrounding gardens, and it is now open to the public as a museum. (The palace is open 09.00–17.00; closed Mon, Thu.)

Beşiktaş

We now come to **Beşiktaş**, where Barbaros Blv. leads inland from the iskele.

Various explanations have been advanced for the name Beşiktaş, or Cradle Stone, the most probable being that it is a Turkish adaptation of the Greek name, Diplokionion, the Twin Columns, from two lofty columns of Theban granite that stood near the shore. In Byzantine times there was a famous church of St. Mamas here, as well as a port, a royal kiosk, and a hippodrome. These have all vanished without a trace, but there are still several Ottoman monuments of some interest in the vicinity.

In the centre of the park by the iskele there is a statue of Hayrettin Paşa, the famous Ottoman admiral, known in the West as Barbarossa. The statue, a vivid and lively work by the Turkish sculptor Zühtü Müridoğlu, was erected in 1946 on the third centenary of Barbarossa's death. **Barbarossa's türbe** is at the far southwest corner of the park, directly opposite his statue. This is one of the earliest works of Sinan, dated by an inscription over the door to 1541–42. The structure is octagonal in plan, with two rows of windows. The türbe was restored in the early 1970s; the upper row of windows was filled in with stained glass; and the dome was well repainted with white arabesques on a rust-coloured ground. Three catafalques occupy the centre of the türbe, and in the little garden outside there is a cluster of handsome sarcophagi in each of which are planted purple irises.

Across the avenue from Barbarossa's türbe, on the northwest corner of the intersection, we see **Sinan Paşa Camii**, a brick and stone edifice. This is another work of the architect Sinan, built for Sinan Paşa, Ottoman admiral and brother of the Grand Vezir Rüstem Paşa. Inscriptions on the şadırvan and over the entrance portal give the date of completion as 1555–56, two years after the death of its founder. The mosque is interesting architecturally, though not particularly attractive. Its plan is essentially a copy of the ancient Üç Şerefeli Camii, built in Edirne in 1447. Its central dome rests on six arches, one incorporated in the east wall, the others supported by four hexagonal pillars, two on the west, one each to north and south; beyond the latter are side aisles each with two domed bays. Thus far the plan is almost like that of Üç Şerefeli, but while there the western piers are incorporated into the west wall, here Sinan has added a sort of narthex of five bays, four with domes, the central one cross-vaulted. The proportions are not very good and the interior seems squat and heavy.

The same indeed is true of the courtyard, where the porticoes are not domed but have steeply sloping penthouse roofs, with the cells of the medrese occupying three sides.

There are also **two Greek churches** in Beşiktaş, both of them dedicated to the Panaghia (Blessed Virgin).

Beşiktaş to Ortaköy (c 2.2km)

About 500m beyond Beşiktaş we pass the **Çırağan Palace Hotel**, the main building of which is the rebuilt Çırağan Sarayı.

Çırağan Sarayı was built during the reign of Abdül Aziz and was completed in 1874; the Sultan died there on 4 June 1876, five days after he had been deposed. His death was officially declared to be a suicide, but the suspicious circumstances suggested to many of his contemporaries that he had been murdered. His nephew and successor, Murat V, was so mentally disturbed at the time of his accession that he proved unable to rule, whereupon he was deposed in favour of his brother, Abdül Hamit II. For the next three decades Murat and his family were kept as virtual prisoners in Çırağan, living in primitive conditions.

Murat died there in 1905, after which the palace was abandoned for a few years. Then, after the Constitution of 1908, Çırağan was restored and used for a time to house the new Turkish Parliament. The last act in the tragedy of this ill-starred palace occurred one night in January 1910, when Çırag˘an was totally gutted in a disastrous fire, leaving only a blackened shell. The palace was completely rebuilt in the 1980s and reopened as a hotel, along with a casino built in the same style.

A few hundred metres beyond Çırağan the shore highway passes on its left the entrance to **Yıldız Park**, the site of *Yıldız Palace** and its imperial kiosks and gardens.

■ **Admission.** Yıldız Park is open every day from 09.00–17.00. Şale Köşk and the Marangozhane are open 10.00–16.00; closed Mon, Thu.

The gardens here, originally known as Çırağan, are first mentioned in Ottoman history during the reign of Murat IV, who bestowed them on his daughter Kaya Sultan and her husband Melek Ahmet Paşa. After their time the gardens reverted to the imperial family. Ahmet III gave the gardens to his son-in-law, the Grand Vezir Nevşehirli Damat Ibrahim Paşa, who here hosted the Sultan and his court in some of the most flamboyant spring fêtes of the Lale Devri, the Tulip Period. The first imperial structure known to have been erected here was a pavilion built for Mihrişah Sultan, mother of Selim III, but this has long since vanished.

Yıldız Sarayı, the Palace of the Star, first began to take form in the upper gardens during the time of Mahmut II, and the buildings that you see here today date from his reign through that of Abdül Hamit II. Abdül Hamit II lived in Yıldız almost exclusively during his reign, preferring its secluded vales to the more exposed locations of Dolmabahçe and the other palaces on the shores of Bosphorus. But this was not just a pleasure dome, for Abdül Hamit, like all of the other Ottoman sultans, had a trade, namely cabinet-making, and he set up workshops on the palace grounds to manufacture both furniture and porcelain of exceedingly high quality for Yıldız Sarayı and the other imperial palaces and pavilions along the Bosphorus.

The pavilions of Yıldız Palace were abandoned after the fall of the Ottoman Empire, but in recent years they have been splendidly restored by the Turkish Touring and Automobile Club, directed by Çelik Gülersoy.

Precincts. The mosque to the right of the park entrance is **Mecidiye Camii**, built in 1848 by Abdül Mecit with a very quaint but ugly minaret in a pseudo-Gothic style.

After entering the grounds of Yıldız Sarayı, we can take any one of a number of very pleasant paths through the park, which is virtually the last extensive tract of woodland left on the European shore of the Bosphorus. A number of kiosks and greenhouses on the palace grounds have recently been converted into **cafés** by the TTOK, including the Malta Köşkü, the Çadır Köşkü, the Lale Sera (Tulip Conservatory), and the Yeşil Sera. The setting of the café outside the Malta Köşkü is superb, with a romantic view of the Bosphorus through a screen of greenery, giving you some idea of how beautiful the shores of the strait were in times past.

The most palatial of the surviving residences at Yıldız Sarayı is **Şale Köşkü** so called because of its resemblance to a Swiss chalet. This consists of two buildings, the first erected in 1889 and the second in 1898; the latter is apparently the work of the Italian architect Raimondo D'Aronco, who brought to Istanbul the Art Nouveau style of architecture under the name of the Stile Floreal. Şale Köşk has some 50 rooms, the largest and grandest being the magnificent Reception Hall, other splendid chambers being the Mother-of-Pearl Hall and the Yellow Parlour. Şale Kösk was used principally as a residence for visiting royalty, most notably Kaiser Wilhelm II, who during his visit with Abdül Hamit in 1895 formed an alliance between Germany and the Ottoman Empire.

Other buildings by D'Aronco are Küçük Mabeyin; Yaveran Dairesi; Usta Kalfalar; Çin Fabrıkası, or Tile Factory; the Limonluk, or Greenhouse; and the Theatre. Among the other buildings of interest are Büyük Mabeyin; Çit Kasrı; Hünkâr Dairesi; and the Marangozhane, or Carpentry Shop, now a museum.

The city of Istanbul has recently opened a new **Municipality Museum** just outside the upper entrance to Yıldız Park. The collection contains mostly works of art from the late Ottoman period, including a number of paintings depicting the Bosphorus and its shores in the latter years of the Empire. (The museum is open 09.30–16.30; closed Thu.)

Outside and to the south of the upper entrance (Dağ Kapısı) on Barbaros Blv. we see the ugly **Hamidiye Camii**, built in 1886 by Abdül Hamit II.

A few yards beyond the lower entrance to Yıldız Park a steep but short street leads to the very picturesque **shrine of Yahya Efendi**, a foster-brother of Süleyman the Magnificent, whom his mother nursed as an infant. Yahya Efendi died in 1570, and so the little külliye, which is a work of Sinan, must date to about that time. The külliye originally included Yahya Efendi's türbe and an associated medrese, but these have been enveloped by various wooden structures of the 19C and it is difficult to see what remains of the medrese, but at least its dershane appears to be intact. The türbe communicates by a large grilled opening to a small wooden mosque with a baroque wooden dome.

The various buildings are picturesque, but the surroundings are even more so: topsy-turvy old tombstones lie scattered among a lovely copse of trees, through which you catch occasional glimpses of the Bosphorus. This is one of the most popular religious shrines in the city, and it is always thronged with pious people at their devotions.

Ortaköy

Some 800m farther along we come to **Ortaköy**. In Byzantine times this village was called Haghios Phocas, after a famous church of that saint which stood here. There is still a Greek **church of Haghios Phocas** (St. Phocas) on the shore road in Ortaköy; this was built in 1856, but its parish undoubtedly dates back to the Byzantine period. Within the village there is another Greek church dedicated to **Haghios Georgios**. A block away from Haghios Phocas we see the Etz Ahayim ('Tree of Life') Synagogue. The original synagogue here dates back to the Byzantine era, though the present building dates only from 1913.

Although Ortaköy is now part of the urban mass of Istanbul, it still has a village atmosphere about it, and in recent years it has become something of a local **arts and crafts centre**; a number of its old houses have been restored, particularly in the area around the ferry-landing, where there are numerous outdoor cafés, bars and restaurants.

The most prominent monument in Ortaköy is **Mecidiye Camii**, a charming baroque mosque dramatically situated on the promontory just upstream from the ferry-landing. The mosque was built for Sultan Abdül Mecit in 1854 by Nikoğos Balyan, architect of Dolmabahçe Camii and Dolmabahçe Palace. But Mecidiye Camii is a much better building than either of those two edifices; although the style as usual is hopelessly mixed, there is a genuinely baroque verve and movement in the undulating walls of the tympana of the great dome arches.

On the shore road in Ortaköy there is an **ancient hamam** that appears to have been wholly overlooked by writers in modern times. This was built by Sinan for Hüsrev Kethüda, who served as steward for the Grand Vezir Sokollu Mehmet Paşa; unfortunately there is no inscription to date the hamam. As so often happens, the façade on the street has been hidden by a modern stucco house-front built against it.

The interior of the hamam, which is a double bath, is curious and unlike any other by Sinan. From a camekan of the usual form (though confused by a modern gallery), you enter a rather large soğukluk consisting of a central area in two unequal bays each covered by a cradle-vault; at one end are the lavatories, at the other a bathing-cubicle. From the central area the hararet is entered. This, instead of being the usual large domed cruciform room, consists of four domed areas of almost equal size. The first two of these communicate with each other by a wide arch. Here, instead of the central göbektaşı, there is a raised marble sofa or podium against one wall, with domed bathing cubicles leading from it.

Ortaköy to Arnavutköy (c 2.3km)

Just beyond Ortaköy we pass under **Atatürk Köprüsü**, the first of the Bosphorus bridges, which was opened in 1973 on the 50th anniversary of the founding of the Turkish Republic. At the time this was the fourth longest suspension bridge in the world, 1074m in length between the two great piers on the opposing continental shores, and with its roadway 64m above the water.

Kuruçeşme, the next village along the European shore, was until recent years disfigured by the coal, sand and gravel depots that lined its waterfront. But these depots have now been removed and replaced by two parks that together extend along almost the entire shore from Ortaköy to Arnavutköy, the next village beyond Kuruçeşme, making this one of the prettiest stretches of the European shore of the middle Bosphorus.

There are three old churches in Kuruçeşme, two of them Greek and one Armenian. The Greek churches are Haghios Demetrius and Haghios Ioannis Prodromos, both of which are first mentioned in 1684. The present **church of Haghios Demetrius** dates from 1798, while **Haghios Ioannis** was rebuilt in 1835. Both of them have sacred springs, that of Haghios Demetrius being one of the most renowned in the city, dating back to Byzantine times. The Armenian church is known as Surp Haç (Holy Cross); this may also date from the Byzantine era, though the present edifice is due to a rebuilding in 1834 by Karabet Balyan. The wooden **Kuruçeşme Camii** on the shore road was built in the 18C by Tezkireci Osman Efendi.

The next village is *__Arnavutköy__, 'the Albanian Village'. The shore road has now been extended out from the shore to run outside the very picturesque old wooden houses along the sea in the village. The interior of the village is also quite charming and picturesque, with old wooden houses lining lanes festooned with vines.

There are two Greek churches in Arnavutköy, which still has a small Greek community. The largest of the churches, near the shore road, is the **Taxiarkes**, dedicated to the Archangels Michael and Gabriel. The other, dedicated to **Profitas Elias** (The Prophet Elijah), has a renowned ayazma beside the church, which has an old Greek graveyard behind it and a Greek taverna across the road.

On the highest hill above Arnavutköy, in a superb position, are the buildings of **Robert College**, an American coeducational lycée, founded in 1871 as the American College for Girls. This was the first modern lycée of its kind in Turkey and produced many women who played a leading part in the life of their country, the most famous being the writer Halide Edib Adıvar, prominent in the Turkish Nationalist movement. In 1971, on the occasion of its centenary, the American College for Girls was amalgamated with the boys' lycée of the old Robert College, a little farther up the Bosphorus, with the new institution taking the latter name and occupying the site above Arnavutköy. From the grounds of the school there is a superb view of this part of the Bosphorus and its shores.

Arnavutköy to Rumeli Hisarı (c 3km)

The point that separates Arnavutköy harbour from the bay of Bebek, the next village on the European shore, is called **Akinti Burnu**, the Cape of the Current. This is the deepest part of the Bosphorus, which here reaches a depth of some 100m at the centre of the strait. The current is extremely powerful, making it very difficult for rowing boats and sailing vessels to round the point.

Bebek

After rounding Akinti Burnu we come to **Bebek Bay**, one of the most beautiful havens on the Bosphorus. Lush rolling hills with groves of umbrella pines and cypresses rise up to form a verdant background to the bay, a green frieze of trees between the blues of sea and sky. As the road enters the village we pass the huge Art Nouveau palace known as **Hidiv Sarayı**. This was formerly the residence of the Khedive of Egypt, the Ottoman viceroy, and now it serves as the summer home of the Egyptian consulate. The palace was built in 1902 by Raimondo D'Aronco in the Stile Floreal.

On the water's edge just past the ferry landing there is a little **mosque** built in 1913 by Kemalettin Bey, a leader of the neo-classical school of Turkish architecture. Like most of Kemalettin Bey's buildings, it is a little lifeless and dull, although the setting is quite pretty.

Bebek was in times past one of the prettiest villages on the Bosphorus, but it has been somewhat spoiled by high-rise apartments and numerous restaurants, most notably a McDonald's. Nothing can detract from its superb setting however, and the promenade by the shore on either side of the ferry-landing takes you along a particularly beautiful part of the strait.

There are still a few **old wooden houses** of the late Ottoman era in the back streets of Bebek. The oldest is the **Kavafyan Konağı** on Manolya Sok., the Street of Magnolia. The house was built in 1751 by the Kafayan, an Armenian family who still own the house today. There is also a Greek church in the village, **Haghios Charalambos**, which in times past was a dependency of the Iviron Monastery of Mount Athos in Greece.

On the hill between Bebek and Rumeli Hisarı, the next village on the European shore, stand the buildings of **Boğaziçi Universitesi**, the University of the Bosphorus. This new Turkish university was established in 1971, occupying the buildings and grounds of the old Robert College.

Robert College, which in its time was the finest institution of higher education in Turkey, was founded in 1863 by Cyrus Hamlin, an American missionary who had baked bread and washed clothes for Florence Nightingale's hospital in Üsküdar. The College was named after Christopher Robert, an American philanthropist who provided the initial funds to build and run the institution. During the 108 years of its existence the College had among its staff and graduates a number of important men (and women after 1960), including several who played a leading role in the cultural and political life of Turkey, as well as Greece and Bulgaria. Its graduates number two Prime Ministers of Turkey: Bülent Ecevit and Tansu Çiller, the latter being the first woman to hold this post.

The site of the University is superb, and its lovely terrace commands a stunning view of this exceptionally beautiful stretch of the Bosphorus. Just below the terrace there is an attractive old house that once belonged to Tevfik Fikret (1867–1915), for many years professor of Turkish Literature at Robert College, and one of the leading poets of his time. The house is called Aşıyan, or the Nest, and it has been converted into a museum to exhibit memorabilia of Tevfik Fikret. (Aşıyan is open 09.00–17.00; closed Thu, Sun.)

The point below Aşıyan is known as **Kayalar**, or the Rocks. This gives its name to **Kayalar Mescidi**, the little wooden mosque beside the road at the point. The original mosque on this site was built in the 17C by Nişancı Sitki

Mehmet Paşa. The present building was erected in 1877 by Şeyh Ahmet Niyazi Efendi, head of a tekke of the Kadiri dervishes.

**Rumeli Hisarı (fortress)

We now come to the narrowest part of the Bosphorus, which is here about 700m wide. We then pass directly under the walls of Rumeli Hisarı, the magnificent fortress that dominates the European shore of the strait.

■ **Admission.** Rumeli Hisarı is open 09.30–17.00 every day except Mon, and also when performances are being held.

It was here that Darius chose to cross the Bosphorus in his campaign against the Scythians in 512 BC. This crossing was accomplished on a bridge of boats designed by Mandrocles of Samos. While his army, estimated to be 700,000 strong, crossed the strait, the Great King watched from a stone throne cut into a cliff on the European shore. This throne, which was located about where the north tower of the fortress now stands, was later flanked by two columns raised to commemorate the historic crossing; these were still standing in early Byzantine times.

Soon after he succeeded to the throne in 1451, Mehmet II began preparations for the long-awaited siege of Constantinople. His first step was to cut off the city from its sources of grain on the shores of the Black Sea; to do this he decided to build a fortress on the European shore of the middle Bosphorus, directly across from Anadolu Hisarı, the fortress constructed on the Asian shore by Beyazit I in the late 14C. He demanded from Constantine XI Dragases a plot of land on which to build his fortress, and the Emperor was powerless to disagree.

The young Sultan himself selected the site, drew the general plan of the fortress, and hired 1000 artisans and 2000 labourers for the task, which began in April 1452. He entrusted the construction of each of the three main towers of the fortress to one of his chief vezirs: the north tower to Saruca Paşa, the sea-tower to Halil Paşa, his Grand Vezir, and the south one to Zaganos Paşa. The three of them strove to complete their task with the greatest speed and efficiency, while the Sultan himself assumed the overall supervision of the project. As a result the project was completed early in August 1452, less than four months after it had been started.

The castle was then garrisoned with a force of Janissaries, whose bombardiers trained their huge cannon on the strait, warning foreign captains not to try and get through to Constantinople from the Black Sea. One Venetian captain made the attempt, but his boat was sunk by the Turkish artillery, and then he and his surviving crewmen were impaled. As a result, Constantinople was cut off from the Black Sea, a factor that contributed to its eventual capture by the Turks in 1453. After the Conquest the fortress lost its military importance and it became a mere garrison post and prison, particularly for foreign ambassadors and prisoners of war.

Rumeli Hisarı was well restored in 1953, in connection with the 500th anniversary of the Conquest of Constantinople, and today it is used for performances associated with the Istanbul Festival.

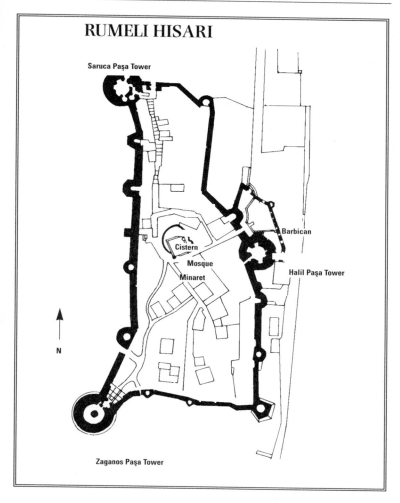

The Fortress. The fortress spans a steep valley with two tall towers on opposite hills and a third at the bottom of the valley at the water's edge, where there is a sea gate protected by a barbican. A curtain wall, defended by three smaller towers, joins the three major ones, forming an irregular figure some 250m long by 125m broad at its maximum. The north tower, built by Zaganos Paşa, was used as a prison in Ottoman times; this is open to the public, and includes a small museum showing objects used by the Janissaries. The area inside the fortress has been made into a park, and the circular cistern on which once stood a small mosque (part of the minaret has been left to mark its position) has been converted into the acting area of a Greek-type theatre.

The **cemetery** under the walls of Rumeli Hisarı is the earliest Turkish burial-

Interior of the Rumeli Hisari , the castle of Europe

ground on the European side of the city, its oldest tombstone dating back to 1452. The little mosque on the shore beneath the castle is **Hacı Kemaleddin Camii**. This was originally founded by Hacı Kemaleddin, perhaps during the reign of Mehmet II (1451–81), and then in 1746 it was rebuilt by Mahmut I. On the ground floor there is an ayazma dedicated to St. John, still sacred to Greeks though it is in a mosque and revered by Muslims as well.

Beyond the fortress we come to the village of **Rumeli Hisarı**, one of the most picturesque on the Bosphorus. The mosque on the corner opposite the iskele is **Ali Pertek Camii**. This was founded by Ali Pertek, an admiral in the reign of Murat IV (1623–40), and it was rebuilt in the 1960s. Within the village there is an Armenian church dedicated to **Surp Santuht** (St. Santuht), still used by the small Armenian community that has lived in Rumeli Hisarı since at least the time of the Conquest. The original church on this site may have been founded in Fatih's time, though the oldest inscription bears the date 1756. This inscription appears on one of the Armenian tombstones used to built the present church in 1856.

Rumeli Hisarı to Emirgan (c 2km)

Just upstream from the village of Rumeli Hisarı we pass under **Fatih Sultan Mehmet Köprüsü**, the second Bosphorus Bridge. This was opened in the summer of 1988, exactly 2500 years after Darius constructed his bridge of boats across the same stretch of the Narrows.

The next village after Rumeli Hisarı is **Baltalimanı**; this is named after the Ottoman admiral Balta Oğlu, who built Fatih's fleet here at the outset of the siege of Constantinople in 1453. As we approach the village we pass the large seaside palace known as **Mediha Sultan Sahilhanesi**. This was built in the mid 19C by Sarkis Balyan for Mustafa Reşit Paşa, who served six terms as Grand Vezir during the reign of Abdül Mecit (1839–61).The palace is now used as a hospital.

After Baltalimanı we come to **Boyacıköy**, a pretty village with many old

Ottoman houses along its back streets. Within the village there is an Armenian church dedicated to Surp Yerits Mangants (The Three Holy Infants). This was originally constructed in wood in 1844; the present church is due to a rebuilding in brick in 1884.

There is also a Greek church dedicated to the **Panaghia Evangelistria**, the Annunciation of the Virgin.

The next village is **Emirgan**, named after the Persian prince Emirgüne, who in 1638 surrendered the Persian city of Erivan to Murat IV without a fight. Emirgüne later became the Sultan's favourite in drinking and debauchery, and was rewarded with the gift of a palace in this village. On the left side of the shore road, not far from the iskele, there are the remains of a handsome old **yalı**, or seaside mansion. This is believed to stand on the site of the palace erected by Murat IV for Emirgüne; parts of the structure may go back to that time, but most of it dates to the 19C, when a new or at least rebuilt mansion was erected by a Şerif of Mecca named Abdullah Paşa. The mansion, now known as the **Şerifler Yalısı**, has been restored as a museum, but it has not yet been opened to the public.

The village square is very picturesque, with outdoor cafés and teahouses shaded by giant plane trees. Beside the square stands a baroque **mosque**, partly of wood, built in 1781–82 by Abdül Hamit I. It consists of a large rectangular room, almost square, but curiously asymmetrical, and its décor is quite elegant in its baroque way.

Just above the village are the famous **tulip gardens of Emirgan**, which are at their most glorious during the annual Tulip Festival in April. The Turkish Touring and Automobile Club has now restored a number of old Ottoman structures around the Emirgan gardens, converting them into cafés known as Pembe Köşk, Sarı Köşk, Beyaz Köşk, and the Kır Kahveleri.

Emirgan to Tarabya (c 4.5km)

After leaving Emirgan the road curves to the left as it approaches the deeply indented bay of Istinye. At the intersection, the highway on the left leads inland to **Levent**, the suburb that occupies the heights above the European shore of the middle Bosphorus. A signpost on the upper highway in Levent directs you to **Maslak Kasrı**, an imperial Ottoman lodge originally set in spacious park lands with a view of the upper Bosphorus and its entrance from the Black Sea. Maslak Kasrı is built on a site first used as a country retreat during the reign of Mahmut II, though the present buildings appear to date mainly from the time of Abdül Aziz.

The various buildings of Maslak Kasrı, which has recently been restored and opened as a museum (open 09.00–17.00; closed Mon, Thu.), are the Kasrı Hümayun, or Imperial Lodge, which now serves as a museum; the Mabeyin Hümayun, or State Hall, now a conservatory; the Çadır Pavilion, which is used as a café and bookshop; and the Paşalar Dairesi, or Pashas' Quarters, which houses the administrative staff of the museum.

We now enter **Istinye**, which has become much more attractive since the removal of the dry-docks that took up much of the bay. Petrus Gyllius writes of Istinye that 'after the Golden Horn it must be acknowledged the largest bay and the safest port of the entire Bosphorus, rich as this is in bays and ports'. The Turkish name Istinye is a corruption of the Greek Sosthenion; according to one version of the legend Jason and the Argonauts erected a statue here, in thanksgiving (in Greek, sosthenion) for aid given by a winged genius of the place against their enemy on the opposite shore, King Amycus, ruler of the savage Bebryces (see Beykoz, below).

There is a **Greek church** in Istinye dedicated to the Archangels Michael and Gabriel.

The Istiniye iskele is just beyond the far end of the port. Between here and Yeniköy, the next village, there is a line of handsome yalıs, many of them dating from the 19C.

*Yeniköy

We then come to Yeniköy, one of the prettiest villages on the Bosphorus. Yeniköy was known in Byzantium as Neapolis, its name having the same meaning in Greek and Turkish: New Town. There are a number of handsome yalıs along the seafront around the iskele, the oldest being the **Dadyan Yalısı**, built by an Armenian family in the late 18C.

Within the village there are **four churches**, three of them Greek and the other Armenian. The Greek churches are dedicated, respectively, to Haghios Georgios, Haghios Nikolaos, and the Panaghia, while the Armenian church is dedicated to Surp Migirdiç. The oldest of these are the churches of Haghios Georgios and Haghios Nikolaos, which are both mentioned as early as 1652. There is also a **synagogue** on the shore road by the iskele; this was founded in 1870 by Count Abraham de Kamondo, who had a summer home in Yeniköy

At the northern extremity of the village we see the summer residence of the old embassy of Austria-Hungary. This was presented by Abdül Hamit II in 1883 to the Emperor Franz Josef I.

Beyond that is the hamlet of **Kalender**, named after the mendicant order of dervishes who once had a tekke here. Here we see the **Huber Köşkü**, a palatial mansion built in the late 19C and restored early in the 20C by Raimondo D'Aronco. After further restoration in 1985 this became an official residence of the President of Turkey. A little farther on is the summer embassy of Germany, which was presented by Abdül Hamit I in 1880 to Kaiser Wilhelm II.

**Tarabya

We now approach the deeply indented bay of Tarabya. Tarabya once vied with Bebek in its claim to be the most beautiful village on the Bosphorus, and for centuries it has been celebrated for its crescent-shaped azure bay. But now, while still lovely, it is suffering from the same ravages of tourism that are spoiling Bebek, with the proliferation of expensive restaurants and the erection of a luxury hotel. The village retains, in a slightly modified form, its old Greek name, Therapeia (cure, healing): this name was apparently given to it by the Patriarch Atticus (406–25), because of its salubrious atmosphere. The ancient name of the village was Pharmakeus, the Poisoner, based on the legend that Medea, in her pursuit of Jason, there threw away the poison with which she had intended to kill Jason.

By the intersection at the beginning of Tarabya we see the Greek **church of Haghia Paraskevi**, built in the mid 19C. In the courtyard of the church there is an ayazma, also dedicated to Haghia Paraskevi, whose shrines are often associated with sacred springs.

Elsewhere in Tarabya there is another Greek **church** dedicated to Haghia

Paraskevi, as well as one dedicated to Haghios Konstantinos (St. Constantine the Great).

Tarabya to Büyükdere (c 2km)

Beyond Tarabya the shore road is lined with the **summer embassies** of several European powers, some of which have lovely gardens. The first is the summer residence of the Italian Embassy, built in 1906 by Raimondo D'Aronco. Beyond it is the French Embassy, formerly the yalı of the Ypsilanti family, presented by Selim III in 1807 to Napoleon Bonaparte. Then comes the Russian Embassy, built in 1840 for General Nikolai Ignatiev, the Czar's ambassador to the Porte.

The next village beyond Tarabya is **Kireçburnu**, a small cluster of houses and fish restaurants at a bend in the Bosphorus. This was known in Byzantium as Kledai tou Pontou, the Keys of the Pontus; here for the first time on the journey up the strait you can see directly into the Black Sea.

We then come to **Büyükdere**, a big village along the northern side of a large bay. Its Turkish name means Large Valley, while in Byzantium it was known as Kalos Agros, the Beautiful Meadow. It is indeed a very lovely and fertile valley with fine old trees through which a road leads into the Belgrad Forest.

> The **Belgrad Forest**. The forest takes its name from the village of Belgrad that once stood in its midst. This was founded by Süleyman the Magnificent after his conquest of Belgrad in 1521, when he transported a number of the inhabitants of that city and settled them here to look after the reservoirs and aqueducts with which the forest abounds. The village of Belgrad became a popular summer retreat for European residents of Istanbul in the Ottoman period, particularly in times of plague. Lady Mary Wortley Montagu lived there during her stay in Istanbul, 1716–18, and in the letters which she later published her encomiums made the village famous. The village was abandoned in late Ottoman times and has now vanished.
>
> The aqueducts and reservoirs that are scattered here and there throughout the Belgrad Forest are very impressive indeed. Many of these were built for Süleyman the Magnificent by Sinan during the period 1554–65, some of them replacing or restoring Byzantine works. The nearest aqueduct to Büyükdere is at the top of the hill along the road leading inland from the Bosphorus. This grand structure was founded by Mahmut I and completed in 1732, and conveys the waters from his reservoir and several others to the distribution centre in Taksim Square.

There is another church dedicated to **Haghia Paraskevi** in Büyükdere, which still has a small Greek community. This is one of the oldest churches on the upper Bosphorus, first mentioned in 1604. There is also an Armenian church dedicated to Surp Boğos (St. Paul). This was originally a small chapel erected by Boğos Bilezikçiyan in 1847; then in 1893 the architect Kirkor Hürmüzyan expanded it into a stone church in the Gothic style.

Near the far end of the village we come to the oldest of the European **summer embassies**, that of Spain. The Spanish ambassador, Juan de Bouligny, bought this mansion from the Franciscans in 1783, so that his legation could escape the cholera epidemic then raging in Istanbul.

A short way farther along we come to the **Azaryan Yalısı**. This was built in the late 19C by an Armenian named Manuk Azaryan Efendi, who served in both the Parliament and the foreign service during the last years of the Ottoman Empire. Today the yalı houses the ****Sadberk Hanım Museum**, a unique and rich collection of antiquities and Turkish works of art. The museum was founded by Sadberk Koç, late wife of Vehbi Koç, one of Turkey's leading businessmen, who died in 1995. The museum opened in 1980 under the direction of their daughter Sevgi Gönül. (The museum is open 10.30–17.00 every day except Wed; closed in Feb.)

The archaeological section of the museum has some 7000 antiquities arranged in chronological order beginning with the Late Neolithic and Early Chalcolithic periods and going on through the Bronze Age, the Assyrian Trade Colonies, the Hittites, the Urartians, the Phrygians, the Mycenaeans, and the successive periods of Greek and Roman history, ending in the Byzantine era. Among the exhibits are terracotta figurines, pottery and ceramics, jewellery, inscribed tablets, glass and crystal objects, ivories, and objects made from bronze, silver, gold and electrum.

The Turkish and Islamic Art section has exhibits ranging in date from the Early Islamic era through the Ottoman period. The objects include metalwork, imperial monograms in silver, jewel-encrusted timepieces, jewellery, Chinese porcelains, and Turkish tiles and pottery from Iznik, Kütahya and Çanakkale. On the upper floor there are dioramas of traditional Turkish scenes, including a bridal shower and a circumcision bed. There are also beautiful examples of Ottoman costumes and Turkish embroideries.

Büyükdere to Rumeli Kavağı (c 6km)

After Büyükdere we come to **Sarıyer**, the largest village on the European shore of the upper Bosphorus. The most picturesque part of the village is on the shore behind the mosque, where there is a small port for the fishermen who work in the upper Bosphorus and the Black Sea. The ***fish-market** is particularly colourful, and on the pier are a number of good restaurants where you can dine on the day's catch, with a splendid view of the Asian shore of the upper Bosphorus. There are more fish restaurants along the shore in **Yeni Mahalle**, the next village, where there is a Greek church dedicated to Haghios Ioannes Prodromos.

At the main intersection in Sarıyer a signposted highway leads to the beach resort at **Kilyos**, a village on the Black Sea (c 15km).

Sarıyer and Yeni Mahalle constitute the last heavily settled area on the European shore of the Bosphorus, for above them there are only the two tiny fishing villages of Rumeli Kavağı and Rumeli Feneri. The coast road runs only as far as Rumeli Kavağı, from where a new highway runs inland, with one branch going to Kilyos and the other to Rumeli Feneri, which is at the very beginning of the Bosphorus. The ferry goes only as far as Rumeli Kavağı, so that those wishing to explore the upper Bosphorus must hire a motor boat there or in Sarıyer.

About midway between Sarıyer and Rumeli Kavağı on the coast road we see on the right the **türbe** of a Muslim saint known as Telli Baba. This is one of the most popular Muslim religious shrines in the city, and it is much frequented by women who pray to the saint for a husband. Those who are successful return to give thanks to the saint, usually fastening on his tomb strands of gold wire.

Rumeli Kavağı consists of a small cluster of houses and fish restaurants around the ferry-landing. On the Asian shore directly opposite are the ruins of a medieval fortress (see below), which, together with a castle on the European side, made up the principal Byzantine defences and customs control points on the upper Bosphorus. Of the European castle only a few scattered ruins remain; these are on the hill above Rumeli Kavağı and are known locally as **Kara Taş**, or Black Stone. The batteries below the castles on either side are relatively modern Turkish works; they were built in 1783 by Toussaint and strengthened in 1794 by Monnier, two French military engineers in the Ottoman service.

The villages of Rumeli and Anadolu Kavağı are probably to be identified with the ancient Serapion and Hieron, respectively. These were the Byzantine toll and customs control points, and a chain was strung between them to prevent ships from passing to and from the Euxine without paying their fees. Both of these posts were guarded by fortresses on the hills above; that on the European side was built by Manuel I Comnenus (1143–80) and called the Castle of the Incorporeal Saints, while the one on the Asian side, founded at some time early in the dynasty of the Palaeologues, was called the Castle of Hieron.

In the 14C the Genoese seized both fortresses from the Byzantines, after which they collected the tolls and customs fees from shipping in the Bosphorus, further contributing to the decline of the Byzantine Empire. Mehmet II captured both fortresses in 1452; they then fell into ruins in the peaceful centuries after the Conquest.

Rumeli Kavağı to Rumeli Feneri (7km)

An excursion by boat along the shores of the upper Bosphorus is one of great delight, for both shores are wild, rugged and desolate, but extremely beautiful. Now for the first time on the Bosphorus you find sandy beaches hidden away in secluded coves; grey herons haunt the cliffs, black cormorants dive into the limpid water, and schools of dolphins often gambol by. Petrus Gyllius who explored this coast in the mid 15C, identified a number of sites on the upper Bosphorus with the mythical voyage of Jason and the Argonauts. These identifications, though based on myth, add romantic interest to this excursion.

Some 5–6km up the Bosphorus by sea from Rumeli Kavağı we come to a strangely shaped and craggy point; in Turkish this has the appropriate name of Garipçe, which means strange or curious. There is a fairly well-preserved **Ottoman fortress** here; this was built in 1773 for Mustafa III by the Baron de Tott, another French military engineer in the Turkish service.

The ancient name of this place was Gyropolis, the Place of Vultures. It received its name through its association with the myth of King Phineus, the blind old prophet who was the son-in-law of Boreas, god of the North Wind. It seems that Phineus was tormented by the Harpies, two winged monsters who, every time a meal was set before the King, would swoop down upon it, snatch away most of the food, and render what was left inedible. As a result, Phineus had almost wasted away by the time the Argonauts arrived on their journey up the Bosphorus in quest of the Golden Fleece.

Among them were Zetes and Calais, the winged sons of Boreas, who took pity on their brother-in-law, King Phineus, flying up into the air to chase away the Harpies for ever. In return the grateful Phineus advised the Argonauts about the rest of their journey, particularly on how to avoid the baleful Symplegades, also known as the Cyanean Rocks. These were two huge rocks at the mouth of the Bosphorus, which were supposed to clash together with great violence, thus making it extremely perilous for ships to enter or leave the strait. Phineus told the Argonauts to let loose a dove which would fly between the Symplegades; if it was caught they were to give up their journey, but if it got through safely they were to wait till the rocks opened again and then row their hardest. They did so, the clashing rocks just shaved off the tail feathers of the dove and the Argo got safely through, with only some slight damage to its stern-works.

At the end of the Bosphorus we come to ***Rumeli Fenerı**, a picturesque fishing village that takes its name from the lighthouse (in Turkish, fener) on this last promontory on the European (in Turkish, Rumeli) shore of the strait. The rocks that Gyllius identified as the Symplegades are now connected to the mainland by a concrete mole, which extends southward to protect the harbour of Rumeli Feneri. On the headland beyond the lighthouse, looking out over the Black Sea, there are the remains of a fort built in 1769 by a Greek engineer.

The rock formation that Gyllius identified as the **Symplegades** is divided by deep fissures into several parts. On the peak of the highest rock are the remains of the so-called **Pillar of Pompey**. This is not really a column base but an ancient altar, decorated with a garlanded ram's head and other reliefs now much worn; it once had a Latin inscription, no longer legible, the transcription and interpretation of which are debated. Certainly neither altar nor column had anything to do with Pompey, and it is not known who first gave it this misleading name: it was after the time of Gyllius, however, since he does not mention it. He thought that the altar was probably a remnant of the shrine to Apollo which Dionysius of Byzantium says the Romans erected on one of the Cyanean Rocks. The column itself, with its Corinthian capital, toppled down in April 1680 and had utterly disappeared by 1800.

There is now a simple fish restaurant under the Clashing Rocks, with its tables set up on the mole, commanding a full view of the mouth of the Bosphorus and the Black Sea.

Anadolu Feneri to Anadolu Kavağı (c 7km)

The Asian shore of the upper Bosphorus is very imperfectly known and seems to have been rarely visited even by the few travellers who write about it. The only safe guide is Gyllius, for he alone appears to have explored the region in detail. Even his account, however, is not altogether free from difficulties, for he never gives the Turkish names of places in this region, perhaps because in his time they did not have any. Nevertheless, there are three places in his narrative that can be identified with certainty: the Promontarium Ancyraeum, the Promontarium Coracium, and the Fanum Jovis; and from these the others can be worked out.

The Ancyraean Cape is **Yum Burnu**, Cape of Good Omen, which is at the mouth of the Bosphorus. In the time of Gyllius it was called Cape Psomion, but anciently it was known as Ancyraean, the Cape of the Anchor, taking its name from the legend that it was here that Jason took on a stone anchor for the Argo.

The bay to the south of Yum Burnu is now called **Kabakoz Limanı**, the Harbour of the Wild Walnuts. In Gyllius' time it was known as the Bay of Haghios Sideros (that is, St. Anchor: the half-remembered story of the Argonautic anchor had given rise in the minds of the medieval Greeks to an apocryphal holy man). On the south this bay is bounded by a point not named by Gyllius but nowadays called **Anadolu Feneri Burnu**, after the lighthouse on the promontory above. Below the lighthouse the village of **Anadolu Feneri** clings perilously to the cliff. Just south of this is the bay that Gyllius calls Ampelodes; this is now known as **Çakal Limanı**, the Bay of Jackals, fringed by savage and rocky precipices.

The next promontory beyond this, unnamed by Gyllius, is now called **Poyraz**. (In Turkish, Poyraz is the fierce northeast wind that howls down the Bosphorus from the Black Sea in winter; its Greek name is Boreas, the Greek god of the winds.) On Poyraz Burnu, just opposite Garipçe, is a **fortress** built in 1773 by Baron de Tott for Mustafa III, a twin of the fortress across the strait; there is also a small village on the cape. The long sandy beach to the south is now known as **Poyraz Limanı**; the Greeks of Gyllius' time called it Dios Sacra, 'because', as he writes, 'I suppose, there was once an altar here either of Jove or of Neptune, the other Jove'.

This bay is bounded on the south by **Fil Burnu**, Elephant Point; Gyllius writes that in his time it was called Coracium. The long stretch of concave coast is now called **Keçili Limanı**, the Harbour of the Goats, but it is so rugged and precipitous that it can hardly be called a harbour.

You now come to the place that Gyllius called the Fane of Jove, by which he meant the temple of Zeus Ourios, Zeus of the Favouring Winds. In the temple there was a Hieron, or sacred precinct, where there were shrines of the Twelve Gods. Keçili Limanı is bounded on the south by a cape still known by a version of its ancient name, **Yoros Burnu**, doubtless from Ourios. According to one version of the myth, this shrine was founded by Jason on his return from Colchis with the Golden Fleece.

In Byzantine times the name Hieron applied to the toll and customs station on the Asian shore at this point, which was guarded by the huge *****fortress** on the hill above. This fortress is often called 'the Genoese Castle'; but it is actually Byzantine in foundation, although the Genoese may have repaired or rebuilt it, to a certain extent, when they took control of it in the 14C. Gyllius rather oddly describes this castle as small, though it is in fact the largest fortress on the Bosphorus, enclosing almost twice the area of Rumeli Hisarı; doubtless he was thinking not of the long surrounding walls but only of the citadel itself, probably the only part garrisoned in his day.

The fortress was garrisoned by the Turkish army up until a few years ago, but now it is open to the public; it is an easy walk from Anadolu Kavağı and is a wonderful spot for a picnic, commanding a superb view of the upper Bosphorus and its mouth on the Black Sea.

Anadolu Kavağı to Beykoz (c 7km)

Below the fortress to the south is the village of **Anadolu Kavağı**, the last stop of the ferry on the Asian side. The fortifications here, like those at Rumeli Kavağı, were built in 1783 by Toussaint and increased in 1794 by Monnier. To the south of the village is the hill known as **Yuşa Tepesi**, the Hill of Joshua, though the Joshua in question seems not to have been Judge of Israel but a local Muslim saint named Yuşa Baba. The hill is over 200m high, the second highest on the Bosphorus after Büyük Çamlıca (see below). Anciently it was called the Bed of Hercules, but in modern times it has been known to Europeans as the Giant's Grave. On top of the hill there is a Muslim shrine dedicated to Yuşa Baba, whose lengthy grave leads the faithful to believe that he was a giant.

Opposite Büyükdere the coast forms a long shallow bay with rather dangerous sand banks in the sea and a rugged and inhospitable coast line. At **Selvi Burnu**, Poplar Point, somewhat disfigured now by oil tanks, the coast turns east to the charming valley of the **Tokat Deresi**. Here Fatih built a royal kiosk, as did Süleyman the Magnificent, at a later date. Gyllius described the later building as a 'royal villa shaded by woods of various trees, especially planes'; he goes on to mention the landing stairs, 'by which the King, crossing the shallow shore of the sea, disembarks into his gardens'. It is from these landing stairs that the place gets its modern name, **Hünkâr Iskelesi**, the Emperor's Landing-Place, which in turn gave its name to the historic peace treaty signed here in October 1833 between Russia and the Ottoman Empire. The palace that now stands on the site was built in the mid 19C for Abdül Mecit I by the Armenian architect Sarkis Balyan; it presently serves as a children's hospital.

The large village of **Beykoz**, Prince's Walnut, is still pretty despite the existence of several factories and depots nearby. South of the iskele there is a handsome old seaside mansion, the **Halil Ethem Yalısı**, built in the second half of the 19C. On the main square there is an extraordinary *fountain. This was built in 1746 by one Ishak Ağa, Inspector of Customs; it forms a domed and columned loggia, and is quite unlike any other çeşme in the city. Within the village there is a Greek church dedicated to Haghia Paraskevi.

Gyllius was at pains to show that Beykoz was the home of the savage King Amycus, ruler of the barbarous people known as the Bebryces. When strangers landed on this coast Amycus forced them to box with him. Amycus and his opponent both wore the nail-studded gloves known as the cestus, but since Amycus, the mighty son of Poseidon, was the best boxer in the world, he always killed his man. However, when the Argonauts landed, Amycus challenged Polydeuces (in Latin, Pollux), who turned out to be an even greater boxer than he, and the King finally met his death.

Beykoz to Anadolu Hisarı (c 7km)

South of Beykoz the ferry passes **Incir Köyü**, Figtree Village. Here we see the charming valley of Sultaniye Deresi, where Beyazit II laid out extensive gardens.

A little farther on is **Paşabahçe**, the Paşa's Garden, named after the palace and gardens established here by Hezarpare Ahmet Paşa, Grand Vezir under Murat IV. The village mosque is an undistinguished structure built in 1763 by Mustafa III. On the seashore is the **Paşabahçe glass factory**, world famous for its fine crystal and glassware, which can be purchased at an outlet shop in the entrance lobby. Within the village there is a Greek church dedicated to **SS. Constantine and Helena**.

The next village is **Çubuklu**, a pleasant hamlet in a verdant setting. In Byzantium this was known as Eirenaion, or Peaceful, and it had a very famous monastery founded in 420 by St. Alexander for his order of Akoimetai, the Unsleeping, who prayed in relays throughout the day and night. Half a century later a branch of this order was installed in the newly founded monastery of St. John of Studius in Constantinople (see chapter 15), where they became renowned for their piety and scholarship.

On the hill above the village is the **palace of the Khedive of Egypt**, the hereditary Viceroy under Ottoman rule; its distinctive tower is one of the most conspicuous landmarks on this part of the Bosphorus. The palace was built in 1900 by the Italian architect Dello Seminati for Abbas Hilmi Paşa, the last Khedive; for such a late date it has considerable charm. The palace has been restored by the Turkish Touring and Automobile Club and is now a hotel.

The next village is **Kanlıca**. Kanlıca has been famous for its delicious yogurt since at least as far back as the mid 17C, when Evliya Çelebi praised it as being the best in Istanbul. The local yogurt is served in several little restaurants around the very attractive square beside the ferry-landing.

On the far side of the square there is a mosque which is a minor work of Sinan; an inscription over the entrance portal records that it was founded in 1559–60 by the Vezir Iskender Paşa. It is of the very simplest type, with a wooden porch and a flat wooden roof; but both porch and roof are clearly modern reconstructions. According to Evliya Çelebi, it originally had a wooden dome, which would have made it much more attractive. The founder's türbe is nearby.

There are a number of Ottoman **yalıs** in Kanlıca. North of the iskele are Asaf Paşa Yalısı and Yağa Şefik Paşa Yalısı; to its south are Hacı Ahmet Bey Yalısı, Ertem Pertev Yalısı, Ferruh Efendi Yalıları, and Vecihi Paşa Yalısı, also known as the Prenses Rukiye Yalısı.

Between Kanlıca and Anadolu Hisarı we pass again under Fatih Köprüsü, the second Bosphorus Bridge. Just beyond we see the very elegant **Hekimbaşı Salih Efendi Yalısı**, built in the mid 19C for the personal physician of sultans Abdül Mecit and Abdül Aziz.

A short way beyond we see what remains of the most historic house on the Bosphorus; the *Amcazade Hüseyin Paşa Yalısı. Hüseyin Paşa, the fourth member of the illustrious Köprülü family to serve as Grand Vezir, is thought to have built this yalı in 1698, the year in which he represented Mustafa II in the negotiations between the European powers and the Ottoman Empire at Carlowitz. The final articles of the Peace of Carlowitz were signed in this yalı on 26 January 1699. All that remains of the original house is the wreck of a once very beautiful room built out on piles over the sea, ruined almost beyond redemption.

A short way farther along we pass the Zarif Mustafa Paşa Yalısı, originally built in the early 18C and reconstructed in its present form in the 19C.

The iskele in **Anadolu Hisarı** is just north of the mouth of **Göksu Deresi**, one of the two little rivers which in late Ottoman times were known as the **Sweet Waters of Asia**; the second of these streams, Küçüksu, is a few hundred metres to the south.

Just beside the iskele, to the north, is the ****fortress of Anadolu Hisarı**, one of the most romantic sights on the Bosphorus, a medieval castle which well deserves its Turkish name: Güzelce, the Beautiful One. The fortress was built in 1397 by **Sultan Beyazit I**. It was rebuilt and perhaps extended by Mehmet II in 1452, when he was constructing the great fortress of Rumeli Hisarı across the Bosphorus. The fortress is a small one, consisting of a keep and its surrounding wall together with an outer wall or barbican guarded by three towers. Parts of the barbican have been demolished, but the rest of the fortress is in fairly good condition.

Next to the Anadolu Hisarı iskele we see the **Bahreli Sedat Bey Yalısı**. South of the iskele, at the mouth of the Göksu, is the **Komodor Remzi Bey Yalısı**, recently restored by Erdal İnönü, former Deputy Prime Minister.

Anadolu Hisarı to Üsküdar (c 11km)

The next ferry stop is at **Küçüksu**. This is named for the second of the two streams that make up the Sweet Waters of Asia, which in Ottoman times was a favourite resort of the beau monde. Just south of the iskele we see ***Küçüksu Kasrı**, a small rococo palace on the lip of the sea. This was erected on the site of several earlier imperial kiosks by Nikoğos Balyan in 1856–57 for Abdül Mecit. (Küçüksu Kasrı is open 09.00–16.00; closed Mon, Thu.)

On the seashore near the palace is the baroque ***fountain of the Valide Sultan Mihrişah**, built in 1796. It is square with upturned eaves and colonettes set in its corners, with the spigots and their basins framed in round arches. The situation of the fountain is extremely picturesque, and has been a favourite subject for painters and engravers.

Just beyond the Sweet Waters we see the ***Kibrisli Yalısı**, the longest seaside mansion on the Bosphorus. It was originally built in the mid 19C by the Grand Vezir Izzet Mehmet Paşa, who sold it to the Grand Vezir Kibrisli ('from Cyprus') Mehmet Emin Paşa. A short way farther along is the **Abud Efendi Yalısı**, built in the mid 19c by Karabet Balyan for Altunizade Necip Bey, who sold it to Mehmet Abud Efendi. Just beyond that is the beautiful ****Kırmızı** (Red) **Yalı**, built in the mid 19C. It is named for the Ostrorogs, a noble French-Polish family who moved to Turkey in the late Ottoman period. The last of the line, Count Jean Ostrorog, died here in 1975.

The next ferry stop is **Kandilli**, where the waters of the Bosphorus rush past the point with such speed that the Turks call this the Devil's Current. At the point is the **Edip Efendi Yalısı**, the only Ottoman yalı to survive a fire that destroyed all of the other seaside mansions in Kandilli. On the hill above is the **palace of Adile Sultan**, sister of Abdül Aziz; this was built in 1856 and restored after a fire in the 1980s, now serving as a secondary school for girls. Within the village there is a Greek **church** dedicated to Christos Metamorphosis (The Transfiguration of Christ).

The next ferry stop is at the adjacent hamlet of **Vaniköy**. Above Vaniköy is the tower of the **Istanbul Rasathane**, an astronomical observatory and meteorological station. The Rasathane has a small but very interesting exhibition of the antique astronomical instruments used by the 16C Turkish astronomer Takiuddin.

The large and imposing building on the shore south of Vaniköy is the **Kuleli Naval Officers' Training College**. The original military training school and barracks here were built c 1800 by Selim III, as part of his attempted reform of the Ottoman armed forces. The present structure dates from an extensive rebuilding and enlargement by Abdül Mecit I, completed in 1860. The older building served as a military hospital in 1855–56, during the Crimean War. It was one of two hospitals which at that time were under the supervision of Florence Nightingale, the other and larger one being the Selimiye Barracks in Üsküdar.

It was more-or-less on this site that the Empress Theodora, wife of Justinian the Great, established her famous home for reformed prostitutes; the institution was called Metanoia, or Repentance. Procopius, the court chronicler, writes in his 'Secret History' that some of the women 'threw themselves from the parapets at night and thus freed themselves from an undesired salvation'.

The next ferry stop is at **Çengelköy**, the Village of the Hooks. According to Evliya Çelebi, the village took its name from the fact that shortly after the Conquest Fatih found a store of Byzantine anchors here. The village is exceptionally pretty and has a very picturesque square on the sea, shaded by plane trees and graced by a baroque fountain. The Greek church in the village is dedicated to St. George. South of the iskele we see the handsome *Sadullah Pasa Yalısı, dating from the late 18C.

The ferry stops next at **Beylerbey**, just above the first Bosphorus bridge. Adjoining the iskele is **Beylerbey Camii**, built in 1778 by Mehmet Tahir Ağa for Abdül Hamit I. It is an attractive example of the baroque style, its dome arches arranged in an octagon, vigorously emphasised within and without, its mihrab in a projecting apse, richly decorated with an assortment of tiles of various periods from the 16C–18C. The mimber and Kuran kursu are unusually elegant and beautiful works, both of them of wood inlaid with ivory.

It has two minarets, the second one added later by Mahmut II. The lower part of each minaret consists of a base of square cross-section above which there is a bulbous foot, rather like a flattened bell-jar and from which rises the fluted shaft, with a single şerefe and a bulbous stone crown with a tall horned alem, or crescent-like symbol. This is the first appearance of this type of minaret which, particularly its bulbous foot, became a characteristic feature in mosques of the late 18C and the 19C.

**Beylerbey Sarayi

Beyond the village and almost directly under the Bosphorus bridge, we come to Beylerbey Sarayı, the largest Ottoman palace on the Bosphorus after Dolmabahçe.

■ **Admission**. The palace is open 09.30–16.00; closed Mon, Thu.

The palace and the village were named for a Beylerbey, an Ottoman title that literally means Lords of Lords; this was Mehmet Paşa, Governor of Rumelia in the reign of Murat III. Mehmet Paşa built a mansion on this site, and though it eventually vanished, the name Beylerbey lived on. The first sultan to reside here was Mahmut II, who built a summer palace that was destroyed by fire in the mid 19C.

The present Palace of Beylerbey was built for Abdül Aziz in 1861–65 by Sarkis Balyan. The palace was used mainly as a summer lodge and as a residence for visiting royalty, one of the first being the Empress Eugénie of France, who stayed here in 1869; later visitors included the Emperor Franz Josef I of Austria, the Shah Nasireddin of Persia, and King Edward VIII of England and Mrs Simpson. Abdül Hamit II lived out the last years of his life in Beylerbey after his return in 1913 from exile in Salonica, dying here in 1918.

Interior. The palace is divided into the usual selamlık and harem. The building is in three storeys, although only the two upper floors are visible along the Bosphorus façade. The ground floor houses the kitchens and other service departments of the palace; the state rooms and imperial apartments are on the two upper floors, a total of 26 elegantly appointed chambers, including six grand salons, with a magnificent spiral staircase leading upwards from the reception hall that divides the selamlık from the harem.

Beylerbey is as sumptuously furnished and decorated as Dolmabahçe; its adornments include Hereke carpets; chandeliers of Bohemian crystal; French clocks; vases from China, Japan, France, and the imperial Ottoman workshops at Yıldız, which also manufactured all of the furniture; and it is also decorated with superb murals done by European painters such as Ayvazovski.

The structures in the garden behind the palace include the Mermer (Marble) Köşk, the Sarı (Yellow) Köşk, and the Ahır (Stable) Köşk, where the royal stud were housed. Two smaller kiosks flank the main façade of the palace along the sea, the southernmost one now standing almost directly under the Bosphorus Bridge.

After leaving Beylerbey the ferry once again passes under the Bosphorus Bridge, after which it passes the **Fethi Ahmet Paşa Yalısı**, also known as the Pembe (Pink) Yalı. This was originally built in the 18C, and then restored in the second quarter of the 19C by the vezir Fethi Ahmet Pasa.

The next ferry stop is at ***Kuzguncuk**, the most delightful village on the Bosphorus. The village was noted in times past for its multi-ethnic character, with Turks, Greeks, Armenians and Jews living here together as friendly neighbours, but now the numbers of the minority communities have diminished considerably. Besides the village mosque, there are still two Greek churches, one dedicated to St. George and the other to St. Panteleimon, as well as an Armenian church and two synagogues, Beth Yaakov and Virano.

During Ottoman times Kuzguncuk had one of the largest Jewish communities in the city, at its peak numbering some 10,000, so that it was called 'little Jerusalem'. The Jewish cemetery on the hill above Kuzguncuk is one of the oldest burial grounds in the city, with tombstones dating back to the 16C.

From Kuzguncuk the ferry heads down along the last stretch of the Asian shore of the lower Bosphorus. The shore here has been ruined by the intrusion of modern apartments, factories and depots of various kinds, but the hills above are still beautiful. The tallest of these is Büyük Çamlıca (262m) (see p 292). Finally the ferry pulls in to the iskele at **Üsküdar**, ending our long journey up and down the Bosphorus.

20 · Üsküdar and Kadıköy

The two most important Asian suburbs of the city are Üsküdar, at the mouth of the Bosphorus, and Kadıköy, farther to the south on the Asian shore, both of them served by ferries from the Golden Horn.

> Üsküdar is ancient Chrysopolis, the City of Gold, founded by the Athenians under Alcibiades in 409 BC. In later Byzantine times it was known as Scutari, a name that lingered on until fairly recent times. Kadıköy is ancient Chalcedon, founded by the Megarians c 680 BC, some two decades before Byzantium. Both cities were eventually absorbed by Byzantium and became suburbs of Constantinople. They were both taken by the Ottomans long before the fall of Constantinople, and under Turkish rule they came to be known as Üsküdar and Kadıköy, respectively.

Üsküdar

The focal point of Üsküdar is **Iskele Meydanı**, the great square beside the ferry-landing. On the north side of the square we see ***Iskele Camii**, a stately imperial mosque on a high terrace. The mosque was built in 1547–48 for Mihrimah Sultan, daughter of Süleyman the Magnificent; the architect was Sinan, who would later build another mosque for the princess on the Sixth Hill (see chapter 16). The exterior is very imposing because of its dominating position high above the square and its great double porch, a curious projection of which covers a charming fountain. The interior is perhaps less satisfactory, for the central dome is supported by three instead of the usual two or four semi-domes; this gives the mosque a rather truncated appearance, which is not improved by the universal gloom. Perhaps it was the darkness of the interior here that made Mihrimah insist on floods of light when, in 1562, she commissioned Sinan to build her mosque on the Sixth Hill.

The medrese of the külliye is to the north, a pretty building of the rectangular type, now used as a clinic. The primary school is behind the mosque, built on sharply rising ground so that it has very picturesque supporting arches; it has recently been restored and is now a children's library. On leaving the mosque terrace you find at the foot of the steps the very handsome baroque ***fountain of Ahmet III**, dated 1726.

Passing the fountain and entering the main avenue of Üsküdar, we soon come, on the left, to a supermarket housed in the remains of an ancient hamam. The owner calls it **Sinan Hamam Çarşısı**, thus ascribing the bath to Sinan; this is probably not so, though it certainly dates from his time. It was a double bath, but the main entrance chambers were destroyed when the street was widened.

A little farther on there is an ancient and curious **mosque** built by Nişancı Kara Davut Paşa toward the end of the 15C. It is a broad shallow room divided into three sections by arches, each section having a dome, an arrangement unique in Istanbul.

Across the street and opening into the square is the large complex called **Yeni Valide Camii**. This was built in 1708–10 by Ahmet III, who dedicated it to his mother, the Valide Sultan Rabia Gülnuş Ümmetullah. At the corner is the Valide's charming open türbe, looking like a large aviary, and next to it a grand sebil. On entering the gate from the square we see a very attractive façade, a later addition, which is the entrance to the imperial loge. The mosque itself was built in the very last phase of the classical period, and just before the baroque influence had come to enliven it. In plan it is a variant of the octagon-in-a-square theme, decorated with inferior tiles of late date. Walking through the outer courtyard, we come to the main gate, over which is the mektep. Outside the gate stands the large imaret with a çeşme at the corner; this is of later date than the rest of the külliye and is fully in the baroque style.

We now return to the seafront, where we begin walking along the promenade that skirts the end of the Bosphorus. On the promontory beyond the port we come to ****Şemsi Paşa Camii**. This is one of the most delightful of the smaller mosque complexes in the city, built of glittering white stone and standing in a very picturesque location right at the water's edge. Built by Sinan for the Vezir Şemsi Paşa in 1580, the mosque is of the simplest type: a square room covered by a dome with conches as squinches. Şemsi Paşa's türbe opens into the mosque itself, from which it is divided by a green grille, a most unusual and pretty feature. The well-proportioned medrese forms two sides of the courtyard, while the third side consists of a wall with grilled windows opening directly onto the quay and the Bosphorus. The külliye has been beautifully restored in recent years.

We now cross the highway to Şemsi Paşa Caddesi, which we follow halfway up a low hill to an ancient mosque. This is **Rum** (the Greek) **Mehmet Paşa Camii**, built in 1471. Mehmet Paşa, the founder, was a Greek who converted to Islam and became one of Fatih's vezirs This is the most Byzantine in appearance of all the early mosques in the city: most notably the high cylindrical drum of the dome, the exterior cornice following the curve of the round-arched windows, and the square dome base broken by the projection of the great dome arches. Internally the mosque has a central dome with smooth pendentives and one semidome to the east, like Atik Ali Paşa Camii; but here the side chambers are completely cut off from the central area. Behind the mosque is Mehmet Paşa's gaunt türbe.

We leave the mosque complex by the back gate and follow the winding street outside, keeping firmly to the right. This eventually brings us to an imposing baroque mosque known as **Ayazma Camii**. Built in 1760–61 by Mustafa III and dedicated to his mother, the Valide Sultan Mihrişah, it is one of the more successful of the baroque mosques, especially on the exterior. A handsome entrance portal opens onto a courtyard from which a pretty flight of semicir- cular steps leads up to the mosque porch; on the left is a large cistern and

Şemsi Paşa Camii

beyond that an elaborate two-storeyed colonnade gives access to the imperial loge. The upper structure is also diversified with little domes and turrets, and many windows give light to the interior. The interior, as in many of the baroque mosques, is less successful, though the grey marble gallery along the entrance wall, supported by slender columns, is effective. At the back of the mosque there is a picturesque graveyard with some interesting old tombstones.

Leaving by the south gate and following the street to the east, we come to Doğancılar Cad., with two pretty baroque **çeşmes** at the intersection. We turn right here and continue to the intersection with Salacak Iskelesi Cad., where on our left we see a **türbe.** This severely plain tomb was built by Sinan for Hacı Mehmet Paşa, who died in 1559. It stands on an octagonal terrace covered with tombstones and overshadowed by a dying terebinth tree.

We continue to the intersection of Tunus Bağı Cad. and Halk Cad., where we turn left. We then take the third turning on the right followed by the first on the left. which leads to an elaborate and delightful külliye, the *Ahmediye mosque and medrese*.

Built in 1722 by Eminzade Hacı Ahmet Paşa, Comptroller of the Arsenal under Ahmet III, this is perhaps the last building complex in the classical style, though verging toward the baroque. Roughly square in layout, it has the porticoes and cells of the medrese along two sides; the library, one entrance portal, and the mosque occupy a third side, while the fourth has the main gate complex with the dershane above and a graveyard alongside. The whole plan is, however, very irregular because of the alignment of the surrounding streets and the slope of the ground.

The dome of the little mosque is supported by scallop-shell squinches and has a finely carved mimber and Kuran kursu. The library and the dershane over the two gates are the most attractive features of the complex and show great ingenuity of design. The whole külliye ranks with those of Amcazade Hüseyin Paşa and Bayram Paşa as being among the most charming and inventive in the city.

At the southeast corner of the courtyard a stairway under the dershane leads to the street below. A short, narrow street opposite the outer gate leads to a wider avenue, Toptaşı Cad., the Avenue of the Cannon Ball. We turn right here and follow the avenue for about 600m, as it winds uphill through a picturesque old neighbourhood.

**Atik Valide Camii

Towards the top of the hill and somewhat toward the left we come to Atik Valide Camii, the great mosque complex that dominates the skyline of Üsküdar.

> The imperial külliye of Atik Valide Camii was built by Sinan in 1583 for the Valide Sultan Nur Banu, wife of Selim II and mother of Murat III. This is the most splendid and extensive of all Sinan's constructions in Istanbul with the sole exception of the Süleymaniye. In addition to the mosque itself, the külliye consists of a medrese, a hospital, an imaret, a school for reading the Kuran, a caravansarai, and a hamam. All of these buildings are still in existence and most are in good condition, though several now form part of a prison and cannot be visited. Altogether this is certainly one of the half-dozen most impressive monuments of Ottoman architecture in the whole of Turkey.

Exterior. The precinct is entered by an alley beside the mosque graveyard. This is one of the most beautiful of all the mosque courtyards in the city, a grandly proportioned cloister with domed porticoes supported on marble columns; in the centre are the şadırvan and a copse of ancient plane trees and cypresses. The mosque is entered through an elaborate double porch, the outer one with a penthouse roof, the inner domed and with handsome tiled inscriptions over the windows.

Interior. The prayer hall is a wide rectangular room with a central dome supported by a hexagonal arrangement of pillars and columns; to the north and south there are side aisles, each with two domed bays. The aisles were added at a later date, and although, when closely examined, the arrangement leads to certain anomalies, the general impression is very attractive. There are galleries around three sides of the room, and the wooden ceilings under some of them preserve that rich painting typical of the period: floral and arabesque designs in black, red and gold. The mihrab is in a square projecting apse entirely revetted in magnificent tiles of the best Iznik period; notice also the window frames of deep red conglomerate marble with shutters richly inlaid with mother-of-pearl. The mihrab and mimber are fine works in carved marble.

Precincts. The **medrese** of the complex stands at a lower level than the mosque and is entered by a staircase in the west wall of the courtyard. Its courtyard is almost as pretty as that of the mosque itself; it is oddly irregular: there are five domed bays to the south but only three to the north. The **dershane** is in the centre of the west side in the axis of the mosque, though at an obtuse angle to

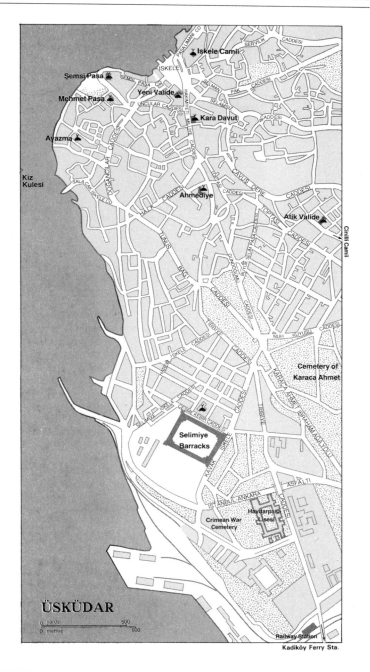

İskele Camii

Şemsi Paşa

Mehmet Paşa

Yeni Valide

Kara Davut

Ayazma

Kız Kulesi

Ahmediye

Atik Valide

Çinili Camii

Cemetery of Karaca Ahmet

Selimiye Barracks

İstanbul-Ankara

Crimean War Cemetery

Haydarpaşa Lisesi

Railway Station

Kadiköy Ferry Sta.

ÜSKÜDAR

0 yards 500
0 metres 500

it, and it projects out over the street below, which passes under it through an archway.

Leaving the medrese by the gate in the south side, you can walk around the building and pass under this picturesque arch. At the next corner beyond it stands the large **hospital**, also highly irregular in plan but quite as attractive as the other buildings. These various irregularities are partly due to the alignment of the surrounding streets and the varying level of the terrain, but Sinan may also have decided to utilise these features to give variety and liveliness to his design.

The other buildings of the külliye are either part of the prison or are in a half-ruined condition. The double hamam has lost its two large entrance chambers and the rest is used as a carpenter's shop, while the caravansarai is partly incorporated into the prison, partly used as a storehouse.

The street to the east of Atik Valide Camii leads after a walk of about 1km to **Çinili Cami**, the Tiled Mosque. This small complex was built in 1640 by the Valide Sultan Kösem, mother of Murat IV and Crazy Ibrahim. The mosque, in a pretty garden filled with flowers and trees, is small and simple: a square room covered by a dome. The mosque is decorated both on the façade and in the interior by a revetment of tiles; these date from just after the best period but they are still quite fine, chiefly pale blue and turquoise on a white ground. The mimber of white marble has its own carving very prettily picked out in gold, red and green, and its conical roof is tiled. The porch of the mosque is a baroque addition, as is the minaret, of which the şerefe has a corbel of very pretty folded-back acanthus leaves, unique in the city.

In the courtyard there is a very fine şadırvan with a huge witch's cap for a roof, and a tiny triangular shaped medrese, sloping headlong downhill. Just outside the precinct is a handsome mektep and not far off there is a large hamam, both of which are part of the külliye.

The street outside the mosque, Çavuş Dere Cad., winds downhill toward the centre of Üsküdar, and in about 1.5km it reaches Iskele Meydanı, where this itinerary began.

Environs of Üsküdar

There are several interesting and pleasant excursions in the vicinity of Üsküdar. These places can easily be reached by bus or taxi from Iskele Meydanı, or, if you have the time and energy you can stroll to them through the town, for none is at any great distance.

We follow Sahil Yolu, the seaside avenue that skirts the end of the Bosphorus and then heads south along the Marmara shore. Near the old Salacak iskele we stop to look out at *Kız Kulesi, the Maiden's Tower, which stands on a tiny offshore islet.

The Turkish name of the islet is derived from a legend concerning a princess who was confined there by her father to protect her from the fate foretold by a dire prophecy: that she would die from the bite of a serpent. However, the princess was eventually bitten by the serpent, which had been smuggled out to the islet, and she died instantly. In English the place is usually called Leander's Tower, in the mistaken notion that Leander drowned here in his attempt to swim the strait to see his lover Hero, although this legendary tragedy should be located near Abydos in the Hellespont.

According to Nicetas Choniates, Manuel I Comnenus (1143–80) built a small fortress on the islet, using it to attach one end of the great chain which he stretched across the mouth of the Bosphorus, fastening the other end at a tower just below the acropolis. Since then the islet has served as the site of a lighthouse, semaphore station, quarantine post, customs control point, and a home for retired naval officers. The present quaint structure dates from the 18C; it is presently being restored for use as a restaurant and café.

A short way farther along we see a splendid old red mansion perched on the cliff above the shore road. This is the **Muharrem Nuri Birgi Yalısı**, believed to date from the 18C, superbly restored in 1968–71.

Büyük Çamlıca. Büyük Çamlıca, the Great Hill of Pines, is the highest peak in the immediate vicinity of Istanbul; its summit, surmounted by television antennae, making it the most prominent landmark along the lower Bosphorus. The peak is about 4km east of Iskele Meydanı, and is approached by the main highway leaving Üsküdar in that direction.

There is an extremely pleasant café and teahouse on the summit, which commands an extraordinary view of Istanbul, the Golden Horn, and the lower Bosphorus. A new museum was opened in the park in 1991. This is the **Aydınlatma ve Isıtma Araçları Müzesi** (Lighting and Heating Systems Museum, whose exhibits are from the private collection of Mehmet Yıldız. Some 2500 objects range from oil-lamps of the Neolithic period to modern light sources and heating devices.

Two late Ottoman edifices in the vicinity are the Abdülmecid Efendi Köskü, a small palace once used by Abdül Mecit (II), the last Caliph; and the **Abdülaziz Av Köskü**, a hunting lodge built in 1856.

There are also two old Armenian churches in this area. One of these is the **church of Surp Haç**, founded in the 17C and then rebuilt in brick in the mid 19C by the architect Serveryan, with the stone campanile added in 1882. The second is the **church of Surp Karabet** (St. Karabet), first built in wood in the 16C; then, after being destroyed by fire in 1847, it was rebuilt in stone in 1888, with two flanking campaniles. Besides these there is also a Greek church dedicated to **Profitis Elias**.

Karaca Ahmet Cemetery (Mezarlık). This historic old Turkish burial-ground is located in the hills above Üsküdar, some 1.5km from Iskele Meydanı, approached via Doğancılar Cad. and Tunus Bağı Cad.

According to tradition, the cemetery was founded here at the time of the Turkish conquest of the surrounding area, in the mid 14C; however, the oldest inscribed tombstone is dated 1521. The cemetery is named after Karaca Ahmet, a sainted warrior from the time of Orhan Gazi (1326–62), who was killed and buried here at the time of the Turkish conquest of

Chrysopolis and Chalcedon. As so often happens, Karaca Ahmet's grave was miraculously discovered in later times, revealed in a dream to a dervish. A türbe was then erected to house the saint's remains (the present structure is a modern one, dating to the 19C), and alongside it a monument in the form of a cupola was built to honour his favourite horse, whose skeleton was also found on the spot. As time went on many of the famous men and women of the Ottoman Empire chose to be buried here, their türbes and tombstones now shaded by spectral cypresses on this very picturesque hill above Üsküdar.

Haydarpaşa. The most prominent monument along the Marmara shore south of Üsküdar is the enormous four-towered structure in Haydarpaşa, the district just to the north of Kadıköy. This is the **Selimiye Barracks**, famous in history as the site of Florence Nightingale's hospital during the Crimean War.

The barracks owe their name to the fact that the original military residence hall here, a wooden structure, was built by Selim III in 1799 to house the men of his New Army, the modern force with which he hoped to replace the Janissaries. But these barracks burned down in 1808, shortly after Selim had been deposed and killed in a Janissary insurrection. New stone barracks were erected on the site by Mahmut II in 1828, within two years after he finally destroyed the Janissaries. This building had only a single wing; the other three wings were added by Abdül Mecit I in the period 1842–53.

During the Crimean War the barracks served as a British military hospital; during the first months of its operation conditions there were so bad that the death toll reached the appalling rate of more than 20 per cent of the patients admitted. In October 1854 Florence Nightingale organised a party of 38 nurses, mostly from various religious orders, for service in the Crimean War. When her party arrived in Istanbul the following month she took charge of the medical services at the barracks in Scutari, as it was then called, and also at the other military hospital at Kuleli on the Bosphorus. Before she left Istanbul, in the summer of 1856, shortly after the end of hostilities, the death rate at the two hospitals under her charge in the city had dropped to 2 per cent.

After the war the Selimiye Barracks was once again used to house Turkish soldiers, a function it still performs today. Consequently, it is not normally open to the public, but permission to visit Florence Nightingale's former quarters can sometimes be obtained by applying to the officer in charge.

The Barracks. The building consist of four enormous wings, each of three storeys, surrounding a vast quadrangular parade ground; at the corners there are five-storeyed towers with tall turrets above, the one to the northeast rising above the chambers where Florence Nightingale lived when she was directing the hospital here. One of the downstairs rooms in this tower has been converted into a **museum** in her honour by the Turkish Nurses Association.

Opposite the main entrance to the barracks is the **Selimiye Camii**, the mosque that Selim III built for the men of his new army. Constructed in

1803–04, it is the last and one of the most handsome of the baroque mosques. Not only are its proportions and details most attractive, but it is placed in an exceptionally lovely garden shaded by three of the finest old plane trees in the city. The interior of the mosque is a little stark, though of impressive proportions. The western gallery, the mihrab, and the mimber are all of highly polished grey marble and give the place a certain charm.

The next prominent building to the south of the Selimiye Barracks is the **Haydarpaşa Lycée**, a huge building with twin towers flanking its entrance. This was built in 1894 to house the Military Medical Academy, which remained here until 1933, after which it became a secondary school for boys.

Farther to the south we see the **Haydarpaşa Railway Station**, a huge building with a façade flanked by twin towers. This was built in the years 1906–08 by the German architects Otto Ritter and Helmut Cuno. The tiled ferry station in front of it was built in 1915–17 by the Turkish architect Vedat Tek.

The **Crimean War Cemetery** is almost hidden away to the east of the railway station, in the angle formed by the two highways that intersect there. The cemetery was founded as a burial place for the British soldiers who died in the Selimiye Barracks when it was being used as a hospital during the Crimean War, and among the tombstones there are a number marking the graves of some of Florence Nightingale's nurses. Also buried here are British soldiers who fell at Gallipoli and others who died in the Middle East during World War II, along with British and other civilians who have died in Istanbul during the past century.

The principal funerary monument is an obelisk of grey Aberdeen granite, with, in several languages, an inscription paying tribute to the dead by Queen Victoria. There is also a plaque dedicated by Queen Elizabeth II, honouring the pioneering nursing work done by Florence Nightingale and her staff during the Crimean War.

Kadıköy

A short distance to the south of the Haydarpaşa Train Station we come to the **Kadıköy ferry station**. A new and very attractive **park** has been created around the Kadıköy iskele, including a playground, a bird-market, and a **theatre** dedicated to the popular Istanbul playwright Haldun Taner. Across the shore road from the ferry-station the old Kadıköy street market has now become an attractive **pedestrian mall**. The mosque on the shore road directly opposite the ferry station is **Iskele Camii**. This was erected in 1761 by Mustafa III; after being destroyed by fire it was rebuilt in 1858 by Abdül Mecit, and it was restored most recently in 1975.

Continuing into the market quarter we come to a little square flanked by two churches, one of them Greek and the other Armenian.

The one on the left is the Greek **church of St. Euphemia of Chalcedon**. This is believed to be on the site of the original church of St. Euphemia, founded early in the Byzantine period. Euphemia was martyred c 300 in Byzantium and became the patron saint of Chalcedon. The church dedicated to her here was the site of the historic Council of Chalcedon in 451. Euphemia's remains were removed to Constantinople when the Persians occupied Chalcedon early in the

7C, and her casket is now in the church of St. George in the Greek Patriarchate (see chapter 14).

The present church was founded in 1694 and was rebuilt in 1830. It has recently been superbly restored, using a number of columns and other architectural members from an earlier Byzantine structure. In the narthex there is a painting by a local artist, dated 1882, showing the Council of Chalcedon in session in the original church of St. Euphemia.

The church on the right is Armenian, dedicated to **Surp Takavor** (Christ the King). The church was founded in the 17C and was rebuilt in its present form in the mid 19C.

One block to the east of St. Euphemia we come to **Osman Ağa Camii**. This is the oldest mosque in Kadıköy, founded in the reign of Ahmet I (1603–17). The founder, an Egyptian named Osman Ağa, also built the nearby fountain, which is dated 1620.

One block farther to the east brings us to the Armenian church of **Surp Levon** (St. Leo). This is the only Armenian Catholic church on the Asian side of the city, all of the others being Gregorian. The present church was built in the mid 19C by the architect Boğos Bey Maksadar, replacing an earlier wooden structure.

Elsewhere in Kadıköy there are two more **Greek churches**, one dedicated to St. Ignatius and the other to the Holy Trinity.

21 · The Princes' Isles

Ferries leave from one of the terminals in Eminönü for the Princes' Isles (Adalar) (Atlas 16), the little suburban archipelago just off the Asian coast of the Marmara. The group consists of nine islands, all but four of them tiny. The nearest is some 15km from the Galata Bridge, the farthest about 30km, though in spirit they seem at a far greater remove than that, they are so different in atmosphere and appearance from the rest of the city.

Ferries stop at the four largest and most populous of the islands, the closest of which is **Kınalı**, followed by **Burgaz**, then **Heybeli**, and finally **Büyükada**, the largest in the archipelago. In summer months there are occasional ferries stopping at **Kaşık** and **Sedef**. **Tavşan** and **Sivri** are uninhabited, while the only residents on **Yassı** are the staff at the military installation there.

History

In the medieval Byzantine period the archipelago was known as Papadonisia, the Isles of the Monks, from the many monasteries that had been established there. These monasteries became famous because of the many emperors and empresses of Byzantium who were shut up there after losing their thrones, along with numerous ecumenical patriarchs deposed in the frequent religious controversies that divided the Greek Orthodox Church.

According to the Byzantine chronicler Cedrenus, Justin II built himself a palace and a monastery on the largest of the isles in 569. This island was called Megale, or the Great Island, but soon after the royal palace was built it became known as Prinkipo, the Isle of the Prince. Later, the entire archipelago came to be called the Princes' Isles.

The first regularly scheduled ferry service to the islands began in 1846. This brought a large influx of visitors who built summer houses on the four largest islands, and many of them eventually settled in as year-round residents. These were largely well-off Greeks, but included substantial numbers of Armenians, Jews, resident foreigners, and a few wealthy Turkish families. The ferries also brought crowds of people on weekend holidays in the summer months, particularly to Büyükada, resulting in the construction of hotels, restaurants, cafés and bathing establishments.

The rapid development of tourism in recent years has, to a certain extent, spoiled the natural beauty of Büyükada, particularly in the town and along the northern shore of the island. However, the hilly interior and its southern coast are relatively untouched; large parts of the other islands are also unspoiled. Motor vehicles are not permitted on the islands, and the only public transport is provided by phaetons, picturesque horse-drawn vehicles which can be hired at the ferry-landings. The absence of automotive traffic has done much to preserve the natural beauty of the isles, making them sybaritic retreats from the crowded and polluted metropolis on their western horizon.

Kınalı

The ferry calls first at Kınalı, some 15km from the Galata Bridge. The island takes its Turkish name (Henna-Red) from the colour of the sandstone cliffs that plunge into the sea at its eastern end. The island has for centuries been inhabited principally by Armenians, and today they still make up most of its population.

The Greeks have always called the island Proti, or First since it is the nearest in the archipelago to the city. In Byzantine times there were two monasteries on the island, one of them dedicated to the Panaghia and the other to the Transfiguration, and there was also a convent of unknown name. All three of these establishments housed royal exiles at one time or another. These included Michael I (811–13); the family of Leo V (813–20); Romanus I Lecapenus (919–44) and his sons Stephen and Constantine; the Empress Theophano, widow of Romanus II (959–63) and Nicephorus II (963–69); and Romanus IV Diogenes (1067–71).

Kınalı is a rather bare and barren isle, but it has a few sandy coves where you can picnic, and it has fine views from the summits of its three bare hills: Çınar Tepesi, Teşvekiye Tepesi, and Monastir Tepesi. Otherwise there is little to do on the island, which has no hotels and restaurants.

Almost nothing remains of the two Byzantine monasteries on the island and the medieval nunnery has vanished without a trace. The modern Greek **church of the Panaghia**, which can be seen to the left of the ferry-landing, a few streets in, is believed to stand on, or near, the site of the Byzantine monastery of the same name. Around the church, and also in a nearby park, there are architectural fragments that almost certainly belonged to the Byzantine monastery.

The second street to the south of the church, Kınalı Fırın Sok., leads inland past a Byzantine cistern thought to have supplied water to the monastery of the Panaghia.

It was undoubtedly from here that the British Admiral Duckworth obtained water for his fleet when he anchored off Kınalı, during his show of force against Istanbul in 1827. While watering his fleet Duckworth learned that a party of Turkish troops had taken refuge at the Monastery of the Transfiguration, which was just a short distance outside the town to the southwest. He thereupon ordered a bombardment which utterly destroyed the monastery, which had probably been in existence for a thousand years.

One block beyond the cistern the street leads to a path which heads out into the countryside. A short way along, on the left, is the modern Monastery of the Transfiguration; this was founded in the mid 19C by Simon Sinosoğlu to replace the Byzantine structure destroyed by Duckworth. A bust of Sinosoğlu stands beside the church, which has a superb iconostasis of dark wood and some fine icons. All that remains of the Byzantine monastery that stood on this site are a few fragments, the most notable of which is a large Byzantine capital.

The path passes between Monastir Tepesi (to the south) and Teşvekiye Tepesi (to the north), after which it turns right to pass between Teşvekiye Tepesi (to the east) and Çınar Tepesi (to the west). From either of these two hills, both of which are 115m in elevation, there is an excellent and unobstructed view of the two tiny isles to the southwest: Sivri (to the right) and Yassı (to the left).

Sivri and Yassı

In Byzantium Sivri was known as Oxya and Yassı as Plate: the Turkish and Greek names are descriptive and mean the same thing in each case: the first meaning Pointed and the second Flat. Sivri is nothing more than a tall craggy reef rising to a height of 90m, taller than any of the Seven Hills of Constantinople. Because of its remoteness and barreness this and its flat neighbour Yassı have been used for centuries solely as places of exile and imprisonment.

During the last century of Ottoman rule Sivri was used on several occasions to dispose of the street dogs of Istanbul, who were rounded up in their thousands and left to starve and tear each other to pieces. Yassı formerly boasted what Murray's 'Handbook' of 1892 describes as 'a dilapidated Anglo-Saxon castle' built by Sir Henry Bulwer, English ambassador to the Sublime Porte and brother of the novelist Bulwer-Lytton; here he is popularly supposed to have engaged in nameless orgies.

Some remains of this castle were still visible until 1960, but it has been largely engulfed in the buildings erected for the trial of the deposed Turkish Prime Minister, Adnan Menderes, and 14 of his associates. After a lengthy trial they were all convicted and sentenced to death, but 12 of the sentences were commuted to life imprisonment and only Menderes and two of his former ministers suffered the death penalty. They were hanged on the night of 16–17 September 1961 on the island of Imralı, farther west in the Marmara.

*Burgaz

The second large island at which the ferry stops is Burgaz, some 4km from Kınalı by sea. This island, which is inhabited principally by Greeks, is one of the most pleasant in the archipelago; it is as beautiful as the two larger and more popular isles to its east, Heybeli and Büyükada, but it has fortunately escaped virtually all of the ravages of uncontrolled development and tourism.

In antiquity the island was known as Panormas, but in Byzantine times it was called Antigone, and it is still known by this name by its Greek inhabitants. Burgaz, its Turkish name, is a corruption of pyrgos, the Greek word for tower; this stemmed from the fact that there was a watch-tower atop the summit of the island, a landmark which continued to be noted by travellers as late as the early 19C. During Byzantine times the island had a large monastery dedicated to the Transfiguration, but it is not known to have housed any imperial exiles.

The only famous personage exiled on Antigone during the Byzantine period was St. Methodius, Patriarch of Constantinople, who was imprisoned here by Michael II during the years 822–29. After the death of Methodius in 846 he was recognised as a saint in the Greek Orthodox Church, and a shrine was built over the dungeon on Antigone by the Empress Theodora, widow of the Emperor Theophilus (829–42). Later, a church dedicated to St. John the Baptist was built around the shrine, fragments of which can still be seen today.

The town of Burgaz is the prettiest in the isles, with white and pastel houses ringing a crescent bay. The most prominent landmark in town is the high dome of the Greek **church of St. John the Baptist**. This is a modern structure, but it stands on the site of the Byzantine church of the same name that was built over the shrine dedicated to St. Methodius. According to tradition, the shrine occupies the dungeon where the saint was imprisoned; it is approached by entering the narthex and passing between the two columns on the left, from where a stairway leads down into the subterranean chamber.

One block beyond the church on Çayır Sok. we find the former home of Sait Faik (1907–54), the famous Turkish writer. The house is now a **museum**, exhibiting memorabilia of Sait Faik. The house is open to the public on Tue–Fri 09.00–13.00 and 14.00–17.00, Sat 09.00–13.00; closed Sun, Mon.

At the south end of the village the second road in from the seashore leads to a path that runs around the southern side of the island. This leads up the slopes of the heavily wooded **Christos Tepesi**, the highest peak on the island (170m). There we find the modern Greek **church of Haghios Christos**, surrounded by some impressive architectural fragments from a large medieval sanctuary, which is probably the Monastery of the Transfiguration. According to tradition, this was founded by Basil I (867–86), and it appears to have stood until 1720, when it was probably demolished by the Turkish authorities.

From the north side of the village a paved road leads out to the northern and western sides of the island. Just as the road leaves the village it passes on the right a modern Greek church dedicated to St. George, beside which there is a café pleasantly situated by the sea.

A narrow strait, less than 1km wide, separates Burgaz from Heybeli, the next island-stop on the ferry. On the way across the ferry passes the tiny islet of **Kaşık**, or Spoon, a name vaguely suggested by its topography. Its Greek name is Pitta and it is the smallest of the nine islands in the archipelago, too minute to support a monastery. In recent years a number of villas have been built on the islet, and in summer months there is a motor launch which makes a few trips a day there from Burgaz.

Heybeli

This is perhaps the most beautiful of all the Princes' Isles, although many would argue in favour of its neighbour, Büyükada. The village is a pretty cluster of white-washed stone houses and pastel-hued villas on the eastern side of the island.

The island has always been known to the Greeks as Halki, a name bestowed upon it in antiquity because of its copper-mines, long ago exhausted. Its general outline as seen from the sea, two symmetric hills separated by a rounded valley, is responsible for its Turkish name, which derives from heybes, or saddle-bag.

In Byzantine times there were two monasteries on the island. One of these was the Monastery of the Holy Trinity, founded in 857 by the Patriarch Photius. This institution, which has vanished without a trace, is believed to have stood on Ümit Tepesi, the northernmost of the hills on Heybeli, which is now surmounted by the impressive buildings of the Greek Orthodox School of Theology, founded in 1841. According to tradition, the original monastery on this site was founded in 857 by the Patriarch Photius, one of the intellectual giants in Byzantine history. Photius, was deposed by Michael III in 886 and exiled to the monastery he had founded on Halki, where he died four years later. This monastery continued in existence until the construction of the present School of Theology, which is also dedicated to the Holy Trinity. This school operated until 1971, when it was closed by an act of the Turkish Parliament. However the establishment itself continues to function as a scholarly institution, for its library has a particularly rich collection of Byzantine manuscripts.

The second of the two Byzantine monasteries on Halki stood on the western slope of Değirmen Tepesi, the more westerly of the two peaks that flank the village across from Ümit Tepesi. This monastery, which was dedicated to the Panaghia Theotokou, the Mother of God, was founded by John VIII Palaeologus (1425–48), and was the last monastic establishment to be founded in the Byzantine Empire. The original monastery was destroyed by fire in 1672; it was rebuilt but then wrecked in the anti-Greek riots in 1821. The monastery was abandoned at that time, but in 1833 the building was restored and converted into a Greek commercial school; this continued in operation until 1916, when it was converted into an orphanage. In 1942 the building and grounds were taken over by the Turkish government, and from that time on it has been part of the Turkish Naval Academy.

The only part of the original Byzantine structure that seems to have survived is the church of the Panaghia Kamariotissa, which served as the monastery chapel. This was founded some time between 1427 and 1439 by Maria Comnena, third wife of John VIII Palaeologus and the last Empress of Byzantium. This church remained in the hands of the Greek community until 1942, when it too was taken over by the Turkish government.

The buildings and grounds of the **Turkish Naval Base** are to the left of the ferry-landing. Until recently this was the site of the Turkish Naval Academy, which has now been moved across to the mainland. Beyond the base a road leads to the Greek church of St. Nicholas on the southeast coast of the island.

A paved road leads around the coast of Heybeli, with a branch road cutting across the waist of the island. Phaetons can be hired near the ferry-station; to go all the way around the island tell the driver 'Büyük (Grand) Tour', or to circle only the northern half say 'Küçük (Small) Tour'.

The most interesting spot on the island is at the intersection of the coast road and the road leading across the waist of the island. To the right of the intersection are the buildings and grounds of the inland branch of the Turkish Naval Base, where the monastery of the Panaghia Kamariotissa once stood.

Normally civilians are not permitted on the grounds of the Base, but sometimes the officer in charge will allow you to see the **church of the Panaghia Kamariotissa**, the former chapel of the monastery. The chapel is of the quatrefoil or tetraconch type; that is, with a central dome surrounded by four semidomes over exedrae, three of which project from the outside of the building, with the fourth being contained within the narthex. This is the only Byzantine church of the tetraconch type that has survived in the city.

Buried in the courtyard of the church are seven Patriarchs of Constantinople. Four of them died violently in the 17C–18C. The most famous of these is the celebrated Cyril Lucaris, six times Patriarch of Constantinople and once of Alexandria. He was executed by Murat IV on 25 June 1638, after which his body was flung into the Bosphorus. His corpse was washed ashore several days later, and was then taken secretly to Halki for burial at the church of the Panaghia Kamariotissa. Thus ended the remarkable career of the man whom Pope Urban had called 'the son of darkness and the athlete of Hell'.

On the hillside, above the entrance to the Naval Base, there is a very interesting old **graveyard**. The most striking sepulchral monument there is a large statue of an angel holding the imperial Russian coat of arms, which, like that of Byzantium, is inscribed with the figure of a double-headed eagle. This is a memorial to the three hundred or so Russian soldiers who died in the nearby monastery, imprisoned there after having been captured in the Russo-Turkish war in 1828. Only the names of the officers are inscribed on the monument.

The most interesting tombstone in the cemetery is that of Edward Barton, the second ambassador from Queen Elizabeth I to the Sublime Porte. The tomb is inscribed with Barton's coat-of-arms and a long inscription in Latin. There are many mistakes in the inscription, but it seems to be intended to read something like this:

'TO EDWARD BARTON/THE ILLUSTRIOUS AND SERENE/AMBASSADOR OF/THE QUEEN OF THE ENGLISH/A MAN MOST PREEMINENT/WHO ON HIS RETURN FROM/THE WAR IN HUNGARY/WHITHER HE HAD ACCOMPANIED/THE INVINCIBLE EMPEROR/OF THE TURKS/DIED IN THE 35TH YEAR OF HIS AGE/AND OF OUR SALVATION 1597/THE 15TH DAY OF SEPTEMBER'. The Emperor to whom the inscription refers is Sultan Mehmet III.

*Büyükada

The ferry finally stops at Büyükada, the Greek Prinkipo, the largest and most populous of the Princes' Isles. When people visit the islands they nearly always come here; it is the summer resort par excellence.

During Byzantine times there were at least four monasteries and a convent on Prinkipo. The convent sheltered several imperial exiles during the medieval period. It had originally been founded by Justinian in the mid 6C, but it was completely rebuilt and considerably enlarged in the last years of the 8C by the Empress Eirene (797–802), one of the very few women to rule Byzantium in her own right. In 797 Eirene usurped the throne from her son, Constantine VI, whom she mutilated so badly that he died a few days later. The Emperor left behind a young daughter, the Princess Euphrosyne, whom Eirene banished to her convent on Prinkipo so that she could not contest the throne. In 802 Eirene was herself deposed and exiled to Lesbos, where she died shortly afterwards. Her body was then taken to Prinkipo to be buried in the garden of her convent.

Euphrosyne remained in the convent on Prinkipo for 26 years, while five emperors in turn succeeded one another on the throne of Byzantium. The last of these ephemeral emperors, Michael II, the Stammerer, suddenly grew tired of his old wife, the Empress Thecla, in the year 829. Rumour reached him of the pretty princess-nun who had been locked up all these years on Prinkipo. So he sent for her, and after banishing Thecla to the convent on Prinkipo married Euphrosyne. Later that same year Michael died and was succeeded by his son Theophilus. The new Emperor showed himself a loyal son, for he restored his mother Thecla to the palace and sent Euphrosyne back to her convent on Prinkipo.

Two centuries later, in 1041, this same convent sheltered for a time the Empress Zoë after she had been exiled by her adopted son, Michael V, the Caulker. She was freed from the monastery a few weeks later however, when the people of Constantinople deposed Michael and raised Zoë and her sister Theodora to the throne, where they ruled in their own right for a few months before being succeeded by Constantine IX, whom Zoë married.

Anna Dalassena, mother of the future Alexius I Comnenus, was imprisoned in the convent for a few months in 1060, before being allowed to return to the capital. In 1115 the Empress Eirene, wife of Alexius I, entered the convent voluntarily so that she could be near her husband, who was suffering a slow and painful death in one of the monasteries on Prinkipo. He died there in 1118.

The island consists of two large hills separated in the middle by a broad valley, so that the road around it makes a figure eight. There are phaetons for hire in the main square, and here again one asks for 'Büyük Tour' for a ride all the way around the island or 'Küçük Tour' to go around the northern half only. You should really take the Grand Tour, for the southern end of the island is almost totally unspoiled and in places it is extraordinarily beautiful. But the best way to tour the island is on foot, for you can then wander off on pathways up into the hills or down to the sea, where there are secluded coves, ideal for picnicking.

Before leaving the village we will stroll around to look at some of the beautiful old Büyükada houses. The most prominent is the **Splendid Hotel** at 23 Nisan Cad., built in 1911 by the Greek architect Kaludi Laskaris for Sakizli Kazım Paşa. One house of historic interest is the **Izzet Paşa Köşkü** at 55 Çankaya Cad., built in the latter half of the 19C by the Greek banker Konstantinos Ilyaso. Toward the end of the 19C the house passed to Izzet Paşa, head of the secret police during the reign of Abdül Hamit II. Leon Trotsky lived here during the first years of his exile on Büyükada (1929–33), and it was here that he began to write his monumental *History of the Russian Revolution*.

Nearby is the **Con Paşa Köşkü**, the grandest of all the old mansions on Büyükada. This was built in the late 19C by the Greek architect Achilleus Politis for Con Paşa (Tarasivolos Yannaros), an Ottoman statesman of Italian-Greek ancestry.

Another very interesting house is on an unnamed street in the back of town; this is the **mansion of the Papal Nuncio**, the representative of the Vatican in Istanbul. The most notable of the Papal legates who lived here was Angelo Giuseppe Roncali, the future Pope John XXIII, who was Nuncio in Istanbul during the years 1934–44.

Both of the island's hills are surmounted by monasteries. The one on **Isa Tepesi**, the Hill of Christ, is dedicated to the **Transfiguration**. Virtually nothing is known of the history or date of foundation of this monastery, other than that it was restored in 1597; the present buildings date from the 19C. It is well worth climbing the hill to see the monastery, for it is in a very picturesque location in the midst of a pine forest.

Yüce Tepe, the southern hill, is also thickly forested; it rises to an altitude of 202m, the highest in the archipelago. The picturesque ***Monastery of St. George**. stands in a beautiful clearing at the top of the hill.

There is evidence that there was a monastery on this site as early as the 12C, though most of the present structure is modern. The monastery is known to the Greeks as Haghios Georgios Coudonas, St. George of the Bells. One version of the legend that explains the foundation of the monastery has it that a shepherd was grazing his flock on the hill when he heard the sound of bells coming from under the ground. When he dug down he found an icon of St. George, which he and the other islanders enshrined on the spot.

The present structure consists of six separate chapels on three levels, the older sanctuaries being on the lower levels. On the ground floor is the caretaker's house and a chapel of St. George, built early in the present century. A flight of stairs leads down to the first level below. Just beside the steps is a chapel of the Blachernitissa, Our Lady of Blachernae. Beyond that is a shrine of St. Charalambos, and past that is another chapel of St. George. Small iron rings set into the floor of these chapels were for controlling the madmen who were brought here in the hope of being cured, for in Byzantine times the monastic complex included an insane asylum. The room at the bottom of the stairs is a tiny shrine with an ayazma, a sacred spring. Beyond the ayazma you come to the final chapel, dedicated to the Twelve Apostles.

The building to the west of the church is a hostel for those who come to visit the monastery on the feast days of the several saints who have sanctuaries here. The most important of these festival days is that of St. George, 23 April, when hundreds of pious Greeks flock to visit the church. On that day the small café to the east of the church provides food and drink for those who visit the shrine, in a setting of incomparable beauty.

From the summit of Yüce Tepe we can see the two tiny islets beyond Büyükada, **Sedef Adası**, or Mother-of-Pearl Island (to the east), and **Tavşan Adası**, Rabbit Island (to the south). In Byzantine times Sedef was known as Terebinthos and Tavşan was called Nyandros. Tiny as they are, both islets were the sites of religious establishments in Byzantium, with a monastery on Terebinthos and a convent on Nyandros. Both of them were founded in the mid 9C by the famous Patriarch Ignatius, eldest son of Michael I. Ignatius served as Patriarch until his death in 877, after which his remains were brought back for burial in his monastery on Terebinthos. He is now venerated as a saint in the Greek Orthodox Church.

Both Sedef and Tavşan can be reached by boats hired at the port in Büyükada. Sedef now has a colony of summer villas, but Tavşan is uninhabited. On Tavşan there are still some scattered ruins of the convent founded by the Patriarch Ignatius.

The History of Istanbul

The founding of Byzantium

There is archaeological evidence of human settlement on the acropolis above Saray Burnu dating back to the sixth millennium BC. However, virtually nothing is known of this prehistoric settlement, and the history of the city really begins with the founding of the Greek city-state of Byzantium in the 7C BC. According to tradition, the eponymous founder of Byzantium was Byzas the Megarian, who established a Greek colony on the acropolis above the confluence of the Bosphorus and the Golden Horn c 658 BC. Before setting out, Byzas had consulted the Delphic oracle, who advised him to settle 'opposite the Land of the Blind'. The oracle was referring to the residents of Chalcedon, a Greek colony established c 675 BC on the Asian side of the strait. The implication is that the earlier settlers must have been blind not to have seen the much greater advantages of the site on the European side. A city built there would be more defensible, since the steep acropolis was bounded on two sides by deep waters, and its short landward exposure could be protected by strong walls. The city would then be in a position to control all shipping passing between the Aegean, the Propontis and the Pontus, while its situation on the principal crossing-point between southeast Europe and Asia Minor would put it astride the main land routes that developed between the continents.

Byzantium became a centre for trade and commerce, acquiring wealth from its fisheries and the customs fees it charged on shipping through the Bosphorus. The city was taken by the Persian king Darius in 512 BC, when he crossed the Bosphorus on a bridge of boats at the outset of his campaign against the Scythians, an incident mentioned by Herodotus.

The Classical Period (480–323 BC)

Byzantium remained in Persian hands until 477 BC, when an allied Greek force under the Spartan general Pausanias freed the city. Byzantium was alternately allied with Athens and Sparta during the Peloponnesian War, which was fought in the years 431–404 BC. The Athenians took Byzantium from the Spartans in 409 BC, at which time Athens founded Chrysopolis, the City of Gold, on the Asian shore opposite the confluence of the Bosphorus and the Golden Horn, the present site of Üsküdar. Byzantium retained its independence throughout the rest of the classical period, withstanding a year-long siege by Philip II of Macedon in 341–340 BC. Despite their spirited resistance to King Philip, the Byzantines avoided conflict with his son and successor Alexander the Great, who began his invasion of Asia with a victory over the Persians at the battle of the Granicus in 334 BC.

Hellenistic (323–130 BC) and Roman (129 BC–AD 330) periods

After Alexander's death in 323 BC, Byzantium was involved in the events following on the collapse and dismemberment of his empire and the subsequent eastward expansion of Rome. Byzantium became part of the Roman Province of Asia after its establishment in 129 BC, and for more than three centuries afterwards it enjoyed a respite from war, sheltered by the mantle of the Pax Romana.

In the closing years of the 2C AD Byzantium was swept up once again in the tides of history when it became involved in the civil war between the Emperor Septimius Severus and his rival, Pescennius Niger, supporting the latter. After Septimius Severus defeated and killed Pescennius Niger in 194 he returned to punish the Byzantines, putting their city under siege. After finally taking Byzantium in 196, the Emperor tore down the city walls, massacred all those who had supported his rival, and burned the city to the ground. A few years afterwards, however, Septimius realised the imprudence of leaving so strategic a site undefended, and rebuilt the city on an enlarged scale, enclosing it on its landward side with a new line of walls. The walls of Septimius Severus are thought to have begun at the Golden Horn a short distance downstream from the present Galata Bridge, and to have ended at the Marmara below the Hippodrome. The area thus enclosed was twice as great as in the original town of Byzantium, which had comprised little more than the acropolis itself.

At the beginning of the 4C AD Byzantium played an extremely important role in the climactic events then taking place in the Roman Empire. After the retirement of Diocletian in 305, his successors in the Tetrarchy, the two co-emperors and their caesars, fought bitterly with one another for control of the Empire. This struggle was eventually won by Constantine, Emperor of the West, who in 324 defeated Licinius, Emperor of the East. The final battle took place in the hills above Chrysopolis, just across the Bosphorus from Byzantium, where Licinius had his last base. On the following day Byzantium surrendered and opened its gates to Constantine, now sole ruler of the Roman Empire.

During the first two years after his victory Constantine conceived and put into operation a scheme that profoundly influenced the world for the next millennium: reorganising the Roman Empire and shifting its capital to Byzantium. After Constantine made his momentous decision he set out to rebuild and enlarge the old town of Byzantium to suit its imperial role. The project began on 4 November 326, when the Emperor personally traced out the limits of the new city. The defence walls with which Constantine enclosed the capital extended in a great semi-circle from the Golden Horn to the Sea of Marmara, quadrupling the area of the city. The imperial building programme proceeded rapidly, and in less than four years the new capital was completed. On 11 May 330, in a ceremony in the Hippodrome, Constantine dedicated the city of New Rome and proclaimed that thenceforth it would be the capital of his empire. However, in popular speech the new capital soon came to be called Constantinople, capital of the Byzantine Empire.

Constantinople, the city of Constantine

The empire ruled by Constantine and his successors turned out to be quite different from the old Roman Empire. The new realm, which later historians called the Byzantine Empire, adopted Christianity as the state religion and Greek as the official language, changes which were effectively completed during the reign of Theodosius II (408–450).

By the time of Theodosius II the capital had grown considerably in population, expanding well beyond the limits established by Constantine. Because of this, and also because of the threat of barbarian invasions, the Emperor decided to build a new and stronger line of walls a mile farther out into Thrace. The first phase of these walls was completed in 413 and the final phase in 447, just in time to turn aside the advancing hordes of Attila.

The Theodosian walls enclosed seven hills, the same number as in Rome. The First Hill, so called, is the acropolis above Saray Burnu. The next five hills are low and broad peaks on the undulating ridge that runs from the acropolis out to the Theodosian walls, while the Seventh Hill has its peak far off in the southwest corner of the old city, sloping down to the Marmara shore. Although the contours of these hills have been obscured by modern roads and buildings, they can still be discerned and form convenient reference-points for studying the old city.

Theodosius II also built a splendid new cathedral dedicated to Haghia Sophia, the Divine Wisdom. Completed in 415, it replaced an earlier church of the same name which had been built by the Emperor Constantius (337–61) and burned down during a riot in 404.

The reign of Justinian the Great (527–65)

A new epoch in the history of the city began in 527, when Justinian succeeded his uncle Justin I (518–27) to the throne. A few years before becoming emperor Justinian fell in love with a reformed courtesan named Theodora, and in 525 he married her. When he succeeded to the throne Theodora became his Empress, becoming the power behind the throne.

Even before his accession, when he served as Caesar under his uncle Justin, Justinian laid the foundation for the grand design that would be carried out during his reign, the reconquest of the lost dominions of Rome. He was fortunate to have in his service one of the greatest generals in Byzantine history, Belisarius, who in 526 began his illustrious career by leading Justin's army against the Persians. This campaign was prosecuted with even greater vigour the following year, when Justinian succeeded his uncle as Emperor.

In 532 Justinian was very nearly overthrown in a revolt that broke out among the factions in the Hippodrome. This insurrection is known as the Nika Revolt, from the rallying-cry of 'Nika' (Victory) that the mobs shouted as they stormed the royal palace on the First Hill, confident that they would succeed in overthrowing the Emperor. At the height of the rebellion, when the rebels were almost in control of the capital, Justinian was on the point of giving up his throne and fleeing for his life. But Theodora persuaded him that it would be nobler to stay and fight on, even if it meant their death. After five days of bloody fighting the revolt was put down by Belisarius, who trapped and slaughtered 50,000 of the rebels in the Hippodrome.

When the revolt ended most of the buildings on the First Hill were in ruins, including the royal palace and the church of Haghia Sophia. Justinian immediately began a programme of reconstruction, and within five years he had rebuilt all of the buildings destroyed in the Nika Revolt, erecting a new church of Haghia Sophia, which the Emperor dedicated on 26 December 537.

During the course of Justinian's long reign Belisarius and his other generals succeeded in regaining much of the former territory of the Roman Empire. By 565 the borders of Justinian's realm extended around the Mediterranean, including Palestine, Syria, Asia Minor, Greece, the Balkans, Italy, southern Spain, the North African littoral, Egypt, and the Mediterranean islands, an area only slightly smaller than that of the Roman Empire in the time of Augustus. But the strength of the empire had been sapped by the enormous expenditure of wealth and manpower in the campaign of reconquest. Taxation had been exorbitant and many lives had been lost in the endless wars of Justinian's reign.

The struggle for survival

During the half-century after Justinian's death the great empire that he created was almost destroyed, attacked by enemies on all sides and torn apart by internal strife. The low point came with the reign of Phocas (602–10), whom historians generally consider to be the worst emperor ever to sit upon the Byzantine throne. Phocas was overthrown and succeeded by Heraclius, who defeated the Persians and the Avars when they were almost on the point of capturing Constantinople in 626. During the remaining years of the reign of Heraclius he won back from the Persians all of the territory they had conquered, and at the same time he drove the Avars out of the southern Balkans, so that the empire seemed secure at the time of his death in 641.

After the final defeat of the Persians the next enemies to appear were the Arabs, who first swept across Asia Minor in 674, putting Constantinople under siege for four years. The Byzantines withstood this siege, driving off the Arab fleet with their flame-throwers spewing the terrible 'Greek Fire'. The Arabs besieged the capital a second time in 717–18, during the reign of Leo III, but once again they were driven off with heavy losses.

The reign of Leo III marked the beginning of the most serious internal conflict in Byzantine history, the Iconoclastic Crisis, which lasted for more than a century. The iconoclasts were adamantly opposed to the presence of figurative paintings in the churches of Byzantine, and while they were in power virtually all such icons were destroyed, and at the same time many of the monasteries of the empire were closed and their monks imprisoned and persecuted. The crisis came to an end in 845, when a council of the Greek Orthodox Church permanently restored icons to the churches of the empire and reopened the monasteries.

The next threat came from the Bulgars, who rose to dominance in the Balkans early in the 9C, besieging Constantinople unsuccessfully in 814, 913 and 924. The climax of this struggle came with the campaigns of Basil II, who ruled from 976 until 1025, the longest and most illustrious reign in the history of the Byzantine Empire. In 995–1001 Basil defeated the Arabs and drove them out of southern Asia Minor for ever, and in 1014 he annihilated the Bulgar army and permanently ended their threat to Byzantium, a feat for which he received the title of Bulgaroctonus, the 'Bulgar-Slayer'.

When Basil died in 1025 he left behind him an Empire that stretched from the Caucasus and Persia to the Adriatic and from the Holy Land to the Danube. This represented the zenith of Byzantine power in the late medieval period, for thenceforth its fortunes inexorably declined.

The dynasty of the Comneni

The death of Basil II in 1025 marked a turning-point in the history of the Byzantine Empire. His passing was followed by a half-century of steady decline, in which a series of weak and ineffective emperors proved unable to deal with the mounting internal troubles of the Empire, at a time when new and stronger enemies were appearing on all sides and threatening the very existence of Byzantium. The nadir of this decline came in 1071, when a Byzantine army led by the Emperor Romanus IV Diogenes was annihilated by the Selçuk Turks at Manzikert in eastern Asia Minor. This opened up all of Asia Minor to the Selçuks, who overran Asia Minor as far as the Sea of Marmara. With them came hordes of nomadic Turcoman tribesmen, who divided up the former Byzantine territory in Asia Minor into a mosaic of Turkish beyliks, or principalities. In the same year, 1071, the Normans captured Bari, thus ending Byzantine rule in Italy.

Although the Empire had now lost forever its possessions in Italy, the Byzantines still maintained close political and economic ties with several Italian city-states, particularly Venice. During the reign of Basil II, Doge Pietro Orseolo obtained commercial concessions for Venice in Constantinople, a development that had important consequences. These concessions included reduced customs fees for Venetian traders, and also gave them a small strip of territory extending from the Golden Horn, where they could build docks for their ships, warehouses for their goods, and houses for their merchants. The Byzantines later gave similar concessions to Amalfi, Pisa and Genoa. Amalfi and Pisa acquired strips of territory on the Golden Horn beside those of the Venetians, while the Genoese were given Galata. The Byzantines derived some commercial and political advantage from these concessions at first, but later the Italians and other Latins in Constantinople became virtually independent of the Empire. This was particularly true in Galata, which became a semi-autonomous city-state governed by an official sent out annually from Genoa. With their stronger fleets the Italians were able to flout the laws and regulations of the Empire with impunity. This led to a great deal of friction between the Byzantines and the Latins, and was a contributory factor in the eventual downfall of Byzantium.

In 1081, a decade after the catastrophic defeat at Manzikert, Alexius I Comnenus became Emperor of Byzantium. Throughout the next century he and his son and grandson, in turn, successfully defended the Empire against the incursion of the forces that were hemming it in on all sides, using diplomacy and an enlightened foreign policy to great advantage. When Alexius first came to the throne, the Selçuk Turks and their Turcoman vassals were in complete control of virtually all Asia Minor, with their capital at Nicaea. When the armies of the First Crusade reached Constantinople in 1096, on their way to the Holy Land, Alexius took the opportunity to use their help in regaining the territory that Byzantium had lost to the Turks. Their first success came in June 1097, when they captured Nicaea, the Selçuk capital. The Crusader leaders returned the city to Alexius and marched on, while the Emperor and his troops hastened to occupy all of the former Byzantine cities abandoned by the fleeing Turks.

Alexius I died in 1118 and was succeeded by his son John II, who has been acclaimed by both his contemporaries and by modern historians as the finest ruler in the illustrious dynasty of the Comneni. John continued his father's foreign policy, applying clever diplomacy and the judicious use of military force against his opponents. When John died in 1143 all of the Empire bequeathed to him by his father was intact, and in addition he had regained southern Asia Minor, extending the borders of the Empire in that direction as far as Syria. John was succeeded by his son, Manuel I, who in a reign of 37 years (1143–80) preserved the Empire he had inherited and added to it Dalmatia, Croatia and Bosnia. When he died the borders of the Empire stretched from Syria to Hungary and from central Asia Minor to the Adriatic, including Cyprus, Crete and the Aegean isles.

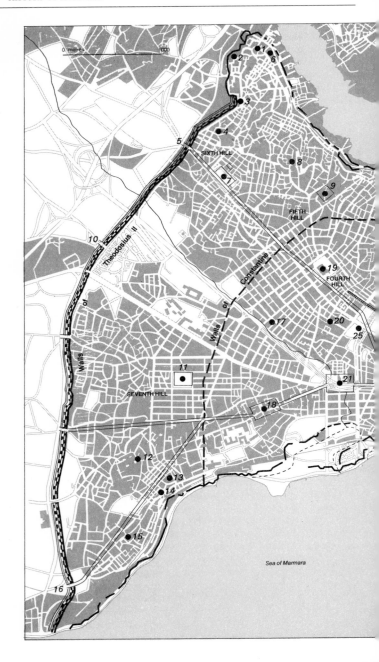

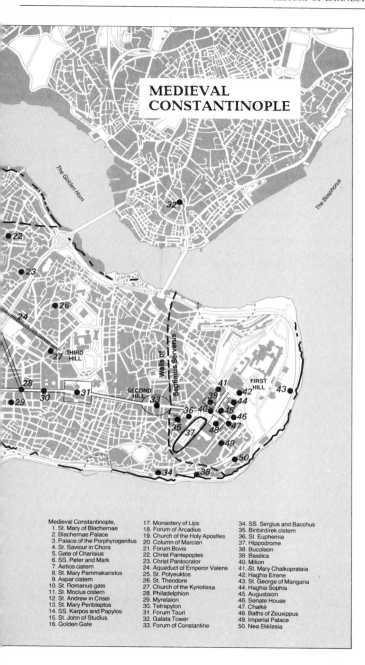

MEDIEVAL CONSTANTINOPLE

Medieval Constantinople,
1. St. Mary of Blachernae
2. Blachernae Palace
3. Palace of the Porphyrogenitus
4. St. Saviour in Chora
5. Gate of Charisius
6. SS. Peter and Mark
7. Aetios cistern
8. St. Mary Pammakaristos
9. Aspar cistern
10. St. Romanus gate
11. St. Mocius cistern
12. St. Andrew in Crisei
13. St. Mary Peribleptos
14. SS. Karpos and Papylos
15. St. John of Studius
16. Golden Gate

17. Monastery of Lips
18. Forum of Arcadius
19. Church of the Holy Apostles
20. Column of Marcian
21. Forum Bovis
22. Christ Pantepoptes
23. Christ Pantocrator
24. Aqueduct of Emperor Valens
25. St. Polyeuktos
26. St. Theodore
27. Church of the Kyriotissa
28. Philadelphion
29. Myrelaion
30. Tetrapylon
31. Forum Tauri
32. Galata Tower
33. Forum of Constantine

34. SS. Sergius and Bacchus
35. Binbirdirek cistern
36. St. Euphemia
37. Hippodrome
38. Bucoleon
39. Basilica
40. Milion
41. St. Mary Chalkoprateia
42. Haghia Eirene
43. St. George of Mangana
44. Haghia Sophia
45. Augustaion
46. Senate House
47. Chalkè
48. Baths of Zeuxippus
49. Imperial Palace
50. Nea Ekklesia

Manuel Comnenus was succeeded by his 12-year-old son, Alexius II. Since Alexius was too young to rule in his own right his mother, the Empress Mary of Antioch, acted as regent. This led to a power vacuum that was filled by Andronicus Comnenus, younger brother of the late Emperor Manuel, who was serving as governor of the Pontus. Andronicus revolted and took control of Constantinople, where in September 1183 he was crowned as co-Emperor with Alexius, whom he murdered shortly afterwards. Two years later Andronicus himself was overthrown and murdered, ending the illustrious dynasty of the Comneni.

The dynasty of the Angeli

Andronicus was succeeded by Isaac II Angelus, the founder of the brief dynasty of the Angeli. Isaac was a totally incompetent ruler who gave free play to the corrupt and divisive elements that were threatening to destroy the empire. In 1195 Isaac II was deposed by his elder brother, Alexius III, who imprisoned him along with his eldest son, Prince Alexius, and blinded him so that he would not be tempted to try to regain power. Then in 1202 Prince Alexius escaped and fled to the West, where he sought help in restoring his father and himself to the throne.

He went first to Pope Innocent II, who earlier that year had declared another Crusade, the Fourth, to free the Holy Land from the Moslems. When the Pope appeared unwilling to help him he went to the court of Philip of Swabia, his brother-in-law. Philip agreed to support him, and suggested that Alexius should present his case to the leaders of the Fourth Crusade: Enrico Dandolo, Doge of Venice, and Count Boniface of Montferrat. After the Pope's proclamation, the Crusaders had assembled in Venice, from where the Doge's fleet would transport them to Egypt to begin their campaign. But the Crusaders proved unable to pay for their passage, and there was an impasse until Dandolo suggested that they might make good the deficiency by helping the Venetians recapture the Dalmatian seaport of Zara (the modern Zadar), a former possession of theirs that had gone over to the Hungarians.

The Crusaders agreed, and in November 1202 began their sacred mission with the capture and sack of the Christian city of Zara, an outrage for which they were all excommunicated by the Pope. The Latins were wintering in Zara when a messenger arrived from the court of Philip of Swabia, carrying Alexius's appeal that the Crusaders restore his father and him to the throne of Byzantium. Alexius promised enormous sums of money to the Latins for their support, and Dandolo persuaded the Crusaders to agree.

The Latins, accompanied by Alexius and his blind father, set sail from Zara in spring 1203, arriving in the port of Constantinople on 24 June of that year. As soon as their fleet appeared, Alexius III fled with the imperial treasury and the crown jewels. The Crusaders captured Galata and encamped outside the land walls of Constantinople, while Dandolo and the other Latin leaders negotiated with the Byzantines. Threatened by the vastly superior force of the Crusaders, the Byzantines agreed to restore Isaac II and to make his son co-emperor as Alexius IV. Immediately after his coronation, Alexius tried to pay the indemnity that he had promised the Crusaders, but he found that the treasury was empty. Under pressure from Dandolo, Alexius attempted to raise the money by imposing confiscatory taxes on the Greek population of the capital. But this lost him what little public support he had, and in January 1204 he and his father were deposed and lost their lives in a popular revolt. They were replaced by Alexius V Ducas Murtzouphlos, who repudiated the agreement that Alexius IV had made with the Crusaders. This led the Latins to attack Constantinople, and on 13 April 1204 they breached the sea-walls along the Golden Horn and took the city by storm. They proceeded to sack the capital, stripping it of its wealth, its art treasures and its sacred relics, sending their loot back to western Europe and leaving the city a burned-out ruin. The Latins then began their occupation of Constantinople, a hiatus in the history of the Byzantine Empire.

The Latin occupation and the Empire of Nicaea

Soon after their capture of Constantinople, the Latins divided up the territory they had seized from the Byzantines. The Venetians were awarded three-eighths of the capital and the church of Haghia Sophia, along with various ports and islands. Half of the conquered Byzantine territory outside the capital was given to various Crusader knights as fiefs, while the other half and the remaining five-eighths of Constantinople became the property of Count Baldwin of Flanders. On 16 May 1204 Baldwin was crowned in Haghia Sophia, now a Roman Catholic cathedral, and took the title of Emperor of Rumania, as the Latins called their new empire. The territory of this empire originally consisted of Thrace and the northwest corner of Asia Minor, as well as a few Aegean isles. But in the subsequent half-century the Latin Empire steadily lost territory to its neighbouring states in Europe and Asia, so that by the middle of the 13C it was so small and weak that it lay open to conquest by those around it.

When Constantinople fell to the Latins in 1204, fragments of the Byzantine Empire continued in existence in several parts of Greece and Asia Minor, ruled by various members of the former royal families of Byzantium. As the Latin Empire progressively weakened, these Byzantine principalities contended with one another for the great prize, the recapture of Constantinople and the restoration of the Byzantine Empire. The most fortunately placed of these states was the Empire of Nicaea, which was founded in 1204 by Theodore I Lascaris, a son-in-law of Alexius III Angelus. Nicaea, the capital, was only a short distance from Constantinople, and the Empire shared a common border to its north with the Latin Empire. Under the extremely able leadership of Theodore I (1204–22) and his son-in-law and successor, John III Ducas Vatatzes (1222–54), the Empire of Nicaea flourished and its boundaries expanded, so that by the middle of the 13C they included all of western Asia Minor from the Black Sea to the Aegean as well as most of the offshore islands. By that time the Latin Empire had shrunk to little more than Constantinople and the European littoral of the Sea of Marmara, the Bosphorus and the Dardanelles.

When John III died in 1254 he was succeeded by his son Theodore II (1254–58). Theodore was a very effective ruler and a highly cultured man, a student of the scholar Nicephorus Blemmydes. During Theodore's brief but brilliant reign Nicaea became a cultural centre of such importance that scholars of the time referred to it as a second Athens. The cultural revival that started there later gave rise to a renaissance of learning in Byzantium. But Theodore died of epilepsy at the age of 37. He was succeeded by his seven-year-old son, John IV, for whom a regent, George Muzalon, had been appointed by Theodore on his death-bed.

But Muzalon was extremely unpopular with the aristocracy, and nine days after his appointment he was murdered, and the aristocracy appointed as regent the ablest and most distinguished man among them, Michael Palaeologus. Early in 1259 he was crowned co-emperor as Michael VIII, the young John IV by then being a virtual prisoner. Two years later, on 25 July 1261, Michael's commanding general captured Constantinople with a small force and with hardly any opposition, for the Latin Empire had been moribund and was now dead. On 15 August Michael VIII made his triumphal entry into Constantinople with his court and army, after which he rode at the head of a joyous procession to Haghia Sophia, where a service of thanksgiving was held. The legitimate emperor, the young John IV, took no part in the celebrations connected with this great event, for he remained a prisoner, and a few weeks later Michael had him blinded and sequestered in a monastery, where he spent the rest of his days in obscurity.

The Byzantium renaissance and the rise of the Osmanlı Turks
The cultural renaissance that had started in Nicaea continued in Constantinople during the reigns of Michael VIII and his successors, the Palaeologi, the last dynasty to rule Byzantium. This renaissance gave birth to great scholars like Gemisthus Plethon, who were important influences on the Italian Renaissance, and it also produced masterpieces of art far surpassing anything created in the history of the Empire. But the Empire under Michael VIII was merely a fragment of what it been in its prime, comprising only western Asia Minor, Thrace, Macedonia, parts of the Peloponnesus, and a few of the Aegean islands.

At the beginning of the 14C a new power arose in western Asia Minor, one which would eventually destroy the Byzantine Empire and all of the other surviving medieval states in western Asia and southeastern Europe. These were the Osmanlı Turks, better known to Westerners as the Ottomans. The Osmanlı were named after their first leader, Osman Gazi (Gazi was an honorific title meaning 'Warrior for the Faith'). Between 1288 and 1326 Osman Gazi headed a small tribe of nomadic Turks from central Asia who had been settled in western Asia Minor by the Selçuks in the first half of the 13C. At that time the Osmanlı controlled a few square miles of farmland and pasturage as vassals of the Selçuks, and their little beylik shared a common border with the Empire of Nicaea, whose capital was only a day's ride from their territory.

The Osmanlı gained their independence when the power of the Selçuks was broken by the Mongols in the second half of the 13C. Under Osman Gazi they began to expand their borders westward, and by the time he died in 1326 their forces were besieging the Byzantine city of Brusa (Bursa), a few miles from the Sea of Marmara. Shortly after Osman's death Brusa was captured by his son and successor, Orhan Gazi, who established his capital there. Orhan Gazi is considered to be the first Ottoman Sultan, for during the 36 years of his reign the Osmanlı forces conquered most of western Asia Minor and penetrated Europe as far as Bulgaria.

The Byzantines could do little to stop this expansion; when the Turks began to penetrate Europe the Empire was engaged in the most serious civil war in its history. In this struggle, which lasted from 1341 to 1347, the forces of the legitimate Emperor, John V Palaeologus, were arrayed against those of the usurper,

John Cantacuzenos, who actually brought the Turks over into Europe as his allies. John V eventually emerged victorious, but by that time the Turks had established a permanent foothold in Thrace and were beginning to move northward. In 1361, the year before Orhan Gazi died, his son Murat captured the Byzantine city of Adrianople on the border between Thrace and Bulgaria. Murat succeeded his father as Sultan in 1362 and soon afterwards shifted his capital from Brusa to Adrianople (which in Turkish became Edirne), for the Thracian city now became the base for the annual campaigns in which the Ottoman armies penetrated ever deeper into southeastern Europe.

The last Byzantine century

From the mid-14C onwards the fortunes of the Byzantines declined with the rise of the Osmanlı, who extended their empire deep into the Balkans, defeating allied Christian armies at Kosova in 1389 and Nicopolis in 1396. Beyazit I besieged Constantinople in 1394, building the fortress of Anadolu Hisarı on the Asian side of the Bosphorus at the narrowest point of the strait. The siege was lifted in 1402, when Beyazit was defeated by Tamerlane at the battle of Ankara and died in captivity. This gave Byzantium a reprieve as Beyazit's sons fought a war of succession that lasted until 1413, when Mehmet I became sultan. The Osmanlı resumed their expansion under his successor Murat II (1421–51), who decisively defeated allied Christian armies at Varna in 1444 and at the second battle of Kosova in 1448.

During the first half of the 15C Byzantium made several futile attempts to obtain help from western Europe. The most notable of these efforts began in 1437, when John VIII Palaeologus travelled to the West to ask for assistance from the Pope and the princes of western Europe. At the Council of Ferrara-Florence, which met from April 1438 until July 1439, the Emperor John and his Patriarch agreed to the Pope's terms, promising to bring the Greek people and clergy with them into union with Rome. But the Emperor gained nothing from this surrender, for not only did help for Byzantium never materialise in the West, but his own people and clergy completely repudiated the agreement.

John died childless and was succeeded by his younger brother Constantine XI Dragases (a name he derived from his mother's family). At the time of his accession Constantine was Despot of the Morea (the Peloponnesus), the only remaining Byzantine possession outside the capital. He was crowned Emperor of Byzantium in Mistra on 6 January 1449, after which he set out for Constantinople by sea, arriving there two months later. He took up the hopeless task that had occupied his late brother all through his long reign, attempting to gain help from the West to save Byzantium from the Turks who encircled it. He tried to persuade the people and clergy of the capital to agree to union with Rome, but the Greek hatred of the Latins was so great that this only turned the populace against him. As one of his highest court officials said to Constantine at the time, when asked to support the Emperor's policy of union with Rome: 'I would rather see the Moslem turban in the midst of the city than the Latin mitre'.

The fall of Byzantium

Murat II died on 13 February 1451 and was succeeded by his son, Mehmet II, then only 19 years old. Immediately after his accession Mehmet began preparations for the long-awaited siege of Constantinople. After organising his government and his military forces, Mehmet set up his military headquarters in Thrace, just a few miles from Constantinople. He then demanded and received from Constantine a plot of land on the European shore of the Bosphorus, just opposite the fortress. There in the summer of 1452 Sultan Mehmet proceeded to build an enormous fortress called Rumeli Hisarı, just opposite Anadolu Hisarı. These two fortresses enabled him to control the Bosphorus and cut off Constantinople from the Black Sea, depriving the city of the shipments of corn that were its main food supply.

In March 1453 the Ottoman navy sailed through the Dardanelles and the Sea of Marmara and anchored within sight of Constantinople, which was now completely cut off from the outside world. During the first week of April Mehmet massed his forces in Thrace and marched them into position before the Theodosian walls, beginning the siege of the city with a tremendous bombardment from his artillery park of giant cannon. The siege continued for seven weeks, with almost continual bombardment and with frequent attacks on the walls by the Turkish infantry. The Byzantines and their Genoese allies, outnumbered more than ten to one, defended the city valiantly, commanded by the Emperor and his Genoese commander, Giustiniani. In the early weeks of the siege the Byzantines were able to keep the Turks out of the Golden Horn by stretching an enormous chain across its entrance, but one night the Sultan had the ships of his fleet placed on rollers and pulled across the ridge above Galata, so that by morning they were all in the Golden Horn. This put the Byzantines at an even greater disadvantage, for they were now forced to take men from their already inadequate ranks on the Theodosian walls to defend the sea-walls along the Golden Horn. But they fought on, though the walls were breached in many places, repelling attacks that often took the Janissaries, the elite corps of the Turkish army, into the inner line of defences.

The Sultan decided to make a final all-out attack in the early morning hours of Tuesday, 29 May. The attack began with the heaviest artillery barrage of the siege, followed by repeated attacks by waves of Turkish infantry who hurled themselves against the walls, but still the defenders managed somehow to repel them. The Sultan then threw in his main reserve, the Janissaries, one contingent of which managed to scale the walls at their weakest point. During the fighting there Giustiniani received a fatal wound and was carried away by his men. This proved to be the turning-point in the battle, for the defenders now became disheartened and were no longer able to hold back the Janissaries, who poured through a breach in the walls. Constantine fought on with his men until he was killed beneath the walls of his fallen city.

Istanbul, capital of the Ottoman Empire

All resistance ceased within a few hours, and by noon the city was completely in Turkish hands. Then, in keeping with Muslim practice, the Sultan turned his soldiers loose to loot the city for three days, as they stripped it of all its wealth and took as slaves most of the young and able Greeks who had survived the siege. Early in the afternoon Sultan Mehmet rode triumphantly into the city, acclaimed by his soldiers as Fatih, or the Conqueror, the name by which he would thenceforth be known. He rode to Haghia Sophia, which was filled with terrified refugees who were being carried off into slavery by Turkish soldiers. Fatih had the building cleared and ordered that it be converted into a mosque at once. This was done, and on the following Friday the Sultan attended the first Islamic service in what the Turks now called Aya Sofya Camii, the Mosque of Haghia Sophia.

The rebuilding and repopulation of the city

Soon after his capture of Constantinople Fatih began to repair the damage it had sustained during the siege and in the decades of decay before the Conquest. A year or so later he transferred his government from Edirne to Constantinople, which thus became the capital of the Ottoman Empire. At about that time he constructed a palace on the Third Hill of the city, in the quarter later known as Beyazit. Some years later he built a second and more extensive palace, Topkapı Sarayı, on the acropolis above the confluence of the Bosphorus and the Golden Horn. By 1470 he had completed the great mosque complex that bears his name, Fatih Camii, the Mosque of the Conqueror. Many of Fatih's vezirs followed his example, building mosques and pious foundations of their own, each of which soon became the centre of its neighbourhood, together developing into the new Ottoman city that the Turks came to call Istanbul. Fatih also repeopled the city, which had lost much of its population in the decades preceding the Conquest, bringing in Turks, Greeks and Armenians from Anatolia, the Asiatic part of Turkey. During the last decade of the 15C large numbers of Sephardic Jewish refugees from Spain were welcomed to the Empire by Beyazit II (1481–1512), Fatih's son and successor, and many of them settled in Galata and Stamboul. By the end of the 15C Istanbul was a thriving and populous city, once again the capital of an empire.

The reign of Süleyman the Magnificent

Beyazit II was succeeded by his son Selim I (1512–20), who extended the bounds of the Ottoman Empire through the Middle East into Egypt with his capture of Cairo in 1517, after which he and his successors added the title of Caliph to that of Sultan.

Selim was succeeded by his eldest son, Süleyman, who came to be known in the West as the Magnificent. During Süleyman's long reign, 1520–66, the Ottoman Empire reached the peak of its fortunes and became the most powerful state in the world. Süleyman personally led his armies in a dozen victorious campaigns, failing only in his attempt in 1529 to take Vienna, which thereafter set the limit to Ottoman expansion into Europe. At the same time his fleet, commanded by pirate-admirals like Kılıç Ali Paşa and Barbarossa, was conquering the Aegean islands and extending the borders of the Empire along the coast of North Africa as far as Tunis and Algiers. Loot from these campaigns, and tribute and taxes from conquered territories, enormously enriched the Empire, and much of this wealth was used by Süleyman and his vezirs to adorn Istanbul with palaces, mosques and pious foundations. The grandest of the structures built during this epoch is the Süleymaniye, the mosque complex completed for the Sultan in 1557 by his Chief Architect, the great Sinan.

According to Islamic law, the Sultan and any other Muslim was allowed four wives, though he could have as many concubines as he wished. The two women who headed the Sultan's harem were his mother, the Valide Sultan, and his chief wife, the First Kadın. Early in Süleyman's reign he took as his First Kadın a woman whom he called Haseki Hürrem, better known in the West as Roxelana.

Süleyman was so in love with her that he put aside all the other women in his harem and lived with her alone. Roxelana's rival for Süleyman's affections was his Grand Vezir, Ibrahim Paşa, a Greek convert to Islam who had been the Sultan's intimate companion since the early years of his reign. So Roxelana set out to eliminate Ibrahim, persuading Süleyman that his wealthy and powerful Grand Vezir was taking on airs of royalty and had designs on the throne. In the year 1536, after an intimate supper in the palace with his beloved friend, Süleyman gave orders to his mutes to strangle Ibrahim in his sleep.

Roxelana's sinister influence over Süleyman continued until her death in 1558. During her last years Roxelana was concerned because her eldest son, Selim the Sot, was not first in line to succeed Süleyman as sultan. The heir-apparent was Prince Mustafa, an able and very popular young man. Roxelana plotted with her son-in-law, the Grand Vezir Rüstem Paşa, and they convinced Süleyman that Mustafa was planning to overthrow him and usurp the throne. Süleyman had Mustafa strangled by his mutes, while he himself looked on through a screen. Thus Selim became the heir-apparent, succeeding Süleyman as Sultan on his death in 1566. Historians consider this to be the turning-point in the history of the Ottomans, for with Selim's reign the Empire began its long and steady decline.

The reign of the women

During Selim's reign, 1566–74, the Sultan left all affairs of state to his Grand Vezir, Sokollu Mehmet Paşa, while he himself caroused with his women and his favourites in the Harem. Sokollu Mehmet, who had become Grand Vezir in the last year of Süleyman's reign, was one of the most capable men who ever held that office. And it was because of his leadership that the Empire still continued to expand during Selim's alcoholic reign, in the course of which the Turks conquered Cyprus and Georgia.

Selim's First Kadın was a woman called Nur Banu, who used his drunkenness to take complete charge of the Harem, running its affairs and those of the palace to her own advantage. Historians refer to this as the beginning of the 'Reign of the Women', a period in which a series of strong and determined women in the Harem took over control of the palace from their weak and dissolute sultans. The two most powerful women in the Harem were invariably the Valide Sultan and the First Kadın, the mother of the reigning sultan and his principal wife, between whom there were often violent struggles for power.

When Selim died on 21 December 1574, after falling in his bath while in a drunken stupor, Nur Banu had all but one of his five sons strangled so that her own child, Murat III, would succeed him as Sultan. Nur Banu corrupted her son by supplying him at a very early age with all of the beautiful women that she could buy in the Istanbul slave market, so that while he spent his time with them she would be free to run the palace. Sokollu Mehmet Paşa continued to serve as Grand Vezir during the early years of Murat's reign, but when he was assassinated in 1578 Nur Banu became the power behind the throne. She eventually lost power to her son's First Kadın, a Venetian girl named Safiye, whose influence over Murat was so great that she persuaded him to adopt a more favourable policy toward her native city.

When Murat died, on 16 January 1595, Safiye had all but one of his 19 brothers strangled so that her son, Mehmet III, would become Sultan. Safiye ruled the palace as Valide Sultan until 1602, when she was strangled by one of her rivals in the Harem. Mehmet III died the following year and was succeeded by his eldest son, Ahmet I, this time without bloodshed. Ahmet, who was only 13 years old at the time he became Sultan, soon fell under the influence of his First Kadın, a Greek girl named Kösem, who was herself only in her early teens when she first entered the Harem. Kösem, the most powerful and fascinating woman in the history of the Ottoman Empire, ruled in the Harem until Ahmet's premature death in 1617. She was then banished from Topkapı Sarayı to the Old Palace in Beyazit, the traditional fate for the women of departed sultans other than the Valide Sultan.

She remained sequestered there until 1623, when her eldest son, Murat IV, became Sultan, at which time she made her triumphant return to Topkapı Sarayı as Valide Sultan. She ruled the Harem throughout Murat's reign and that of her second son, Crazy Ibrahim (1640–48). Kösem even managed to cling to power during the early years in the reign of her grandson, Mehmet IV (1648–87), but in 1652 she was strangled on the orders of the Sultan's mother, Turhan Hadice. This ended the Reign of the Women, and thenceforth the Harem ceased to play a dominant role in the history of the Ottoman Empire.

The decline of the Ottoman Empire

Another turning-point in Ottoman history came in 1683, when the Turks failed in their second attempt to take Vienna. The tide of Ottoman expansion had turned, and thereafter the Turks began to lose more battles against their European foes than they won. By the end of the 17C the fortunes of the Ottoman Empire had declined to the point where its basic problems could no longer be ignored, even in the palace. The Empire gave up large parts of its Balkan territories after losing wars with European powers. Within, the Empire was weakened by anarchy and rebellion, particularly among the subject Christians in the Balkans, who now began to nourish dreams of independence.

During the second half of the 18C the Ottoman Empire was strongly influenced by developments in western Europe, particularly by the liberal ideas that brought about the French Revolution. This eventually led to a movement of reform in the Ottoman Empire. The first Sultan to be deeply influenced by these Western ideas was Selim III (1789–1807). Selim attempted to improve and modernise the Ottoman army by reorganising it along European lines. By this means he hoped to protect the Empire from further encroachments on the part of foreign powers and from anarchy and rebellion within its own borders. But Selim's efforts were resisted and eventually frustrated by the Janissaries, who felt that their privileged position was being threatened by the reforms. The Janissaries were finally crushed in 1826 by Mahmut II (1808–39), who instituted an extensive programme of reform in all the basic institutions of the Ottoman Empire, remodelling them along Western lines. This programme continued for a time during the reigns of Mahmut's immediate successors, Abdül Mecit (1839–61) and Abdül Aziz (1861–76). The reform movement (in Turkish, Tanzimat), culminated in 1876 with the promulgation of the first Ottoman constitution and the establishment of a parliament, which convened on 19 March 1877. But the following year the constitution was revoked and the parliament dissolved by Abdül Hamit II (1876–1909), who ruled as an autocrat for the rest of his reign, trying to preserve the disintegrating Ottoman Empire.

The last years of the Ottoman Empire

The reform movement had came too late to prevent the dismemberment of the Ottoman Empire, which in the 19C lost considerable territory as the subject peoples of the Balkans fought wars of national liberation to free themselves from Turkish domination. Between 1804 and 1878 five independent states came into being on what had been Ottoman territory in the Balkans: Serbia, Greece, Montenegro, Romania, and Bulgaria. The Ottoman Empire was the Sick Old Man of Europe and it seemed to be just a matter of time before it would pass on.

In 1909 the Young Turks deposed Abdül Hamit and restored parliament and the constitution. But this second experiment in Ottoman democracy lasted little longer than the first, for the Young Turks under the leadership of Enver Paşa set up a military dictatorship in which neither the Sultan, Mehmet V (1909–18), nor the people had any voice in the government. In 1912 the Greeks, Serbs and Bulgars inflicted a severe defeat on the Turks in the First Balkan War, in which the Ottoman Empire lost virtually all of Macedonia and Thrace, its last remaining territories in Europe. In 1913 the Balkan allies fell to fighting among themselves, and in the process the Turks regained eastern Thrace.

In 1914 Enver Paşa brought the Ottoman Empire into the First World War on the side of Germany, a decision that proved to be a fatal mistake. For when the war ended the Ottoman Empire was in ruins, its armies defeated in Palestine and the Caucasus, and with Istanbul occupied by an Allied army. A Greek army landed in Smyrna (modern Izmir) in May 1919 with the approval of the USA, France and Great Britain, and soon afterwards began advancing into western Asia Minor as far as the Sea of Marmara. The defeated Ottoman army was in no position to resist them, and so on 10 August 1919 Sultan Mehmet VI (1918–22), a puppet of the Allies, was forced to agree to an armistice. In doing so he put his signature to the Treaty of Sèvres, by which the Ottoman Empire lost all of its territory except Istanbul and that part of Anatolia which was not occupied by the Greeks and the other Allies.

However, the great mass of the Turkish people in Anatolia refused to comply with the terms of the armistice or of the Treaty of Sèvres. They rallied to the banner of Turkish Nationalism under the leadership of Mustafa Kemal Paşa, later to be known as Atatürk, who in 1919, in a conference in Sivas, called upon his fellow Turks to embark upon their own war of national liberation. In the following year Atatürk presided over a meeting in Ankara of the new Turkish National Assembly, which formed a government in opposition to the Sultan's puppet regime in Istanbul. The Turkish Nationalists then defeated the Greeks in several engagements, and by September 1922 the Greek army was forced to withdraw from Anatolia. During the following year more than a million Greeks were forced to leave Asia Minor and to resettle in mainland Greece, part of a population exchange for Turks living in Greek territory. This was one of the results of the Treaty of Versailles, signed in July 1923, which established the boundaries of Turkey as they are today except for the Hatay province, annexed in 1939.

Meanwhile, the Turkish National Assembly had on 1 November 1922 declared that the Osmanlı sultanate no longer existed, whereupon Mehmet VI fled from Istanbul aboard a British warship. His younger brother Abdül Mecit (II) succeeded him as Caliph, an institution that was abolished in 1924, when he too was forced to flee from Turkey. The climax of these developments came on 29

October 1923, when the Turkish National Assembly proclaimed the founding of the Turkish Republic, with Atatürk as its first President. At the same time the Assembly declared that Ankara was the capital of the new nation. Soon afterwards the embassies of the great European powers packed up and moved to new quarters in Ankara, leaving their old mansions along the Grande Rue de Pera in Istanbul. And so for the first time in sixteen centuries Istanbul was no longer the capital of an empire.

Modern Istanbul

The modern metropolis of Istanbul has changed greatly since the days when it was the capital of the Ottoman Empire. When the Republic of Turkey was founded in 1923 the population of Istanbul was about half a million, while in 1996 it was more than twelve million and increasing rapidly, the bounds of the city extending up the Bosphorus to within sight of the Black Sea and stretching for miles along both the European and Asian shores of the Marmara. In 1923 almost half of the population was non-Turkish, with large numbers of Greeks, Armenians and Jews, but now only very small percentages of the ethnic minorities remain.

In 1973, on the fiftieth anniversary of the founding of the Turkish Republic, the first Bosphorus Bridge (Boğaziçi Köprüsü) was built across the strait, linking the European and Asian suburbs of the city between Ortaköy and Beylerbey. Then in 1988 a second bridge (Fatih Sultan Mehmet Köprüsü) was built across the strait between Rumeli Hisarı and Anadolu Hisarı, spanning the Narrows at the same point where the Persian emperor Darius built his bridge of boats across the Bosphorus in 512 BC.

In recent years many of the Byzantine and Ottoman monuments of Istanbul have been restored and opened to the public, and numerous new museums have been founded as well, dealing with all aspects of the city's life, past and present. During the past decade new parks and promenades have been created along the Golden Horn and the Bosphorus, opening up those historic waterways to the people of Istanbul and their visitors, restoring the faded beauty of what the Byzantine historian Procopius called the city's 'encircling garland of waters'.

The Byzantine Emperors

324–337	Constantine the Great	565–578	Justin II
337–361	Constantius	578–582	Tiberius II
361–363	Julian the Apostate	582–602	Maurice
363–364	Jovian	602–610	Phocas
364–378	Valens	610–641	Heraclius
379–395	Theodosius the Great	641	Constantine II
395–408	Arcadius	641	Heracleonas
408–450	Theodosius II	641–668	Constantine III
450–457	Marcian	668–685	Constantine IV
457–474	Leo I	685–695	Justinian II
474	Leo II	695–698	Leontius
474–491	Zeno	698–705	Tiberius III
491–518	Anastasius I	705–711	Justinian II (second reign)
518–527	Justin I	711–713	Phillipicus Bardanes
527–565	Justinian the Great	713–715	Anastasius II

715–717	Theodosius III		Botaniates
717–741	Leo III	1081–1188	Alexius I Comnenus
741–775	Constantine V	1118–43	John II Comnenus
775–780	Leo IV	1143–80	Manuel I Comnenus
780–797	Constantine VI	1180–83	Alexius II Comnenus
797–802	Eirene	1183–85	Andronicus I
802–811	Nicephorus I		Comnenus
811–813	Michael I	1185–95	Isaac II Angelus
813–820	Leo V	1195–1203	Alexius III Angelus
820–829	Michael II	1203–04	Isaac II Angelus
829–842	Theophilus		(second reign)
842–867	Michael III	1203–04	Alexius IV Angelus
867–886	Basil I	1204	Alexius V Ducas
886–912	Leo VI		Murtzupholos,
912–913	Alexander	1204–22	*Theodore I Lascaris
913–959	Constantine VIII	1222–54	*John III Ducas
	Porphyrogenitus		Vatatzes
919–944	Romanus I	1254–58	*Theodore II Lascaris
	Lecapenus	1258–59	*John IV Lascaris
959–963	Romanus II	1259–82	Michael VIII
963–969	Nicephorus II Phocas		Palaeologus
969–976	John I Tzimisces	1282–1328	Andronicus II
976–1025	Basil II		Palaeologus
1025–28	Constantine VIII	1328–41	Andronicus III
1028–34	Romanus III		Palaeologus
	Argyrus	1341–91	John V Palaeologus
1034–41	Michael IV	1347–54	John VI Cantacuzenos
1041–42	Michael V	1376–79	Andronicus IV
1042	Theodora and Zoe		Palaeologus
1042–55	Constantine IX	1390	John VII Palaeologus
1055–56	Theodora (second reign)	1391–1425	Manuel II Palaeologus
1056–57	Michael VI	1425–48	John VIII Palaeologus
1057–59	Isaac I Comnenus	1448–53	Constantine XI
1059–67	Constantine X Ducas		Dragases
1067–71	Romanus IV Diogenes		
1071–78	Michael VII Ducas	(*Reigned in Nicaea)	
1078–81	Nicephorus III		

The Ottoman Sultans

1288–1326	Osman Gazi	1421–51	Murat II
	(Chieftain, but not	1451–81	Mehmet II, the
	Sultan)		Conqueror, known in
1326–62	Orhan Gazi		Turkish as Fatih
1362–89	Murat I	1481–1512	Beyazit II
1389–1403	Beyazit I	1512–20	Selim I
1403–13	Interregnum	1520–66	Süleyman the
1413–21	Mehmet I		Magnificent

1566–74	Selim II	1754–57	Osman III
1574–95	Murat III	1757–74	Mustafa III
1595–1603	Mehmet III	1774–89	Abdül Hamit I
1603–17	Ahmet I	1789–1807	Selim III
1617–18	Mustafa I	1807–08	Mustafa IV
1618–22	Osman II	1808–39	Mahmut II
1622–23	Mustafa I (second reign)	1839–61	Abdül Mecit I
1623–40	Murat IV	1861–76	Abdül Aziz
1640–48	Ibrahim the Mad	1876	Murat V
1648–87	Mehmet IV	1876–1909	Abdül Hamit II
1687–91	Süleyman II	1909–18	Mehmet V
1691–95	Ahmet II	1918–22	Mehmet VI
1695–1703	Mustafa II	1922–24	Abdül Mecit (II)
1703–30	Ahmet III		(Caliph only)
1730–54	Mahmut I		

Byzantine Architecture and Art

Byzantine churches

The oldest surviving church in Istanbul is St John of Studius, built in 463. The church is a basilica, a plan that was developed in Hellenistic and Roman times, and which in the early Byzantine period was the one most widely used for ordinary churches. The typical **basilica** is a long, rectangular building divided by two rows of columns into three parts, a wide central nave flanked by an aisle on either side, while at the eastern end of the nave a semicircular projection forms the apse. The entrance, at the western end opposite the apse, is generally preceded by a vestibule, or narthex, and sometimes by an outer vestibule, the exonarthex, which in turn opens into a large arcaded courtyard, the atrium.

The early **Byzantine basilicas** had pitched roofs and flat ceiling. Later, most notably in the reign of Justinian the Great, a major innovation was made by introducing a dome. Two outstanding examples of the domed basilica survive in Istanbul, the churches of Haghia Eirene and Haghia Sophia, both completed in 537. In Haghia Eirene the nave is covered on the east by a large dome, and on the west by a smaller and slightly elliptical domical vault, otherwise it is a very typical basilica. In Haghia Sophia the enormous central dome is supported to east and west by two semidomes of equal diameter, and there are other modifications that superficially conceal its basic plan, which is that of a basilica.

The other type of classical building sometimes used for early Byzantine churches was of a centralised plan, either round or polygonal. In Istanbul the most famous and beautiful example of this type is the church of SS. Sergius and Bacchus, built by Justinian in 527.

The period from the beginning of the 7C to the middle of the 9C may be called the **Dark Ages of Byzantium**. Little or no building of new churches was done, and virtually all the existing figurative mosaics and frescoes in the churches and monasteries of the Empire were destroyed because of the Iconoclastic movement. When Byzantine architecture began to revive in the second half of the 9C, a new type of church building came into being, one generally known as the **cross-domed church**. In this type a central dome is surrounded on the axes of the building by four long barrel vaults resting on four strong corner piers, thus forming an internal cross; on three sides there are aisles and galleries, so that the exterior is rectangular. At the eastern end the wide central apse is flanked by two smaller side apses; thenceforth three apses became the rule, required by the developed ritual; and at the west there is the usual narthex.

Another type is known as the **four-column church**, though some authorities consider this to be a mere development of the cross-domed type. Its most striking internal features are the four columns that here take the place of the corner piers of the earlier types as supports for the dome. These churches are all small and tall, more-or-less square externally, but preserving the cruciform plan within. There are no galleries, except sometimes over the narthex, but the four corners of the cross are occupied by domed bays or by domical vaults on high drums; these, together with the central dome, form a quincunx, by which name this type is sometimes known. The four-column church appeared in Constantinople in the 9C–10C and thereafter became almost standard; its small size was suitable to the declining revenues of the shrinking Empire, while its internal form provided ample areas for mosaic and fresco decoration.

All the Byzantine churches in Constantinople were built of brick, including Haghia Sophia, and they were generally little adorned on the exterior, depending for their effect on the warm brick colour of the walls. Towards the end of the Empire, in the 13C–14C, exteriors were sometimes enlivened by polychrome decoration in brick and stone.

Decoration in Byzantine churches

As if to compensate for the relative austerity of the outside, the interior of the churches blazed with colour and life. The lower parts of the walls up to the springing of the vaults were sheathed in marble, while the vaults, domes and upper walls were covered in gold mosaic. The most magnificent example of **marble revetment** is that in Haghia Sophia, where a dozen different kinds of rare and costly marbles are used, the thin slabs being sawn in two and opened out to form intricate designs. Haghia Sophia was of course unique, though there may have been a few other churches of Justinian equally lavishly covered with marble. But even the humbler and smaller churches of a later period had their revetment, largely of the common but attractive greyish-white marble from the nearby quarries on the Isle of Proconnesus in the Marmara. Most of the churches surviving in Istanbul have lost this decoration, but an excellent example survives almost intact in St. Saviour in Chora (Kariye Camii).

The **mosaics** of the earlier Byzantine period seem to have consisted chiefly of a gold ground round the edges of which, emphasising the architectural forms, were wide bands of floral decoration in naturalistic designs and colours; at appropriate places there would be a simple cross in outline. Large areas of this simple but effective decoration survive from Justinian's time in the dome and the aisle vaults of Haghia Sophia. It appears that in Haghia Sophia, at least, there were originally no pictorial mosaics. In the century following Justinian's death, however, picture mosaics became the vogue and an elaborate iconography was worked out which regulated which parts of the Holy Story should be represented and where the various pictures should be placed in the church building.

Then came the Iconoclastic Age, when all of these pictorial mosaics were ruthlessly destroyed, so that only one or two survive in Istanbul from before the mid 9C. From then onwards there was a revival of the pictorial art, still in the highly stylised and formal tradition of the earlier period, and all the great churches were again filled with holy pictures. A good idea of the stylistic types in favour from the 9C–12C can be seen in examples uncovered in Haghia Sophia.

But in Istanbul the most extensive and splendid mosaics date from the last great flowering of Byzantine culture before the Turkish Conquest in 1453. At the beginning of the 14C were executed the long cycles of the life of the Blessed Virgin and of Christ in St. Saviour in Chora, which have been so brilliantly restored by the Byzantine Institute. To this date also belong the glorious frescoes in the side chapel of that church, and the series of mosaics in the side chapel of the church of the Pammakaristos (Fethiye Camii). The art of these pictures shows a decisive break away from the hieratic formalism of the earlier tradition, breathing the very spirit of the Renaissance as it was beginning to appear at the same date in Italy. In Byzantium it had all too short a life.

Ottoman Architecture and Art

Mosques

The mosques of Istanbul fall into a small number of fairly distinct types of increasing complexity. The simplest of all, used at all periods for the less costly buildings, is simply an oblong room covered by a tiled pitched roof; often there was an interior wooden dome but most of these have perished in fires and have been replaced by flat ceilings. Second comes the square room covered by a masonry dome resting directly on the walls. This was generally small and simple but could sometimes take on monumental proportions, as in the mosque of Selim I. Occasionally, as there, mosques had side rooms used as tabhanes, or hospices for travelling dervishes. Later, in the 18C–19C, a more elaborate form of this type was adopted for the baroque mosques, usually with a small projecting apse for the mihrab, the niche that orients the faithful toward Mecca.

The next two types of mosque both date from an earlier period and are rare in Istanbul. Third is the two-domed type, essentially a duplication of the second, forming a large room divided by an open arch, each unit being covered by a dome. It is derived from a style common in the Bursa period of Ottoman architecture, and hence is often known as the 'Bursa type' (see the plan of Mahmut Paşa Camii on p 116). A modification occurs when the second unit has only a semidome. Mosques of this type always have side chambers. A fourth type, of which only two examples occur in Istanbul, also derives from the earlier Selçuk and Ottoman periods: a rectangular room covered by a multiplicity of domes of equal size supported on pillars; this is often called the great-mosque or Ulu Cami type.

The mosques of the **classical period** (c 1500–1650)—what most people think of as 'typical' Ottoman mosques—are rather more elaborate than their predecessors. They derive from a fusion of a native Turkish tradition with certain elements of the plan of Haghia Sophia. The great imperial mosques have a vast central dome supported to east and west by semidomes of equal diameter. (All mosques face in the direction of Mecca, which in Istanbul is approximately southeast, but for simplicity this Guide will follow the convention that they face east.) This strongly resembles the plan of Haghia Sophia, but there are significant differences, dictated partly by the native Turkish tradition, partly by the requirements of Islamic ritual.

In spite of its domes Haghia Sophia is a basilica, clearly divided into a nave and side aisles by a curtain of columns, on both ground floor and gallery level. The mosques suppress this division by getting rid of as many of the columns as possible, thus making the interior almost open and visible from all parts. Moreover, the galleries, which in Haghia Sophia are as wide as the aisles, are here reduced to narrow balconies against the side walls. This is the plan of Beyazit Camii and the Süleymaniye. Sometimes this centralisation and opening-up is carried even further by adding two extra semidomes to north and south, as at the mosques of the Şehzade, Sultan Ahmet I, and Yeni Cami.

A further innovation of the mosques is the provision of a monumental exterior in attractive grey stone with a cascade of descending domes and semidomes balanced by the upward thrust of the **minaret** or minarets. The smaller mosques have a single minaret which is almost always on the right side of the entrance, while the larger imperial mosques may have two, four, or even six, as

Sultan Ahmet I Camii, in which case they rise from the corners of the building and/or the courtyard. These minarets often have elaborately sculptured serefes, or müezzin's balconies.

Almost all mosques of whatever type are preceded by a porch of three or five domed bays and generally also with a monumental courtyard, the **avlu**. This is usually surrounded on three sides with a domed arcade and with a monumental gateway opposite the main doorway to the mosque. In the centre of the courtyard there is usually a **şadırvan**, or ablution fountain, where the faithful perform their abdest, or ritual washings, before going into the mosque to pray. The stone platform on the side of the courtyard next to the mosque is called the **son cemaat yeri**, literally the place of last assembly. When the mosque is full on the occasion of the Friday noon prayer, latecomers perform their devotions on this porch, usually at one of the niches flanking the doorway leading into the mosque.

The **interior furnishings** of all mosques are essentially the same. The most important element is the mihrab, a niche set into the centre of the wall opposite the main entrance. In the imperial mosques of Istanbul the mihrab is invariably quite grand, with the niche itself made of finely carved marble and with the wall around it sheathed in ceramic tiles. To the right of the mihrab is the mimber, or pulpit. At the time of the noon prayer on Friday the imam, or preacher, mounts the steps of the mimber and gives the weekly sermon, or hutbe. To the left of the mihrab, often standing against the main pier on that side, is the Kuran kursu, where the imam sits cross-legged while he reads the Kuran to the congregation. And to the right of the entrance in the larger mosques there is usually a raised platform, the müezzin mahfili, where the müezzins kneel when they are chanting the responses to the prayers of the imam.

In the imperial mosques there is always a hünkar mahfili, or royal loge, a chamber screened off by a gilded grille so that the Sultan and his party would be shielded from the public gaze when they attended services. This royal enclosure is usually in the far left corner of the gallery as one faces the mihrab, and it often had its own entrance from outside the mosque.

The Külliye

All imperial mosques and most of the grander ones of the great men and women of the Empire form the centre of a külliye, a whole complex of religious and philanthropic institutions comprising a vakif, or pious foundation, often endowed with great wealth. The founder invariably built his **türbe**, or mausoleum, in the garden or graveyard behind the mosque; these are simple buildings, square or polygonal, covered by a dome and with a small entrance porch, sometimes beautifully decorated inside with tiles.

Of the utilitarian institutions, almost always built around four sides of a central arcaded and domed courtyard, the commonest is the **medrese**, or college. The students' cells, or hücre, each had its dome and fireplace. The cells opened off the courtyard, which usually had a central fountain, and in the middle of one side of the portico was the large domed dershane, or lecture hall. Sometimes the medrese formed three sides of a mosque courtyard, while elsewhere it was an independent building, occasionally with an unusual shape, such as in the octagonal medrese of Rüstem Paşa. These medreses functioned at several academic levels, some being mere secondary schools, others teaching more advanced subjects, while still others were colleges for specialised studies such as law, medicine, and the hadis, or traditions of the Prophet. There were also primary schools, or **sibyan mektebi** (sometimes simply called a mektep), which were usually small buildings with a single domed classroom and sometimes an apartment for the teacher, or hoca.

The larger imperial foundations included a hospital, or **darüssifa**, a **caravansarai**, and a public kitchen, or **imaret**. Large institutions like the Süleymaniye also included an insane asylum, or **timarhane**. The caravansarai was built to the same general plan as the medrese, with the domed rooms around the central courtyard serving to house and feed travellers. The imarets had vast domed kitchens with very distinctive chimneys and large vaulted refectories. They provided free food for all the people associated with the külliye, as well as for the poor of the neighbourhood. All of the other institutions were free too, and in the great days of the Ottoman Empire they were very efficiently managed. In recent years many of them have been restored and are again serving the people of Istanbul, with Ottoman hospitals operating as clinics, schoolhouses functioning as children's libraries, and medreses being used as research centres, libraries, and student dormitories.

The kütüphane and the tekke

Sometimes these pious foundations were not part of a mosque complex, but were independent institutions. One example was the Ottoman library, or **kütüphane**, of which three charming examples from the 18C are still functioning in the city. Another such institution was the **tekke**, or dervish monastery, of which there were more than 300 housing the members of the 17 different religious orders represented in Istanbul. All of these were closed when the dervish orders were banned in the early years of the Turkish Republic, and most of the buildings have since been destroyed or have fallen into ruins. One of them, the tekke of the Mevlevi dervishes in Tünel, has recently been restored and is now open to the public, revealing yet another aspect of the life of old Istanbul.

The han

Another very important institution was the **han**, whose function closely paralleled that of the caravansarai. Like so many Ottoman structures, the han was built around one or more courtyards, but in two or three storeys, with the lower chambers used as stables for the horses and camels of the caravans that brought goods to Istanbul and the upper ones serving as guest-rooms for the merchants and as storage places for the wares that they sold there. These hans were virtually self-sufficient institutions, complete with kitchens, dining-halls, baths, toilets, blacksmith, and a mosque, and they were the mainstay of Istanbul's commercial life all through the Ottoman period. There are scores of these monumental old Ottoman hans still operating in Istanbul, some of them as much as five centuries old, and they are among the most picturesque sights in the old city.

Hamams

One of the most important of these Ottoman foundations was the **hamam**, or public bath, whose revenues were often used to pay for the upkeep of the other institutions in a külliye. There are well over one hundred of these old Ottoman hamams still functioning in Istanbul.

Turkish hamams are built to the same general design as the baths of ancient Rome. Ordinarily, a hamam has three distinct sections. The first chamber that you enter is the camekan, the Roman apoditarium. This is a reception chamber and dressing-room, a place in which you can relax and sip tea after bathing. Next comes the soğukluk, anciently known as the tepidarium, a chamber of intermediate temperature that serves as an anteroom to the bath, keeping the cold air out on one side and the hot air in on the other. Finally there is the hararet, or steam-room, the Roman calidarium.

The camekan is usually the most monumental chamber in a Turkish hamam. It is typically a vast square room covered by a dome on pendentives or squinches, with an elaborate fountain in the centre; round the walls there is a raised platform where the bathers undress and leave their clothes. The soğukluk is almost always a mere passageway, which usually contains the lavatories. In most Turkish baths the most elaborate chamber is the hararet, perhaps the most beautiful example of which is that in the Cağaloğlu Hamamı. In the centre of the hararet there is usually a large marble platform, the göbektasi, or 'belly-stone', which is heated below by a wood fire in the furnace room, the külhan. The patrons lie on the belly-stone to sweat and to be massaged before bathing at one of the wall-fountains in the side chambers.

Çeşme/fountains

Turkish fountains, or çeşme, are ubiquitous; there are more than 700 in Istanbul dating from Ottoman times, and even one or two that may date from before the Turkish Conquest. The most monumental of these are the imperial **street-fountains**, such as the splendid çeşme of Ahmet III beside the main entrance to Topkapı Sarayı. This huge structure is really a composite of the two basic types of fountains to be seen all over Istanbul. These are the sebil, or fountain house, which occupy the four corners of the structure, and the çeşme, the wall-fountains on each of the four sides.

The **sebil**, which is often used to adorn the corner of a mosque precinct, is usually a domed structure with three or more grilled openings in its facade. In Ottoman times these sebils were staffed with attendants who passed out cups of water free to thirsty passers-by. There are scores of these old Ottoman sebils still standing in Istanbul, and although none of them is still serving its original purpose, they remain an adornment to the city.

The most common type of Turkish fountain is the simple **çeşme**. In its most basic form a çeşme may consist of a mere niche set into a wall, with water flowing from a spout into a marble basin. The water-spout is set into a marble tablet called the mirror-stone, which is often decorated with floral or geometrical designs in low relief. The niche is usually framed in an arch, while the facade of the surrounding wall is decorated in the same design as the mirror-stone. At the top of this facade there is always a calligraphic inscription giving the name of the donor and the date of construction. The older inscriptions are often in the form of chronograms, in which the numerical values of the Arabic letters give the date of foundation. These chronograms became a favourite art form for Ottoman poets, and they vied with one another in composing clever and original epigrams, which would not only give the name of the donor and the date of foundation but would also advertise the poetic talents of the composer.

Ottoman Architectural Forms

In Ottoman architecture there are no 'orders' as these are understood in the West, such as the Doric, Ionic, and Corinthian orders in ancient Greek architecture. Nevertheless, in the great period of Ottoman architecture there were two recognised types of **capital**: the stalactite and the lozenge. The stalactite is an elaborate geometrical structure composed chiefly of triangles and hexagons, which is built up so that it resembles a stalactite formation or a honeycomb. It is derived directly from Selçuk architecture and is used not only for capitals but often for portal canopies, cornices, and even pendentives and squinches. The lozenge capital, apparently introduced by Sinan or anyhow not much used before his time, is a simple structure of juxtaposed lozenges. Neither capital is very satisfactory compared with those of the ancient Greek orders, because both, especially the lozenge, give a too-smooth and weak transition from the cylinder of the column to the square of the impost. In the baroque period of Ottoman architecture bad imitations of Western types of capitals came into vogue, almost all of them hopelessly weak.

And until the baroque period all Turkish **arches** had not been round like the Roman ones but pointed like the Gothic, and sometimes of the ogive or 'broken' type that is often so effectively used by Sinan. It should also be noted that the Ottoman **dome** resembles the hemispherical Roman, Byzantine, and Syrian type, not the more common Western ovoid type created by Brunelleschi, which is structurally double. Even when Ottoman domes are double, as in some türbes, each dome is structurally independent.

Turkish tiles

Of decoration applied to architecture, far and away the most brilliant and striking is Turkish ceramic tiling. Only fairly recently have the full importance and uniqueness of Turkish tiles been recognised: they used often to be called Rhodian ware or else lumped together with Persian pottery. Even though the potters were sometimes Persian—as well as Greek, Armenian, and Turkish—the Ottoman tiles were altogether different from Persian ceramics. They were manufactured chiefly at Iznik, the ancient Nicaea, but also sometimes at Kütahya and Istanbul.

Broadly speaking, there are three periods of Turkish ceramics represented in Istanbul. In the early period, from the Conquest to the mid 16C, the tiles were extremely plain and without design. These early Turkish tiles were usually hexagonal, a deep blue or a lighter green or turquoise, and sometimes overlaid with an unfired pattern in gold. More interesting are the tiles in the cuerda seca technique. Here, instead of a painted design covered by a transparent glaze, the glazes themselves were coloured and the colours were prevented from running into each other by a hair-like dividing line of permanganate of potash outlining the design (hence the name cuerda seca, dry cord); if visible at all this line is deep purple or black. The predominating colours of these tiles are apple-green and bright yellow with subordinate blues and mauves. They are very beautiful and very rare in Istanbul, and the only extensive examples are in the türbe of Prince Mehmet at the Şehzade Camii and in the porch of the Çinili Kösk.

About 1550 this lovely technique gave place to the no less beautiful and more famous Iznik style, where the design is painted on the clay and covered with an absolutely transparent glaze. Here the predominant colours are: on the purest, most unblemished white ground, deep blue, light blue, shades of green, and above all the matchless tomato red. This was made with a clay known as Armenian bole, found near Erzurum in eastern Anatolia. It has to be laid on very thickly so that it protrudes from the surface of the tile like sealing-wax. The technique of using it successfully is extremely tricky, so much so that it was only completely mastered toward 1570 and lost again in about 1620, so that the absolutely perfect tiles of this type are confined to this half-century. In tiles before or after this period the bole tends to be a bit muddy and brownish and lacking in clear outline. But at their best the Turkish tiles in the period 1550–1620 are incomparably beautiful.

After that the quality of Turkish tiles began to decline, like most other things in the Empire. A short revival was made about 1720 at Tekfursarayı in Istanbul, but this hardly outlasted the first generation of craftsmen. Thereafter inferior European tiles or even more inferior imitations of them became the vogue. There has been a considerable and praiseworthy revival of the old style in recent years, so that really good modern tiles (now made at Kütahya) are sometimes hard to distinguish, at first glance, from the great ones.

Sinan the Architect

No discussion of Ottoman architecture would be complete without at least a brief biography of the great Sinan, who created most of the masterpieces founded by Süleyman and his immediate successors. Sinan was born of Christian parents, presumably Greek, in the Anatolian province of Karamania in about 1492. When he was about 20 he was caught up in the devşirme, the annual levy of Christian youths who were taken into the Sultan's service. As was customary, he became a Muslim and was sent to one of the palace schools in Istanbul. He was then assigned to the Janissaries as a military engineer and served in four of Süleyman's campaigns. Around 1538 Süleyman appointed him Chief of the Imperial Architects, a post he held for half a century, continuing to serve under Süleyman's two immediate successors, Selim II and Murat III. Sinan built his first mosque in 1538, in Aleppo, and the following year he erected his first mosque in Istanbul; this was Haseki Hürrem Camii, commissioned by Süleyman for his wife Roxelana. In the following half-century he was to adorn Istanbul and the other cities of the Empire with an incredible number of mosques and other structures.

The 'Tezkere-ül Ebniye', the official list of Sinan's accomplishments, credits him with 81 large mosques, including 42 in Istanbul, 50 mescits, or smaller mosques, 55 medreses, 7 Kuran schools, 19 mausoleums, 15 public kitchens, 3 hospitals, 6 aqueducts, 32 palaces, 6 storehouses, 22 public baths, and 2 bridges, a total of 323 structures, of which 84 still remain standing in Istanbul alone. He was nearly 50 when he completed his first mosque, 65 when he completed the Süleymaniye, the crowning glory of Ottoman architecture in Istanbul, and he was 84 when the Selimiye mosque complex in Edirne was completed, a work that is generally agreed to be the supreme masterpiece in the history of Ottoman architecture. Sinan did not pause even then, but continued to work as Chief Architect, and built a half-dozen of Istanbul's finer mosques for the Sultan's vezirs.

Koca Mimar Sinan, or Great Sinan the Architect, as the Turks call him, died in 1588 at the age of 96 (100, according to the Islamic calendar) just a few days after completing his last project, a new gate in the Byzantine sea-walls along the Golden Horn. He was then buried in a mausoleum that he had constructed himself in the shadow of the Süleymaniye, his greatest work in Istanbul. Sinan was the architect of the golden age of the Ottoman Empire, and his monuments are the magnificent buildings with which he adorned its capital.

Glossary

The following are some Turkish words and technical terms in architecture that are used frequently in the text. Turkish words enclosed in parentheses are the form that they take when they are modified by a preceding noun; e.g. Sultan Ahmet Camii = the Mosque of Sultan Ahmet, whereas Yeni Cami - the New Mosque.

ambo, a raised pulpit from which the Epistle and the Gospel were read

ambulatory, a covered passageway around the apse of a church behind the altar

antae, projecting pilasters ending the lateral walls of a Greek temple; columns between the antae are said to be in antis

apse, the circular or polygonal termination of a church sanctuary

arcade, a range of arches supported on piers or columns

architrave, the beam or lowest division of the entablature, which extends from column to column

arcosolia, burial niches

atrium, the forecourt of a church

avlu, the forecourt of a mosque

ayazma, a holy well

barbican, an outwork of a fortress, designed to protect a gateway

barrel vault, a continuous vault of semicircular cross-section

bema, a raised stage reserved for the clergy in a Byzantine church

bedesten, a multi-domed building, usually in the centre of a Turkish market, where valuable goods are stored and sold

buttress, a mass of masonry built up against a wall to resist the outward pressure of an arch or vault

camekan, the reception or dressing room of a Turkish bath

cami (camii), a mosque

capital, the crowning feature of a column or pilaster

çarşı (carşışı), a Turkish market

çeşme (çeşmesi), a Turkish fountain

ciborium, a canopy supported by columns over an altar, also called a baldachino

corbel, a block of stone or wood, often carved or moulded, projecting from a wall, and supporting the beams of a roof, floor, vault or other architectural member

cornice, the crowning or upper portion of the entablature

crenellations, the indentations in the parapet of a fortress wall

cross vault or **groin vault**, vaults characterised by arched diagonal groins, which are formed by the intersection of two barrel vaults

cupola or **dome**, a spherical roof, placed over a circular, square, or polygonal chamber

curtain wall, a defence wall linking towers in a fortress

dado, the portion of a pedestal between its base and cornice. The term also applies to the lower portion of walls when decorated separately

darülhadis, a college of advanced studies in the religious law (Şeriat) of Islam

darülkura, a school for learning the Kuran

darüşşifa, an Ottoman hospital

dershane, the lecture hall of a medrese

devşirme, periodic levy of Christian youths inducted into the Ottoman army

diaconicon, in Byzantine churches, the sacristy

domical vault, a dome rising direct on a square or polygonal base, the curved surfaces separated by groins

entablature, the upper part of an Order of architecture, comprising architrave, frieze and cornice, supported by a colonnade

epistyle, the Greek word for the architrave

exedra, a semicircular niche

exonarthex, the outer vestibule of a church

extrado, the outer curve of an arch

eyvan, a vaulted or domed recess open on one side

faience, glazed earthenware, often ornamented, used for pottery or as revetment on the walls of a building

fresco, the term originally applied to painting on a wall while the plaster is still wet, but often used for any painting not in oil colours

frieze, the middle division of a classical entablature, often decorated with carvings in low relief

göbektaşi, the 'belly-stone', the heated stone platform in the hot-room of a Turkish bath

Grand Vezir, the Sultan's chief minister

groin, the curved edge formed by the intersection of two vaulting surfaces

hamam (hamamı), a Turkish bath

han (hani), an Ottoman inn for travellers

hararet, the steam room of a Turkish bath

harem, the female quarter of a Turkish home or palace

hisar (hisarı), an Ottoman fortress

hünkâr kasri, royal pavilion attached to an imperial mosque

hünkâr mahfili, the Sultan's loge in an imperial Ottoman mosque

hücre, a student's cell in a medrese

hypocaust, a series of small chambers and flues through which the heated air was distriuted to the rooms of a bath

iconostasis, the screen between the nave and chancel of a Greek church, invariably decorated with icons, or holy pictures

imam, the cleric who presides over public prayers in a mosque

imaret, the public kitchen in an Ottoman pious foundation.

impost, the member, usually formed of mouldings, on which an arch rests

intrado, the inner curve of an arch

iskele (iskelesı), quay

kadın, woman, the wife of a Sultan

kible, the direction of Mecca

konak, an Ottoman mansion

köşk (köşkü), a Turkish kiosk or pavilion

külliye (külliyesı), an Ottoman mosque complex or pious foundation

kursu or **kuran kursu**, the chair on which the imam, or preacher, sits when he is reading the Kuran to the congregation

kütüphane, Turkish library

lintel, the horizontal timber or stone, also known as the architrave, that spans an opening

lunette, a semicircular window or wall-panel let into the inner base of a concave vault or dome

medrese (medressesı), Islamic school of higher studies

mektep, an Ottoman primary school, also called sibyan mektebi

mescit (mescidi), a small mosque

metatorium, in Haghia Sophia, an enclosure set aside for the Emperor and the Patriarch when they were participating in the liturgy

mihrab, the niche in the wall of a mosque that indicates the kible, the direction of Mecca

mimber, the pulpit in a mosque

minaret, the spire, beside a mosque, from which the müezzin, or chanter, gives the call to prayer

mosaic, decorative surfaces formed

by small cubes (tesserae) of stone, glass, or marble

müezzin, cleric who chants the responses to the prayers of the imam in a mosque and gives the call to prayer from the minaret

müezzin mahfili, the raised platform where the müezzins chant their responses to the prayers of the imam

muvakithane, the house of the müneccim, or mosque astronomer

namazgah, an outdoor place of prayer

narthex, the arcaded entrance porch of a Byzantine church

ocak, a Turkish fireplace

oda (odası), in Turkish, room or chamber

ogive arch, a pointed arch

opus Alexandrinum, a mosaic inlaid in a stone or marble paving

opus sectile, ornamental paving or wall covering made from marble slabs cut in various shapes, usually geometric

Order, an Order in ancient Greek architecture comprised a column, with base (usually), shaft and capital, the whole supporting an entablature

parecclesion, side chamber in a church, often used as a funerary chapel

pendentive, the triangular curved overhanging surface by means of which a circular dome is supported over a square or polygonal chamber

penetralia, in architecture, the innermost parts of a building, especially of a temple or palace

peristyle, a range of columns surrounding a courtyard

pier, a mass of masonry, as distinct from a column, from which an arch springs

pilaster, a rectangular feature in the shape of a pillar, but projecting only about one-sixth of its breadth from a wall

porphyry, a hard, red or purple rock

portico, a colonnaded space, with a roof supported on at least one side by columns

refectory, the dining-hall in a monastery, convent, or college

revak, in Turkish, a domed or vaulted colonnade enclosing a porch

revetment, a facing of stone, marble, or ceramic tile upon a wall

şadırvan, an ablution fountain in the courtyard of a mosque

saray (sarayı), an Ottoman palace

sebil, an Ottoman fountain-house from which water is distributed free to passers-by

selamlık, the male quarters of an Ottoman home or palace

semahane, the dancing room of a Mevlevi dervish lodge

şerefe, the balcony of a minaret, where the müezzin gives the call to prayer

şeriat, the sacred law in Islam

şeyülislam, head of the Islamic religious hierarchy

sibyan mektebi, see mektep

soğukluk, the chamber of intermediate temperature in a Turkish bath

soffit, the ceiling or underside of any architectural member

son cemaat yeri, the raised front porch of a mosque where latecomers pray

squinch, a small arch, bracket, or similar device built across each angle of a square or polygonal structure to form an octagon or any appropriate base for a dome

surbase, a moulding at the base of a pedestal, podium, or wall

suterazi, a Turkish water-control tower

synthronon, tiers of seats for the clergy around the apse of a church

tabhane, a hospice for travelling dervishes

taksim, a Turkish water-distribution system

tekke, a dervish lodge

timarhane, an Ottoman insane asylum
tip medrese, an Ottoman medical school
trabeate, arranged with beams and lintels rather than arches
türbe (türbesı), an Ottoman mausoleum
tympanum, the space enclosed by an arch
vakıf, the deed of an Ottoman pious foundation

Valide Sultan, the mother of a reigning Sultan
vault, an arched covering in stone or brick over any building
Vezir, one of the Sultan's ministers
voussoirs, the truncated wedge shaped blocks forming an arch
yalı (yalisı), an Ottoman mansion on the Bosphorus
zaviye, religious establishment to accommodate pilgrims

Suggested reading

The following is a selective list of books in English about Istanbul. This is not meant to be a definitive bibliography, but rather an introduction to the history, archaeology, art, architecture and folklore of the city.

History

Alderson, A.D., *The Structure of the Ottoman Dynasty*, Oxford, 1956

Allom, Thomas and Walsh, Robert, *Constantinople and the Scenery of the Seven Churches of Asia Minor*, London, 1839

Amicis, Edmondo de, *Constantinople*, tr. Maria Horner Lansdale, Philadelphia, 1896

Atil, Esin, *The Age of Süleyman the Magnificent*, New York, 1987

Babinger, Franz, *Mehmet the Conqueror and his Time*, tr. Ralph Manheim, ed. William C. Hickman, Princeton, 1978

Baker, G. P., *Justinian*, New York, 1931

Balfour, Patrick (Lord Kinross), *Atatürk, The Rebirth of a Nation*, London, 1964; *The Ottoman Centuries*, London, 1977

Barker, John W., *Justinian and the Later Roman Empire*, Madison, Wisconsin, 1966; *Manuel II Palaeologus (1391–1425)*, New Brunswick, New Jersey, 1968

Baynes, Norman H., *Constantine the Great and the Christian Church*, London, 1929

Bowder, Diana, *The Age of Constantine and Julian*, London, 1978

Brand, Charles M., *Byzantium Confronts the West, 1180–1204*, Cambridge, Mass., 1968

Browning, Robert, *The Emperor Julian*, Berkeley, California, 1972

Busbecq, Ogier Ghislain de, *Turkish Letters*, Oxford, 1927

Cantemir, Demetrius, *The History of the Growth and Decay of the Ottoman Empire*, London, 1734–35

Comnena, Anna, *The Alexiad*, tr. Elizabeth Dawes, London, 1928

Downey, Glanville, *Constantinople in the Age of Justinian*, Norman, Oklahoma, 1960

Freely, John, *Istanbul, the Imperial City*, London, 1996

Freeman, Kathleen, *Greek City States*, London, 1950

Haldon, J.F., *Byzantium in the Seventh Century*, Cambridge, 1990

Haslip, Joan, *The Sultan: The Life of Abdül Hamit II*, London, 1958

Hussey, Joan, *The Byzantine World*, London, 1957

Imber, Colin, *The Ottoman Empire, 1300–1481*, Istanbul, 1990

Inalcık, Halil, *The Ottoman Empire: The Classical Period, 1300–1600*, tr. Norman Itzkowitz and Colin Imber, London, 1973

Jenkins, Romilly, *Byzantium, the Imperial Centuries, AD 610–1071*, London, 1966

Kazhdan, Alexander, and Constable, Giles, *People and Power in Byzantium*, Cambridge, Mass., 1982

Knolles, Richard, *History of the Othman Turks*, London, 1603

Kritovoulos of Imbros, *History of Mehmed the Conqueror*, tr. Charles T. Riggs, Princeton, 1954

Lewis, Bernard, *The Emergence of Modern Turkey*, Oxford, 1961; *Istanbul and the Civilization of the Ottoman Empire*, Norman, Oklahoma, 1963

Lewis, Geoffrey, *Turkey*, New York, 1964

Lewis, Raphaela, *Everyday Life in Ottoman Turkey*, London, 1961

Lybyer, A.H., *The Government of the Ottoman Empire in the Time of Suleiman the Magnificent*, Cambridge, Mass., 1913

Magdalino, Paul, *Tradition and Transformation in Medieval Byzantium*, Brookfield, Vermont, 1991

Nicol, Donald M., *The Last Centuries of Byzantium, 1261–1453*, Cambridge, 1972

Norwich, John Julius, *Byzantium: The Early Centuries*, London, 1988; *Byzantium: The Apogee*, London, 1991; *Byzantium, The Decline and Fall*, London, 1995

Ostrogorsky, George, *History of the Byzantine State*, tr. Joan Hussey, Oxford, 1956

Palmer, Allan, *The Decline and Fall of the Ottoman Empire*, London, 1992

Procopius of Caesarea, *Works*, tr. H.B. Dewing, London, 7 vols, 1914–40

Psellus, Michael, *Chronographia*, tr. E.R.A. Sewter, London, 1953

Rice, Tamara Talbot, *Everyday Life in Byzantium*, New York, 1967

Runciman, Steven, *Byzantine Civilization*, London, 1933; *The Fall of Constantinople, 1453*, Cambridge, 1965; *A History of the Crusades*, Cambridge, 3 vols, 1952–54

Rycault, Paul, *The History of the Present State of the Ottoman Empire*, London, 3 vols, 1670

Shaw, Stanford J. and Shaw, Ezel Kural, *History of the Ottoman Empire and Modern Turkey*, 2 vols, Cambridge, 1976–77

Shaw, Stanford J., *Between Old and New, the Ottoman Empire under Selim III*, Cambridge, Mass., 1971

Sphrantzes, George, *The Fall of the Byzantine Empire: a Chronicle*, ed. and tr. Marios Philippides, Amherst, Mass., 1980

Thévenot, M. de, *Travels into the Levant*, London, 1687

Toynbee, Arnold J., *Constantine Porphyrogenitus and his World*, Oxford, 1973

Vasiliev, A.A., *History of the Byzantine Empire*, Madison, Wisconsin, 2 vols, 1952

Wittek, Paul, *The Rise of the Ottoman Empire*, London, 1938

Art and Architecture

Aslanapa, Oktay, *Turkish Art and Architecture*, London, 1971

Davis, Fanny, *The Palace of Topkapı*, New York, 1970

Gilles, Pierre (Petrus Gyllius), *The Antiquities of Constantinople*, New York, 1988

Goodwin, Godfrey, *A History of Ottoman Architecture*, London, 1971; *Sinan*, London, 1993; *The Janissaries*, London, 1994

Krautheimer, Richard, *Early Christian and Byzantine Architecture*, Baltimore, 1965

Kuran, Aptullah, *The Mosque in Early Ottoman Architecture*, Chicago, 1968; *Sinan, The Grand Old Man in Ottoman Architecture*, Washington, DC, 1986

Lethaby, W.R. and Swainson, H., *The Church of Sancta Sophia*, Constantinople, New York, 1894

Mainstone, Rowland J., *Haghia Sophia, Architecture, Structure and Liturgy of Justinian's Great Church*, London, 1988

Mango, Cyril, *The Brazen House, A Study of the Vestibule of the Imperial Palace of Constantinople*, Copenhagen, 1954; *Byzantine Architecture*, New York, 1976; *Byzantium, The Empire of the New Rome*, London, 1980; *Byzantium and its Image*, London, 1984

Matthews, Thomas F., *The Early Churches of Constantinople*, London, 1971

Necipoğlu, Gülrü, *Architecture, Ceremonial and Power: The Topkapı Palace in the Fifteenth and Sixteenth Centuries*, New York, 1991

van Millingen, Alexander, *Byzantine Constantinople, The Walls of Constantinople and Adjoining Historical Sites*, London, 1899; *Constantinople*, London, 1906; *Byzantine Churches in Constantinople, Their History and Architecture*, London, 1912

Istanbul Past and Present

Çelik, Zeynep, *The Remaking of Istanbul*, London, 1986

Dallaway, James, *Constantinople Ancient and Modern*, London, 1797

Diehl, Charles, *Byzantine Empresses*, tr. Harold Bell and Theresa de Kerpely, New York, 1963

Dwight, H.G., *Constantinople*, Old and New, New York, 1915

Evliya Efendi (Evliya Çelebi), *A Narrative of Travels* [the Seyahatname], tr. Joseph von Hammer, London, 1834

Freely, John, *Stamboul Sketches*, Istanbul, 1974; *Istanbul, The Imperial City*, London, 1996

Grosvenor, E.A., *Constantinople*, 2 vols., Boston, 1896

Haider, H.R.H. Princess Musbah, *Arabesque*, London 1944

MacFarlane, Charles, *Istanbul in 1828*, London, 1829

Mansel, Philip, *Constantinople, City of the World's Desire, 1453–1924*, London, 1995

Miller, Barnette, *Beyond the Sublime Court*, New Haven, 1931; *The Palace School of Mohammed the Conqueror*, Cambridge, Mass., 1941

Montagu, Lady Mary Wortley, *The Complete Letters of Lady Mary Wortley Montague*, Vol. 1, 1708–20, ed. Robert Halsband, Oxford, 1965

Pardoe, Julia, *The City of the Sultan and domestic manners of the Turks in 1836*, 3 vols, London, 1836; *Beauties of the Bosphorus*, London, 1839

Penzer, N.M., *The Harem*, London, 1965

Pierce, Leslie P., *The Imperial Harem*, Oxford, 1993

Sumner-Boyd, Hilary and Freely, John, *Strolling Through Istanbul*; Istanbul, 4th edn, 1988

Walsh, Robert, *A Residence at Constantinople*, London, 1836

Travel Literature

Ash, John, *A Byzantine Journey*, New York, 1995
Cuddon, J.A., *The Owl's Watchsong*, London, 1960, reprinted 1986
Freeley, John, *Stamboul Sketches*, Istanbul, 1973
Liddell, Robert, *Byzantium and Istanbul*, London, 1956
Pereira, Michael, *Aspects of a City*, London, 1968
Seal, Jeremy, *A Fez of the Heart*, New York, 1995
Stoneman, Richard, *Across the Hellespont, A Literary Guide to Turkey*, London, 1987

Books in English by Modern Turkish Authors

And, Metin, *Dances of Anatolian Turkey*, Ankara, 1959; *Karagöz*

Turkish Cuisine

Eren, Neşet, *The Art of Turkish Cooking*, New York, 1969; *The Delights of Turkish Cooking*, Istanbul, 1986
Orga, Irfan, *Turkish Cooking*, London, 1951

Index

A

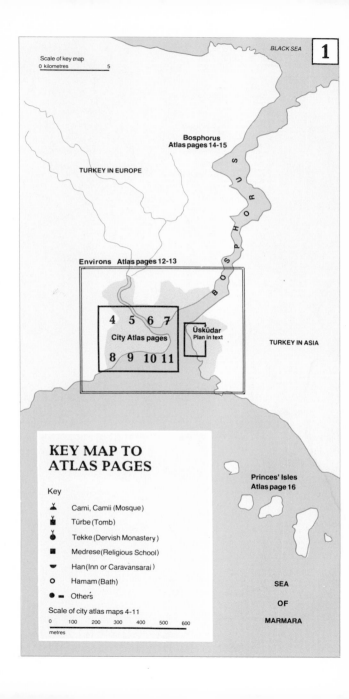

BLACK SEA

1

Scale of key map
0 kilometres   5

Bosphorus
Atlas pages 14-15

TURKEY IN EUROPE

B O S P H O R U S

Environs Atlas pages 12-13

4   5   6   7
City Atlas pages
8   9   10   11

Üsküdar
Plan in text

TURKEY IN ASIA

KEY MAP TO ATLAS PAGES

Key

    Cami, Camii (Mosque)

    Türbe (Tomb)

    Tekke (Dervish Monastery)

    Medrese (Religious School)

    Han (Inn or Caravansarai)

○   Hamam (Bath)

● ▬   Others

Scale of city atlas maps 4-11

0   100   200   300   400   500   600
metres

Princes' Isles
Atlas page 16

SEA

OF

MARMARA

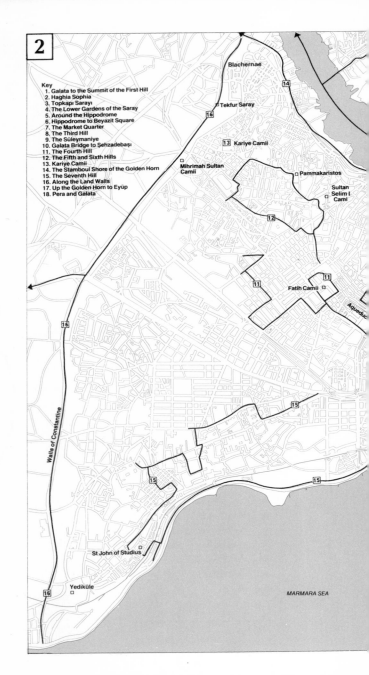

2

Blachernae

14

Tekfur Saray

16

13   Kariye Camii

□ Pammakaristos

Mihrimah Sultan
Camii

Sultan
Selim I
Camii

12

11

11

Fatih Camii

Aqueduc

Walls of Constantine

16

15

15

15

St John of Studius

16   Yedikule

MARMARA SEA

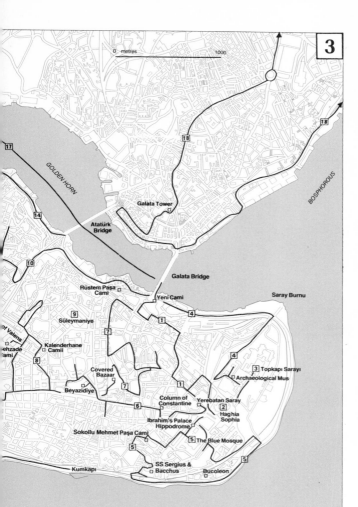

3

0 metres 1000

GOLDEN HORN

BOSPHORUS

17

14

Atatürk
Bridge

Galata Tower

10

Galata Bridge

Rüstem Paşa
Cami

Yeni Cami

Saray Burnu

9

Süleymaniye

1

4

7

or Valens

Kalenderhane
Camii

4

ehzade
ami

8

3 Topkapı Sarayı

Archaeological Mus

Covered
Bazaar

7

Beyazidiye

1

6

Column of
Constantine

Yerebatan Saray

2

Ibrahim's Palace
Hippodrome

Haghia
Sophia

Sokollu Mehmet Paşa Cami

5

5 The Blue Mosque

5

Kumkapı

SS Sergius &
Bacchus

Bucoleon

PLAN OF ROUTES

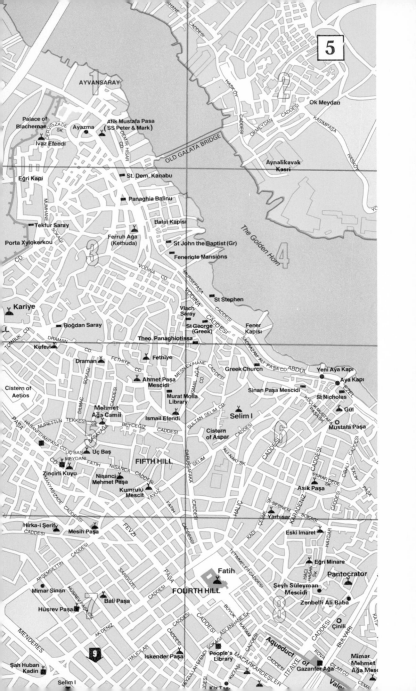

5

AYVANSARAY

Ok Meydan

Palace of
Blachernae

Ayazma

Atik Mustafa Pasa
(SS Peter & Mark)

KASIMPASA

Ivaz Efendi

OLD GALATA BRIDGE

Aynalikavak
Kasrı

Eğri Kapı

St. Dem. Kanabu

Panaghia Balinu

The Golden Horn

Balat Kapısı

Tekfur Saray

Ferruh Aga
(Kethuda)

St John the Baptist (Gr)

Porta Xylokerkou

Feneriote Mansions

Kariye

St Stephen

Boğdan Saray

Vlach
Saray

St George
(Greek)

Fener
Kapısı

Theo. Panaghiotissa

Kefevi

Draman

Fethiye

Greek Church

Yeni Aya Kapı

Aya Kapı

Cistern of
Aetios

Ahmet Paşa
Mescidi

Murat Molla
Library

Sinan Paşa Mescidi

St Nicholas

Gül

Mehmet
Aga Camii

Ismail Efendi

Selim I

Mustafa Paşa

Uç Baş

Cistern
of Aspar

Zincirli Kuyu

Nişanci
Mehmet Paşa

FIFTH HILL

Kumrulu
Mescit

Asik Paşa

Yarhisar

Hirka-i Şerify

Mesih Paşa

Eski Imaret

Egri Minare

Fatih

Pantocrator

Mimar Sinan

FOURTH HILL

Seyh Süleyman
Mescidi

Bali Paşa

Zenbelli Ali Baba

Hüsrev Paşa

Çinili

9

Şah Huban
Kadin

Iskender Paşa

People's
Library

Aqueduct of

Mimar
Mehmet
Aga Mesc

Selim I

Gazanfer Aga

Valer

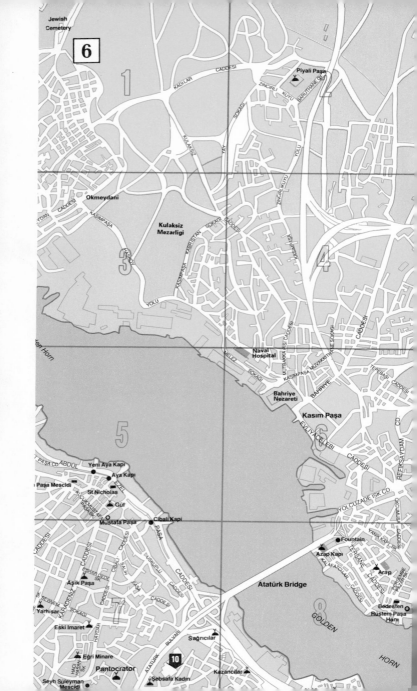

Jewish Cemetery

6

1

KADILAR CADDESİ

ZİNCİRLİ KUYU

BARUTHANE CD

Piyali Paşa

SOKAĞI

TAY

KULAKSIZ

ZİNCİRLİ KUYU YOLU

KASIMPAŞA

Okmeydani

AYDIN CADDESİ

KASIMPAŞA

CADDESİ

Kulaksiz Mezarligi

SOKAĞI

CADDESİ

3

KAPTAN PAŞA

KABRISTAN

4

KASIMPAŞA

CADDESİ

YOLU

MELEZ

KUTBAKKALİSİ CADDESİ

MUYAORTHANE SOKAĞI

TEPEBAŞI CADDESİ

Naval Hospital

SOKAĞI

KASIMPAŞA

BAHRİYE

Bahriye Nezareti

Golden Horn

5

Kasım Paşa

EVLİYA ÇELEBİ

CADDESİ

REFİKSAYDAM CD

Ç PAŞA CD ABDÜL

Yeni Aya Kapı

KVÇ KULAKSIZ PAŞA

Aya Kapı

İMRET

YOLCUZADE İSK CD

ORTMİSLİ CADDESİ

Paşa Mescidi

St Nicholas

Gul

Fountain

YANIK KAPI

Mustafa Paşa

PAŞA

Cibali Kapı

Azap Kapı

KALAFATÇILAR

TERSANE CADDESİ

BOSNA SOKAĞI

Arap

CADDESİ

EBUSKUPALI CADDESİ

SALİH

CİBALI DEDE

CADDESİ

CADDESİ

DİDRİRİ

CADDESİ

Aşik Paşa

ERHAT DEDE

Bedesten

Rüstem Paşa Hani

ŞEBNEM

KADENDERİZ

SOKAĞI

CADDE-8

Yarhisar

HAYDAR

Atatürk Bridge

8

GOLDEN

Eski İmaret

Sağıcılar

ATATÜRK BULVARI

Egri Minare

HACI İLBAY HSK CD

10

HORN

Pantocrator

Seyh Süleyman Mescidi

Sebsafa Kadın

Kazancılar

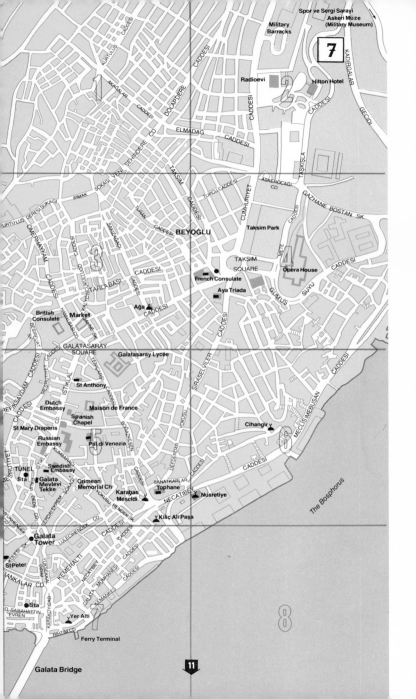

Spor ve Sergi Sarayı
Askeri Müze
(Military Museum)

Military
Barracks

7

KADIRGALAR GECIDI

Radioevi

Hilton Hotel

KURTULUS CADDESI

AKAÇALAR CADDESI

DOLAPDERE CD

ŞEHİT DERE CD

ELMADAĞ CADDESI

TAKSİM CADDESI

CADDESI

TAŞKIŞLA CD

TÜRKÇÜ CADDESI

IRMAK SOKAĞI

YENİ ŞEHİT DERE

ASKEROCAĞI CD

GAZHANE BOSTAN SK

CUMHURİYET CD

TURAN CD

SAKIZAĞAÇ

PERES SOKAĞI

URTULUS CD

BEYOGLU

ÖMER HAYAM CD

Taksim Park

MEŞE CADDESI

Opera House

TAKSİM
SQUARE

CADDESI

TARLABAŞI CADDESI

OPTIULUDERE

CADDESI

French Consulate

GÜMÜŞ

SUYU

CADDESI

Aya Triada

Ağa

British
Consulate

Market

HAMALBAŞI CD

İNÖNÜ CD

CADDESI

BEŞİRLAT SK

**GALATASARAY
SQUARE**

Galatasaray Lycée

SIRASELVİLER CADDESI

MİS SK

ASMALI MESCİT

YENİÇARŞI CD

İSTİKLAL CD

BESTEKAR CD

ŞAHKULU

BOĞAZKESEN CD

OĞUL SK

DEFTERDAR

CADDESI

REFIK SAADAM CADDESI

St Anthony

Dutch
Embassy

Maison de France

Spanish
Chapel

St Mary Draperis

Russian
Embassy

Pal. di Venezia

Cihangir

MECLİSİ MEBUSAN CADDESI

TÜNEL
Sta

Swedish
Embassy

Galata
Mevlevi
Tekke

Crimean
Memorial Ch

SANATKARLAR

Tophane

KUMBARACI

NECATİBEY CADDESI

Karabaş
Mescidi

HENDEK SK

KEMERALTI CADDESI

YÜKSEK KALDIRIM

LÜLECİHENDEK CD

HENDEK SK

Kılıç Ali Paşa

Nusretiye

The Bosphorus

MEŞRUTİYET CADDESI

DEBE CD

SERDAR EKREM

**Galata
Tower**

LÜLECİHENDEK CD

St Peter

ANKALAR CD

Sta

NECATİBE

KARANTİNA CD

D. SABAHATTİN
EVREN

KARAKÖY CD

BİLLTİM CD

MUMHANESİ CD

EMEKSİZ

DALFA

Yer Altı

Ferry Terminal

Galata Bridge

11

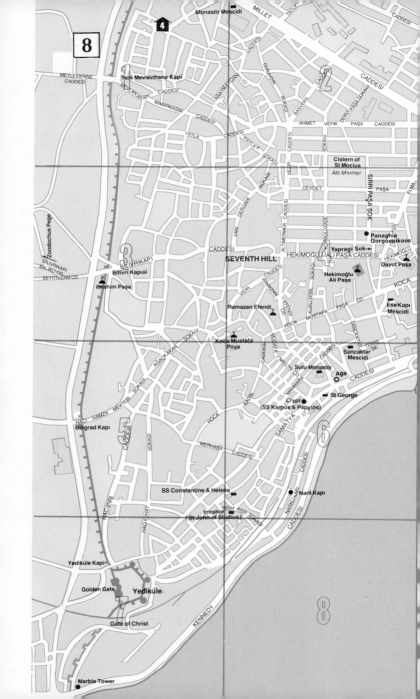

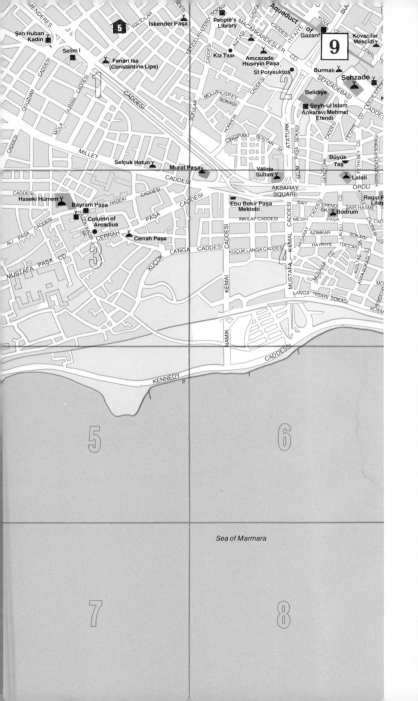

Şah Huban
Kadin

Selim I

Fenari Isa
(Constantine Lips)

İskender Paşa

People's
Library

Kiz Taşı

Amcazade
Hüseyin Paşa
St Polyeuktos

Aqueduct of
Gazanf

Kovacılar
Mescidı

9

Burmalı

Şehzade

Belidiye

Şeyh-ul İslam
Ankaravi Mehmet
Efendi

Büyük
Taş

MILLET

Selçuk Hatun

Murat Paşa

CADDESI

Valide
Sultan

Laleli

AKSARAY
SQUARE

ORDU

Haseki Hürrem

Bayram Paşa

Column of
Arcadius

Ebu Bekir Paşa
Mektebi

Ragip P

Bodrum

INKILAP CADDESI

Cerrah Paşa

CERRAH

LANGA

CADDESI

KÜÇÜK LANGA CADDES

KÜÇÜK

MUSTAFA PAŞA CD

KEMAL

HAYRIYE

LANGA HISARI SOKAGI

MUSTAFA

KEMAL

NAMIK

CADDESSI

KENNEDY

5

6

Sea of Marmara

7

8

GOLDEN

Rüstem Paşa Hanı

HORN

Tatmisal

Eski Imaret

HAYDAR

6

BULVARI

Sağrıcılar

10

ATATÜRK

Pantocrator

Kazancılar

KATIP

Ahi Celebi

Zindan Kapı

Şeyh Süleyman Mescidi

Şebsafa Kadın

Kantarcılar Mescidi

Tahtakale

Rüstem Paşa

KANTA

CELEBI

BULVARI

Zenbelli Ali Baba

Çinili

KARMANI

Siyavuş Paşa

Timurtaş

Hurmalı

Yeni C

Atif Efendi Library

FETVA

CADDESI

Balkapan

Mısır Çarşısı (Spice Bazaar)

Aqueduct of

CADDESI

ITFAIYE

KOVA

Mimar Mehmet Ağa Mescidi

Vefa

PROF

SINAN

Samanveren

Yavaşça Şahin

CADDE

Gazanfer Ağa

CEMAL

Kilisi

Süleymaniye

Valens

Ekmekcizade Ahmet Paşa

ONAR CD

ISMETIYE CD

VASIF

ASIR

zade Paşa

Burmali

SEHZADEBASI

KREZLI MESCIT SOKAGI

Valide

Kürkcü

Rüstem Paşa

olyeuktos

Şehzade

SÜLEYMANIYE CADDESI

TACIRHANE

Büyük Yeni

Küçük Yeni

Belidiye

Kalenderhane

BOZDOGAN-KEMERI

University of Istanbul

Tower

FUAT PASA

SULTAN MEKTEBI SK.

Şeyh-ul Islam Ankaravi Mehmet Efendi

THIRD HILL

BESIM OMER PASA CADDESI

CAKMAKCILAR YOKUSU

TIGCILAR CADDESI

Mahmut Paşa

Kuyucu Murat Paşa

UNIVERSITE

BAKIRCILAR CADDESI

Bit Pazar

Kapalı Carsi

See large scale plan

Büyük Taş

Institute of Turkology

Beyazidiye

Sahaflar Carsisi

Nuruosmaniye

KILICILAR SK

SEREF

Laleli

ORDU

BÜYÜK

Beyazidiye

BEYAZIT MEYDANI

SECOND HILL

NURUO

AKSARAY SQUARE

GENÇTÜRK

FETHIBEY SOKAGI

HARIKZADELER SOKAGI

Forum of Theodosius

Ali Paşa of Çorlu

Koca Sinan Paşa

Atik Ali Paşa

Vezir Han

SAIT

Ragip Paşa

Hasan Paşa

Simkeşhane

YENICERILA

Cemberlitaş

SAIR HASMET SOKAGI

Kara Mustafa of Merzifon

Mehmet Paşa A

şa

SK

Bodrum

Ottoman Library

MESIH

DER INKITU SK

AZIMKAR

NISANCA BOSTANI SK

Gedik Paşa

SINAN HAMMI SOKAGI

CADDES

CADDESI

HAYRIYE

TUCCARI

SK

TURNALI

MITHAT PASA CADDESI

Gedik Ahmet Paşa

KUCUKSU

PERTEV PASA SOTU

OZDAHRE CES

MOLLATASI

TURKELI

IBRAHIM PASA

TIYATRO

SARAYICI SOKAGI

NEVI

LANGA

HISARI SOKAGI

Nişanci Mehmet Paşa Camii

Sokollu Mehmet Paşa

Ösbekler

ALISAN SOKAGI

Panaghia Elpida

Haghia Kyriaki

KADIRGALIMANI CD

KADIRGA LIMAN MEYDANI

KUMKAPI MEYDANI

KÜCÜK

Cardakli

CADDESI

Kumkapi

KENNEDY

7

8

SEA

OF

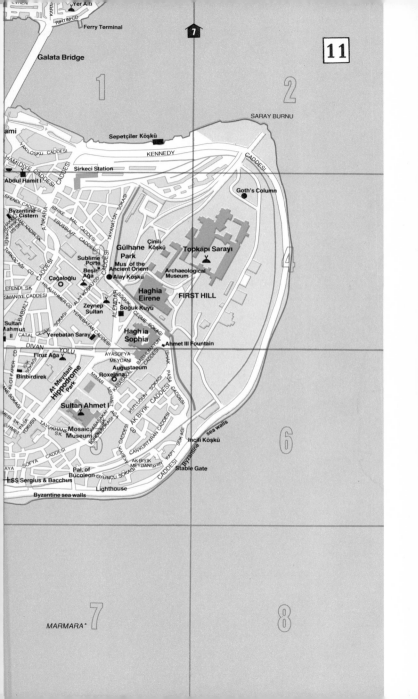

Yer Altı

Ferry Terminal

Galata Bridge

1

2

SARAY BURNU

ami

Sepetçiler Köşkü

YALI KÖŞKÜ CADDESI

KENNEDY

HAMIDIYE CADDESI

CADDESI

Sirkeci Station

CADDESI

Abdul Hamit I

Goth's Column

EFENDI CADDESI

Byzantine
Cistern

ROYAL NADIR SK

ANKARA

İBNİCE

MAL

EBUSSUUT CADDESI

Çinili
Köşkü

TURKOCAĞI

CADDESI

Gülhane
Park

Sublime
Porte

Mus of the
Ancient Orient

TAYAHATUN SOKAĞI

Topkapı Sarayı

Cağaloğlu

Beşir
Ağa

ALAY KÖŞKÜ SK

Alay Köşkü

Archaeological
Museum

4

EFENDI SK

HILALI AHMER CAD

Zeynep
Sultan

ALEMDAR

SOĞUK

Haghia
Eirene

FIRST HILL

SMANIYE CADDESI

BABIALI

Soğuk Kuyu

ÇEŞME SOKAĞI

Sultan
Mahmut
II

ÇATAL SK

MERBATAN CADDESI

Yerebatan Saray

Haghia
Sophia

Ahmet III Fountain

DIVAN

YOLU

Firuz Ağa

AYASOFYA
MEYDANI

BABIHUMAYUN

ISHAK

Augustaeum

İSKELE SK

Binbirdirek

At Meydanı
Hippodrome
Park

MİMAR

Roxelana

KABASAKAL

PAŞA CADDESI

Sultan Ahmet I

MEHMET

KUTLUGUN

AK BIYIK

CADDESI

SOKAĞI

Mosaic
Museum

TAVUKHANE
SK

CANKURTARAN CADDESI

İncili Köşkü

6

SOFYA

CADDESI

AK BIYIK
MEYDANI

CADDESI

Byzantine sea walls

Pal. of
Bucoleon

OYUNCU SOKAĞI

Stable Gate

SS Sergius & Bacchus

Lighthouse

Byzantine sea walls

7

MARMARA

8

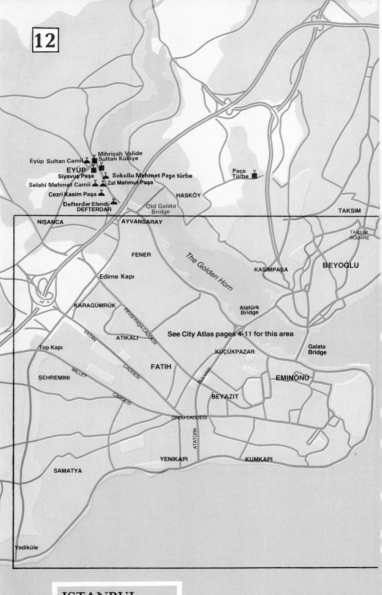

12

Eyüp Sultan Camii

Mihriçah Valide
Sultan Külliye

EYÜP

Siyavuş Paşa

Sokollu Mehmet Paşa türbe

Selahi Mehmet Camii

Zal Mahmut Paşa

Paça
Türbe

Cezri Kasim Paşa

Defterdar Efendi
DEFTERDAR

Old Galata
Bridge

HASKÖY

NİŞANCA

AYVANSARAY

TAKSİM

FENER

The Golden Horn

KASIMPAŞA

TAKSİM
SQUARE

Edirne Kapı

BEYOĞLU

KARAGÜMRÜK

FEVZİPAŞA CADDESİ

Atatürk
Bridge

VATAN

ATIKALI

See City Atlas pages 4-11 for this area

Galata
Bridge

Top Kapı

CADDESİ

FATİH

KÜÇÜKPAZAR

BULVARI

EMİNÖNÜ

ŞEHREMİNİ

MİLLET

CADDESİ

BEYAZIT

ORDU CADDESİ

ATATÜRK

YENİKAPI

KUMKAPI

SAMATYA

Yediküle

ISTANBUL
Environs

0 metres   500   1000   1500

Sea of Marmara

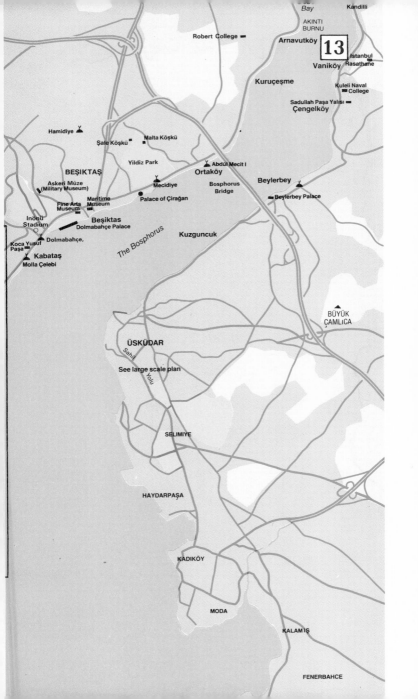

Bay

Kandilli

AKINTI
BURNU

Robert College

Arnavutköy

13

Vaniköy

Istanbul
Rasathane

Kuruçeşme

Kuleli Naval
College

Sadullah Paşa Yalısı
Çengelköy

Hamidiye

Şale Köşkü

Malta Köşkü

Yıldız Park

Abdül Mecit I

BEŞIKTAŞ

Ortaköy

Bosphorus
Bridge

Beylerbey

Askeri Müze
(Military Museum)

Mecidiye

Fine Arts
Museum

Maritime
Museum

Palace of Çirağan

Beylerbey Palace

İnönü
Stadium

Beşiktas
Dolmabahçe Palace

Dolmabahçe,

The Bosphorus

Kuzguncuk

Koca Yusuf
Paşa

Kabataş

Molla Çelebi

BÜYÜK
ÇAMLICA

ÜSKÜDAR

Sahil

See large scale plan

Yolu

SELIMIYE

HAYDARPAŞA

KADIKÖY

MODA

KALAMIŞ

FENERBAHÇE

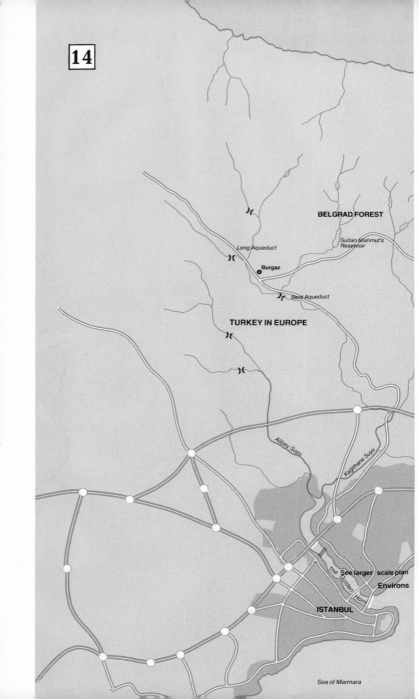

BELGRAD FOREST

Sultan Mahmut's
Reservoir

Long Aqueduct

Burgaz

Bent Aqueduct

TURKEY IN EUROPE

Alibey Suyu

Kağıthane Suyu

The Golden Horn

See larger / scale plan

Environs

ISTANBUL

Sea of Marmara

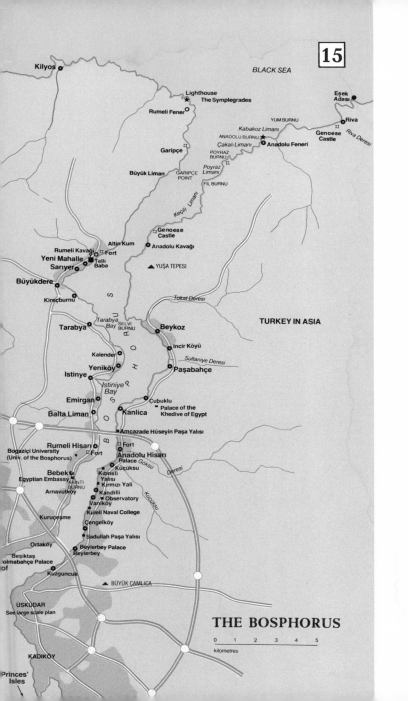

15

BLACK SEA

Kilyos

Lighthouse
The Symplegrades

Eşek
Adası

Rumeli Feneri

Riva

YUM BURNU

Kabakoz Limanı

Genoese
Castle

Riva Deresi

ANADOLU BURNU

Garipçe

Çakalı Limanı

Anadolu Feneri

POYRAZ
BURNU

Büyük Liman

GARIPÇE
POINT

Poyraz
Limanı

Poyraz Limanı

FIL BURNU

Keçili Limanı

Genoese
Castle

Altin Kum

Anadolu Kavağı

Rumeli Kavağı

Fort

YUŞA TEPESİ

Yeni Mahalle

Telli
Baba

Sarıyer

Büyükdere

Kireçburnu

Tokat Deresi

TURKEY IN ASIA

Tarabya
Bay

SELVI
BURNU

Beykoz

Tarabya

Kalender

İncir Köyü

Sultaniye Deresi

Yeniköy

Paşabahçe

İstinye

İstinye
Bay

Emirgan

Çubuklu

Palace of the
Khedive of Egypt

Balta Liman

Kanlıca

Amcazade Hüseyin Paşa Yalısı

Rumeli Hisarı

Fort

Boğaziçi University
(Univ. of the Bosphorus)

Fort

Anadolu Hisarı

Palace

Göksu Deresi

Bebek

Küçüksu

Egyptian Embassy

Kıbrıslı
Yalısı

AKINTI
BURNU

Kırmızı Yali

Arnavutköy

Kandilli

Vaniköy

Observatory

Kuruçeşme

Kuleli Naval College

Küçüksu Deresi

Çengelköy

Ortaköy

Sadullah Paşa Yalısı

Beşiktaş

Beylerbey Palace

Dolmabahçe Palace

Beylerbey

of

Kuzguncuk

BÜYÜK ÇAMLICA

ÜSKÜDAR
See large scale plan

THE BOSPHORUS

0   1   2   3   4   5

kilometres

KADIKÖY

Princes'
Isles

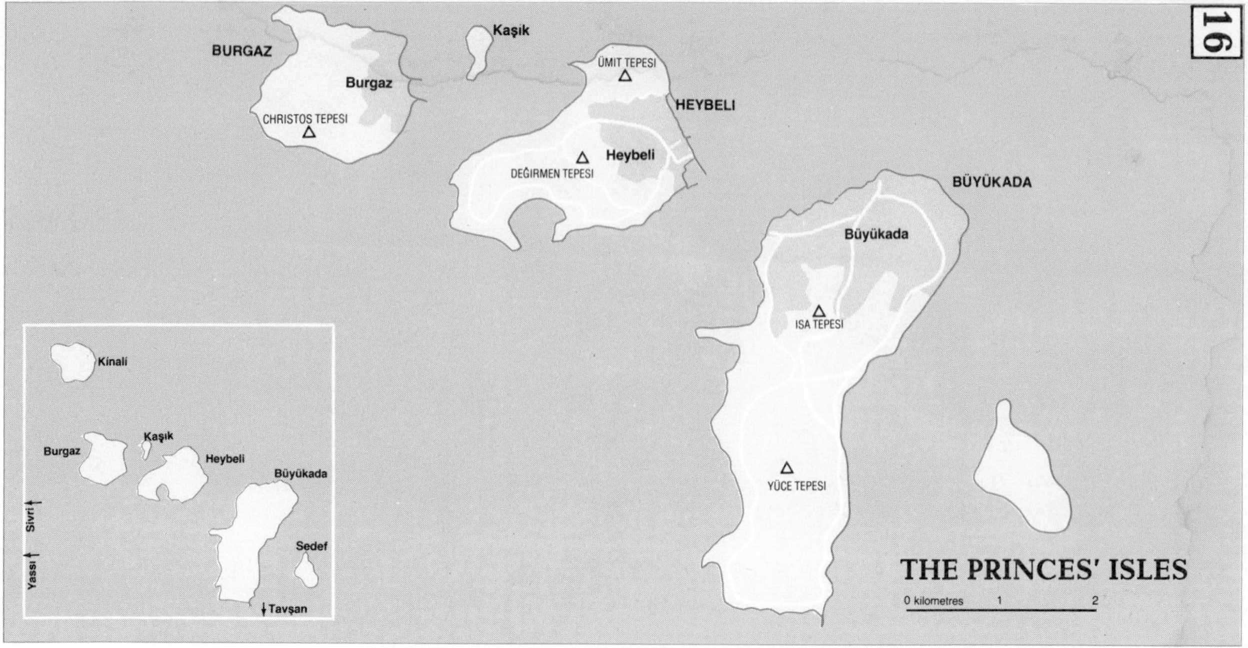

THE PRINCES' ISLES

0 kilometres 1 2

BÜYÜKADA

Büyükada

△ ISA TEPESI

△ YÜCE TEPESI

HEYBELI

ÜMIT TEPESI △

Heybeli

△ DEĞIRMEN TEPESI

Kaşik

Burgaz

BURGAZ

CHRISTOS TEPESI △

Kinali

Kaşik

Burgaz

Heybeli

Büyükada

Sedef

↓ Tavşan

Yassi ↓

Sivri ↓